Policy Reform and Chinese Markets

ADVANCES IN CHINESE ECONOMIC STUDIES

Series Editor: Yanrui Wu, *Associate Professor in Economics, University of Western Australia, Australia*

The Chinese economy has been transformed dramatically in recent years. With its rapid economic growth and accession to the World Trade Organisation, China is emerging as an economic superpower. China's development experience provides valuable lessons to many countries in transition.

Advances in Chinese Economic Studies aims, as a series, to publish the best work on the Chinese economy by economists and other researchers throughout the world. It is intended to serve a wide readership including academics, students, business economists and other practitioners.

Titles in the series include:

High-Tech Industries in China
Chien-Hsun Chen and Hui-Tzu Shih

Economic Growth, Transition and Globalization in China
Edited by Yanrui Wu

The Chinese Business Environment
An Annotated Bibliography
Fuming Jiang and Bruce W. Stening

China's Capital Markets
Challenges from WTO Membership
Edited by Kam C. Chan, Hung-gay Fung and Qingfeng 'Wilson' Liu

China's Accession to the WTO
Impacts on China and the Asia-Pacific Region
Edited by Tianshu Chu and Kar-yiu Wong

Market Development in China
Spillovers, Growth and Inequality
Edited by Belton M. Fleisher, Haizheng Li and Shunfeng Song

The Dynamics of Chinese Regional Development
Market Nature, State Nurture
Jane Golley

Policy Reform and Chinese Markets
Progress and Challenges
Edited by Belton M. Fleisher, Nicholas C. Hope, Anita Alves Pena and Dennis Tao Yang

Policy Reform and Chinese Markets

Progress and Challenges

Edited by

Belton M. Fleisher
The Ohio State University, USA and IZA, Germany

Nicholas C. Hope
Stanford Center for International Development, USA

Anita Alves Pena
Colorado State University, USA

Dennis Tao Yang
Virginia Polytechnic Institute and State University, USA and The Chinese University of Hong Kong, China

ADVANCES IN CHINESE ECONOMIC STUDIES

Edward Elgar
Cheltenham, UK • Northampton, MA, USA

Published by
Edward Elgar Publishing Limited
Glensanda House
Montpellier Parade
Cheltenham
Glos GL50 1UA
UK

Edward Elgar Publishing, Inc.
William Pratt House
9 Dewey Court
Northampton
Massachusetts 01060
USA

A catalogue record for this book is available from the British Library

Library of Congress Cataloguing in Publication Data

Policy reform and Chinese markets : progress and challenges / edited by
Belton M. Fleisher ... [et al.].
     p. cm. – (Advances in Chinese economic studies series)
  Includes bibliographical references and index.
  1. China–Economic policy. 2. China–Economic conditions. 3.
Capitalism–China. I. Fleisher, Belton M.
   HC427.95.P637 2008
   338.951–dc22

                                                                    2007039492

ISBN 978 1 84720 396 0

Printed and bound in Great Britain by MPG Books Ltd, Bodmin, Cornwall

Contents

Contributors

Pieter Bottelier is an economist and China scholar. He is the author of many articles on China's economic reforms. Since he retired from the World Bank in 1998, he has been an Adjunct Professor at The Johns Hopkins School of Advanced International Studies (SAIS) in Washington DC. He also taught courses on China's economy at Harvard's Kennedy School of Government and at Georgetown University. He is a Senior Advisor on China to The Conference Board. His World Bank career (1970–98) included a posting as Chief of the World Bank's Resident Mission in China (1993–97). He studied economics at the University of Amsterdam and at MIT.

Busakorn Chantasasawat has a PhD in international economics from the University of California, Santa Cruz. She has worked as a visiting fellow at the East Asian Institute (EAI), National University of Singapore and the Hong Kong Institute of Economics and Business Strategy (HIEBS).

Belton M. Fleisher attended Stanford University, where he received his PhD in 1961. He was on the faculty of the University of Chicago 1961–65 and joined the Ohio State University faculty in 1965, where he is professor of economics. In 1989 and 1990, he taught economics at the Renmin University of China in Beijing. Since 1990, his research has focused on economic growth and labor and productivity in the Chinese economy. He currently serves as a co-editor of *China Economic Review* and he is Vice President of the Chinese Economists Society.

K.C. Fung is a Professor of Economics at the University of California, Santa Cruz. His research areas are in international trade, multinational corporations, the WTO and the economies of the Asia/Pacific. He was a senior economist at the White House Council of Economic Advisors in both the Bush and Clinton administrations. He is a co-founder of Santa Cruz Center for International Economics (SCCIE) and a Senior Research Fellow at the Hong Kong Institute of Economics and Business Strategy (HIEBS).

Ross Garnaut is Professor of Economics in the Division of Economics of the Research School of Pacific and Asian Studies, and Chairman of the China Economy and Business Program at the Australian National University. He was Australia's Ambassador to China from 1985 to 1988. His research interests are the Australian economy, regional economic integration and the Chinese economy.

Nicholas C. Hope is director of the Stanford Center for International Development. Prior to joining Stanford in 2000, he had a lengthy career at the World Bank, holding positions that included chief of the external debt division, director of the resident staff in Indonesia, and country director, China and Mongolia. A Rhodes Scholar from Tasmania in 1965, he received his PhD in Economics from Princeton University in 1975. His research interests include banking and enterprise reform in China.

Hitomi Iizaka is research fellow at the Hong Kong Institute of Economics and Business Strategy (HIEBS). She is also a visiting assistant professor at the University of Hong Kong. She received her PhD from the University of California, Santa Cruz. Her research interests are in international trade, economic development and growth and the economies of the Asia Pacific region.

Lawrence J. Lau is Vice-Chancellor of The Chinese University of Hong Kong. Prior to assuming this distinguished office in 2004, he had a long career at Stanford University, holding several positions that included those of the Kwoh-Ting Li Professor of Economic Development, Co-Director of the Asia-Pacific Research Center, and Director of the Stanford Institute for Economic Policy Research. Known for developing one of the first econometric models of China, he is a prolific writer who specializes in economic development, economic growth, and the economies of East Asia, including especially China. Professor Lau obtained his undergraduate education at Stanford and his PhD in economics from the University of California Berkeley.

Vlad Manole is a Senior Economist with The Conference Board. He has served as a consultant to the World Bank and the United Nations, working on a variety of international trade issues and migration. He wrote research and policy papers on the impact of tariffs on trade liberalization, tariff aggregation, developed models to analyze the effects of human and social capital on the patterns of migration, and analyzed the productivity of commercial banks in emerging markets. He holds a PhD in Economics from

Washington University, St Louis, and an MS in Applied Mathematics from the University of Bucharest.

Will Martin is a Lead Economist at the Development Research Group of the World Bank. He specializes in analysis of trade policy reforms in developing countries, with an emphasis on reforms related to the WTO and a primary regional focus on East Asia. He has studied and written on China's trade policy since the late 1980s. He received his PhD from Iowa State University following training in Economics at the Australian National University and in Agricultural Science at the University of Queensland. He has been a Guest Professor at Renmin University.

Bruce M. Owen is the Morris M. Doyle Professor in Public Policy in the School of Humanities and Sciences and Director of the Public Policy Program at Stanford University. He is also the Gordon Cain Senior Fellow in Stanford's Institute for Economic Policy Research and Professor (by courtesy) in the Department of Economics. He is the author or co-author of numerous articles and eight books; his research interests include regulation and antitrust, economic analysis of law, economic development and legal reform, and intellectual property rights.

Anita Alves Pena is an Assistant Professor of Economics at Colorado State University. She received her PhD and MA in Economics from Stanford University and BA in Economics from The Johns Hopkins University. She worked as a graduate assistant at the Stanford Center for International Development from 2004 to 2007. Her research interests are in public economics, economic development and labor economics.

Eswar S. Prasad, who headed the IMF's China Division during 2002–04, is the Tolani Senior Professor of Trade Policy at Cornell University. He received his PhD from the University of Chicago. His research has spanned a number of areas including labor economics, business cycles, open economy macroeconomics, and the Chinese economy. His research has been published in top academic journals and has been cited frequently in major international newspapers. He has testified before various US congressional committees (on China).

David Roland-Holst is an Adjunct Professor of Agricultural and Resource Economics at UC Berkeley and the James Irvine Professor of Economics at Mills College. One of the world's leading authorities on empirical policy modeling, he has extensive research experience on international trade, development and environmental economics having undertaken applied research in over 25 countries. Professor Roland-Holst holds a PhD from the University of California, Berkeley.

Andrew Sheng is one of Asia's leading advocates for financial sector reforms in the region and has a wealth of experience in the field. He has served as Chief Economist and Assistant Governor at Malaysia's central bank, senior manager at the World Bank and Deputy Chief Executive at the Hong Kong Monetary Authority before his eventual appointment as Chairman of the Securities and Futures Commission of Hong Kong (SFCHK), a position he held for seven years. He has served as Adjunct Professor at Tsinghua University and as the Tun Ismail Ali Professor of Monetary and Financial Economics at the University of Malaya.

Alan Siu is an Associate Professor of the School of Economics and Finance at the University of Hong Kong. He is the Deputy Director of the Hong Kong Institute and Business Strategy, and Executive Director of the Hong Kong Centre for Economic Research. His research interests are the economics of research and development, productivity growth, technical change and statistical computation.

Ligang Song is Associate Professor at Crawford School of Economics and Government, and Director of the China Economy and Business Program at the Australian National University. His research interests are international trade and development studies and the Chinese economy.

Su Sun has a PhD in economics from the University of Michigan and is a Senior Economist at Economists Incorporated, an economic consulting firm headquartered in Washington DC. Mr Sun's consulting experience is primarily microeconomic and econometric analyses in antitrust litigation and other regulatory matters. He has a special interest in China's antitrust development and has written and spoken on such issues in both English and Chinese.

Kong-Yam Tan is currently Professor of Economics and Director of the Asian Research Centre at the Nanyang Technological University in Singapore. He was a senior economist at the World Bank office in Beijing from June 2002 to June 2005. Prior to that, he was the chief economist of the Singapore government at the Ministry of Trade and Industry. He is a graduate of Princeton (1975–79, class of 1931 scholar) and Stanford University (1980–83). His research interests are in international trade and finance, economic and business trends in the Asia Pacific region and economic reforms in China.

Yuan Wang is a senior executive at China's State Development Bank. She was previously an Adviser on China Policy at the Securities and Futures Commission of Hong Kong. She also worked at China's Ministry of Finance, the World Bank office in Beijing and the People's Bank of China.

Shang-Jin Wei is Professor of Finance and Economics and N.T. Wang Professor of Chinese Business and Economy at Columbia University's Graduate School of Business, and Director of the Working Group on the Chinese Economy and Research Associate at the National Bureau of Economic Research (US), Research Fellow at the Center for Economic Policy Research (Europe) and Special-appointment Professor of Finance at Tsinghua University (China). He previously was Assistant Director and Chief of the Trade and Investment Division at the International Monetary Fund, Associate Professor of Public Policy at Harvard University's Kennedy School of Government, and the New Century Chair at the Brookings Institution. He holds a PhD in economics and MS in finance from the University of California, Berkeley. His research in the areas of international finance, trade, development, and the Chinese economy has been published in top academic journals and reported in *Financial Times*, *The Economist*, *Business Week* and other media outlets.

Geng Xiao is Director of the Brookings-Tsinghua Center and Senior Fellow at the Brookings Institution. From 1992 until joining Brookings in 2007, Xiao taught at the University of Hong Kong and was the founding Deputy Director of the University's Institute for China and Global Development. Xiao obtained his BS from the University of Science and Technology of China and his PhD in economics from UCLA. In the 1990s Xiao worked for the World Bank, UNDP and Harvard Institution for International Development. During 2000–2003, Xiao served as Adviser and Head of Research for the Securities and Futures Commission of Hong Kong.

Dennis Tao Yang is Professor of Economics at Virginia Polytechnic Institute and State University and The Chinese University of Hong Kong. He is also Senior Fellow at the Center for China in the World Economy at Tsinghua University and Senior Advisor on China to The Conference Board. He obtained his undergraduate education at UCLA and his PhD from the University of Chicago. Professor Yang's main research interests are in economic development and growth, labor and demographic economics, and especially the Chinese economy. He currently serves on the Editorial Boards of several international economic journals.

Yang Yao is Professor of Economics and Deputy Director of China Center for Economic Research at Peking University. His major research areas are transition and development in China.

Xiaobo Zhang earned a BS in mathematics from Nankai University, China; an MS in economics from Tianjin University of Economics and Finance, China; and an MS and PhD in applied economics and management from Cornell University. Currently, he is a senior research fellow at the International Food Policy Research Institute (IFPRI) and the leader of IFPRI's China Program. He served as the president of the Chinese Economists Society (CES) from 2005 to 2006. He has published over two dozen papers in the fields of income distribution, growth and public investment.

Wentong Zheng is an associate attorney at the Washington, DC office of Steptoe & Johnson, LLP. He graduated from Stanford University in 2005 with a PhD degree in Economics and a Juris Doctor degree. He served as an Executive Editor of *Stanford Law Review* for the academic year 2004–05. While focusing on international trade litigation and policy advocacy in his law practice, he has a broad interest in China's legal and economic developments, including China's efforts to enact a new antitrust law.

Introduction and Acknowledgements

China's long-running experiment in replacing a failing command economy with a home-grown version of the market variety is unfinished. But it is already a resounding success if more than a quarter century of an average annual growth rate exceeding 9 percent is the criterion by which to judge. At the end of 2006, the Chinese economy was the world's fourth largest, and China has become the third largest trading nation measured by the sum of merchandise exports and imports. Poverty levels have fallen dramatically within China as income per person – below US$200 when reform began in 1978 – has risen to about US$2000 in 2006.

Still, in the Chinese way, progress is gradual and uneven, and many challenges remain. The chapters in this volume – revised versions of papers first presented in the annual conferences on Chinese policy reform hosted by the Stanford Center for International Development (SCID) at Stanford University from 2003–05 – analyze aspects of China's experiment with market reform and propose ways of responding to those challenges in several important policy areas. The contributing authors owe an intellectual debt to the other participants in SCID's conferences, most of whom have been influential scholars with extensive knowledge of China or senior Chinese officials either currently or formerly in positions of authority with influence over policy decisions. In their roles as formal discussants of papers, chairs of sessions, or commentators from the floor, conference participants have influenced the authors' thinking and contributed positively to the revisions of the original papers.

The book comprises selected chapters that evaluate a variety of legal, regulatory, and economic aspects of China's transition from a command to a market economy. Just as progress in market reform in China is uneven, so is the coverage of the included chapters. As editors, we have generally followed the following organizing principles: broad survey material is presented first (Chapters 1 and 2) as an introduction to the major issues that China is tackling, followed by institutional concerns in enabling markets to perform better (Chapters 3 through 5), then chapters analyzing specific emerging factor and goods markets (Chapters 6 through 8), and concluding with four chapters (9 through 12) that consider how the international market system helps shape the evolving Chinese market system. China's accession to the World Trade Organization (WTO) and the impact that will have on market development is a pivotal event motivating the discussion in most chapters.

The volume begins with a general survey of China's transition to a market economy. In Chapter 1, Nicholas C. Hope and Lawrence Lau present a general overview of developments in Chinese markets for goods (agricultural and industrial), services and production factors (labor, credit, securities, and land) over the period of China's accession to the World Trade Organization (WTO). The authors describe remaining market fragmentation and suggest broad policy measures to further China's transition to a market economy. Chapter 2 focuses more specifically on the progress in reform of China's enterprise system. Authors Ross Garnaut, Ligang Song and Yang Yao describe the measures officials are taking to equip formerly uncompetitive state-owned enterprises (SOEs) with the characteristics, including especially changes in ownership structure, that they need to compete effectively in China's modern markets. They analyze how China's 'privatization process' and the restructuring of SOEs have affected the performance of the enterprise system since the mid-1990s.

Chapter 3, by Bruce M. Owen, Su Sun and Wentong Zheng, reviews the recent history of competition policy (antitrust) law in China in the context of the country's unique economic, legal, and regulatory characteristics. They find that the new antitrust law has much merit, especially its focus on reducing the anticompetitive behavior of favored enterprises and government bodies. The acid test of its ability to support more effective market competition lies in the ability and the willingness of the bureaucracy to enforce the law appropriately. And Andrew Sheng, Geng Xiao, and Yuan Wang build on their growing body of work on the role of secure property rights in nurturing economic development in Chapters 4 and 5. They first consider the relationship between transaction costs, wealth creation, and property rights infrastructure, and then in Chapter 5 take up the relationship between effective corporate governance and the development of the capital market.

The evolving Chinese labor market is the main concern of Chapter 6, the first to investigate a major factor market. Belton M. Fleisher and Dennis Tao Yang analyze the changing distribution of jobs in China and other key transformations in China's labor force since the beginning of reform. They pose the questions of what are the implications of economic reform for labor-market institutions, what are the current conditions of the labor markets, and what challenges remain. They also explore the implications of establishing markets for land on the mobility of the rural labor force.

In a contribution updated through the early months of 2007, Pieter Bottelier, in Chapter 7, finds much cause for optimism in the potential for rapid development of China's debt markets. As the government continues its emphasis on reforming China's financial system, the growing diversification of debt instruments, emergence of a meaningful yield curve for government bonds, increased willingness to let markets determine key interest rates, and improving supporting infrastructure all indicate that the debt markets are poised for a breakthrough. He anticipates a broader and deeper corporate bond market that would help mitigate financial risk and add stability to the financial system, and identifies sub-national bonds as the important missing component in the supply of Chinese securities.

In Chapter 8, Xiaobo Zhang and Kong-Yam Tan take up the issue of whether Chinese domestic markets are becoming more integrated or the reverse. Hope and Lau, in their chapter, concluded that more research would be needed to arrive at firm conclusions about whether goods markets were becoming better unified across China. The analysis of Zhang and Tan provides additional evidence to support the view that Chinese goods markets increasingly exhibit the characteristics of a single market as the scope for rent-seeking behavior is reduced. They conclude, however, that distortions in the factor markets have encouraged rent seekers to shift their attention especially to the capital market where distortions continue to create opportunities for capturing rents. They recommend further reforms of the capital markets to promote competition.

Chapters 9–12 comprise the last section of the book and examine China's changing patterns of trade and capital flows during the phasing in of the reforms agreed as conditions for China's accession to the WTO. In Chapter 10, Will Martin and Vlad Manole investigate China's emergence as a (perhaps, the) major exporter of manufactured goods. The authors compare China's experience to those of other low-income exporters and examine the emergence of new exports, especially skill-intensive manufactures, during the reform period using data on export shares by sector and technology level.

David Roland-Holst analyzes in Chapter 10 the impact of China's rapid emergence as a major trading power on the economies of its neighbors. He uses a forecasting model to consider how a variety of East-Asian trade regimes might emerge and how integration with the Chinese economy could become a primary driver of economic growth in neighboring countries. There will be implications for exchange rate arrangements and probable benefits to China with the introduction of greater flexibility of the price of its currency; in time, the Chinese yuan might emerge as the anchor for a regional currency block.

In Chapter 11, Eswar S. Prasad and Shang-Jin Wei take a cross-country perspective in examining the evolution of capital flows into China. They describe and explain how the pattern and volume of capital inflows have changed, and identify a transformation early in this century as years of undocumented capital outflow yielded to undocumented inflow, presumably in anticipation of a rise in the value of the Chinese currency. They find little evidence to support the notion that China is welcoming export-oriented foreign direct investment (FDI) and manipulating its currency to maintain export-driven growth, and consider the scope for China to ease capital controls. Finally, in Chapter 12, Busakorn Chantasasawat, K.C. Fung, Hitomi Iizaka and Alan Siu investigate the determinants of FDI into China and the role FDI plays in overall capital formation. They examine the extent to which investment flows into China encourage complementary investment in neighboring countries to supply resources to meet Chinese demand, and also whether FDI drawn to China as a platform for processing trade diverts similar investment from China's neighbors. They conclude that policy and institutional factors in China's neighbors have a much greater effect on their ability to attract FDI than Chinese actions.

Overall, this book provides a multi-faceted, wide-ranging assessment of the progress of market reforms in China. It should provide valuable insight to policy makers, business planners, students and researchers interested in China, as well as to anyone interested in the world economy.

The editors greatly appreciate the financial contributions that supported the conferences from which the selected chapters were drawn. Our gratitude goes to Burton and Deedee McMurtry and Stanley Wang, to Doll Capital Management (DCM), Exxon-Mobil Corporation, the Koret Foundation, W.I. Harper Group, Warburg Pincus, and to Stanford University. We also thank the dedicated editorial staff at Edward Elgar Publishing Ltd, especially Alan Sturmer and Alexandra O'Connell, for unending patience and support of this project. Mark F. Owens typeset this manuscript and contributed to its editing.

1. China's Transition to the Market: Progress and Challenges

Nicholas C. Hope and Lawrence J. Lau[1]

1. INTRODUCTION

In the quarter century since China began to dismantle its command economy and rely more on markets, China has vaulted into the front ranks of the world's rapidly growing economies. Chinese nominal GDP reached almost two and a quarter trillion US dollars in 2005, with a 10.9 percent annualized growth rate reported in the first half of 2006. Per capita GDP for China's 1.3 billion people exceeded US$1700 in 2005; it was only US$206 in 1980. At the same time, the composition of GDP has changed, with the share originating in primary industry falling from 30 percent in 1980 to 13 percent in 2005, and that of tertiary industry rising from 21 percent to 40 percent in the same period (Table 1.1). The share of GDP originating in secondary industry was fairly stable at just under half.[2]

China's international trade has expanded even faster than the economy, with merchandise exports and imports together reaching US$1.42 trillion in 2005, 23 percent higher than in 2004, which had already seen growth of 36 percent over 2003. China's integration with the international economy, as measured by the share in GDP of total merchandise trade, has progressed rapidly, from only 14 percent in 1980, to 32 percent in 1990 and 64 percent in 2005. At the same time, the composition of merchandise trade has undergone a pronounced shift from primary products towards manufactures, which were half of exports (two-thirds of imports) in 1980 but nine-tenths of exports (four-fifths of imports) in 2000 and 94 percent of exports (78 percent of imports) in 2005 (Table 1.2). During this period, petroleum changed from a major earner of foreign exchange to a substantial net import.

More than two-thirds of Chinese GDP now originates in the broadly defined private (non-state) sector, which predominates even more as a source of jobs. With agriculture diminishing in importance, most new jobs

Table 1.1:   Composition of Gross Domestic Product (percent of total)

	1980	1985	1990	1995	2000	2005
Primary Industry	29.9	28.2	26.9	19.8	14.8	12.6
Secondary Industry	48.2	42.9	41.3	47.2	45.9	47.5
Tertiary Industry	21.9	28.9	31.8	33.0	39.3	39.9
Trillion Yuan	0.46	0.90	1.87	6.08	9.92	18.31

Source: China Statistical Yearbook 2006.

Table 1.2:   Composition of China's Merchandise Exports and Imports
           (percent of total)

	1980		1990		2000		2005	
	Exp	Imp	Exp	Imp	Exp	Imp	Exp	Imp
Primary Goods	50.3	34.8	25.6	18.5	10.2	20.8	6.4	22.4
Manufactures	49.7	65.2	74.4	81.5	89.8	79.2	93.6	77.6

Source: China Statistical Yearbook, various years and authors calculations.

are in the service sector. Moreover, the recent progress in restructuring mainly small- and medium-sized state-owned enterprises (SOEs), and in many cases transferring their ownership to private firms, is remarkable (Garnaut et al., 2005). By the end of 2001, 'about 80 percent of SOEs had undergone some form of *gaizhi* ..., and 70 percent of the *gaizhi* cases involved the transfer of ownership from the state to private owners.'[3] After a slow beginning in the mid-1990s, the doctrine of 'retaining the large and letting go the small' has gained momentum: the central government intends to maintain its ownership and control of a thousand or so of the largest SOEs, while allowing the others to pass to the control of lower-level governments or private interests.[4]

Undoubtedly, progress in *gaizhi* has been accelerated by the increasing official recognition of the essential role of the private sector in sustaining China's rapid growth. Early examples were provided in two speeches by former President and Party Secretary, Jiang Zemin: in the first speech he welcomed private entrepreneurs to party membership,[5] and in the second he stressed the importance of the non-state sector in 'promoting economic growth, creating jobs, and invigorating markets.'[6] Although the transformation of the enterprise system has not been free from problems, its speed confirms that, in China, gradual does not mean slow.

China's generally impressive macro-economic performance has been accomplished against a backdrop of continuing but still incomplete reform. Since the blueprint for a 'socialist market economy' was announced in

November 1993, considerable progress has been made on an ambitious agenda for economic reform, but much is left to do in improving the performance of state enterprises, and in reforming the financial system and the social safety net. Even where positive steps have been taken (restoring the health of the public finances, improving the framework for the conduct of monetary policy, freeing markets), further reforms are needed.[7] Moreover, the adjustments required to accommodate the profound changes that are resulting from accession to the World Trade Organization (WTO) serve only to emphasize that Chinese reform is very much an ongoing process.

This chapter considers the progress China has made in one important aspect of its reforms: the extent to which Chinese markets now function efficiently. It serves as an introduction to the more detailed analyses of particular markets found in the body of the volume. It takes a broad brush view of the evolution of markets, investigating conditions in selected markets for goods, services, and factors of production and presenting conclusions in a highly aggregated way about broad classifications of goods, services and factors. More specifically, the chapter considers developments in the markets for agricultural goods, industrial goods, retailing services, labor, credit, stocks, bonds, and land. Many of those markets are treated in more depth in subsequent chapters, and some of the conclusions of those chapters are also included to complete the picture painted here. Any student of Chinese reform would conclude that China has benefited greatly from its experiments with markets, and has largely succeeded in eliminating administered pricing. China now relies on the forces of supply and demand to determine prices to varying degrees: predominantly in the goods markets, increasingly in the markets for services, and considerably, albeit partially, in the markets for factors of production.

Much remains to be done, however, to improve the efficiency of Chinese markets. Some policies, laws, regulations and rules still need amendment and many of them need to be implemented more consistently, with less scope for regional discretion. Market-supporting institutions, especially the legal system, also need to improve performance greatly. The continuing priorities for China's governments are to eliminate barriers to the greater integration of the domestic markets; to encourage foreign participation in the Chinese economy and closer ties with global markets; to supply better information about economic conditions to all market participants; and to continue to experiment by introducing complementary markets and market supporting services.

2. LIBERALIZING CHINESE MARKETS

The strategy of improving economic incentives by allowing prices to be determined in progressively freer markets has been at the heart of Chinese reforms. Over more than a quarter century, China has made steady progress in freeing domestic markets, so that prices are now much more closely aligned with economic costs. Similar progress has been made in reducing the barriers to international trade so that Chinese domestic prices are increasingly better aligned with international prices. One result has been significant efficiency gains in China's use of resources, thereby spurring growth. Of the former centrally planned economies, China can claim to have been among the most successful in transitioning from a centrally planned to a predominantly market economy.[8] Although China retains the formal mechanisms of the central plan, the eleventh Five-Year Plan (2006–10) is indicative, not mandatory; reference to it in official pronouncements on the economy has become rare. And, with some exceptions noted below, the rate of interest and the exchange rate are the only prices that are still administratively determined on the margin, though lending rates, in particular, now convey considerable flexibility to banks. Significantly, what was in former times the State Planning Commission is, since March 2003, the State Development and Reform Commission.

2.1. How did China Make the Transition?

Under central planning, enterprises and households are assigned rights to and obligations for fixed quantities of commodities at fixed prices. Rights and obligations are specific to individual enterprises and households, and there are governmental sanctions if they fail to fulfill those obligations. In converting its planned economy to a market economy, China faced two principal challenges: the replacement of (i) administrative allocation by market allocation, and (ii) administered prices by market prices. The ease with which those requirements can be stated contrasts starkly with the complexity of implementing them in a country as big as China.[9]

The Chinese solution was the ingenious 'dual-track' approach, under which two mechanisms were phased in to allocate each product. The 'plan track' – the pre-existing central plan – remained, and its rights and obligations continued to be enforced by the government. At the same time, a 'market track' was introduced for output above the planned amounts. On the margin, all markets were immediately open, with prices determined by supply and demand. Under the dual-track system, producers were given both autonomy and incentive to organize their production to enable them to participate in the market, provided their obligations under the plan were fulfilled. Consumers were completely free to plan their consumption and participate in the market, given allocated consumption goods and fulfillment of labor obligations.

Changes on the margin allowed incentives to respond to prices that align with economic costs, without excessive dislocation or damage to those unable to take advantage of the new arrangements. The profits and losses (and taxes and subsidies) of enterprises under the central plan remained the same before and after the initiation of the dual-track reform. Continued planned deliveries of consumer goods enabled authorities to maintain the pre-reform standard of living as a floor. At the same time, differences between plan and market prices made lump-sum transfers feasible, creating scope to compensate people disadvantaged by reforms. No one was worse off, producers and consumers enjoyed autonomy and incentive on the margin, beneficiaries of the process supported further reform, and potential opponents were bought off, thus minimizing opposition.[10]

Table 1.3 illustrates the progress through 2001 of the dual-track approach in selected goods markets. In the broadly defined markets for agricultural goods, industrial goods, and retail sales, the plan-track was phased out quickly. When reform began in 1978, the shares of output value sold at market prices rose from close to zero to 88 percent, 81 percent and 94

Table 1.3: *Phasing Out the Dual-Track (percent of output value, selected years)*

	1978	1985	1991	1993	1995	1998	1999	2001
Agricultural Products								
Plan price	94.4	37.0	22.2	10.4	17.0	9.1	6.7	2.7
Guide price	0.0	23.0	20.0	2.1	4.4	7.1	2.9	3.4
Market price	5.6	40.0	57.8	87.5	78.6	83.8	90.4	93.9
Industrial goods								
Plan price	100.0	64.0	44.6	13.8	15.6	9.6	9.6	9.5
Guide price	0.0	23.0	19.0	5.1	6.5	4.4	4.8	2.9
Market price	0.0	13.0	36.4	81.1	77.9	86.0	85.6	87.6
Total Retail Sales								
Plan price	97.0	47.0	30.0	4.8	8.8	4.1	3.7	2.7
Guide price	0.0	19.0	25.0	1.4	2.4	1.2	1.5	1.3
Market price	3.0	34.0	45.0	93.8	88.8	94.7	94.8	96.0

Note: 'Guide prices' are government-administered prices, but with reference to market supply and demand.

Source: *Price Yearbook of China* (various years).

percent, respectively, by 1993. They continued to rise to 94 percent, 88 percent and 96 percent, respectively, by 2001. Taking a guarded view of developments, one can summarize the experience as one of rapid conversion to market pricing through 1993, with only slow progress (and even regress in the inflationary period 1993–95) thereafter. Although broad classes of markets are essentially free to set prices according to supply and demand, small but persistent elements of planned pricing continued into the new century.

The government also maintained its influence over the grain market during the reform period. In 1978, state procurement – all at plan-determined prices – accounted for 16 percent of a domestic grain production of 305 million tons. By 1987–88, total annual production had risen to about 400 million tons of which the state procured 24 percent, albeit with only 13 percent procured at plan-determined prices. By 1995, grain production increased to 470 million tons, of which state procurement accounted for 20 percent, evenly split between the quota (procured at approximately 60 percent of the free market price) and negotiated purchases (procured at approximately 90 percent of market price). Only 30 percent of total production was marketed outside the village of origin, meaning that government grain enterprises were procuring an astonishing 65 percent of grain output sold outside the village of its production (World Bank, 1997). In 2002, grain production was 457 million tons.[11] Minister Ma Kai announced a fall of 26.4 million metric tons in 2003, which together with the widening gulf between urban and rural incomes has prompted even greater attention to agricultural reforms as indicated by Premier Wen (5 March 2004, Report: pages 16–18).[12] Although many of the initiatives he announced were welcome, in particular the increase in investment for agriculture, the enhancement of agricultural research and extension services, reform of agricultural taxes and charges, and direct income subsidies for poor farmers, the emphasis on putting more land into grain production was hard to reconcile both with the elimination of controls on grain purchases and markets and with China's undertakings on agriculture for its accession to the WTO.

The grain market clearly continues to be affected by the effective monopsony power of state interests, despite competition between government enterprise and private retailers who purchase their stocks mainly from state-owned enterprises. In the interests of 'price stabilization' provinces have stored vast quantities of grain, an increasingly (and massively) inefficient way of ensuring that local officials can cope with localized harvest failures and other events that might threaten continuity of food supply. Those objectives could be achieved with much lower stocks,

Table 1.4: *Growth of the Non-State Sector in Retail Sales (percent of total)*

Ownership type	1979	1998
Collective	43.1	16.6
State	54.0	20.7
Individual	0.2	37.1
Joint	0.0	0.6
Other	2.6	25.2

Source: *China Statistical Yearbook* (various years).

which could be (and increasingly are) maintained more efficiently by private traders under more competitive market conditions.

2.2. Diversifying Ownership

The move to market pricing has been fostered by the rapid diversification of ownership. In 1979 total retail sales were dominated by state-owned (54 percent) and collectively-owned (43 percent) enterprises, but their combined share had fallen to only 37 percent in 1998, when individually owned ventures also accounted for 37 percent of total sales and other ownership forms for the remaining quarter.[13]

To a large extent, the perception is that progress in freeing domestic markets for other services is impressive too, though there are occupations where, similar to wholesale and retail distribution, competition has been limited until very recently. Public utilities, financial services, and such professional services as accounting and audit, marketing, legal, and management consulting are areas where entry barriers until very recently have impeded competition, especially from abroad. Partly for that reason, the negotiations for WTO accession targeted service markets to a marked degree, and heightened competition in the markets for services, especially financial services, will be one of the more beneficial outcomes of China's WTO accession. At the same time, accommodating foreign competitors in areas where domestic suppliers of services have been notably inefficient will require sustained efforts to improve local firms' performance, if their inability to compete is not to lead to pressures to re-impose protection.[14]

3. HOW COMPLETE IS MARKET REFORM?

The general current perception is that China's markets for final goods are largely free, despite a sense that pervasive protectionism lingers at the local level. The dual-track system of prices introduced in the mid-1980s to facilitate China's transition from a centrally planned to a socialist market economy has essentially been phased out. For almost all goods sold in Chinese markets, the forces of demand and supply have been the primary determinants of market prices for a decade or more. What remains is a single-track, market-based system, with some important exceptions: the prices of natural gas, petroleum, edible oils, grains, tobacco, water, salt, and products related to national security are still administered to a greater or lesser extent.

Although markets now determine the prices of virtually all goods in China that does not mean that all markets are competitive, or that all prices are determined by marginal costs. Moreover, there are questions about the extent to which China comprises a single market. In part, those questions reflect an explicit policy from the early communist years of establishing self-contained regions within China to ensure the continuing supply of essential commodities in the event of an invasion or foreign occupation of part of the country. Subsequently, a rudimentary distribution system contributed to the isolation of markets. Even now, transport and other distribution costs are a significant constraining factor in integrating national markets. Opinion differs about the extent to which domestic markets are now integrated, and, even if they are mainly integrated for final goods, factor markets are still fragmented to a marked extent.

There is a body of anecdotal and other evidence that points to widespread protection of local markets, even as similar evidence points to the increasing availability of goods produced throughout China in most local markets. Local officials can and do create barriers to firms from elsewhere in China in order to reserve local markets. A range of instruments is used: licenses that can be withheld arbitrarily; technical, health or other standards; levies imposed on goods as they transit provincial boundaries; or explicit subsidies (or tax concessions) to firms that 'buy local.' Central authorities have consistently opposed local protectionist forces, with recent additional emphasis occasioned by the provisions for unrestricted market access under the accession agreement for the WTO, but the fight to integrate the market continues.

Some analysts conclude, nevertheless: 'Such comparative data as are available should convince us that China has the basic characteristics of a single country, rather than an international trading union.' Using data from 1987 and 1992, Naughton (2003) further finds that there are only 'two provinces for which foreign trade is more important than domestic interprovincial trade ... Guangdong and Fujian.' Others have reached opposing conclusions based on trade across provincial borders, as well as on the comparison of price data within and between provinces, with particular emphasis on 'spatial discontinuities implied by provincial borders' (Poncet, 2003a). Some researchers conclude that not only has the general lack of integration of regional markets that the World Bank noted in its study in 1994 been sustained, but also the forces impeding internal trade flows might have intensified in the 1990s (Young, 2000; Poncet, 2003b). In Chapter 8 of this volume, Xiaobo Zhang and Kong-Yam Tan examine more recent contributions to this debate. Although the studies they cite still seem insufficiently authoritative to admit firm conclusions, they do provide some persuasive evidence to suggest that the domestic goods markets now exhibit less rather than more fragmentation and are becoming better integrated.[15]

Chinese tariffs are low by the standards of many developing countries, all the more so as the further reductions agreed under the WTO protocols are implemented. The US Trade Representative's office estimated for US exports that, in 2007, tariffs on major industrial goods would fall to 7 percent compared with 25 percent in 1997, and to 14 percent from 31 percent for agricultural goods.[16] Moreover, most non-tariff measures, notably including licenses, quotas, and tendering arrangements, were eliminated at accession. China negotiated some exceptions, with quotas remaining on processed petroleum (until 2004), rubber products (2004), and automobiles and automotive parts, for which quotas were progressively liberalized then eliminated in 2005.

But tariffs, quotas and other impediments to international trade are often augmented by additional policies that have the effect of protecting the domestic market. Huang et al. (2003, pp. 6–7) show that domestic taxation policy serves to protect Chinese agriculture. They cite national regulations requiring imported goods (not for immediate re-export) typically to be subject to value-added tax in the range 13–17 percent. Traders who procure agricultural commodities directly from farmers are exempted from the tax. When applied to soybeans, Huang et al. (2003) conclude that domestic producers receive price protection in the domestic market of about 10 percent. A noteworthy conclusion of the same paper is that most of China's agricultural markets appear to be 'well-integrated into the economy' in the sense that, despite remote locations and the high costs of reaching distant markets, movements in border prices for undifferentiated agricultural commodities (such as soybeans and maize) correlate with price movements in local markets.

In several service sectors, as Table 1.5 illustrates, China chose to liberalize over time. Supply of wholesale and retail trade services was restricted at first to joint ventures, which were subject also to geographic limitations. Foreign-owned insurers were limited as to the kinds of insurance they could provide: for example, reinsurance and certain forms of

Table 1.5: *Examples of China's Limitations on Access to Service Markets*

Sector	Cross-border supply	Consumption abroad	Commercial presence	Presence of natural persons
Insurance	Unbound, with exceptions	None	Subject to 3-year geographic and scope liberalization, 5-year capital liberalization	Unbound
Banking	Unbound, with exceptions	None	Subject to 5-year liberalization	Unbound
Retail services	Unbound except for mail order	None	Subject to 5-year liberalization	Unbound
Wholesale distribution	Unbound	None	Subject to 3-year liberalization	Unbound
Transport	Unbound	None	Subject to limitations on foreign ownership	Unbound
Telecom.	Subject to regulations	None	Subject to 3-year geographic and ownership limitations	Unbound

Note: Natural persons, as defined by the WTO, are citizens or permanent residents of a member country.

Source: Schedule of Specific Commitments: People's Republic of China, World Trade Organization, 2002. (Document code: GATS/SC/135.)

transportation insurance were forbidden. Initially, they were allowed to operate only in certain large cities, e.g. Shanghai and Dalian, but these restrictions lapsed three years after accession. Foreign-owned banks initially were circumscribed in their ability to offer domestic currency services, but the scope of services and geographic regions in which they were allowed to operate were greatly extended over five years, and eliminated from January 2007. Most restrictions on transportation services were lifted at the time of accession, but the maritime and aviation sectors were open only to new entrants with minority foreign ownership. Rail and road transport were scheduled for complete liberalization within three years.

There were important provisions as well to introduce freer markets and greater competition for state trading companies, which had to become more independent and make price decisions on a commercial basis. Competition in international trade was intensified in four stages. At accession, all Chinese enterprises were allowed to trade subject to capital requirements that were to be lowered over time. In 2003, joint ventures with minority foreign ownership were able to trade. In 2004, joint ventures with majority foreign ownership acquired trading rights. Finally, in 2005, all Chinese and foreign companies, as well as many individuals, were able to engage in international trade.

An interesting development was China's entry into a closer economic partnership agreement (CEPA) with Hong Kong (see note 13). That agreement extended the provisions of the WTO accession preferentially to Hong Kong, with most taking effect from the beginning of 2004. The Deutsche Bank analyst Jun Ma (2003) listed the many examples of products of Hong Kong origin that became tariff-exempt from January 2004, and characterized China's offer of tariff liberalization measures as 'more generous than ... expected.' But he also viewed the concessions made on access to China's service sectors as having greater long-term impact for the Hong Kong economy. Using fairly restrictive criteria to define a venture as having its origin in Hong Kong, those ventures that qualified enjoyed preferential treatment compared to other nationals' firms, and were allowed to enter Chinese service sectors selectively either earlier than provided for in the WTO accession protocols or with less stringent requirements for entry, or both.

For example, Hong Kong banks with minimum assets of US$6 billion were eligible to open branches in China, compared with a minimum asset requirement of US$20 billion for other foreign banks. And Hong Kong representatives in Chinese representative offices of Hong Kong law firms were required to reside in China for only two months a year compared with six months for similar representatives of other nationalities. As a result of CEPA, there was scope for Hong Kong based companies to benefit significantly from the advantages of an early start. And China also might have benefited from yet another example of 'gradualism,' this time as it applied to adjustment to increased competition from foreign firms under the provisions of the WTO.

Finally, China still restricts rights to land ownership, and the documents for its accession to the WTO made clear that all land is owned by the State. Individuals and businesses could lease land, but subject to term limitations. For residential purposes, the limit is 70 years. For commercial, tourist, and recreational purposes, the limit is 40 years. For all other uses, including educational, cultural, and industrial purposes, the limit is 50 years.

4. THE OVERALL IMPACT OF THE WTO

China's accession to the WTO raised its own questions about how well

Chinese markets for goods and services work, and how they would handle the heightened competitive pressures engendered by both the entry of foreign enterprise into activities previously denied to them, and the further reduction of trade protection. Ianchovichina and Martin (2004) estimated that China's weighted average tariff would fall from 13.3 percent in 2001 to 6.8 percent by the end of the implementation period. They regarded this as a significant reduction in protection, but a minor one compared with the decline in tariff levels achieved over the decade preceding WTO accession. By implication, the adjustment to the post-WTO regime should have been routine, given what had taken place before. On the other hand, the commitments made to open trade in services were more dramatic and therefore were likely to have a more disruptive impact on domestic suppliers of those services (Bhattasali et al., 2004).

Within China, local officials were particularly concerned about the effects on agricultural output and the implications for employment and incomes in rural areas. The work of Huang et al. (2003) suggests that undifferentiated agricultural commodities were likely to be the hardest hit by foreign competition, particularly products that had been favored with protection from policies not principally directed at international trade, but inadmissible under the rules of the WTO. Ianchovichina and Martin projected that beverages and tobacco would be among the sectors that faced considerable pressure to adjust. Most analysts agree that the automotive sector would go through a major realignment, mainly because of policies that fostered a proliferation of uneconomically-sized automotive assemblers throughout China, a result of the flawed notion that China needed to promote 'pillar industries.' The automotive sector currently enjoys booming demand, but an excess of domestic producers also faces intense competitive pressure from imports as protective barriers are rolled back, adding to the incentive to rationalize the domestic assembly of cars.

The work of Martin and others has demonstrated that China's compensation for the inevitable adjustment costs of WTO entry would lie in the gains from further specialization according to comparative advantage. The benefits to China from further opening would be considerable, substantially higher, as one should expect from what is essentially a unilateral action on China's part, than those accruing to other countries from Chinese accession. Other analysts have pointed to the impetus that China's accession to the WTO has given to globalization more generally, and particularly to the presumption that initiatives to liberalize further global trading arrangements should occur in multilateral negotiations despite the disappointments of Doha.

The potential efficiency gains to China from competition in the provision of services clearly are considerable. But many domestic suppliers in such sensitive areas as banking, insurance, telecommunications, retailing and logistics could fare poorly in direct competition with foreign suppliers. One can anticipate therefore that Chinese officials might take advantage of all recourse offered to them under the WTO to continue to shield domestic suppliers from the full force of competition. To an extent, this was done already in the provisions for graduated elimination of ownership and geographical restrictions on the activities of foreign service-providers. But one suspects that Chinese banks, for example, have still been unable to work off the legacy effects of an underdeveloped credit culture and non-performing loans to SOEs, despite Government actions to remove most non-performing loans from their balance sheets, to inject new capital, and to allow strategic investment from foreign banks and investors in off-shore share issues.[17] As 2007 begins, Chinese officials still could be seeking compromises in several areas to slow the entry of foreign competitors, effectively trading off the early realization of substantial efficiency gains against the perceived subsequent benefit of maintaining competitive domestic suppliers of important classes of financial services.

5. ISSUES IN CHINA'S FACTOR MARKETS

Most observers still consider that China's factor markets function much less freely than markets for goods and services, even allowing for recent measures that have enhanced factor mobility. The prices of labor, capital and land all remain subject to distortions caused by restrictions on mobility, ill-defined property rights,[18] administered allocation and pricing, and other interventions designed to affect 'market' outcomes.

5.1. The Labor Market

The development of labor markets has been impeded by direct (administrative) restraints on the ability of workers to relocate within China, as well as indirect ones mainly related to the lack of portability of benefits. The most noteworthy among these are health benefits, housing and pensions. Xin Meng (2000) summarizes the non-existence of a functioning labor market before reforms began in 1978 as follows: 'The main characteristics of (China's) labor arrangements before (1978) were the segregation of the rural and urban economies, the extreme immobility of labor and the disincentives implanted in the income distribution system.'

More recently, Fleisher and Yang (Chapter 6 in this volume) point to the extreme divergence of urban and rural incomes, which places China among those countries where the ratio of urban to rural income is greatest (approximately 3), as *prima facie* evidence of the barriers that still impede labor mobility. They cite similarly wide divergences in the productivity of labor in agricultural compared with non-agricultural occupations, true of both urban and rural areas. But, notwithstanding the market impediments that remain, they also point to important successes in labor market reform. Chief among those successes are the decline of the planning framework for enterprise employment, the diminishing importance of the state sector and collectives as suppliers of jobs and output, the profound changes in work incentives for both rural and urban employees and their managers, and growing integration of product and labor markets nationwide.[19] They cite estimates that attribute from a sixth to a fifth of China's annual growth in the reform era to the movement of labor from lower to higher productivity occupations.

Differences in productivity of urban and rural workers are not the only indicator of a major source of inefficiency in allocating labor. Within rural areas, large productivity differentials persist between agricultural and non-agricultural activities. Fleisher and Yang identify three factors that comprise persistent impediments to the mobility of rural labor. First, they note, farm families enjoy land-use rights 'but not rights of alienation.' Families leaving the land forego future earnings from their land holdings, meaning that wages in new employment must compensate for their loss; they would accept lower wages if they could sell their land-use rights. Labor mobility is impeded further by the requirement that households sell part of their grain output in quantities and at prices determined by the government, which limits their ability to reallocate family labor to other jobs.[20] The rural reform program foreshadowed in Premier Wen Jiabao's speech on 5 March 2004 (see note 10) probably included greater mobility of rural labor amongst its objectives.

The other two factors discussed by Fleisher and Yang are local protection and the *hukou* system.[21] They cite a survey reported by the Development Research Center of the State Council in 2003 that identified 'intervening in the labor market' as the form of protection most commonly used by officials to benefit local enterprises. Moreover, long-time residents are favored in both pay and benefits relative to those who come from elsewhere seeking employment. The *hukou* system is less constraining than in the past, with residency typically being granted in smaller cities and towns to those who have secure jobs and the means to acquire housing in the locality. Migration to the larger cities still is severely restricted, and people who move there seeking jobs are unable to secure all of the benefits for their families that registered residents enjoy.

In recent years, labor scarcity in rapidly growing cities in Eastern provinces has been a spur to reform. In particular, shortages of senior managerial and technical skills seem to be contributing to the emergence of greater mobility and more extensive recruitment of those skills nationwide and even internationally (ADB, 2003). Senior officials of less developed provinces have begun to express unease about the 'brain drain' of their graduates to employment with enterprises, including foreign-invested ones, located in the coastal region. More generally, the onset of reforms involved significant restructuring of the broad labor market, parallel to the dual-track reforms in the markets for goods and services. In 1978, three-fifths of the non-farm workforce was employed in the state sector, and all state workers were guaranteed permanent employment. By 1997, the share of permanent state employees in the non-farm workforce had fallen below one in six, reflecting the dramatic increase in total employment of the non-state sector (from 40 to 70 percent) as well as the increasing use of contract employees by the state. In 1997, more than half of state employees were contract workers.

The State Statistical Bureau ceased reporting the breakdown between contract and non-contract employees in state employment in 1998, presumably because the distinction vanished with the civil service reform in that year. This reform essentially made all state employees contract employees, and sharply reduced their number. By 2000, there were 107 million employees of urban enterprises with labor contracts and, even for rural collective enterprises, the number of contract employees reached 23 million. This compares with total employment in 2000 of 721 million. By 2002, total employment reached 737 million, with 248 million employed in urban areas.[22] By 2005, total employment was 758 million, with 273 million urban employees.[23]

Lay-offs in the state sector caused a contraction of almost 30 million workers in the non-farm state workforce by 2000, when the share of non-state workers rose to 76 percent, and a further nine million plus state sector jobs had been lost by 2002, when the corresponding share of non-state workers reached 78 percent. These numbers probably exaggerate the true flexibility of the labor markets, as governments at all levels continue to monitor closely the firing practices of enterprises, and intervene when employees threaten to become restive.

Nevertheless, in the early years of the new century there was considerable progress in developing the (urban) labor market, with pilot efforts to standardize and modernize employment practices in 100 cities nationwide. Municipal employment analysis of supply and demand conditions began to be reported in 62 of the cities, and 64 of them offered real-time information networks. Services offered under the pilot included assistance in locating jobs, occupational training, employment counseling, and social security benefits, including pensions, basic health care, unemployment insurance (all compulsory), disability insurance and maternity benefits. Coverage under all five benefit programs costs employers around 30 percent of the worker's wage, with the worker's contribution somewhat over a third of the payment made by the enterprise or work unit. Essentially, China has been transitioning in the customary gradual way from a system of guaranteed employment with little choice of employer, into one that offers considerable choice between employment opportunities but at the cost of security of long-term employment.

5.2. Credit Markets

China's debt markets comprise predominantly bank loans, and bonds and bills; in 2006, loans were still about four times the volume of debt securities (excluding PBC bills) notwithstanding the rapid expansion of the latter from 1998. Bonds and bills are dominated by issues of the Central Government and its agencies, despite recent rapid growth in the inter-bank market for corporate bills, and a pick up in the issuance of corporate bonds that might accelerate further as the right to authorize bond issues passes from the NDRC to the CSRC.[24] Recent experiments in liberalizing lending rates for bank loans included provision in October 2004 for banks to adjust lending rates freely, but deposit rates are still largely administered. As well, the interest rates on Government bonds at time of issuance have been remarkably similar no matter what their maturity. Both in access to bank credits and in issuance of bonds, borrowers other than the Government and state-owned enterprises are severely disadvantaged. One has to conclude, therefore, that the debt markets have far to go before they conform to the ideal of competitive markets.

Even though the four large state-owned commercial banks (SCBs) are no longer formally servants of the credit plan, they still allocate the bulk of their lending to state-owned enterprises (SOEs). Many SOEs are loss-making, and use bank credit to meet current obligations to their workers and pensioners without much attention to repayment. Despite their indifferent performance, the SCBs continue to dominate the domestic credit market. They accounted for more than 60 percent of domestic banking assets in 2001, when three of them – the Industrial and Commercial Bank of China (ICBC), the Bank of China (BOC), and the China Construction Bank (CCB), in that order – were among the 50 largest global banks, and all four (the other being the Agricultural Bank of China (ABC)) were in the top ten banks in Asia by asset size (Solvet, 2002).[25] They continued to account for 60 percent of banking assets at the end of 2003, and 55 percent at the end of 2004.[26] Along with the state policy banks (since 1994) and the four asset management companies (AMCs – set up in 1999 to deal with some of the bad loans on the books of the four SCBs and the China Development Bank (CDB)), the SCBs comprise overwhelmingly the core of the Chinese banking system, notwithstanding the recent emergence of many smaller banks and increasing activity from foreign banking interests.[27]

The SCBs were, and to a considerable extent remain, hamstrung by the legacy of the plan. Analysts in the early years of the new century variously estimated non-performing loans (NPLs) to comprise a quarter to a half of the SCBs' portfolios, with the official figure at the bottom of the range. For example, Solvet (2002, page 41) put the figure at about a third of outstanding loans, and assumed a recovery rate of about 20 percent (consistent with the experience of the AMCs) to project system-wide losses of about 30 percent of GDP in 2001. Solvet was one of several analysts at that time who concluded that the big four banks would be unlikely to be able to restore themselves to profitability and financial health simply by growing their way out of their problems.[28] Essentially, the SCBs were insolvent, as subsequently recognized in the Government's actions to remove more non-performing loans from the SCBs' portfolios, and to recapitalize them through direct injections of equity, the sale of minority investments to strategic foreign investors and to public share offerings for CCB and BOC (in 2005) and ICBC (in 2006). Despite their portfolio problems, the SCBs are highly liquid and have continued to lend vigorously, consistent with an economy where the M2/GDP ratio exceeds 160 percent (2005).

To encourage better lending performance by the SCBs, the People's Bank of China (PBC) established targets for non-performing loans in each of the four large SCBs of 15 percent by the end of 2005. The official aggregate ratio for the SCBs' NPLs was 30 percent at the end of 2001, and was approaching 20 percent by the end of 2003.[29] Setting aside concerns about the accuracy of the official figures, as some observers put the ratio of NPLs far higher, one might question whether banks went about reducing their NPLs in the right way. Credit expansion in 2002–03 picked up strongly, and much of the improvement in the banks' portfolio performance might have resulted from the youth of the portfolio rather than improvements in the lending practices of the banks.

Many analysts, including in particular the authors of this chapter, would argue the need to ensure that banks are free to make decisions based solely on commercial considerations, as a precondition for a massive, once-for-all capital injection to write off unrecoverable loans and establish a satisfactory capital base for the SCBs. Even when freed from the obligation to prop up shaky SOEs, there is still reason to question the competence of the managers of the four SCBs to reduce loan losses to acceptable levels immediately. But the more radical solutions appearing in the past two to three years might improve the performance of the SCBs and permit them to compete on an equal footing with foreign banks by the second half of this decade. There seems much to commend in the government's experiments in seeking foreign partners who could inject both new capital and management and financial expertise to establish sound practices in the SCBs.

The Government has seemed bent on this path since its announcement, early in January, 2004, that it was injecting US$45 billion from the People's Bank of China's international exchange reserves as new capital to the BOC and CCB, with half of the funds going to each. A company, Central Huijin Investment Ltd., was established to hold the equity in the two banks as its only asset, and its board comprises officials from the PBC, State Administration of Foreign Exchange and the Ministry of Finance. The new company effectively became the largest shareholder in the two banks; possibly, it is a precursor of a financial version of the State-owned Asset Supervision and Administration Commission (SASAC), which was established to discharge the State's ownership functions for the Central Government's SOEs.

The funds injection improved the two banks' balance sheets and along with the credibility provided by reputable strategic foreign investors helped in propelling the BOC and the CCB into successful initial public share issues (IPOs). Those IPOs, together with the later, hugely successful, similar exercise for ICBC, further augmented the banks' capital at comparatively low cost to the Government. By the middle of 2006, all three of the publicly listed banks reported NPL ratios below 5 percent of their portfolios, a result of aggressive removal of NPLs, massive capital injection, and probably some improvement in their selection of borrowers, Many governance issues remain to be resolved, however, and the degree of management autonomy that will be extended to the BOC, CCB and ICBC remains uncertain. What is clear, however, is that until the factors that contribute to the weaknesses of their portfolios are overcome, the SCBs' capacity to compete with better-capitalized foreign banks will be impaired severely. In turn, that might presage a reluctance by the Government soon to allow market forces freely to determine the allocation of credit. In particular, as foreign banks compete for a greater share of the Chinese market, controls on deposit rates are unlikely to be eased.

Lending to private enterprises continues to be a comparatively minor activity of the SCBs, partly because of their weak portfolios, and partly because until October 2004 they had insufficient flexibility to set interest rates at levels that would make such lending profitable when adjusted for transaction costs, monitoring costs, and risk. But the SCBs increasingly do lend for consumer purchases that have an 'investment character.' Consumer lending, which was virtually zero in 1997, grew explosively subsequently and comprised more than 8 percent of financial institutions' portfolios by the middle of 2003. At that time, housing finance accounted for three-quarters of the lending, with the remaining quarter divided between automobile loans and all others. By the end of 2005 according to Moody's, consumer lending had risen to more than 10 percent of the SCBs' portfolios, more than four-fifths of which was mortgages.[30] The rapid growth of consumer lending has helped reduce the share of non-performing loans in SCBs' portfolios, but the development is too recent to judge the longer-term effects on loan performance and portfolio quality.

5.4. Securities Markets

The securities and other asset markets have developed quickly but with a heavy bias towards securities issued by the central government, its specialized financial agencies and listed SOEs. As the markets developed in the 1990s, securities were listed on either or both of two main boards in Shanghai and Shenzhen. Foreigners participated by purchasing 'B-shares,' with 'A-shares' reserved for Chinese nationals. This segmentation of the market persisted until recently. In November 2002, the China Securities and Regulatory Commission (CSRC) promulgated the 'Provisional Measures on Administration of Domestic Securities' Investments of Qualified Foreign Institutional Investors (QFII), which allows qualified foreign fund management institutions, insurance companies, securities companies and other asset management institutions to invest in Chinese securities markets. The QFII will be able to purchase A-shares, treasury instruments, bonds and other financial instruments as approved by the CSRC, up to an investment quota granted/approved by the State Administration of Foreign Exchange (SAFE). Applicants for QFII status must satisfy the CSRC's requirements on assets size, financial and credit standing, and other factors. By August 2003, seven foreign companies – Citigroup Global Markets, Deutsche Bank, Goldman Sachs, HSBC, Morgan Stanley and Co. International, Nomura Securities, and UBS – had received CSRC approval to invest in China's securities markets. China's extraordinary foreign reserve holdings almost surely have played a part in this decision, along with a desire to introduce greater liquidity and fund management expertise into China's capital markets. During 2004, the continuing, heavy volume of capital inflow apparently discouraged further substantial investment approvals; nevertheless, by the middle of 2006, SAFE had approved 40 foreign institutions as QFII for potential investments exceeding eight billion dollars.[31]

The stock market listings are dominated by SOEs, and those markets are unlikely sources of capital for the vast majority of Chinese private ventures in the near term. No more than about 20 privately held firms have been allowed to list, though early in 2004 more than 200 listed firms were regarded as private because of post-listing sales of Government-held, largely legal person, shares. An issue is the extent to which these firms now function as if they are privately owned; in particular, are the firms' managers free to make their own hiring and firing and investment decisions free of official interventions? For most of the more than 1400 firms listed in 2006, the predominant objective seems to have been to attract new funds, an entirely rational response to market prices that have seemed absurdly high in relation to the financial fundamentals of most listed enterprises.[32] Listed SOEs seem disinterested, in particular, in using the discipline of the market to improve their governance, financial transparency and efficiency.

Despite evident problems, especially the comprehensiveness and reliability of the financial information available for listed firms, the Chinese stock markets comprise the third biggest market in Asia (after Japan and Hong Kong), with a daily market turnover of about US$1.5 billion. The market capitalization is approximately equivalent to US$1.14 trillion in 2006, but two-thirds of the stock is in state-owned, non-tradable (or non-circulating) institutional shares.[33] Notwithstanding some glaring deficiencies of the markets, the CSRC impresses as a competent and responsible agency that has introduced a succession of liberalizations of them. The second half of 1999 alone saw the introduction of indexed funds in China and permission for SOEs to trade stocks. Plans to sell some of the Government's share holdings in listed companies to help fund pension obligations had to be shelved, however, in October 2001 when the prospect of such selling led to disorderly markets and consequent investor unrest. As concerns about the treatment of these shares began to recede through 2005, confidence returned to the markets, which once more witnessed the resumption of a steady stream of new issues after June 2006.

Private firms and others under non-state ownership are likely to raise their share in listed companies. But the process, like so many reforms in China, is also likely to be gradual. China's regulators require a lengthy process before stocks can be listed, including a training program for officers of the listing companies on the responsibilities of senior executives of publicly traded companies. The program is a commendable requirement, and can run for as long as a year. The gradual nature of the process leaves the question of how to channel more risk capital to private ventures unanswered. One might conjecture that an even bigger role is emerging for venture capital, and that smaller, regional stock markets can flourish (as already seems to be happening informally) in a manner that helps smaller firms find reliable investment partners.

Until very recently, for almost all enterprises and sub-national governments there was no bond market to speak of. That has begun to change for selected SOEs, 19 of which issued around US$590 million (equivalent) in corporate bonds in 2000, increasing to US$4.3 billion in new issues in 2002 (Bottelier, 2004).[34] Since the central bank law prohibited (in 1995) the funding of governments through credit creation, the central government has been issuing considerable volumes of bonds, in particular to finance infrastructure expenditures in poor western provinces. The policy banks and the AMCs also have issued bonds to fund their activities. Many bond issues are non-tradable placements, usually with banks, and there is no active secondary market for many other securities that have been placed at administered interest rates rather than publicly issued. Bottelier (2004) noted, however, that the absence of secondary market activity in corporate bonds can be attributed to their scarcity: holders of bonds see them as too valuable to trade. The potential market demand for corporate bonds can be inferred from the fact that household savings deposits with the SCBs is more than 300 times the volume of listed tradable corporate bonds.

This adds up to increasingly active primary and secondary markets for debt of the central government and its specialized financial agencies, including the People's Bank of China (PBC), supported by more than 40 primary dealers and a handful of credit rating agencies. Bottelier (2004) contended, however, that the 'legal and regulatory framework for government debt issues and secondary market trading is very limited.'[35] He asserted that the efficiency of the market could be greatly enhanced by reducing fragmentation of regulatory oversight,[36] of government instruments (there are three kinds of government bonds), and of markets (there are three separate markets for government bonds). As well, the market lacks 'sufficient diversity of maturity dates,' efficient clearing and settlement processes (increasingly needed with growing market participation by institutional investors), and 'a truly independent and authoritative bond rating system' (ibid.). Increasingly, the government and other market participants recognize the advantages of a competitive bidding system for bond issuance and trading.

To summarize, the very high savings of the Chinese people provide a ready source of liquidity through vast deposits in the banking system. There seems considerable scope to channel some of those funds directly to enterprises and to well-managed sub-national governments through appropriate debt instruments, given that some potential borrowers are probably inherently more creditworthy than the banks through which the funds are otherwise intermediated. Policy makers should be investigating ways in which more active bond markets can begin to raise the efficiency of the capital markets.[37]

5.5. Land Markets

The Chinese Constitution divides land into two types: urban state-owned and rural collectively-owned. Correspondingly, there are two land usage systems and two land registration systems. For urban state-owned land, usage rights can be transferred from the state to the land users in one of two ways: by administrative transfer, or by remising the user rights at an agreed price. The market for the second kind of transfer is termed the 'first tier land market,' in which prices are determined by negotiation, bidding or auction. The government is the only supplier, but competition can exist on the demand side when prices are set by bidding or auction.

There have been two major reforms in the first tier land market. In 1990, the State Council issued the 'Temporary Regulation on Urban State-Owned Land Usage Right Remising and Transfer,' which allowed ownership and use of the land rights to diverge.[38] Land rights began to be transferred at an agreed price for a specified period. In 2002, the State Council issued the 'Notice for Enhancing the Management of State-Owned Land Assets,' which allowed the Ministry of Land and Resources to invite public bidding and auctions of land use rights in the transfer of state-owned land. The public must be notified in advance of the government's intention to sell those rights, and the price paid for them must be made public.[39]

The result was an immediate abrupt increase in transactions in the first tier land market. In 2002, for example, the number of market-based transactions increased from below 5 percent of the total in prior years to more than 21 percent of total disposition of 83 300 hectares. The value of the market-based transfers exceeded 55 percent of the value of all transactions, which indicates the efficiency gains from allowing the market to price land use rights.[40] In August 2006, however, *The China Daily* quoted statistics from the same source that indicated only 35 percent of 163 000 hectares of government-transferred land in 2005 was dealt through bidding and auction. Even in urban areas, progress in developing a comprehensive land market is slow.[41]

Once the land usage rights are in non-state hands, they can be traded freely in the 'second tier land market,' and rented out or mortgaged at prices determined by market competition. Before 1999, holders of land use rights acquired by administrative transfer had to pay fees before the rights could be sold or leased to others. In 1999, the Ministry of Land and Resources waived the fee requirement where that would help to promote reform of SOEs and the development of the land market. However, governments retain the right of eminent domain, and can reacquire usage rights from firms or individuals ahead of schedule, where needed, for example, to accommodate investments in urban infrastructure.[42] Governments also can adjust transfer prices agreed between market participants, where they deem such an action desirable to moderate fluctuations in land usage prices.

Given the remaining capacity of governments to intervene, the land markets must still operate under considerable uncertainty, which might have been exacerbated by the regulations issued by the Ministry of Land and Resources early in 2003. In what seems to be an attempt to offset a potential 'bubble' in the real estate market, notification has been given to the responsible units at sub-national level to control strictly land development for the building of commercial housing and other commercial uses. In particular, the notification requires the examination of land used for constructing high-tech parks. Those parks that have been built in violation of overall land-use planning will have their land-use rights rescinded, irrespective of how they are designated. Localities cannot arbitrarily revise their land-use plans to accommodate such parks.

The notification also prohibited enterprises and individuals from occupying farmland for the purpose of developing commercial housing. To avoid turmoil in the real estate market, the government guidelines required that authorizations granted for the building of commercial apartments and office buildings should be controlled, and authorizations granted for the construction of villas be suspended. The notification urged local land and resources departments to supervise closely the use of authorized land, to prevent a handful of land developers from occupying large tracts of land, thereby wasting precious land resources and negatively impacting the real estate market. Meanwhile, work on cadastral registration and land management work should intensify, so that essential real estate information can be reliably supplied to the country's financial institutions.

The evident buoyancy of the housing and property markets suggests that land markets are functioning to some degree, despite the evident concerns of authorities to ensure that land is not misused. Real estate developers must be securing sufficiently reliable title to land ownership or lease to persuade bankers that mortgage financing is secure. One can question, however, whether rights to land use are recognized universally. One can also question whether they are so well established that they can be used reliably, for example, by farmers as collateral for borrowing, or be sold by SOEs as a way to reduce their liabilities, or by governments as a way to capitalize pension funds to benefit their employees.

In comparison with the urban market, the market for rural collectively owned land is underdeveloped. There are laws and regulations that specify conditions under which rural land can be converted to commercial use, providing certain examination and approval processes are followed, including the payment of compensation by those acquiring the land-use rights to the collective land owners and former users. But the share of rural land entering true market circulation has been quite low. Local leaders at village or township level retain considerable authority to allocate and reallocate land use rights to households, although rental markets in land use rights are becoming more common. Rozelle et al. (2002) find that rental markets are more common in those villages that have younger leaders and smaller grain quotas. They note as well that both administrative reallocation and rental of land use rights 'are positively correlated with growth in off-farm (employment) opportunities.'[43]

6. REMAINING CHALLENGES

In their evaluation of China's progress in transition to a market economy, Qian and Wu (2003) assert that the core issue among the many reform challenges that China still faces 'is to establish a system of free and competitive enterprises wherein the nature of the government–business relationship is changed to one at arm's length.' This sound conclusion impresses as the pre-condition for the elimination of the remaining fragmentation of China's markets, since the incentive to tilt the playing field in favor of local firms will persist if the interests of local officials and local businesses remain conjoined.

The greater efficiency made possible by the improved incentives embodied in the household responsibility system and its descendants contributed greatly to accelerating China's growth, and growing competition in fair and open markets remains the best approach to ensuring that efficiency continues to improve. The entry into the WTO served to heighten the competitive forces that are essential if China's regions are to specialize according to their international comparative advantage and so form an integrated domestic market in which resources are allocated to their most productive uses.

Two recent surveys (IFC, 2000; ADB, 2003) of China's domestic privately owned firms point to the concerns that entrepreneurs express about the lack of consistency with which local officials interpret and implement policies, laws, regulations and rules governing the conduct of enterprises and the functioning of markets. China has begun the task of reformulating many of its laws and regulations to make them conform to WTO requirements. An associated burden is to educate officials at all levels in the way in which the new laws and regulations have to be interpreted and implemented to meet those requirements. These changes create a general opportunity to make China's institutions more 'market friendly,' and to raise the consistency with which government officials implement policies that affect economic activity. In particular, the commitment under WTO to enable those who contend they are harmed by protection of local markets to appeal to the central government clearly would be of equal or greater value for dealing with solely domestic disputes.

Institutional change in China has evolved in similar fashion to policy change, with gradual adaptation being the norm. The greater openness of the Chinese economy to foreign enterprise probably will heighten concern about how effectively the legal system functions, and foreign firms likely will push for increased transparency in how Chinese courts deal with contractual disputes, bankruptcy, recovery of collateral, and so on. One way to reduce the parochial nature of local court decisions is the suggestion by Qian and Wu (2003) to introduce a 'two-tier judiciary' in which cross-province circuit courts could have jurisdiction over disputes involving agents from two or more provinces. They regard such an institutional adaptation of the legal system as analogous to the similar changes brought about under (i) fiscal reform, with local and national tax bureaus replacing a single tax administration; and (ii) monetary reform, where the PBC established nine cross-provincial branches to replace a system in which every province had a branch of the PBC and local officials applied pressure to local branch managers to supplement liquidity in the local credit market.

A two-tier judiciary might be effective, in particular, in enforcing anti-trust legislation as it emerges (see the discussion of anti-trust issues in Chapter 3), as well as inter-province commerce regulations that would prohibit many of the restrictions used by local officials in the past to protect local markets. Both the Ministry of Commerce and the State-owned Assets Supervision and Administration Commission (SASAC) seem committed to promoting fair competition in a way that ensures the integration of the domestic market, at the same time ensuring that attempts to protect local markets do not cause China to contravene its undertakings to the WTO.[44]

If a solution such as this were introduced to create impartiality in resolving legal disputes across provinces, complementary reform of the legal system within provinces would still be needed. There is a pressing need to streamline the functioning of the commercial and tax courts to ensure consistent and timely resolution of contract disputes between parties within provinces. A particular example is the need for more reliable and expeditious recovery of collateral in the event of loan defaults, especially to the commercial banks. The local courts also have to guarantee to private property the same degree of protection under law that is enjoyed by public property. An important example is intellectual property; increasingly, private companies report infringements of patents, copyrights and trademarks (ADB, 2003).

The pressure on the court system to bring timeliness, impartiality and transparency to the settlement of legal disputes will be mirrored in the similar pressures on regulators to establish standards for the performance of regulated enterprises that will apply nationwide. The regulatory agencies that oversee the financial and capital markets, as well as those that oversee the provision of infrastructure services in such essential areas as power; telecommunications; road, rail, air and sea transport; and water supply, need to ensure that the service and other standards they introduce contribute to the integration of, for example, the national power grid, the inter-bank market, and long-distance freight hauling.

Besides improved legal and regulatory supporting infrastructure for markets, other institutional changes and complementary services also will help to improve market performance. Many analysts point to the inefficiency that still plagues China's internal distribution chains, quite apart from any overt attempts by local officials to hamper free movements of goods into their markets. Nyberg and Rozelle (1999) identify many of the sources of inefficiency in marketing agricultural products.[45] They note that improved marketing efficiency benefits both producers and consumers, as it enables middlemen to pay higher prices for farmers' crops, while at the same time reducing prices to final consumers. The greatest benefits are likely to derive from eliminating state monopolies in procurement and introducing greater competition in wholesale and retail trading, including allowing small traders to procure products directly from farmers or farmer marketing cooperatives.

Competition would encourage improvements in transportation infrastructure and packaging, as well as specialized handling facilities for high-value, perishable products. Nyberg and Rozelle (1999) state: 'Interprovincial barriers to trade in perishable and processed foods include inconsistent weighing, inspection and other procedures, and the lack of national standardized quarantine and phytosanitary inspection certificates and clearance documents.' They go on to describe the idiosyncratic behavior of inspection and control authorities at provincial borders, especially at borders with provinces that produce competing products. This underlines the need to quash local protectionist measures as a prerequisite for improving efficiency in distribution. The entry of foreign expertise as agreed in the WTO negotiations should contribute to very considerable efficiency gains in the transportation and distribution of goods in China.

6.1. Standards and Information

Information lubricates the engine of competitive markets, and there is scope for much greater disclosure of market relevant information in China.[46] The ADB (2003) identifies deficient information as one of the three principal resource constraints on private enterprises (along with access to finance, and to senior management and technical skills). An important area where the need for better information intersects with the need for better market-supporting infrastructure is in the provision of high quality grading, standardization and certification services. Chinese companies that sell into global markets increasingly see the value in seeking ISO9000 or comparable certifications of product quality. China needs similarly reliable domestic standards, uniformly applied and recognized nationwide, to certify the integrity of the product to the consumer.

Certification of quality adds value to a diverse range of goods and services. In the case of professional services, such as accounting, medicine, legal services, and engineering or architectural consultancies, associations of the practitioners often certify that a member of their association is qualified to provide the relevant service. In issuing licenses to prospective suppliers of professional services, Chinese officials could increasingly draw on professional associations to assess the qualifications of applicants. In the longer term, this might allow self-policing associations to establish codes of behavior and service standards for licensed members.

In agriculture and food handling services (restaurants, supermarkets) much of the certification activity is designed to ensure that consumers are supplied with healthy products: standards of hygiene and storage and other practices are such that shoppers can be confident that they do not put their health at risk in consuming the product. But beyond simple considerations of the wholesomeness of products, there is still scope for certifying differences in quality (in rice and wheat, meat, cotton fiber, edible oils, etc.) that justify differences in price. China needs to train many more skilled product graders who can establish reliable standards, so consumers will be assured that identification labels mean what they say. Misrepresentation of standards should be punished under law in the same way that infringements of copyright and other proprietary assets of firms are.

Nyberg and Rozelle (1999) contrast the open access to information in the United States with the situation in China, where 'market information has historically been collected as input for government policy decision rather than to help markets perform more efficiently.' The problem in China is not so much that information does not exist, but that so little emphasis has been placed on making it available in a useful form to market participants. Referring to enterprises' access to information, the ADB (2003) recommends that to improve the availability and quality of information the priorities are (i) to coordinate the responsibilities of different agencies to collect and distribute information; and (ii) to improve the dissemination of information on policies and regulations, internal and external markets, access to technology, availability of training services, and so on. With adequate education of producers and consumers, the Internet is a potentially highly efficient way to inform people about all aspects of participation in markets.

Introducing complementary markets can provide additional information to enhance overall market efficiency. The development of forward and futures markets could play this role, especially in agriculture. But for these markets to develop and flourish there needs to be competition in procurement of agricultural commodities so that large suppliers and large users can make a market. The emergence of chain distributors and such ubiquitous franchises as McDonalds can be expected to create pressures for reliable quality products and secure supplies over time. In turn, that will encourage vertical supply linkages built on longer-term contracts to supply products of appropriate quality to final users and retailers. Increasing competition in the capacity to supply supermarkets, department stores and their like should be a source of substantial efficiency gains in the Chinese economy.

6.2.   Financial and Capital Markets

Better information, greater transparency and complementary service provision have a major role to play as well in improving the functioning of financial and capital markets. High on the priority list is reliable adherence by listed firms to the disclosure provisions of the CSRC. Attempts by the CSRC to encourage better disclosure of real performance seem to have achieved only limited success. Companies have to demonstrate three years of profitable operation before they can be listed on the stock exchanges, which presumably creates incentives for some firms to report profits that otherwise might be hidden to avoid taxes. And the CSRC requirement that firms must pay dividends to stockholders for three consecutive years before they are eligible to make a public issue of additional equity has led many firms to issue what amount to derisory dividends where none were paid out previously (Lau and Wang, 2003). The need is for a culture that emphasizes that firms have to comply with the intent rather than the letter of market regulations: overall, public confidence in the published annual reports and balance sheets of listed firms can hardly be high.

With the emergence of institutional investors and professional fund managers, one can expect that many more stock analysts will be hired by brokerage houses and merchant banks, and their analyses of the inner working of listed companies over time should do much to provide better information to the investing public. Reputable rating agencies would have valuable contributions to make to develop further the market for corporate and sub-national government bond issues, as they begin to be authorized. Another important source of information to facilitate the development of the debt market will be provided by the emergence of a yield curve for different maturities of central government debt – the 'risk-free' debt instrument. Establishing a yield curve will require the Ministry of Finance, the PBC and the specialized financial institutions to issue a wider range of maturities for their instruments and to allow (at least, the bulk of) their issues to be placed according to free bids in regularly scheduled auctions for the securities. That requires greater willingness to allow flexibility in the determination of all domestic interest rates, as well as to continue to phase out the practice of effectively placing government bond issues with the state-owned banks. It also requires active secondary markets, which argues for many more bondholders who will seek advantage in trading bonds in the secondary market. Increasingly, institutional investors can be expected to play an active role. A result of deeper, more active bond markets would be an improved capacity of the PBC to conduct monetary policy through open market operations.

Commercial banks would benefit from even greater freedom to determine lending and deposit rates, but judgments of their current performance based on the scrutiny of stock analysts, rating agencies and others would be likely to be harsh despite evident efforts to improve performance. Little reliable information is available about the loan experience of the banks and, although the business publications are rife with speculation about the share of non-performing loans in the banks' portfolios, there are no authoritative figures, and few believe the official pronouncements. Bank governance and performance would likely improve with more public disclosure of the banks' loan experience. Loan committees might acquire considerably more backbone in resisting the blandishments of officials seeking support for down-at-heel SOEs and other pet projects, if the results of such decisions were given more publicity. The growing presence of foreign interests in the major banks also should help in this regard.

At the same time, banks might finance more private firms if they could recover collateral quickly and at reasonable cost in the event of loan default.[47] They would be aided in making credit decisions by the introduction of some form of credit information system, under the oversight of the CBRC or the PBC. Such a system could supply to banks and enterprises specific information about the borrowing status, loan servicing records and credit standing of prospective clients. A related institutional development would be the introduction of a collateral registration system that would allow banks to determine whether assets offered as collateral for loans were unencumbered or had already been pledged to secure loans (ADB, 2003).

Besides securities, markets for other assets also would perform better if more expertise in asset valuation were available. Specialists in valuing assets could help in the disposition of state-owned assets where that would be desirable either to improve the economic return on those assets, or to raise the revenues needed to capitalize pension and other funds, and so finance the contingent liabilities of China's governments to workers and retirees. Officials would be less reluctant to approve the transfer of public assets to private hands if they had assurance that the prices paid conform to an expert's view of the intrinsic value of the asset and if, by publicizing the appraised value of the assets before disposing of them, officials could thereby deflect accusations of malfeasance in the transfer.

Open auctions could play a much bigger role in establishing working markets for assets. They have been used to a limited extent already: to a greater extent in issuing some government bonds and in allocating exploration blocks to minerals interests, and to a lesser extent in allocating user rights to urban land, and in placing SOEs under private ownership. Auctions of government securities will facilitate the conduct of monetary policy as the capital market develops, and will comprise the principal mechanism for issuing corporate securities through underwriters, who themselves will compete to provide their services. Open auctions of real assets against a disclosed reserve price have great appeal as a transparent way to dispose of public assets efficiently.

7. CONCLUSIONS

How well do Chinese markets function? Where will further market liberalization have the biggest impact in raising efficiency and promoting faster growth? What are the main impediments to reforms and how can they be removed? We draw a few (tentative) conclusions, and advance some hypotheses.

First, by any reasonable criteria, China's progress in re-establishing markets has been highly successful, as demonstrated in particular by the spectacular growth of the economy over more than a quarter century. Aided by very large inflows of foreign direct investment, China has adapted the East Asian model to its advantage, linking its economy to the international economy and building a highly competitive export sector. This has served both to demonstrate the advantages of market-oriented policies and to raise the productivity of resource use throughout the economy. Although China has irrevocably committed to establishing a market economy, the situation is yet to progress to the point where the markets are entrusted with minimum encumbrance to allocate goods, services and factors of production. The Government reserves the right to intervene in markets when developments are not to its liking, even where the better (meaning more market friendly) policy might be to liberalize further rather than to re-impose administrative controls.

Our review suggests that market development has progressed most in the goods markets, with services next, and factor markets still lagging. Despite the significant cracks that now exist in the 'iron rice bowl,' the integration of labor markets, especially, still has far to go – within provinces between the rural and urban work forces, and nationwide. The expectation that the *hukou* system soon will be essentially phased out in coastal provinces might portend a welcome increase in the mobility of rural labor, which would help in the adjustment of the agricultural work force to the WTO-induced changes in agricultural output and trade. Markets for both capital and land seem to function to a degree, with considerable progress in their development since 1993, but both remain underdeveloped. In the case of land, there still seems more to do in providing adequate legal support for user rights.

Second, China's markets, like markets everywhere, thrive where there is free and fair competition. Most Chinese entrepreneurs view their business environment as intensely competitive and, like enterprise owners everywhere, they seek shelter from competitive forces wherever possible. They are frequently successful in that endeavor, with officials of sub-national governments in particular taking steps to protect enterprises that they regard as local. There is insufficient recognition in local government of the advantages of an integrated national market, and in turn a Chinese economy that is integrated with the global economy. The central government has repeatedly emphasized the need to eliminate protection of local markets, and thereby lends support to the notion that the internal Chinese markets would be more efficient if they were better integrated.

To improve the function of China's markets, more of the right sort of competition is needed. We hypothesize that four broad types of government actions can heighten fair competition and improve the way in which Chinese markets work. In the approximate order in which they are likely to contribute to efficiency gains, they are:

- Phase out remaining barriers to the freedom of movement of goods, services and factors of production in the domestic markets
- Roll back the barriers to foreign participation in the Chinese economy in accordance with, but not limited to, the undertakings for accession to the WTO
- Compile and disseminate more information of all kinds to improve participants' knowledge of China's market environment, and

- Experiment more boldly in introducing additional complementary markets (for example, forward markets, markets for derivatives) and market supporting services (rating agencies, specialists in grading products and valuing assets, marketing, communications, transport, handling and distribution services, and more).

Of course, these actions are complementary rather than exclusive, which is a major reason for suggesting that the ranking is approximate. Better internal logistics networks will contribute to a better-integrated domestic goods market, while foreign competition in providing supporting logistics, as well as in supplying goods, will help to lower costs and contribute to market efficiency. Similarly, better information about the availability of jobs and the conditions of employment, as well as about the local housing market, education and health services, could be considered a prerequisite for integration of the labor market. And introducing complementary markets and services would help to generate considerably more useful information for market participants, thereby enhancing competition.

As in all Chinese reforms, further liberalization of markets inevitably will be gradual, which raises the question of how best to sequence new policy initiatives. In important areas: services of all kinds, agriculture, banking and enterprise reform, labor and land markets, credit and capital markets, what genius will be needed to design more of the transitional, 'dual-track' types of policies that have served China so well? Has China progressed to a stage in market reform where the price of benefits for some is considerable pain for others, including governments, which must forego interventions dear to their hearts in the interests of greater economic efficiency? Greater competition in providing services offers potentially great economic benefits because these are areas in which domestic suppliers have been woefully inadequate. But even if, for example, rapid penetration of China's banking system by foreign banks, either independently or as strategic partners with Chinese banks,[48] would improve client services, the Government has to welcome that development despite the fact that domestic banks might be disadvantaged competitors. The historically weak portfolios of the big state-owned banks as well as their fundamental lack of banking skills might encourage the Government to take measures to delay its commitments under the WTO accession until the SCBs are better placed to take on the foreigners. Essentially, approaches need to be found that reap the benefits of early foreign entry as they convey breathing space to the SCBs to clean up their act.

In many cases, however, the Government will need to bite the bullet and accept the consequences of greater reliance on the markets. There the Government still exhibits a deep ambivalence, for example, in its directives to the SASAC, which at the time was feeling its way in supervising 189 central-level SOEs, to improve the performance of those SOEs and at the same time to 'strengthen … the role of the SOE–Party organization in all aspects of major decisions of the enterprises, including the appointment of key enterprise personnel.'[49]

Similarly, as Premier Wen Jiabao (2004) promised reform of the grain distribution system, with all controls over market sales and purchases to be lifted, he gave assurances in the same report that 'grain production capability must be maintained and increased' and 'acreage sown in grain crops will be expanded,' which hardly indicates willingness to allow the markets to determine outcomes.[50] China would be no exception if it over-rides market forces in the interests of food security and other objectives in the agricultural sector, but the contradictory nature of official statements indicates that some distance remains to be traveled to complete market reforms.

NOTES

1. We are grateful to Irena Asmundson, Yo-ling Ma, Anita Alves Pena, Hong Qiao, and Guijuan Wang for preparation of statistical tables and other valuable contributions.
2. *China Statistical Yearbook 2006*.
3. *Gaizhi* means literally 'changing the system.' More details on the process of restructuring of state-owned enterprise are to be found in Chapter 2.
4. About 40 percent of China's SOEs were privatized in 1996–2001 according to Yao and Song (2003). Also see material in Chapter 2.
5. Speech of Jiang Zemin, General Secretary of the Central Committee of the Communist Party of China (CPC), at the Meeting celebrating the Eightieth Anniversary of the Founding of the CPC, 1 July 2001.
6. Speech of Jiang Zemin at the 16th Chinese Communist Party Congress, 11 November 2002.
7. A summary of Chinese policy reforms can be found in Hope et al. (2003).
8. Pomfret (2002) provides an assessment of how countries making the transition from central planning have fared in their efforts to establish market economies.
9. For an accessible discussion of China's planned economy, see Chapter 2 in Chow (2002).
10. See also Lau et al. (2000).
11. Zeng (2003). Subsequently, Premier Wen Jiabao, in his Report to the Second Session of the Tenth National People's Congress on 5 March 2004, foreshadowed sweeping reform of the grain distribution system and state-owned grain enterprises, including: 'All controls over grain purchase and sales markets will be lifted.' (See page 17, English translation.)
12. Ma (2004).
13. Similar changes have occurred in the shares of total gross industrial output (GIO) accounted for by the state sector. Between 1985 and 1999, the share of state-owned enterprises in GIO fell from two-thirds to less than a third, and the ADB (2003) observes: 'the other striking feature is the extraordinary growth in the activity of private firms of all types – from next to nothing in 1985, their share in total (GIO) was rapidly approaching half in 1999.' By 2004, value added in China's manufacturing industry was Rmb 5.2 trillion yuan (33 percent of GDP), compared with Rmb 4.6 trillion yuan (39 percent of GDP) in 2002 (*China Statistical Yearbook*).

14. Arrangements for trade in services are complex. See, for example, Ma (2003) (available at http://ap.research.db.com/) for an analysis of the provisions of the closer economic partnership agreement signed at the end of June 2003 by Hong Kong SAR and China, in particular the liberalization of market access to apply to 17 categories of services.

15. See Chapter 8 of this volume. Zhang and Tan also cite studies that suggest labor markets are better integrated alongside others that point to continuing significant fragmentation in those markets. Similar conflicting results are presented for the extent to which capital markets are becoming better integrated. Their own study indicates better integration of goods markets and the labor market, along with greater fragmentation of the capital market. The inconclusive nature of the analysis calls for more research to settle the issues.

16. More information can be found at: http://www.ustr.gov/regions/china-hk-mongolia-taiwan/accession.shtml and http://www.mac.doc.gov/China/Docs/industryfactsheets/index.htm.

17. See Hope and Hu (2006).

18. See Chapters 4 and 5 of this volume.

19. They observe that the more important changes in incentives include the removal of life-time job security and closer links between remuneration and performance.

20. It also restricts their choice of crops, though plenty of anecdotal evidence suggests that entrepreneurial farmers grow what suits them best and purchase grain in the market to meet their compulsory sales to the state.

21. This is a system that registers citizens according to their locality of origin and links certain benefit rights to that locality. In its strict form relocation without explicit official permission was prohibited, even if rights to community-provided benefits were waived.

22. *China Statistical Yearbook 2003.*

23. The sources for these figures are *China Statistical Yearbook* (various years) and authors' estimates. After 1998 the *China Statistical Yearbook* ceased publishing the number of contract staff and workers in state-owned economic units. The most recent data on total farm and non-farm employment available is 2002. Thereafter, these data were replaced with data on the number of employed persons in urban units by sector. The new data cannot be reconciled with the earlier figures

24. This section draws heavily from Bottelier (2004); see also Chapter 7 of this volume.

25. Solvet provides an excellent survey of the status of banking in China.

26. See Dobson and Kashyap (2006), page 29.

27. The policy banks (in order of asset size) are the China (State) Development Bank, the Agricultural Development Bank of China and the (much smaller) Export Import Bank of China, which together have total assets less than ABC, the smallest of the SCBs. The asset management companies (AMCs) and their partner banks are: Cinda – CCB and CDB; Great Wall – ABC; Huarong – ICBC; and Orient – BOC.

28. The World Bank, Goldman Sachs, Hong Kong, and Nicholas Lardy (2003) all argued at around that time that under reasonable assumptions the SCBs would be unable to reconstitute their capital from their future earnings.

29. China's loan classification system was amended from a four to a five category system in 2001. Under the former system, the NPL ratio would have been lower.

30. Moody's Investors Service Global Credit Research, Banking System Outlook 2006: China, July 2006, Table 7, page 13.

31. A further eight QFIIs were approved by 30 September 2006.

32. About 1224 enterprises (more than 90 percent of which were majority state-owned) were listed on the Shanghai and Shenzhen exchanges at the end of 2002. The CSRC reports 1377 A- or B-share listed companies at the end of 2004 and 1434 listed companies at the end of 2006.

33. On 26 August 2003, *The Wall Street Journal* reported that the market capitalization of the Shanghai and Shenzhen exchanges was equivalent to US$501.6 billion, with shares that could be bought by public investors accounting for 32 percent of the valuation. Of the totality of 1259 listed companies, only 175 had a market capitalization exceeding US$200 million, while 112 companies were in danger of being de-listed for poor earnings performance. Total market capitalization, as reported by the CSRC, at the end of 2006 was

8.94 trillion yuan, or US$1.14 trillion. Of this total, 2.50 trillion yuan (US$320 billion) was circulating (negotiable market capitalization).

34. He notes, however, that the volume of corporate bonds issued in 2002 was only about half as great as in 1992, when local government issues mainly to finance locally-owned SOEs 'was part of the widespread financial irregularities that contributed to overinvestment and high inflation.' After 1996, equity issues became a much larger share of capital market financing than bond issues, partly because (and unlike many other countries' markets) the exceptionally high price–earnings ratios made equity cheaper than debt.

35. Outstanding issues of PBC sterilization bills increased by about Rmb 500 billion yuan in the last three quarters of 2003.

36. Responsibility for regulation and supervision of the market for government bonds is divided between the Ministry of Finance (for new issues), the PBC (for trading in the interbank market) and the China Securities and Regulatory Commission (CSRC) (for trading in the stock market).

37. In Chapter 7 of this volume, Bottelier describes recent developments in the increasingly rapidly evolving bond markets.

38. Ministry of Construction, PRC: www.con.gov.cn/law/other/2000111602.00.htm.

39. See http://home.sinohome.com/home/5249.htm

40. Source: Ministry of Land and Resources, PRC. Note that the 'market price' includes prices set by bidding and auction.

41. See http://www.chinadaily.com.cn/china/2006-08/01/content_654028.htm.

42. On 14 March 2004, the tenth National People's Congress in its second session approved an amendment to the third paragraph of Article 10 of the Constitution of the PRC. It formerly read: 'The State may, in the public interest, requisition land for its use in accordance with the law.' The revision reads: 'The State may, in the public interest and in accordance with the provisions of law, expropriate or requisition land for its use and shall make compensation for the land expropriated or requisitioned.' This amendment indicates a concern at high levels to convey greater certainty to the value of land user rights. See http://english.peopledaily.com.cn/constitution/constitution.html.

43. The italics are ours. See Rozelle et al. (2002). They conclude that 'a solid empirical basis does not currently exist for making an assessment of the impact of the land system on efficiency, equity, and overall development of China's rural sector.'

44. The Ministry of Commerce was formed from the union of the Ministry of Foreign Trade and Economic Cooperation and the Ministry of Domestic Trade in the government reforms emerging from the National People's Congress of March 2003. It also took over some of the functions of the former State Economic and Trade Commission (SETC). The Xinhua News Agency reported on 22 May 2003 that the SASAC has taken over responsibilities for 'the reform and restructuring of [SOEs and] the maintenance and appreciation of state assets value for those state-invested enterprises,' as stated by SASAC Director, Li Rongrong. The SASAC inherited the former SETC's role in these areas, as well as the Ministry of Finance's former responsibility for management of state-owned assets, and the similar responsibilities of the former Work Committee of Enterprises of the CPC Central Committee and the Ministry of Labor and Social Security.

45. See especially Chapter 5: 'The Development of Markets.'

46. Many examples of the role that information plays in efficient markets are available in McMillan (2002). In particular, see Chapter 4.

47. The passing of a new bankruptcy law to take effect from June 2007 should help in this regard.

48. See Hope and Hu (2006).

49. Communication from Hang-Sheng Cheng, President, The 1990 Institute, April 2004.

50. Wen, J. (2004). Op. cit. pages 16–17.

REFERENCES

Asian Development Bank (ADB) (2003), *People's Republic of China: The Development of Private Enterprise*, Manila: Philippines.

Bhattasali, D., L. Shantong and W. Martin (eds) (2004), *Globalization with Chinese Characteristics: Policy and Poverty after China's Accession to the WTO*, Washington, DC: The World Bank.

Bottelier, P. (2004), 'China's emerging domestic debt markets', SCID Working Paper No. 202.

Chow, G.C. (2002), *China's Economic Transformation*, Malden, MA: Blackwell Publishers.

Dobson, W. and A.K. Kashyap (2006), 'The contradiction in China's gradualist banking reforms', paper prepared for the Brookings Panel on Economic Activity.

Garnaut, R., L. Song, S. Tenev, and Y. Yao (2005), *China's Owenership Transformation: Process, Outcomes, Prospects*, Washington DC: World Bank Publications.

Hope, N.C., D.T. Yang and M.Y. Li (eds) (2003), *How Far Across the River: Chinese Policy Reform at the Millennium*, Stanford, CA: Stanford University Press.

Hope, N. and F. Hu (2006), 'Reforming China's banking system: How much can foreign strategic investment help?', in J. Aziz, S. Dunaway and E. Prasad (eds), *China and India: Learning from Each Other – Reforms and Policies for Sustained Growth*, International Monetary Fund.

Huang, J., S. Rozelle and M. Chang (2003), 'The nature of distortions to agricultural incentives in China and implications of WTO accession', paper presented at the international conference on 'Emergent Trilateralism in the Pacific Basin,' University of California Berkeley, 3–4 June 2003.

Inachovichina, E. and W. Martin (2004), 'Economic impacts of China's accession to the World Trade Organization', *World Bank Economic Record*, **18** (1).

Lardy, N. (2003), 'When will China's financial system meet China's needs?', in N.C. Hope, D.T. Yang and M.Y. Li (eds), *How Far Across the River: Chinese Policy Reform at the Millennium*, Stanford, CA: Stanford University Press.

Lau, L., Y. Qian and G. Roland (2000), 'Reform without losers: An interpretation of China's dual-track approach to transition', *The Journal of Political Economy*, **108** (1), 120–43.

Lau, L. and G. Wang (2003), 'Tax policies for enhancing the stabilization of China's stock markets', discussion paper.

Ma, J. (2003), 'CEPA: Gateway for China–Hong Kong integration', Deutsche Bank, Asia-Pacific Equity Research, 7 July 2003.

Ma, K. (2004), 'Report on the implementation of the 2003 Plan for National Economic and Social Development and on the 2004 Draft Plan for National Economic and Social Development', speech delivered at the Second Session of the Tenth National People's Congress, 6 March 2004.

McMillan, J. (2002), *Reinventing the Bazaar: A Natural History of Markets*, New York, NY: W.W. Norton and Company.

Meng, X. (2000), *Labor Market Reform in China*, Cambridge, UK: Cambridge University Press.

National Bureau of Statistics of China (various years), *China Statistical Yearbook*, China Statistics Press.

Naughton, B. (2003), 'How much can regional integration do to unify China's Markets?', in N.C. Hope, D.T. Yang and M.Y. Li (eds), *How Far Across the River: Chinese Policy Reform at the Millennium*, Stanford, CA: Stanford University Press.

Nyberg, A. and S. Rozelle (1999), *Accelerating China's Rural Transformation*, Washington, DC: The World Bank.

Pomfret, R. (2002), *Constructing a Market Economy*, Cheltenham, UK and Northampton, MA, USA: Edward Elgar Publishing Limited.

Poncet, S. (2003a), 'Domestic market fragmentation and economic growth in China', CERDI.

Poncet, S. (2003b), 'Measuring Chinese domestic and international integration', *China Economic Review*, **14** (1), 1–21.

Qian, Y. and J. Wu (2003), 'China's transition to a market economy: How far across the river?', in N.C. Hope, D.T. Yang and M.Y. Li (eds), *How Far Across the River: Chinese Policy Reform at the Millennium*, Stanford, CA: Stanford University Press.

Rozelle, S., L. Brandt, L. Guo and J. Huang (2002), 'Land rights in China: Facts, fictions, and issues', *China Journal*, **47**, 67–97.

Solvet, E. (2002), 'Banking in China', CLSA Emerging Markets.

Wen, J. (2004), 'Report on the work of the government', Speech delivered at the Second Session of the Tenth National People's Congress, 5 March 2004.

World Bank (1994), *China: Internal Market Development and Regulation*, Washington, DC: The World Bank.

World Bank (1997), *At China's Table: Food Security Options*, Washington, DC: The World Bank.

Yao, Y. and L. Song (2003), 'Impacts of privatization and firm performance in China', Stanford Center for International Development, Working Paper No. 179.

Young, A. (2000), 'The razor's edge: Distortions and incremental reform in the People's Republic of China', *Quarterly Journal of Economics*, **115**(4), 1091–136.

Zeng, P. (2003), 'Report on the implementation of the 2002 Plan for National Economic and Social Development and on the 2003 Draft Plan for National Economic and Social Development', Speech delivered at the first session of the Tenth National People's Congress on 6 March 2003.

2. Impact and Significance of State-Owned Enterprise Restructuring in China

Ross Garnaut, Ligang Song and Yang Yao[1]

1. INTRODUCTION

The transformation of China's state-owned enterprises (SOEs) over the past decade has resulted in remarkable changes to the structure of the Chinese economy. *Gaizhi*, the Chinese term meaning 'transforming the system', has become a major phenomenon in most parts of the country and in many cases has involved privatization. The term *gaizhi* is used to describe any form of structural change to a firm, including public offering of shares, internal restructuring, bankruptcy and reorganization, employee shareholding, open sales, leasing and joint ventures. Unlike the mass privatization programs that occurred in Eastern Europe and the former Soviet Union, the Chinese government's *gaizhi* programs have been gradual and low-profile. However, the significance of the Chinese reform should not be underestimated.

Based on a 683-enterprise survey conducted in 11 cities in 2002,[2] this chapter reviews the trends of privatization, discusses the forms of *gaizhi*, analyzes the issues emerging in the process of *gaizhi*, especially the handling of state assets and land-use rights and re-employment, and compares firm performance before and after *gaizhi*. The aim of this chapter is to give the reader an overview of the restructuring process in China, and to analyze some of the key issues.

Several key conclusions have emerged from the study. First, restructuring has become more oriented towards privatization over recent years. Privatization here means an increase in the share of ownership held by private investors. Second, the so-called 'loss of state assets' has occurred mainly in the form of price discounts when selling state assets. Local governments gave discounts and in many cases land-use rights to new owners in exchange for their consent not to sack many workers. Third, restructured or *gaizhi* firms did sack more workers in the year the *gaizhi* took place, but subsequently they maintained a slower rate of employment reduction than pure SOEs. Fourth, *gaizhi*, especially restructuring with privatization, has hardened firms' budget constraint with banks, but has not been effective in hardening firms' budget constraint with the government. Finally, *gaizhi* and privatization have significantly improved firms' profitability, but have not raised investment rates or labor productivity (measured by per-worker sales). This result shows that *gaizhi* and privatization have led firms to abandon the expansionary business model characterizing old-style SOEs and to adopt a new business model that gives top priority to cost savings.[3]

The chapter is organized as follows. The next section reviews China's recent history of SOE reforms. It provides data to gauge the extent of privatization in China. Then, after describing the survey, it analyzes the forms of *gaizhi* and the pace of privatization using the survey data. We then discuss the terms of transfer of state assets and the extent of price discounts in the process of *gaizhi*; analyze the effects of restructuring on employment, giving specific attention to the financial arrangements for worker settlement; and finally consider the impact of restructuring on firms' financial discipline and economic performance.

2. RECENT SOE REFORMS IN CHINA

Reform of China's state-owned enterprises has been much discussed since urban reforms began in 1984. Although there were early calls for privatizing the SOEs, the government's emphasis was initially on boosting performance by changing the SOEs' internal governance and improving the market environment in which they operated. Inspired by the success of the rural household responsibility system, the government introduced a contracting system into the state industrial sector, requiring SOE managers to meet targets for sales, profitability, rates of investment and so on, in return for the enterprise retaining a share of the profits. Studies have found that the contracting system had improved firm performance in the 1980s.[4] The main problem with this system was that managers were rewarded for their successes but not punished for their failures. By the end of the 1980s, leasing was adopted as another approach to reforming SOEs. The first significant lease contract involved the Wuhan Motor Engine Factory in 1986, when three people put up 34 000 yuan as collateral to lease the factory. In May 1988 the State Council issued a regulation on the leasing of small SOEs.[5] A direct consequence was that managers could be recruited from outside the enterprise. Private shareholding was first introduced into SOEs in three Guangzhou firms in 1986, when the employees bought 30 percent of their firms' shares. The first large SOE in which private entities purchased shares was the Shenyang Motor Corporation, which became Shenyang Jinbei Motors when it issued shares to the public in August 1988.[6] The opening of the Shenzhen Stock Exchange in 1990 and the Shanghai Stock Exchange in 1991 enabled a limited number of SOEs to issue shares to the public. Large-scale privatization only started after Deng Xiaoping's famous visit to southern China in 1992. As with many other reform initiatives, privatization started at the local level and was later sanctioned by the central government.

The most important impetus for privatization in the localities was the large amount of debt built up by the state sector. The level of debt was a more pressing problem in small cities. For example, in Zhucheng city of Shandong province, 103 of the 150 SOEs were in the red at the end of 1992, with losses amounting to 147 million yuan − equivalent to the city government's revenue over 18 months.[7] The Shunde municipal government was also encountering a debt problem when it first started privatizing its SOEs in 1992.[8] It was not a coincidence that Shunde and Zhucheng were the two cities that pioneered the privatization of all their state and collective firms.[9]

In 1995, after extensive discussions, the central government decided on the policy of *zhuada fangxiao*, or 'keep the large and let the small go'. The state decided to retain ownership of 500 to 1000 large state firms and to allow smaller firms to be leased or sold.[10] There were good reasons for this decision. In 1997 the 500 largest state firms held 37 percent of the state's industrial assets, contributed 46 percent of all taxes collected from state firms, and totalled 63 percent of the state sector's profits. Small firms owned by local governments had been performing poorly. In 1995, 72.5 percent of local firms were unprofitable, but only 24.3 percent of firms owned by the central government.[11] As Vice-Premier Wu Bangguo said in a speech in December 1997, 'Control of the (500) largest firms means we have a control of the largest chunk of the state economy'.[12]

From the 'let the small go' part of the policy came the term '*gaizhi*', which in Chinese means 'changing the system', but which has increasingly served as a euphemism for privatization, especially in the case of small firms. By the end of 1998, more than 80 percent of state and collective firms at the level of the county or below had gone through *gaizhi*.[13] In cities, *gaizhi* has occurred in two waves. Reform started in the mid-1990s and at first followed the model of employee-shareholding adopted by Shunde and Zhucheng. When these two cities abandoned this model and moved to share concentration and management buy-outs in 1997, other cities followed suit. Management buy-out has been the most common model in the second wave

Figure 2.1: *Firms with State Ownership Control: A Comparison Between National and Sample Average (percent)*

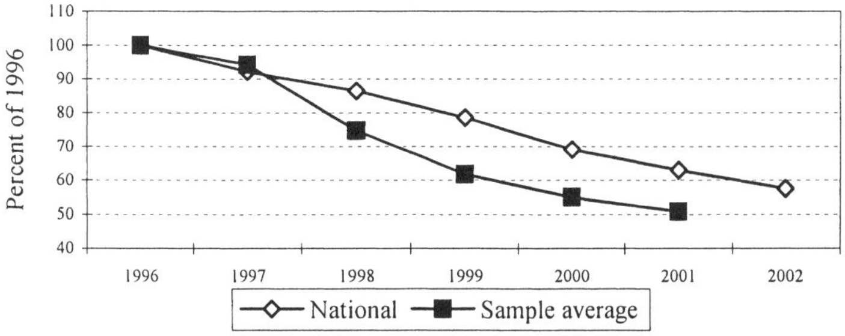

Sources: *China Fiscal Statistical Yearbook: 1997–2003* (Beijing, various years) and the survey data.

of *gaizhi* and has spread to large firms, such as the SOEs listed on the stock market. Privatization has been accepted as the key to urban reform, and the slogan 'the state retreats and the private sector moves forward' has become common in many cities.

Figure 2.1 shows the trend of privatization in the whole country for the period 1996–2002 and in the 11 sample cities for the period 1996–2001. The figure takes the number of state-controlled firms – defined as those with more than 50 percent of their shares controlled by the government – in 1996 as 100 percent, and shows the percentage that remained in public ownership in each subsequent year. On the assumption that the reduction in the number of state-owned firms reflected privatization,[14] more than 40 percent of the SOEs were privatized in China during the period 1996–2002. The pace of privatization was faster in the sample cities. Only about half of the firms controlled by the state in 1996 remained in 2001. Statistically, the falling numbers of SOEs can also be partially explained by a growing number of mergers and acquisitions within the state sector and the use of new categories of firms such as corporatized SOEs. It is noteworthy that 1997 was a turning point for the sample cities. Privatization accelerated considerably following Shunde's and Zhucheng's second wave of *gaizhi* which aimed at consolidating shares in the hands of the management.

There was a debate in 1998–99 on whether management buy-outs had resulted in a 'loss of state assets',[15] that is, whether SOE assets had been appropriated by the management. The debate did not have a real impact on the pace of privatization, although the word 'privatization' has since disappeared from both official and public discourse and been replaced by *gaizhi*.

The trend of privatization shown in Figure 2.1 is also confirmed by other survey studies. A national survey in 1998 showed that one quarter of China's 87 000 industrial SOEs had experienced *gaizhi* and another quarter planned to undertake some form of *gaizhi*. Among the *gaizhi* firms, 60–70 percent had been partially or fully privatized.[16] A 2002 national survey of industrial SOEs estimated that 86 percent had been through *gaizhi* by the end of 2001, and about 70 percent had been partially or fully privatized.[17]

Figure 2.2:   Locations of the 11 Sample Cities

3. THE SURVEY

The survey was funded by the International Finance Corporation and was conducted in the spring of 2002. The 11 sample cities are, from north to south: Harbin, Fushun, Tangshan, Lanzhou, Weifang, Xining, Zhenjiang, Huangshi, Chengdu, Hengyang and Guiyang. They represent a wide spectrum of regions, levels of economic development and conditions for SOEs. The design of the survey aimed at sampling all the SOEs managed by the city governments at the end of 1995. The year 1995 was chosen because large-scale privatization began in the mid-1990s. However, not all

Table 2.1:   *Distribution and Statistics of the Sample Firms*

	No. of firms	% of firms	2001 Statistics			
			Size[a]	Gross value of assets[b] (Million yaun)	Per-worker assets (1000 yuan)	Profit rate (%)[c]
Harbin	120	17.6	302.9	58.0	623.6	−2.3
Fushun	10	1.5	475.5	82.7	677.4	−2.8
Tangshan	59	8.6	1361.2	76.5	229.2	−0.7
Weifang	30	4.4	1049.3	80.6	123.4	3.1
Lanzhou	39	5.7	318.4	54.8	401.0	−3.3
Xining	26	3.8	383.1	71.9	182.5	0.4
Huangshi	79	11.6	345.0	47.1	293.1	0.1
Guiyang	149	21.8	515.7	42.9	118.5	0.7
Zhenjiang	70	10.2	433.8	40.2	244.1	−2.5
Hengyang	57	8.3	330.5	48.0	665.7	−1.2
Chengdu	44	6.4	119.4	10.7	142.9	0.3
Total	683	100.0	463.7	51.2	414.4	−0.01

Notes:
[a]   Size is the average number of on-duty workers.
[b]   Assets include fixed capital, working capital, account receivable and several miscellaneous categories.
[c]   Profit rate is the return to gross assets, that is, it is defined as pre-tax profit divided by the gross value of assets.

Source: Survey.

firms returned the questionnaires. The possibility of bias in sample selection thus presents a potential problem that was considered in the analysis of survey results. Table 2.1 shows the distribution of the 683 sample firms in the cities.

On average, the sample firms were of medium size, but some were quite large, employing close to 10 000 workers. In fact, the average size of the sample firms was more than double the national average of 204 workers in the same year. This is because the sample was drawn from firms managed by the city government and did not include firms managed by city districts and counties, which are usually smaller. Accordingly, the sample firms were quite 'heavy' in the sense that they were highly capital-intensive. On average, per worker assets were 414 400 yuan, most of which were fixed and working capital. Firms in Harbin, Fushun, Lanzhou and Hengyang were particularly 'heavy', as these four cities have a concentration of capital-intensive industries. Many of these industries were undergoing painful restructuring, so it is not surprising that firms in these four cities on average registered a loss. Firms in two other cities, Tangshan and Zhenjiang, also had negative average profit rates. Responding firms in the other five cities had positive profit rates. On average, firms in the sample roughly broke even. It was a tough time in the several years after the Asian financial crisis.

4. FORMS OF *GAIZHI* AND THE EXTENT OF PRIVATIZATION

Different forms of *gaizhi* lead to different outcomes. Public offering, for example, does not change the state's control because the Chinese law requires that, in this process, the state retains the majority of the shares. Internal restructuring does not change the ownership of the assets, but involves reorganization, splitting, debt–equity swap and other restructuring measures within the firm. China's Bankruptcy Law only applies to SOEs. It was not widely applied until the mid-1990s, when the central government began to adopt bankruptcy as a means to restructure SOEs.[18] An ordinary bankruptcy in a market economy would result in the bankrupt firm being dissolved, or at least being subject to fundamental change in ownership and management. But in many recently reported cases, bankrupt firms have continued operating with the same management. This false bankruptcy involves the firm entering bankruptcy and writing off its debts. But it does often result in diversification of the ownership of the firm, leading to partial or full privatization.

Employee-shareholding has been by far the most popular form of *gaizhi* throughout the country. Although proven to be a sub-optimal arrangement in other transitional countries,[19] this form of *gaizhi* carried the least political risk in the early stage of reform. Open sale has become more popular in recent years. The firm is openly sold to insiders or outsiders, sometimes through auction. This is the most radical form of privatization because it can involve the transfer of the firm to a single private owner or a management group. The lease contracts now commonly used in *gaizhi* are quite different from those adopted in the early years of SOE reform. Early lease contracts acted as incentives within the SOE, but now they are used as a substitute for open sale when the buyer(s) do not have cash to buy the firm. Finally, forming a joint venture or merging with a domestic or foreign firm is another approach to *gaizhi*. This type of *gaizhi* helps the firm obtain long-term access to capital and technology.

Table 2.2: Forms of Gaizhi by City (number and percentage)

	No. of gaizhi	Public offering	Internal restrict.	Bnkrpt.	Emp. share.	Open sales	Leasing	Joint venture
Harbin	40	7.5	47.5	2.5	22.5	10.0	10.0	0.0
Fushun	10	0.0	40.0	20.0	20.0	0.0	20.0	0.0
Tangshan	57	8.8	26.3	10.5 ·	15.8	15.8	17.5	7.0
Weifang	34	14.7	14.7	11.8	50.0	2.9	0.0	5.9
Lanzhou	11	0.0	9.1	54.5	27.3	9.1	0.0	0.0
Xining	18	11.1	22.2	50.0	16.7	0.0	0.0	0.0
Huangshi	54	7.4	11.1	5.6	38.9	22.2	13.0	1.9
Guiyang	41	4.9	26.8	7.3	19.5	19.5	17.1	4.9
Zhenjiang	45	8.9	26.7	2.2	44.4	2.2	6.7	8.9
Hengyang	49	4.1	16.3	16.3	6.1	6.1	49.0	2.0
Chengdu	21	4.8	14.3	0.0	38.1	38.1	4.8	0.0
Total	380	7.4	23.2	11.3	27.1	12.4	15.3	3.7

Source: Survey.

In the sample of 683 firms, 375 reported that they had been subject to *gaizhi* by the spring of 2002. Table 2.2 provides a breakdown of the *gaizhi* cases by type and city. It is evident that the southern and southwest cities, Chengdu, Weifang, Huangshi and Zhenjiang in particular, were more likely to adopt employee-shareholding and open sales while the northern cities were more likely to take internal restructuring and bankruptcy. This is largely due to the high concentration and scale of SOEs in the northeast region in comparison with the south where the private sector is relatively more developed and market environments are more competitive. Among the *gaizhi* firms, a total 70 percent of *gaizhi* cases involved the transfer of ownership from the state to private hands.

Of the 85 cases of internal restructuring, 62 percent of SOEs were incorporated, that is, restructured as companies under the law, 19 percent were new establishments emerging from the old firms, 8 percent arranged a debt–equity swap, 6 percent had new investors, and the remaining 5 percent were unclassified. Evidence from other transitional countries suggests that some incorporated SOEs perform better than other firms. This may be because firm-specific characteristics such as pre-privatization performance and firm size were not controlled for in these studies. It is quite possible that the government is more reluctant to privatize larger and better performing SOEs.

Of the 103 cases of employee-shareholding, 53 percent became limited liability companies, 34 percent became cooperatives, and the remaining 13 percent were unclassified. Chinese law does not grant legal status to cooperatives. Interviews with the firms found that most cooperatives wanted to register as limited liability companies, but the limit on the number of shareholders (under 50) prevented them from doing so. Employees in some firms have solved this problem by pooling their shares under the name of an entrusted member.

Insider control is believed to have been one of the main problems with the Russian privatization program because insiders were reluctant to restructure firms.[20] Chinese firms have also been criticized as being controlled by insiders.[21] The lack of transparency in privatization programs may mask corruption and create an unjust allocation of shares within firms. The significant presence of employee-shareholding firms in the 11-city survey confirmed the popularity of insider control as a means of privatization in China.

Insiders also took over a large proportion of those firms that were sold or leased out: 16 of the 26 sales and 15 of the 58 leases involved insiders, mostly managers. Only 16 sales and 20 leases involved a private company. Overall, sales or leases to an outside private firm consisted of only 9.6 percent of the 375 cases of *gaizhi*. In the summary, 10 sale and 19 lease cases were classified as 'other types' of sales and leases. These cases might be a mixture of insider control and outsider participation. If these cases are included, the share of *gaizhi* cases that involved at least partial outsider participation rises to 15 percent. This shows that the private sector has become an active player in *gaizhi*.

Table 2.3[22] shows how preferred forms of *gaizhi* changed over time. More firms have adopted open sales, in most cases the sale of the firm not part of its assets. Before 1995, no firm adopted open sale. Open sales have become a popular way of starting *gaizhi* in 2000. In 2001 and 2002, more than one-fifth of all *gaizhi* cases were open sales. Leasing became popular earlier. In the two most recent years, open-sales, leasing and employee-shareholding were the three most common forms of *gaizhi*.

Together they constituted more than two-thirds of all *gaizhi* cases in those two years. It is noteworthy that the popularity of employee shareholding has declined in recent years. It became the dominant form of *gaizhi* in the late 1990s. Nearly one third in 1999 involved employee shareholding. The ratio declined to less than one quarter in 2002.

Contrary to the steadily increasing importance of open sales and leasing, the incidence of internal restructuring increased at first in the 1990s butrapidly declined in the period 2000–02. Joint ventures were popular before 1996, but have played a rather insignificant role since then. Public offering was significant in the mid-1990s, but declined considerably after

Table 2.3: Forms of Gaizhi by Year (number and percentage)

	<1995	1995	1996	1997	1998	1999	2000	2001	2002
Total number	30	13	40	32	50	53	54	64	34
Public offering	6.7	0.0	15.0	18.8	8.0	9.4	5.6	3.1	2.9
Internal restructuring	20.0	23.1	22.5	37.5	34.0	34.0	20.4	7.8	11.8
Bankruptcy	3.3	23.1	27.5	12.5	2.0	1.9	7.4	18.8	11.8
Employee shareholding	30.0	7.7	17.5	25.0	28.0	30.2	31.5	29.7	23.5
Open sales	0.0	7.7	7.5	3.1	12.0	5.7	14.8	20.3	23.5
Leasing	16.7	7.7	10.0	3.1	16.0	17.0	18.5	20.3	23.5
Joint venture	23.3	30.8	0.0	0.0	0.0	1.9	1.9	0.0	2.9

Source: Survey.

that. Bankruptcy was quite popular in the mid-1990s. This was the time when the Bankruptcy Law began to be seriously implemented and the central government provided large amounts of funds to write off the bank debts of bankrupt SOEs. As a result, many SOEs used bankruptcy as a way to evade repayment of bank debts. A common practice was to file for bankruptcy and establish a new company on the same site.[23] The central government quickly realized the problem and tightened up the regulation, so that the incidence of bankruptcy decreased in the late 1990s. However, as *gaizhi* reached its peak in 2000–01, the incidence of bankruptcy increased again. In the current sample, 18.8 percent and 11.8 percent of the *gaizhi* cases in 2001 and 2002 respectively involved bankruptcy. Evading bank debts was still a significant motivation. The central government had to issue several decrees to block this tendency. The Supreme Court was also involved, issuing a decree making it clear that the evasion of bank debts through bankruptcy was illegal.[24]

4.1. Privatization

Has *gaizhi* led to privatization in the sense of an increase of private participation in the ownership of enterprises' capital? Table 2.4 shows that privatization proceeded rapidly over the sample period 1995–2001. The average proportion of private shares increased from a mere 3.5 percent in 1995 to 33 percent in 2001. The percentage of firms with private shares increased accordingly, from 6.8 percent to 43.6 percent. Privatization accelerated from 1999, the year in which the second wave of privatization

Table 2.4:   Dynamics of Privatization, 1995–2001

Year[a]	1995	1996	1997	1998	1999	2000	2001
Private shares (%)	3.5	4.2	5.5	9.4	14.3	23.9	33.0
Among which shares held by:							
Management	0.0	0.1	0.5	1.2	2.7	6.9	10.0
Employees	0.5	1.0	1.3	2.5	3.8	7.5	9.9
Outsiders	3.0	3.2	3.8	5.6	7.9	9.6	13.1
% of *gaizhi* firms with private shares	6.8	7.8	10.8	16.3	22.9	33.7	43.6
Among which:							
% private shares	54.6	55.6	53.2	59.5	64.0	72.2	76.6
% privately controlled[b]	52.0	51.7	48.7	55.2	59.5	70.7	75.2

Notes:
[a]   A total of 387 firms were used in the calculation.
[b]   Over 50 percent of shares owned privately.

Source: Survey.

began to spread to the whole country. Management, employees and external private persons or firms were private owners of shares, and outsiders were the single largest player in all years.

By the end of 2001, 13.1 percent of shares were held by outsiders. This trend is encouraging, as studies of other transition countries have shown that outsider participation in privatization plays a more significant role than insider participation in the improvement of firm efficiency.[25] Shares controlled by employees and by management increased at similar rates. By 2001, the two parties held almost the same amount of shares on average. Among the firms with private shares, both the amount of private shares and the number of firms in which private shares exceed 50 percent increased during the survey period. By the end of 2001, 76.6 percent of these firms' shares were owned by private persons, and 75.2 percent of the firms had a majority of private shares. Increased private ownership was matched by an increased proportion of firms in which private shareholders owned controlling stakes.

In summary, *gaizhi* has become more radical in that it has involved more privatization in recent years, and outsiders have been playing an increasingly important role in privatization. These trends have had a lot to do with the emergence of the private sector and market liberalization in the country. Market liberalization in the early 1990s abandoned controls on prices and opened up the market to private firms. As a result, SOEs faced increasingly fierce competition from the private sector, and many of them were pushed to the verge of bankruptcy.[26] In addition, banks have become more commercially oriented and have tightened their lending to SOEs.[27] In particular, the People's Bank of China, the central bank, issued stringent regulations related to commercial banks' loan activities in 1998 as a response to the Asian financial crisis. Local governments could no longer use SOEs to finance activities designed to advance their own objectives, such as maintaining employment. This hardened budget constraint has been a major cause for local governments privatising their SOEs.[28] These changes have accompanied the accumulation of wealth in the private sector, which has enabled many private firms to have enough capital to buy SOEs. For example, several large SOEs in Tangshan city have been purchased by private coal mine owners.

5. HANDLING SOE ASSETS

Has the sale of SOE assets been handled with appropriate regard for the public interest? Or have insiders abused their positions to steal state property? These questions have been hotly debated. For example, Ding Xueliang found that restructuring has resulted in the transfer of state assets to a small number of private persons, especially the managers.[29] Our survey provides insights into this important issue. Proper handling of SOE assets is related to the method of sales, asset valuation, and the way that discounts on true value are provided to purchasers. The handling of SOE debts is a related issue. Most SOE debts are owed to banks. Since most banks belong to the central government, local governments deal with debts to banks differently from the assets of SOEs which are owned by local government.

5.1. Practices in the Selling of SOE Assets

Local governments have used a number of methods to transfer state assets in *gaizhi*. The variations can be attributed to applications of discretionary power rather than to explicit policy, although there are some policy differences across regions. The main approach for larger and high-quality SOEs has been to issue equity through the stock market. Firms must meet stringent rules to qualify as listed companies, with the result that only the best-performing can list on the stock market. Current regulations stipulate that the state must hold the majority of shares in those listed companies, which restricts firms from becoming truly independent corporate entities.[30]

For smaller firms, the purchase of equity by insiders is common. Local governments often encourage managers to buy the majority of their firm's shares. Government guidelines suggest that shares sold internally should be distributed according to rank. The largest proportion goes to senior managers, followed by technical personnel and then ordinary employees. To encourage the purchase of shares, employees are able to defer payment of two shares for each share that they buy for cash. If shareholders defer payments, they are able to receive dividends and have voting rights, but have no right to ownership, or to transfer over those shares through sale or bequest. Deferred payments have to be settled within five years. Shares are occasionally distributed to employees in lieu of wages or retirement benefits. Government regulations also allow inventions and other intellectual property rights to be converted to shares after they have been valued and priced, dependent on the agreement of a general meeting of shareholders. The principal managers of the new state-controlled shareholding companies can fund the purchase of up to 50 percent of the shares allocated to them by borrowing from the state asset exit funds (see below), and are obliged to repay the loan with interest within five years.

When an SOE is sold openly, the buyer needs to sign a contract with the government regarding the debts and redeployment of the employees. We found that there are different ways of deciding the price of the assets. When the firm's net asset value is positive, the sale price will be the value of the net assets. When a firm's assets and debts are more or less equal, the firm could be transferred at a zero price. When net assets are negative, the debt may be reduced to make total assets and debts more or less equal. The concession on price could be achieved by giving the new owner free land-use rights, or by making payments from the returns from state assets managed by the provincial or city government asset management agencies which have been established in dealing with state assets sales and transfer at local levels.[31] Another method is to exempt the *gaizhi* firm from income tax until enough value has been transferred to reach zero net asset value.

The local government's main priority is the redeployment of workers who have become redundant in the process. In principle, earnings from asset sales could be used for this purpose. However, this cannot happen in cases where the SOE's net assets are negative. Three government-sponsored funds facilitate and reduce the costs of *gaizhi*: namely, the state asset exit funds; the SOE bankruptcy provisional funds; and the funds to assist retailers to prepare for enterprise reform. State asset exit funds provide a loan to the *gaizhi* firm to meet the costs of redeploying its workers. The loan must be paid back within five years. The funds are managed by authorized state asset-management agencies or by finance departments of local governments. The funding comes from the transfer of ownership rights, sale or lease of state assets.

Not all localities have the same ability to raise funds for *gaizhi*. Richer provinces such as Guangdong have been able to handle the costs of *gaizhi* more proficiently, although even there local officials are concerned about their ability to bear the costs of *gaizhi*, especially the costs of redeploying workers. Those regions where average incomes are low and the number of SOEs high lack adequate government funding to support *gaizhi* programs, and many programs have stalled. Local governments have come under increased pressure to reform their SOEs. There have been calls for greater central government support for poorer regions, or for those with a higher concentration of SOEs.

5.2. Asset Valuation and Price Discounts

The valuation of assets is the key to fair transfers of an SOE to a private investor. Firms must go through three procedures: asset valuation, the demarcation of ownership rights, and the verification of assets. Although asset valuation forms the basis for the sale or transfer of assets, discounts are often given by local governments in exchange for the new owner's consent to employ more workers.

There are several standard methods for valuing business assets: historical cost and multiples of past incomes; replacement cost; multiples of current earnings; and discounted expected cash flows. However, the lack of development of the capital market and other factors such as control over interest rates have prevented China from using some of these more sophisticated methods of asset valuation. The book value of assets is, therefore, commonly used to determine the selling price. This method can either overestimate or underestimate a firm's value, but in the absence of open bidding it remains the easiest way.

Irregularities and weaknesses in the accounting industry often cause distortions in the valuation of SOE assets. The industry is fragmented because valuers specialize in particular areas, such as assets, property, land, mining rights or vehicles. In addition some agencies do not act on a commercial basis but are influenced by local governments or *gaizhi* firms that make requests for a favorable valuation. The choice of a valuer can be made by either the state government or by the firm. The survey found that in the first round of *gaizhi* undertaken by the sample firms, 39 percent of valuers were chosen by *gaizhi* firms, 35 percent by local governments, and the remaining 25 percent jointly by local governments and firms.

Stabilizing employment in the process of *gaizhi* has been strongly emphasized by the central government. It is a political as well as an economic issue. As a result, local governments are prepared to do a great

Table 2.5:   *Discounts Provided to Gaizhi Firms by Cities (numbers and*
                  percentage)

	Number of *gaizhi* firms	Number of rebates	Percent
Harbin	35	2	5.7
Fushun	4	1	25.0
Tangshan	46	8	17.4
Weifang	25	7	28.0
Lanzhou	12	1	8.3
Xining	13	0	0.0
Huangshi	53	19	35.8
Guiyang	30	7	23.3
Zhenjiang	40	12	30.0
Hengyang	38	4	10.5
Chengdu	18	3	16.7
Total	314	64	20.4

Source: Survey.

deal to maintain employment in the process of *gaizhi*. One method that has
been commonly used is to exchange price discounts for the new owner's
agreement to redeploy more workers. Regulations in Harbin, for example,
allow the government to offer discounts when selling SOE assets. Buyers
who purchase the whole business and make a one-off payment can receive a
30 percent discount. Those making a one-off payment covering 60 percent
of total asset value can receive a 10 percent discount. Beyond 60 percent of
the value of assets, a half-percentage point discount can be given for every
percentage point increase in payment. The first payment should not be
below 30 percent of the assessed price, and payments should be made in
installments, with guarantees given before the assets are transferred.

Table 2.5 presents data on the discounts given to *gaizhi* firms by local
governments. The percentage of *gaizhi* cases that involved a discount on the
firm's assets ranged from 5.7 percent in Harbin to 35.8 percent in Huangshi.
It is noteworthy that most firms surveyed did not want to report whether
they had received a discount in *gaizhi*. So the figures reported in Table 2.5
provide only a lower limit to the true situation.

5.3. SOE Debts

Most SOEs hold large debts, which must be dealt with before *gaizhi* is
possible. As mentioned, bank debts generally make up the main item of
enterprise debts, but many enterprises also have unpaid taxes, overdue

wages, pensions and social insurance, and other debts. In the survey, the 493 SOEs that have valid data for 2001 owed a total of 25 billion yuan, of which bank loans with interest made up 15 billion yuan, or 59 percent of the total. Most overdue loans were owed to the four state-owned commercial banks. *Gaizhi* firms have little wish to pay back debts that have been accumulated over time, and the banks lack the means to recover these loans. One example is the Hengdong Cement Factory, which borrowed 14.4 million yuan from the Industrial and Commercial Bank of China for investment in 1995. The factory performed poorly and payments became overdue in 1997. In 2001, four years and several managers later, the overdue amount, including interest, had risen to 15.9 million yuan.

Debt problems have hampered the reform of SOEs, but it is no easy task to resolve the multiple and sometimes competing concerns of *gaizhi* firms, banks and local governments. As one CEO in Harbin pointed out during an interview, *gaizhi* firms are more concerned about the debts owed to employees than about the overdue bank loans, which they see as being owed to the government by the former SOE. Even if they had originally intended to pay off the debt, most *gaizhi* firms find themselves unable to do so as they would struggle to stay in operation and find it difficult to attract new capital. The government has not gone as far as canceling the debts of small and medium-sized enterprises, as it did for the large SOEs. Some medium-sized SOEs in Harbin in 2002 were delaying their *gaizhi* programs in anticipation that the government would extend the debt write-offs and debt–equity swaps to medium-sized SOEs.

As mentioned earlier, bankruptcy is used to escape bank debts. More than 2000 firms have gone through bankruptcy procedures since the Bankruptcy Law was enacted in 1988. In the survey, 90 percent of CEOs of *gaizhi* firms believed that bankruptcy was a feasible means of resolving their enterprise's debt problems. In response, banks have been trying to avoid losses, preferring firms not to be restructured if that is likely to involve bankruptcy. In 2002, the Supreme People's Court ruled that it would not process bankruptcy cases if the main intentions were to escape debts.[32] The central government has also tightened regulations to strengthen the management of debt liabilities and to prevent firms from ignoring their debts.[33] To prevent firms from using *gaizhi* to discharge their bank debts, a register of firms that have tried to avoid debts has been set up, and firms are given a schedule for debt repayment. If firms fail to meet the schedule, they will be unable to apply for new loans or open new bank accounts. Financial institutions can reduce the credit rating, and suspend the review of new projects and the granting of new loans for specific regions, which directly affects local government interests.

Although local banks would like to help *gaizhi* firms by discounting and rescheduling their debts or reducing interest payments, this would not be enough to solve the problems of *gaizhi* firms, as many SOEs were heavily in debt before *gaizhi*. Banks have been asked by the central banking authority to act as true commercial entities, making it difficult for them to give up their rights as creditors. Banks can sue enterprises to recover loans, but lawsuits often end up in a stalemate, with the banks unable to recover the loans and the firms unable to continue with restructuring. Several firms in Harbin said that *gaizhi* programs had stalled pending court decisions over the repayment of bank debts. As one bank manager stated: 'We can sue the debtors in court, but it would not do much to get our money back because we can never get a single cent from the *gaizhi* firms whether we win the lawsuit or not'. In some cases banks have also been reluctant to seize the assets of the *gaizhi* firms, because the revenue might not cover the cost of auctioning the assets. Their only recourse is to refuse to make new loans to firms that default on loan repayments.

Many *gaizhi* firms have not begun real *gaizhi* because they have refused to take over the debts of the old firm. Firms sometimes take other ways of avoiding responsibility for the debts, for instance by setting up a new private firm to lease the assets and employ most of the workers, leaving the old firm to carry the bank debts. In many cases, the old firm is left with few employees to look after the workshops and equipment and is likely to go bankrupt eventually.

In dealing with the debt problems of *gaizhi* firms, the interests of debtors and creditors have to be balanced. In practice, solutions that hurt the interests of either side disproportionately may not be conducive to successful *gaizhi*. While the government needs to tackle the debt problems, it is more important that an environment is created that allows *gaizhi* firms to perform well so that they avoid falling into new debt traps. It is necessary to provide access to bank credit and loans if hard budget constraints are to be imposed on firms. 'The imposition of hard budget constraints on enterprises in the absence of functioning credit may force sound firms into insolvency'.[34]

5.3. Land-use Rights

Land in China is owned by the state or, in rural and suburban areas, by collectives. Before 1995 all land-use rights for SOEs were under government control. The state being the owner of both enterprises and land, the land-use rights were not defined and the land was used free of charge by the SOEs. As a result, much of the land taken by SOEs was underutilized or misallocated. This situation continued until the 1998 Land Law, which defined land as a scarce resource and stipulated that it should be used to generate revenue.[35]

At least four methods are used to deal with land-use rights in *gaizhi*: keeping the appropriation by the firm of the land-use rights (meaning the use free of charge of occupied land); leasing; buying; and converting land-use rights into equity. Despite the government's active encouragement for firms to buy land-use rights, many *gaizhi* firms prefer to maintain their appropriation of the land-use rights. The Regulation on Appropriated Land-Use Rights in SOE Reform, and the document entitled 'Strengthening Land Resource Management and Promoting SOE Reform', issued by the Bureau of National Land Resource Management, have stipulated that some *gaizhi* firms that currently occupy land can use it free of charge on conditions set by the local government.

The usual conditions are: *gaizhi* firms must be operating in sectors stipulated by the government; land in use must be assessed, and any extra land must be returned to the government; the land must be used for production, and the firm's owners cannot change the land use or lease the land to others without the permission of the relevant agency; and land-use tenure is usually set for between five and ten years, depending on the land use. Although land appropriation has restrictions, it can save *gaizhi* firms a great deal of money.

Leasing is a suitable method for *gaizhi* firms that cannot afford to buy granted land-use rights. To reduce the financial pressure, *gaizhi* firms are allowed to pay around 30 percent of the fee up front and the remaining amount on an annual basis. Leasing has many advantages, but different cities have different practices. In some cities, *gaizhi* firms with leased rights were able to mortgage or use the land-use rights as collateral for a loan, while such practice was not allowed in other cities.

Finally, the method of converting land-use rights into equity is rarely used, but can complement other methods; for instance, when the government wants to retain shares in *gaizhi* firms and to take over the management rights, or when joint ventures are formed with foreign companies, it can own part of the firm by converting land-use rights into equity.

The survey demonstrated that maintaining appropriation was the dominant method of acquiring land-use rights in all the cities except Xining, Harbin and Huangshi. Of the 199 *gaizhi* firms that replied to this question, 45 percent favored this method. The second most common method was buying the land-use rights (31 percent), followed by leasing (12 percent) and converting land-use rights into equity (6 percent). The majority of the sample firms, particularly listed companies and restructured firms, obtained land-use rights for free. A high proportion of firms that were sold or leased out purchased the land-use rights. Non-reported cases were high across all forms of *gaizhi* firms.

There have been a number of problems with the way land issues have been dealt with during *gaizhi*. It has been difficult for the local land resource authority to manage the process of pricing the land, and its decision may not reflect the true value of the land. The decision to offer a discount on the price to the *gaizhi* firm has often been made arbitrarily. The different regimes of land-use rights may also create a disincentive for firms to privatise. Private firms will have to pay a significant fee to convert the allocated land-use rights into grant-use rights. Allocated land-use rights also limit the ability of *gaizhi* firms to obtain bank financing or to enter into joint venture arrangements with domestic or foreign partners.

The ability of the local governments to monetize the value of the land is a key factor in implementing the *gaizhi* programs at local level. Many local governments rely on the proceeds from the sale of land-use rights to cover the social obligations related to restructuring. The current attempts by the central government to fight overheating of land prices (in particular due to a booming real estate market) by exercising a tight control on land sales is having an effect on the pace of *gaizhi* programs.

6. FINANCIAL ARRANGMENTS FOR WORKER SETTLEMENT

6.1. The Impact of *Gaizhi* on Unemployment

Enterprise restructuring has been a socially painful process. Between 1995 and 2001, the number of state-owned and state-controlled enterprises in China fell from 118 000 to 47 000 and total employment in the SOE sector fell by 36 million. The number of jobs lost totaled 15 percent of urban employment in 2001. Over-employment had created a massive burden on SOEs now trying to shake off some of its excess workers during the *gaizhi* process. The number of labor disputes of all kinds rose by 12.5 percent in 2000, and by another 14.4 percent in 2001 to reach 155 000. In the first half of 2004 alone, labor disputes arbitration committees at various levels accepted 135 000 labor dispute cases and handled 6640 collective labor disputes, which involved 184 000 persons.[36]

The survey found that both non-*gaizhi* and *gaizhi* SOEs have lost many employees in recent years, suggesting that market competition has been exerting pressures on all firms. Table 2.6 shows the proportions of on-duty employees, and of retired, *xiagang*[37] and discharged workers in 2001 in

Table 2.6:   *Shares of On-duty, Retired,* Xiagang *and Discharged Employees in 2001*

Type of firm	Firms with valid data	Total employees (1000)	On duty (%)	Retired (%)	*Xiagang* (%)	Discharged (%)
Sum of *gaizhi* firms	214	308	57.1	16.0	26.1	0.7
Shareholding companies	32	85	75.1	16.2	7.8	0.9
Limited liability companies	119	190	62.1	17.5	19.2	1.2
Partnerships/ cooperatives	16	11	51.6	24.4	22.8	1.2
Single-owner private firms	2	0.7	37.0	9.3	53.7	0.0
Other	45	21	59.9	12.7	27.2	0.3
Non-*gaizhi* SOEs	280	209	43.9	22.1	32.7	1.3
Total	494	518	56.6	19.1	23.2	1.1

Source: Survey.

both non-*gaizhi* and *gaizhi* SOEs. Note that *xiagang* workers and retired workers were sometimes included in the enterprises' statistics of total employment because these workers were still being partly supported by the firm. The number of retired employees includes all those who retired in previous years. The number of *xiagang* workers includes those laid off in previous years but still listed by the re-employment service center and therefore still counted as employees. The statistics did not include *xiagang* workers who had found employment or had been removed from the re-employment service center after three years. The number of discharged employees only includes those who were discharged in 2001. *Xiagang* workers made up 32.7 percent of employees in non-*gaizhi* SOEs but only 26.1 percent of employees in *gaizhi* firms. This could be because *gaizhi* firms had already shed many of their *xiagang* workers during *gaizhi*.

However, Table 2.7 suggests that *gaizhi* firms performed better in the long run. In the table, estimates are made of the accumulated number of xiagang and discharged employees in sample enterprises over the period 1995–2001. Again there was a significantly higher share of *xiagang*

Table 2.7:   *Accumulated* Xiagang *and Discharged Workers per Firm in the Period 1995–2001*

| | Xiagang[a] | | Discharged | |
	Average number	Per firm (%)[b]	Average number	Per firm (%)[b]
Sum of *gaizhi* firms	417	29	69	4.8
Shareholding companies	319	12	117	4.4
Limited liability companies	527	33	88	5.5
Partnerships/cooperatives	296	43	13	1.9
Single-owner private firms	245	70	0	0.0
Other	238	51	6	1.2
Non-*gaizhi* SOEs	515	69	37	5.0
Total	472	45	51	4.9

Notes:
[a]   The number of accumulated *xiagang* workers is calculated under the assumption that their average stay in the re-employment service centres was three years (reflecting the difficulty of gaining employment and the provision of a subsidy over the period that acts as a disincentive to seek employment).
[b]   Percentage of the average number of total employees in 2001.

Source: Survey.

workers in non-*gaizhi* SOEs compared with *gaizhi* firms (69 percent versus 29 percent). Therefore, even if they shed more workers during the year of *gaizhi*, *gaizhi* firms had accumulated significantly fewer *xiagang* workers after *gaizhi*, which means that *gaizhi* may improve the employment situation in the long run.

6.2.   Re-employment and Compensation to Laid-off Workers

As pointed out by Oi (2005), 'political economy of corporate restructuring in China is shaped by political as well as economical constraints. The political constraint is fear of worker reaction; the economic constraint is a lack of resources to fill the holes in a still-developing national social-welfare safety net, which in practice means having to buy off workers and other 'losers from reform' with acceptable severance packages. Restructuring and privatization remain a patchwork of solutions that push the limits of reform but then must be reined back to accommodate the political as well as economic realities that exist in different localities'.[38]

Re-employment is therefore a desirable solution both for redundant workers and staff members of SOEs and for the state, because it lowers the cost of *gaizhi* and reduces the political as well as economic constraints. This is why most governments give tax holidays and deductions to former SOE employees who start a business or to new enterprises that hire *xiagang* workers to the extent of at least 60 percent of their workforce. Government departments and banks also help these firms with registration and access to bank loans. In some cases the government assists redundant workers to find other work, but this accounts for only a small proportion of employee redeployment. But re-employment is not always possible, and layoffs are unavoidable.

It is a difficult task to determine the level of compensation. As Roland puts it: 'Some of these workers expect to find jobs easily and will not lose much from redundancies, whereas others will have a much harder time and will need to be compensated more heavily to accept being laid off. But if one cannot tell which worker is in which category, then all workers would have to be paid high compensation, because they are indistinguishable and because workers with lower exit costs have an incentive to pretend they have high exit costs'.[39] In reality, the level of compensation depends on the collective bargaining power of the workers and on the resources available to enterprises and local governments. Our interviews show that, while in most cities workers receive compensation equal to three years' salaries, in a few cases, such as Daqing Oil Fields, workers get much higher compensation.

The most common way for local governments to finance the compensation is to use the money raised in selling SOE assets. In many cases, local governments prefer the new owner to hire as many workers as possible in exchange for discounts on the price of assets (including land). Many enterprises are sold at zero value, and in some cases the government pays extra subsidies to cover the redeployment of the employees. One example is the city of Tangshan where buyers of SOEs must agree to take responsibility for all employees and retired workers.[40] The government compensated buyers for the future cost of redeploying workers by reducing the price of the assets on the understanding that no more than 10 percent of employees will be made redundant. The new owners frequently reported that the compensation was inadequate as the cost of redeploying workers was much higher. However, there were also complaints from employees that state assets such as land were being sold too cheaply.[41] In Harbin, the municipal government allowed enterprises going through *gaizhi* to sell part of their assets to compensate employees who are being discharged. Land-use rights can be transferred if funds are inadequate.

Nan'an District of Chongqing City adopted a different approach.[42] The employment contracts of all SOE employees were terminated and workers compensated before the enterprises were sold or went bankrupt, regardless of whether workers will be re-employed by the new owners of the enterprises or not. This makes *gaizhi* much easier and reduces conflicts after *gaizhi*. A large percentage of the district's SOEs have completed *gaizhi*. The proportion of enterprises that has completed *gaizhi* is much smaller in the other districts, which adopted a municipal government policy of redeploying employees after the enterprise goes bankrupt. In these districts, state assets are used to pay off debt, leaving little for employee redeployment. If governments wish to compensate the employees before *gaizhi*, they need the agreement of the creditor banks and usually there needs to be a large positive net value of state assets to cover the costs of employee redeployment. In Nan'an District, land values are high and the sale of land-use rights has financed redeployment.

Guiyang has adopted a policy that allows employees more say. In the city, *gaizhi* plans have to pass a vote of the employee conference or employee representative committee. Employees must agree with the decision to terminate their contracts. They should receive a lump-sum payment of two months' wages for every year of service. Such comparatively generous conditions, not common elsewhere, make the *gaizhi* process more difficult, because employees are likely to block the decision to undergo *gaizhi* until the situation becomes so bad that no wages can be paid. These provisions may explain why the private sector in Guiyang is underdeveloped. Guiyang is also a very poor place in which the social role of SOEs is probably more important than elsewhere. The development of the private sector in the local economy helps provide employment opportunities for redundant state workers and is a crucial factor for the success of *gaizhi*.

7. IMPACTS OF RESTRUCTURING ON FIRM PERFORMANCE

7.1. Financial Discipline

Soft budget constraint has been one of the most serious problems to plague SOEs in the former centrally planned economies. Kornai suggests that a soft budget constraint arises as a consequence of state paternalism towards the socialist firm, so it is expected that *gaizhi*, and privatization in particular, will alleviate the problem.[43] However, a soft budget constraint can also exist in a capitalist economy, due to the banks' and the state's failure to commit to a time-consistent policy.[44] Can we expect *gaizhi* and privatization to improve a firm's financial discipline? Here we compare *gaizhi* and privatized firms with the old-style SOEs using three financial indicators: performance on meeting obligations on bank debts, taxes, and social security. The first indicator reflects the firm's relationship with the bank, and the other two reflect its relationship with the government. When a firm can postpone its due payments to the bank or the government the constraint on its budget is soft. So we study overdue bank debts (overdue bank loan repayments plus the arrears in interest payments), overdue taxes and overdue social security.

Table 2.8 compares *gaizhi* firms with non-*gaizhi* firms with regard to the above three indicators. The first three columns of the table show the percentage of firms with overdue payments; the last three columns show the average amount of overdue payments weighted by appropriate denominators. It is evident that a smaller number of *gaizhi* firms than non-*gaizhi* firms owed overdue bank debts, and the average size of their debts was smaller than non-*gaizhi* firms although the difference seems to have

Table 2.8:   *Financial Discipline:* Gaizhi *Versus Non-Gaizhi Firms*

	1996	1997	1998	1999	2000	2001
% of firms with overdue bank debts[a]						
Non-*Gaizhi*	72.2	73.9	77.3	79.0	79.2	77.3
Gaizhi	50.0	52.7	61.4	61.3	62.8	68.6
% of firms with overdue taxes						
Non-*Gaizhi*	37.5	40.2	43.0	44.9	48.1	51.7
Gaizhi	27.7	34.8	37.2	42.8	44.3	45.1
% of firms with overdue social security						
Non-*Gaizhi*	15.8	19.7	21.9	26.0	30.5	34.2
Gaizhi	15.4	18.0	21.1	26.6	25.5	31.1
Size of overdue bank debts (%)[b]						
Non-*Gaizhi*	76.1	77.7	94.5	102.6	111.5	90.0
Gaizhi	50.0	48.4	55.2	53.7	57.2	78.5
Size of overdue taxes (%)[c]						
Non-*Gaizhi*	4.9	3.8	3.6	2.9	2.8	2.7
Gaizhi	2.3	3.2	2.7	3.1	2.6	2.3
Size of overdue social security (%)[c]						
Non-*Gaizhi*	0.2	0.2	0.2	0.3	0.3	0.4
Gaizhi	0.5	0.4	0.3	0.4	0.4	0.6

Notes:
[a]   Overdue bank debts include overdue bank loans and interests.
[b]   Size of overdue bank debts is defined as the total amount of bank debts divided by the amount of year-end outstanding loans.
[c]   Sizes of overdue taxes and overdue social security are defined as the total amount of overdue taxes and total amount of overdue social security divided by the value of the firm's gross assets, respectively (some firms did not pay taxes in some years, so the denominator uses the value of gross assets).

Source: Survey.

decreased over time. However, this better discipline of *gaizhi* firms may be a result of their reduction of bank and other debts in the year of *gaizhi*. There is a widely shared suspicion that firms use *gaizhi* to evade debts.

Nevertheless, there were only 8.3 percent and 13.6 percent respectively of the *gaizhi* firms in the sample, that reduced their bank debts and all forms of debts in the year of *gaizhi*. So the better performance of *gaizhi* firms was unlikely to have been a result of debt evasion in the year of *gaizhi*. *Gaizhi* has indeed hardened firms' budget constraint with the bank by imposing more discipline on these firms. It has also hardened firms' budget constraint with the government, but to a much lesser extent. A smaller number of *gaizhi* firms owed taxes to the government, and the average size of their overdue taxes was smaller than for other firms, but the differences were much smaller than in the case of bank debts. The advantage of *gaizhi* was even less clear in the case of social security. The percentage of *gaizhi* firms with overdue social security did not significantly differ from that of non-

Table 2.9:   Financial Discipline: Privatized Versus Fully-State Owned Firms[a]

	1996	1997	1998	1999	2000	2001
% of firms with overdue bank debts						
Full state	71.8	73.1	76.4	77.9	76.7	77.0
Privatized[a]	40.0	51.3	63.2	62.8	70.4	66.9
% of firms with overdue taxes						
Full state	36.5	39.7	42.8	45.3	48.4	52.1
Privatized	40.0	41.0	40.4	44.2	45.2	47.2
% of firms with overdue social security						
Full state	16.3	20.0	22.5	27.3	32.1	36.4
Privatized	10.0	17.9	19.3	22.1	18.3	24.6
Size of overdue bank debts (%)						
Full state	75.4	76.4	92.5	99.5	107.8	99.1
Privatized	39.7	45.7	54.8	56.5	62.4	59.5
Size of overdue taxes (%)						
Full state	4.7	3.7	3.4	2.8	2.8	2.8
Privatized	4.6	6.6	5.0	4.9	3.5	3.0
Size of overdue social security (%)						
Full state	0.2	0.2	0.3	0.3	0.4	0.5
Privatized	0.5	0.5	0.3	0.3	0.2	0.3

Notes:
[a]   Privatized firms are firms with any amount of private shares.
[b]   The definitions of the categories are the same as those in Table 2.7.

Source: Survey.

gaizhi firms, and the average size of their overdue social security was even larger than that of non-*gaizhi* firms.

Table 2.9 compares firms in which the private share of ownership is increasing with fully state-owned firms. In this table, a 'privatized' firm is one in which any ownership shares are held privately. The comparison shows results similar to those in the comparison of *gaizhi* and non-*gaizhi* firms, but the advantage of privatized firms over fully state-owned firms has been strengthened in the case of overdue bank debts and overdue social security. This shows that *gaizhi* with privatization works better than *gaizhi* without privatization in terms of hardening firms' budget constraint.

7.2. Efficiency

Gaizhi firms, especially truly privatized firms, were subject to a harder budget constraint than non-*gaizhi* firms. But were they more productive? This sub-section compares *gaizhi* and non-*gaizhi* firms in the sample with regard to three performance indicators: return to assets, per worker sales and new investment. The results are presented in Table 2.10. *Gaizhi* firms are shown to do better than non-*gaizhi* firms with regard to return to assets and marginally better in per-worker sales, but remain indistinguishable from non-*gaizhi* firms with regard to new investment. *Gaizhi* firms' better performance was made possible not so much by more investment, but rather

Table 2.10: *Performance:* Gaizhi *versus Non-*Gaizhi *Firms*

Year	Return to assets[a] (%)		Per-worker sales[b] (1000 yuan)		New investment[c] (%)	
	Non-*Gaizhi*	*Gaizhi*	Non-*Gaizhi*	*Gaizhi*	Non-*Gaizhi*	*Gaizhi*
1996	−1.3	1.8	5.2	4.0	17.0	17.9
1997	−1.4	1.9	4.7	5.4	16.0	21.0
1998	−1.9	1.4	5.2	5.5	16.5	19.2
1999	−1.8	1.5	5.3	5.7	16.8	16.5
2000	−1.8	1.2	5.5	6.1	16.4	16.4
2001	−1.5	0.6	5.9	6.8	17.9	15.3

Notes:
[a] Return to assets is defined as the pre-tax profit divided by the value of the firm's gross assets.
[b] It is defined as sales value divided by on-duty workers. The value of sales is converted to 2001 yuan.
[c] New investment divided by the value of the firm's gross assets.

Source: Survey

Table 2.11:   *Performance: Privatized versus Fully State-Owned Firms*

Year	Return to assets[a] (%)		Per-worker sales[b] (1000 yuan)		New investment[c] (%)	
	Full state	Privatized	Full state	Privatized	Full state	Privatized
1996	−1.2	2.5	5.0	6.8	16.6	20.8
1997	−1.4	3.2	4.7	5.7	15.7	14.7
1998	−1.9	4.2	5.2	6.1	15.8	15.0
1999	−2.0	4.1	5.2	6.9	16.2	12.7
2000	−2.2	3.7	5.1	7.8	16.2	11.4
2001	−2.1	2.4	5.5	7.3	17.8	11.0

Notes:
[a] Return to assets is defined as the pre-tax profit divided by the value of the firm's gross assets.
[b] It is defined as sales value divided by on-duty workers. The value of sales is converted to 2001 yuan.
[c] New investment divided by the value of the firm's gross assets.

Source: Survey.

by efficiency enhancement.

Table 2.11 shows the comparison between privatized and fully state-owned firms. The effect of *gaizhi* was enhanced in terms of return to assets when it was accompanied by privatization, but differences based on ownership are not very significant for per-worker sales, and privatized firms are shown to invest less than fully state-owned firms. The results are subject to one qualification. It is possible that better performing firms have been deliberately chosen to undergo *gaizhi* and privatization either because local governments believe that they can improve performance and receive a higher price by delaying privatization of poorly performing enterprises or simply because better performing firms are easier to privatize. To accommodate this consideration, we calculate the effect of privatization by adopting the difference-in-difference (DID) method. This method compares privatized firms' relative performance before and after privatization, and the relative performance of fully state-owned firms over the same years. The method is an effective nonparametric method to control firm specific characteristics. Figure 2.3 summarizes the results. It shows the average effect of privatization for firms privatized in different years, being arranged by years after privatization.

Two patterns emerge from the figure. First, privatization has a significantly positive effect on return to assets, and this effect increases as time passes. There is clearly a learning process for privatization to become

Figure 2.3: *The Effect of Privatization Calculated by DID Method*

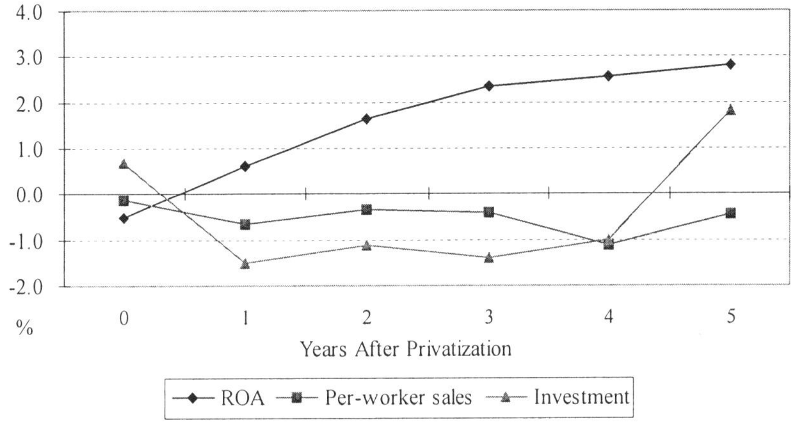

Years After Privatization

—◆— ROA —■— Per-worker sales —▲— Investment

Notes:
The calculation is based on the sample of 387 firms.
ROA stands for return to assets.

Source: Calculated using survey data.

effective in raising profitability. The new owners need to change the management structure, adopt new business models, and possibly shift to a new line of business. Second, privatization does not result in a significant positive, and might in fact have a negative impact on labor productivity and investment. Indeed, *gaizhi* firms perform worse than non-*gaizhi* firms for most years after *gaizhi*. These two results suggest that privatized firms were more conscious than the old-style SOEs about saving costs. It is well known that traditional SOEs were used to an expansionary business model that pays little attention to saving capital, material and wage costs. Privatization changes this model. Firms no longer pursue the goal of high growth in output and investment, but rather focus on a more efficient use of financial and human resources to generate more profits. In other words, the improved efficiency of *gaizhi* firms comes mostly from adopting new technologies, new product combinations and more efficient ways of production.

8.   CONCLUSIONS

This study reveals an accelerating trend of privatization in China. Firms have adopted more radical forms of restructuring in recent years and the extent of privatization has deepened. By 2001, 43.6 percent of the sample firms had introduced private shares, and among these firms two-thirds had a majority of private shares. While restructuring is frequently criticized for leading to the loss of state assets, this chapter finds that the loss has happened mainly in the form of price discounts which local governments gave to the new owners in exchange for their consent not to sack many workers. In other words, the loss of state assets, if any, is partly a result of the government's emphasis on maintaining employment.

Contrary to the conventional wisdom is another finding that *gaizhi*, or restructured firms, have maintained a slower rate of employment reduction than pure SOEs in the years after *gaizhi*, although in the year when *gaizhi* happened they did sack more workers. This shows that privatization has the potential to improve China's employment situation in the long run. This is made possible because privatization has led to efficiency improvements. We have found that *gaizhi*, especially restructuring with privatization, has hardened firms' budget constraints with the banks and significantly improved firms' profitability. As firms' investment rate and labor productivity measured by per-worker sales have not been improved in a significant way, we conclude that the positive effect of *gaizhi* and privatization on firms' profitability has been made possible by firms' shift from the expansionary business model characterizing the old style SOEs to a new business model that gives higher priority to cost-saving.

However, we find that restructuring has not hardened firms' budget constraints with the government. One explanation is that local governments want to trade tax and social security amenities for firms' incentive to maintain employment. This can be a rational choice, as employment is the top priority that the central government puts on restructuring. Another explanation is that local governments themselves have a soft-budget constraint with the central government. Although China has separated local and central taxes, quotas are still placed on local governments regarding the growth of tax revenues. However, these quotas are subject to negotiation. In the case of social security, the central government has established a fund preparing for unexpected payment shortfalls in the social security system. It has also provided funds to individual provinces for them to migrate from the old pay-as-you-go system to the new system with both public and individual accounts.

Two important issues are not studied in this chapter. One is corporate governance. Restructuring will create many firms with dispersed shares held by many small shareholders most of whom are employees. A proper corporate governance structure thus is very important for these firms' future performance. Judging by the findings on private firms,[45] we expect no easy task for privatized SOEs to handle corporate governance issues properly. The other issue is related to the capital market. Currently local capital markets are very thin in China, but we will soon see the demand for opportunities to trade employees' shares obtained through privatization. This increases the need for an efficient local capital market.

NOTES

1. The chapter was originally published in the *China Journal* (Issue 55, 2006). We are grateful to the *China Journal* for giving its permission to reproduce the article with adaptation in this volume.
2. The authors are principal researchers in this survey. The survey adopted a research strategy that combines structured questionnaires distributed to firms selected by random sampling with face-to-face interviews with government officials and enterprise management selected to provide insights into the privatization process and its outcomes. While the sampling provides quantitative data, the interviews reveal rich qualitative information regarding different government policies and various problems that have been encountered in *gaizhi*.
3. For a more comprehensive coverage of these issues, see Ross Garnaut, Ligang Song, Stoyan Tenev and Yang Yao, *China's Ownership Transformation: Process, Outcomes, Prospects* (Washington: International Finance Corporation; the World Bank, 2005).
4. Roger Gordon and Wei Li, 'The Change in Productivity of Chinese State Enterprises, 1983–1987', *Journal of Productivity Analysis*, Vol. 6, No. 1 (1995), pp. 5–26; Theodore Groves, Yongmiao Hong, John McMillan and Barry Naughton, 'Autonomy and Incentives in Chinese State Enterprises', *Quarterly Journal of Economics*, Vol. 109, No. 1 (1994), pp. 183–209; Theodore Groves, Yongmiao Hong, John McMillan and Barry Naughton, 'China's Evolving Managerial Labor Market', *Journal of Political Economy*, Vol. 103, No. 4 (1995), pp. 873–92; Wei Li, 'The Impact of Economic Reform on the Performance of Chinese State Enterprises, 1980–1989', *Journal of Political Economy*, Vol. 105, No. 5 (1997), pp. 1080–106.
5. 'Guanyu xiaoxing guoyou gongye qiye zulin de zhanxing guiding' (Tentative Regulations on the Lease of Small State-owned Industrial Enterprises), State Council, 20 May 1988.
6. Xiao Zhao, 'Jingzheng, gonggong xuanze he zhidu bianqian' (Competition, Public Choice and Institutional Change), CCER Working Paper No. C1999025, 1999, Beijing University.
7. Xiao Zhao, *'Jingzheng, gonggong xuanze'*, p. 21.
8. Yang Yao (2004), pp. 91–101.
9. Shao'an Huang and Jian Wei, 'A Research Report on State-Owned SMEs in Zhucheng', mimeo, School of Economics, Shangdong University, 2001; Yang Yao, 'Privatising the Small SOEs'.
10. In 1994, the State Economic and Trade Commission, sent a report, *'Guanyu gaohuo xiaoxing guoyou qiye de jianyi'* (Suggestions on Revitalizing Small State-owned Enterprises), to then Vice-Premier Wu Bangguo, who was in charge of enterprise reforms. In September 1995 the policy was formally announced by the Central Committee of the Chinese Communist Party in one of its plenaries and went forward as a suggestion for the Ninth Five-Year Plan.
11. Xiao Zhao, *'Jingzheng, gonggong xuanze'*, p. 18.
12. Ibid., p. 25.
13. Ibid., p. 29.
14. This assumption is subject to two qualifications. First, some firms may have vanished not because of privatization but because of simple closing-up, which implies that our measure of privatization is upward-biased. Second, new SOEs may be established over the period, which implies that the measure is downward-biased.
15. Qin Hui (1998), *Jiangzhe xiangzhen qiye zhuanzhi anli yanjiu* (Case Studies of TVE Ownership Transformation in Jiangsu and Zhejiang) (Hong Kong: Chinese University of Hong Kong, 1998).

16. Unpublished report of the National Bureau of Statistics.
17. Unpublished report of the State Economic and Trade Commission.
18. Shanwen Gao and Yang Yao, 'Implementation of Socially Optimal Outcomes in the Process of Dissolving Public Enterprises in China', *China Economic Review*, Vol. 10, No. 1 (1999), pp. 41–58.
19. Simeon Djankov and Peter Murrell, 'Enterprise Restructuring in Transition: A Quantitative Survey', *Journal of Economic Literature*, Vol. 40, No. 3 (2002), pp. 739–92.
20. See Simeon Djankov and Peter Murrell, 'Enterprise Restructuring in Transition', for a survey.
21. Jean C. Oi, 'Patterns of Corporate Restructuring in China: Political Constraints on Privatization', *The China Journal*, No. 53 (January 2005), pp. 115–36.
22. The difference in total number of *gaizhi* firms reported in Tables 2.2 and 2.3 is due to the discrepancies occurred when reporting the numbers across cities (Table 2.2) and years (Table 2.3).
23. Shanwen Gao and Yang Yao, 'Implementation of Socially Optimal Outcomes in the Process of Dissolving Public Enterprises in China', *China Economic Review*, Vol. 10, No. 1(1999), pp. 41–58.
24. The Supreme Court (2001), *Guanyu renmin fayuan zai shenli qiye pochan he gaizhi anjian zhong qieshi fangzhi zhaiwuren taofei zhaiwu de jinji tongzhi* (Urgent Decree for Strictly Avoiding Debt Evasion in Trials of Enterprise Bankruptcy and *gaizhi* Cases in the People's Court), the Supreme Court Decree (2001) No.105.
25. See Simeon Djankov and Peter Murrell, 'Enterprise Restructuring in Transition', for a survey.
26. These competitive forces forced many SOEs to restructure rather than to privatize during the 1980s and 1990s, leading to the emergence of some very successful SOEs, such as Haier, without privatization.
27. Yuanzheng Cao, Yingyi Qian and Barry Weingast, 'From Federalism, Chinese Style to Privatization, Chinese Style', *Economics of Transition*, Vol. 7, No. 1 (1999), pp. 103–31.
28. Kai Guo and Yang Yao, 'Causes of Privatization in China: Testing Several Hypotheses', *Economics of Transition*, Vol. 13, No. 2 (2005), pp. 211–38.
29. See Xueliang Ding, 'The Illicit Asset Stripping of Chinese States Firms', *The China Journal*, No. 43 (January 2000), pp. 1–28.
30. Tenev and Zhang with Brefort, (2002).
31. At the central level, it is the State-Owned Assets Supervision and Administration Commission (SASAC) which is responsible for carrying out enterprise restructuring in those centrally administered, large-size SOEs. SASAC is responsible for regulating the *gaizhi* process. It has promulgated a series of regulations dealing with the transformation of SOEs in response to the 'irregularities' resulting in the loss of state assets since 2003.
32. Clause 12(1), '*Guanyu chuli qiye pochan shenqing wenti de ruogan guiding*' (Regulations on Issues of Processing Applications for Enterprise Bankruptcy), Supreme People's Court, 1 September 2002.
33. See the People's Bank of China, '*Guanyu jiaqiang zhaiwu guanli, jianli fangzhi he chengfa taofeizhai tixi de tongzhi*' (Notice on strengthening management of debt liabilities and building a system of preventing and penalizing the behavior of avoiding financing debts), 7 January 1997.
34. Holger Wolf, 'Transition Strategies: Choices and Outcomes', *Princeton Studies in International Finance*, Vol. 85 (June 1999), p. 4.
35. Anthony Gar On Yeh, 'Dual land market and internal spatial structure of Chinese cities', in Laurence J.C. Ma and Wu Fulong (eds), *Restructuring the Chinese City: Changing Society, Economy and Space*' (London: Routledge, 2005).
36. 'Labor disputes on the rise', *People's Daily*, 1 November 2004.
37. *Xiagang* literally means 'losing the position'. An employee is called a *xiagang* employee if he stops working in the factory but nevertheless keeps a nominal tie with the factory through work registration. In effect, *xiagang* and unemployment are equivalent in terms of the status of the worker, but government policies are different for the two categories of worker. The benefit of being described as *xiagang*, rather than as officially unemployed, is

that people are still counted as employees and may have the chance to resume working the enterprise, although in reality this does not often happen.

38. Jean C. Oi, 'Patterns of Corporate Restructuring in China', p. 135.
39. Gerard Roland (2002), 'The Political Economy of Transition', *Journal of Economic Perspectives*, Vol. 16, No. 1, pp. 29–50.
40. Workers and staff members retired from SOEs are covered by the new pension system. However, pension payments are low, perhaps lower than the common pension rate in SOEs. Enterprises still have to pay the difference between the actual and common pension rate.
41. The survey found only a few cases in different cities of new owners complaining about the overvaluation of state assets.
42. Only face-to-face interviews were conducted but no questionnaires were distributed in this city.
43. Soft budget constraints result from the lack of discipline which derives, for example, from the unenforceability of bankruptcy, together with various subsidies, credits, and price supports provided by the state to SOEs. See Janos Kornai, *Economics of Shortage* (Amsterdam: North-Holland Pub. Co., 1980); Janos Kornai, 'The Soft Budget Constraint', *Kyklos*, Vol. 39, No. 1 (1986), pp. 3–30.
44. M. Dewatripont and Eric Maskin (1995), 'Credit and Efficiency in Centralized and Decentralized Economies', *Review of Economic Studies*, Vol. 62, No. 4, pp. 541–55. Dewatripont and Maskin (1995) borrow the phrase 'time-consistent policy' from macroeconomics. It refers to a situation where it would be optimal for the bank to impose tough financial discipline over the firm, but once the firm becomes insolvent it becomes rational for the bank to issue more credit to enable the firm to bring back some returns.
45. Ross Garnaut, Ligang Song, Yang Yao and Xiaolu Wang, *Private Enterprise in China* (Canberra: Asia Pacific Press, 2001); Neil Gregory, Stoyan Tenev and Dileep Wagle, *China's Emerging Private Enterprises: Prospects for the New Century* (Washington: International Finance Corporation, 2000).

BIBLIOGRAPHY

CCP Central Committee and the State Council (1998), 'CCP Central Committee and the State Council notice on mending basic living security and reemployment for SOE laid-off workers', No. 10, CCP Central Committee Document.

Gao, Shanwen and Yang Yao (1999), 'Implementation of socially optimal outcomes in the process of dissolving public enterprises in China', *China Economic Review*, **10**, 41–58.

Huang, Shao'an and Jian Wei (2001), 'A research report on state-owned SMEs in Zhucheng', mimeo.

Ministry of Labour and Social Security (2001), 'Essentials of the Tenth Five-Year-Plan for Development of Labor and Social Security Projects', 24 April.

Ministry of Labour and Social Security, State Committee for Economic and Trade, Ministry of Finance, Ministry of Education, National Bureau of Statistics, and All China General Trade Union (1998), 'Notice relating to enhancing administration of SOE lay-off employee and establishing reemployment service centres', No. 8, Ministry of Labor and Social Security Document.

Organization for Economic Cooperation and Development (OECD) (1993), *Valuation and Privatisation*, Centre for Cooperation with the European Economies in Transition, OECD.

Roland, Gerard (2002), 'The political economy of transition', *Journal of Economic Perspectives*, **16**(1), 29–50.

State Council (1991), 'State council decision on reforming enterprise employee pension system', No. 33, 26 June.

State Council (1993a), 'Regulations on job-waiting security for employees of state-owned enterprises', 12 April.

State Council (1993b), 'Regulations on redeployment of redundant employees in state-owned enterprises', 20 April.

State Council (1995), 'State Council notice on deepening reform of enterprise employee pension system', No. 6, 1 March.

State Council (1998), 'State Council decision on establishing urban employee basic medical insurance system', No. 44, 14 December.

State Council (1999a), 'Bylaw on unemployment insurance', 22 January.

State Council (1999b), 'Bylaw on urban resident minimal living safeguard', 28 September.

State Council Office (1999), 'State Council Office notice relating to further improving the distribution of lay-off basic living allowance and pension', No. 10, 3 March.

Tenev, Stoyan and Chunlin Zhang with Loup Brefort (2002), *Corporate Governance and Enterprise Reform in China*, Washington, DC: World Bank and International Finance Corporation.

Weitzman, Martin and Chenggang Xu (1994), 'Chinese township village enterprises as vaguely defined cooperatives', *Journal of Comparative Economics*, **18**, 121–45.

Wolf, Holger C. (1999), 'Transition strategies: Choices and outcomes', *Princeton Studies in International Finance*, **85**, June.

Yao, Yang (2004), 'Privatizing the small SOEs', Chapter 7 in Ross Garnaut and Ligang Song (eds), *China's Third Economic Transformation: The Rise of the Private Economy*, London and New York: RoutledgeCurzon.

Zhang, Gang (1998), 'A study on township and village enterprises', PhD Thesis, Stockholm School of Economics: Stockholm.

Zhao, Xiao (1999), 'Competition, public choice and institutional change', CCER Working Paper No. C1999025, Beijing University.

3. Antitrust in China 2006: The Problem of Incentive Compatibility

Bruce M. Owen, Su Sun and Wentong Zheng[1]

1. INTRODUCTION

The Supreme Court of the United States once characterized antitrust law as the 'Magna Carta' of free enterprise. In the US, where antitrust law is most developed, the law has supported capitalist free enterprise in several ways. First, it has sought to protect customers, both individuals and businesses, against the creation and exercise of undue market power. Second, more controversially, it has often served to protect small, inefficient firms from competition. Third, antitrust law is an aspect of competition policy, which refers to broader public policies that seek to promote private competitive markets as alternatives to state-owned, monopoly, or regulated monopoly supply sectors. Antitrust law in the United States is also associated with a particular (common law) legal system, one in which predictability of outcome is given high value, much law is created by judges, private parties have standing to enforce law, and the major effects of public law enforcement are intended to be deterrent rather than direct. However, antitrust is also practiced in 'civil law' jurisdictions, typically by administrative agencies of the executive power, guided by whatever political aims the current government may have.

In the past more than two decades, China has moved pragmatically from an economic system designed in conformity with Marxist–Leninist–Maoist theory to one in which decentralized competitive markets are permitted to determine many important aspects of economic allocation decisions. These economic reforms have not, generally, been accompanied by equally dramatic reforms in legal and political systems. One would expect that a pragmatic policy of increased reliance on capitalist free markets would be accompanied by measures designed to ensure that those markets operate to their maximum potential. This requires, among other things, means of mitigating 'market failures.' By market failures, we mean conditions in which decentralized market decision making does not align individual incentives properly with overall economic welfare. In the West, institutions that mitigate market failure include property rights, contract law, and liability systems, as well as antitrust and regulatory laws. Having decided to rely on markets for certain important purposes, presumably China would be wise to adopt either similar legal remedies for market failures or other institutions whose purposes and effects are the same.

Market reforms such as those that have occurred in China are now commonplace around the globe. Developing countries in what used to be called the 'Third World' have been pushed to introduce reforms by a variety of forces, chief among them the demise of the Soviet Union and the discrediting of communism as an alternative basis for economic organization. Antitrust is often seen as one of the safeguards required to ensure that free markets act as a servant of society, rather than its master. Many, even in long-established market economies, view the market as a dangerous mechanism, which must be harnessed and directed to serve social ends. The famous symbol of this perspective is the Depression-era sculpture next to the Federal Trade Commission Building on Pennsylvania Avenue in Washington DC, depicting a heroic male figure reining in a muscular plow horse.

Scholars who follow regulatory reform have noticed, however, that the model of government regulation as a control on the excesses and failures of private markets can be incomplete and misleading. Often, whatever the intent of the regulators may have been, government intervention ends up protecting incumbent sellers rather than consumers, or, more generally, favors politically influential groups. The political forces at work are essentially the same as those that produce tariffs and quotas on imported goods that threaten domestic producers while benefiting consumers. Further, the tools used by regulators often have unforeseen and unpleasant consequences, and regulations that turn out to have bad effects may be very difficult to change. In consequence, competition policy in developed countries has frequently been aimed as much at government itself as at private monopolies and cartels. This is seen most vividly in the work of the European Commission as it replaces the regulatory interventions of member states in order to promote intra-European markets and competition. The EC has struck down many laws and regulations in member countries that impede imports from other member countries, and it has promoted the privatization of state-owned enterprises, such as telecommunications and airlines, so as to produce a set of pan-European competitors in place of national monopolists. It has now embarked on a similar reform in service industries. Similarly, in the United States, much of the regulatory reform movement that led to the deregulation of trucking, airlines, railroads, banking, professional services and telecommunications in the last 30 years has been motivated and promoted by the antitrust agencies of the US government.

All this has been noted in the market economies. In the developing world, government intervention historically has taken the form of outright ownership of major industries, protectionism, and regulations designed to suppress competition. The first step in reform has been privatization – the sale of government-owned enterprises to private entities. Most often this has happened with little concern for the competitive structure of the post-privatization industry. Examples can be found throughout Latin America, for example, of privatized energy, telecommunications, transport and water companies continuing under private ownership as underperforming monopolies, devoting as much effort to blockading potential competitors as to serving customers efficiently.

China, India and the former Soviet republics relied on state-owned enterprises to an even greater degree than Latin American and other developing countries. Within the socialist economies there is a spectrum of national 'memories' of market systems and accompanying legal institutions. For example, the market economies of Eastern Europe have been more easily restored than those of Russia. China is at the opposite extreme from Eastern Europe on this spectrum, partly because China did not have an extensive commercial economy (and associated legal structures) even before the Maoist period. Enterprise in China today remains, if not state-owned, under the active influence of the state. The principal source of competitive private entrepreneurial activity is from coastal provinces in the southeast where special economic zones were first set up more than two decades ago and local economic controls have been more relaxed, and from foreign direct investors that the central government has permitted to enter domestic markets. A significant part of Chinese domestic production of goods and services still takes place in state-owned enterprises, or SOEs, central or local. The SOEs still dominate China's key industries. Therefore, efforts to promote the use of competitive market solutions to the production and allocation of goods and services must be aimed chiefly at the operation of current and former SOEs.

We turn next to a brief description of the current structure of the Chinese economy.[2]

2. CHINA'S ECONOMIC AND REGULATORY CONTEXTS

Competition policy is not shaped by economic theory alone. The goal, scope, and nature of a country's competition policy is closely tied to the underlying industrial organization and regulatory structure of the country, and is to a large extent determined by the perception of the role of competition by the country's political and economic culture. This is particularly so in the case of China, a country that is undergoing a historic transformation from a centrally planned economy to a market economy. Therefore, to fully understand China's proposed antitrust law, an introduction to China's underlying economic and regulatory structures and the role of competition in China's economy is in order.

2.1. Pre-Reform Economic Structure

Before 1978, China had a centrally planned economy. In rural areas, farms were organized first as cooperatives, then starting in 1958, as communes. The government's planning agency directed communes to plant particular crops, supplied necessary inputs and collected predetermined quantities of outputs at given prices. Under the commune system, the central planning agency could not arrange everything accurately and efficiently, and farmers had little incentive to work hard.

The inefficiency of central planning was repeated in the industrial sector. The government set up plans for production and distribution at virtually all enterprises. The government also set prices for almost all goods and services. Workers were assigned to enterprises by the government and were guaranteed lifetime employment. In order to 'modernize' quickly, priority was given to heavy industries and these industries were heavily subsidized.

Before 1978, China's economy was dominated by the state, and private enterprises played only a negligible role. According to China's State Statistics Bureau, in 1978, private enterprises accounted for only 0.2 percent of China's industrial output, while state-owned enterprises and collectively owned enterprises controlled the rest of the economy.[3] With factories being relegated to units of the state productive machinery, there was essentially no role for competition. At times the government promoted 'labor competition' among factories or productive units in an effort to indoctrinate the populace with communist ideology, but competition motivated by profits was condemned as a symptom of corrupt capitalist systems.

2.2. Post-Reform Economic Structure

In 1978, under Deng Xiaoping's leadership, China began its economic reforms. Reform started in rural areas where population was more dispersed, the commune system had obviously failed, and some reform experiments had already self-started at the village level. Under the newly established household responsibility system, farmers were given much freedom on what to do with their land and got to keep much of what they earned. Then Township and Village Enterprises (TVEs) were formed and collectively owned by the local government. Where they had enough resources and incentives, TVEs grew very quickly to become a significant part of the rural economy and even started to compete with the SOEs.

In contrast, the reform of the SOEs has been more difficult. SOEs reflected the central planning perspective of the past and there were various government agencies whose very existence relied on control over the SOEs. The functioning of SOEs is complex, both because of the lack of management training and because of the need to serve social objectives (e.g., employment stability and benefits, such as provisions for retirement). Major steps were taken to reform SOEs. One example is the contract responsibility system, introduced in 1987, whereby SOEs were given much autonomy and could retain profits after paying taxes to the local government. More recently in 1997 SOEs were restructured into share-issuing companies. The price system was also decontrolled with a transition during which a two-tier price system allowed the coexistence of market prices with government-controlled (subsidized) prices for important goods.

In 1992, China significantly accelerated its pace of economic reform after the inspection tour of the southern regions by its paramount leader, Deng Xiaoping. In the fall of 1992, the 14th Congress of the Chinese Communist Party officially declared that the central goal of China's economic reform is to establish a 'socialist market economy.' In the following decade, far-reaching reform measures were undertaken to overhaul China's SOE sector, taxation, banking, and foreign currency systems. Private enterprises grew rapidly, and large amounts of foreign investment flowed in.

Now, nearly 30 years after the start of economic reform in 1978, China's economic structures have undergone dramatic changes. One of the most significant changes is the decline of the importance of the SOEs and other state-controlled enterprises and the emergence of the country's private sector. According to a national census on the composition of China's economic entities completed in 2003, among three million enterprises that existed on 31 December 2001, SOEs and enterprises with a controlling share held by the State accounted for 56.2 percent of capital invested and 49.6 percent of annual revenue.[4] Anecdotal evidence indicates that since 2001, further economic reform has lowered the share of SOEs in China's economy to about one third.[5] In contrast, when the reform first started in 1978, all enterprises were state-owned.

Despite the increasingly important role of the private sector in China's economy, private enterprises in China are mostly small in size. In fact, 99 percent of the enterprises in China are small or medium size, with most of them funded by private investment.[6] The largest enterprises in China are still SOEs in such industries as electricity, railroads, aviation, telecommunication, and banking, where the state maintains de facto monopolies or dominant firms. According to government statistics, by the end of 2003, China's small- and medium-sized enterprises consisted of 55.6 percent of the country's GDP, 74.7 percent of industrial production value added, 58.9 percent of retail sales, 46.2 percent of tax revenues and 62.3 percent of exports.[7]

2.3. China's Regulatory Structure

Understanding China's current regulatory structure is important for understanding China's competition policy, since direct government regulation and competition policy are often deemed alternative ways for government to control the economy, and China's competition policy is being formulated against the backdrop of its current regulatory structure.

At the same time that China's economic structure is undergoing significant changes, the regulatory structure of China is also being transformed to one more compatible with the requirements of a market economy. Since 1978, the Chinese leadership has gradually recognized the harms of undue state interference with the economy, and has undertaken measures to minimize the abuse of the state power while trying to maintain government control in key industries.

China's need for government regulation, as the term is understood in Western countries, was created by the devolution of economic power and the emergence of private enterprises described above. In the prereform era, China's regulation of the economy was modelled after the former Soviet Union and took the form of direct control of the economic activities of the SOEs. For almost every major industry, a corresponding ministry was created within the government to control, manage, and coordinate the production in that industry. There was no need for separate regulatory agencies; the industries were already regulated in the sense that they were directly owned and managed by the state. It was not until after 1978 that China faced the issue of devising a regulatory system in the modern sense.

Realizing the problems associated with the government's interference with the economy, the Chinese government has made a strategic choice to retreat from the 'non-essential' industries such as machinery, electronics, chemicals, and textiles. Those industries do not tend to create conditions of 'natural monopoly,' do not impinge upon national security and public goods, and usually are not regulated in market economies. In several rounds of government restructuring since 1978, China has gradually dissolved the government ministries overseeing those industries and has replaced them with 'industrial associations' representing various interests in those industries.[8]

In industries considered key to China's national security and economic development, such as electricity, petroleum, banking, insurance, railroads, and aviation, the Chinese government has chosen to retain or strengthen its control. In those key industries, the dominant firms remain mostly state-owned. As a result, the government plays a double role: it is both the owner of the major players and the referee, i.e., the regulator. This dual role is now seen as detrimental to the development of China's market economy. Among the steps that have been taken to address this problem, the foremost was to establish separate regulatory agencies for the key industries and to strip the SOEs in those industries of the regulatory power bestowed upon them in the planned-economy era. In so doing, the Chinese government hopes to separate the government's functions as a player and as a regulator. For example, between 1998 and 2004, China established the Insurance Regulatory Commission, the Banking Regulatory Commission, and the Electric Power Regulatory Commission, which are charged with overseeing the insurance, banking, and electricity industries, respectively. The largest enterprises in those three industries, all state-owned, along with enterprises of other ownership forms that may emerge in the future, are subject to regulation by those new agencies. Additionally, to strengthen government control over SOEs in key industries and to stop the rapid loss of state assets, China in 2003 established the State Assets Regulatory Commission to oversee the operation of state-owned assets by SOEs.

Despite the positive developments in China's regulatory reforms, China's regulatory systems are still beset by abuses of government's regulatory power. The most prominent of those regulatory abuses is the so-called 'administrative monopolies,' i.e., government-created monopolies.

Administrative monopolies are found mostly in three areas. First, in the industries where government ministries have been converted to industrial associations, the industrial associations often permit or encourage anticompetitive practices by their members. Although the government's original intent in organizing those industrial associations was deregulation, in reality many of the industrial associations thus organized are little more than government ministries in disguise. The major participants in those industrial associations are still SOEs subject to the control of the government, and the heads of these associations are often former government officials. Since 1990, amid increasing market competition, many industrial associations adopted industry-wide 'self-disciplinary' prices, functioning as price cartels.[9] To make things worse, this practice was officially sanctioned by the government in 1998.[10] Second, in the sectors where the government has retained its regulatory presence, many of the government ministries or regulatory agencies have 'affiliate companies' and give preferential treatment to them. This problem is particularly serious at the local level. A good example of this phenomenon is that some local civil affair agencies in charge of issuing marriage licenses require applicants to take pictures only at designated photo shops, which are 'affiliates' of the agencies. Third, the governments at provincial and local levels are well known for creating and maintaining barriers to competition from other localities. For example, many local governments force dealers in beer, fertilizer, and medicines to sell only goods that are produced within their own jurisdictions.

Dealing with the problem of administrative monopolies is one of the major goals of China's proposed antitrust law. Given China's current regulatory structure, administrative monopolies are seen as posing a far more significant problem to China's burgeoning market economy than monopolies created by private enterprises.[11] China's proposed antitrust law tries to tackle this problem by subjecting government ministries and regulatory agencies at all levels to the new antitrust regime. Ambitious as that goal is, it remains an open question whether that is politically feasible. As will be discussed in more detail below, the proposed antitrust enforcement agency will be able to bring antitrust enforcement actions against government agencies of the same or even higher rank. Such an institutional arrangement will inevitably set off power struggles among bureaucrats from different government agencies and among vested interests. Indeed, it is believed that it is this very issue – the relationship between the antitrust enforcement agency and other government agencies – that holds up the drafting process of the proposed antitrust law.[12]

2.4.   China's Ambivalance Towards Competition

The scope of China's proposed antitrust law[13] and how strictly the antitrust law will be enforced in practice will depend largely upon the prevailing attitudes in China towards the role of competition in its economic development. Although the doctrine of neoclassical economics that emphasizes free competition has long begun to take hold in China, the attitudes of China's policymakers toward competition are ambivalent at best. On the one hand, Chinese policymakers have recognized the problems created by administrative monopolies, and are also awaking to the challenges posed by the acquisitions of domestic businesses by multinational corporations. On the other hand, for the vast majority of China's small- and medium-sized firms, many Chinese policymakers doubt whether the proposed antitrust law needs to be strictly enforced or even whether an antitrust law is needed at all.

Administrative monopolies have been subject to extensive criticisms by China's policymakers and intellectuals. There is a national consensus that more competition needs to be introduced into the industries that are dominated by the state, and some concrete measures have already been taken to achieve that goal. The restructuring of China's telecommunication industry provides an example of China's commitment to promoting competition in state-dominated industries.[14] Meanwhile, Chinese policymakers are increasingly worried about the acquisition of Chinese businesses by multinational corporations. How to curb the influence of foreign companies and promote the competitiveness of Chinese enterprises has been at the top of China's antitrust policymakers' agenda.[15]

However, there are fierce debates about whether China really needs an antitrust law for its millions of small- and medium-sized enterprises, both state-owned and private. The opinion that appears to have gained the upper hand is that for China's small- and medium-sized enterprises, the problem is not the lack of competition, but too much competition. Chinese policymakers are very concerned about what they call the 'repetitive investments at low levels' made by small businesses, and have blamed China's small- and medium-sized companies for engaging in 'suicidal' competition. At times the government even took measures to prohibit some forms of competition that it considered harmful to the national economy. For instance, in 1999, the Bureau of Civil Aviation issued an order prohibiting airlines from offering air ticket discounts, citing the adverse effect of price competition on the healthy development of the airline industry.[16]

Therefore, there are tensions between China's determination to fight administrative and foreign monopolies and its unwillingness to take on its small- and medium-sized enterprises. Most likely, those tensions will be reflected in the enforcement of the antitrust law. Besides these tensions, the government may also be concerned about the loss of a policy tool. Lacking effective macroeconomic policy tools to finetune the economy, China's economic policymakers tend to micromanage the economy by directly controlling the scale of investment at the local level (for example, by ordering local governments and banks not to approve new investment proposals and loan requests). This is likely to undermine the proposed antitrust law.

Another concern may be the impact of competition on the survival of SOEs that employ many workers. As noted above, pensions and other social security programs have been funded and administered in the past by the SOEs, and there is as yet no mechanism to supply such benefits to former employees of defunct SOEs. Large and failing SOEs often receive 'policy loans' from state-owned banks at low interest rates that are often not expected to be repaid, while small private enterprises face much difficulty in financing, paying much higher interest rates (sometimes plus the cost of side payments to bank officials). If such subsidies become targets of antitrust, then there is a policy problem that cannot be resolved by the competition authority acting alone.

3.   CHINA'S LEGAL CONTEXT

The passage and enforcement of laws in China have been largely carried out by the Communist Party through its political leadership and organizational structure. Since the economic reforms started in 1978, some reforms of the legal system have taken place. Within the Party's organizational structure and in the legislature, the National People's Congress, indirect elections have been used to a large extent. The National People's Congress has also gradually increased its independence. In rural areas, direct elections have been conducted at the village level for more than a decade.

The focus of China's legislature in most of the past 20 years has been on economic laws, most notably contract law, bankruptcy law, corporate law, foreign investment law, securities law, and the like. These laws have provided a framework under which market activities are facilitated, transaction costs are reduced and disputes may be resolved. However, economic behavior and expectations cannot be and have not been changed by passing laws alone. Both the enforcement agencies and adjudicating body are under direct control of the political leadership at all levels of the government, and there are serious deficiencies and often corruption in enforcement. People are still used to conducting economic activities through social networks. Moreover, judges and lawyers are not well trained. This situation, however, is improving, as the government is pushing for legal reform and the role of lawyer has gradually become more important and professional in recent years.

From an economic perspective, law is a potentially powerful tool for aligning the economic incentives of individuals with the conditions required for greater economic efficiency.[17] This tool works by its influence on the expectations of economic agents concerning the future consequences of their economic decisions. Individual agents form expectations about future events based on information available at the time a decision is made. One dimension of such expectations is the legal significance of decisions that the agent may make, or that others may make in reaction to that decision. The decision to enter into a contract for the purchase of goods to be delivered in the future, for example, obviously depends in part on the role that the legal system will play in the event of various contingencies, both those contemplated in the contract and those not contemplated. Other things equal, if the legal system's reaction to any contingency is difficult to predict, the risk associated with any given contract will increase, and a higher expected return will be required to make the transaction worth bearing that risk. Thus, if the legal system provides a predictable set of contract enforcement remedies, more transactions will be entered into than otherwise, increasing output, social welfare and economic growth. In the antitrust area, to use a more relevant example, entry by firms seeking to compete with an SOE will be more likely than otherwise if the entrants expect the competition agency to protect them effectively from potential predatory responses from the SOE.

In addition to reducing the risks associated with economic activity, the legal system can mitigate market failures, often more effectively than direct regulation of economic activity. Competition law is a leading example. Monopolies, cartels, and practices associated with them are a source of market failure; their reduction improves economic efficiency. Antitrust law can reduce this cost to society by imposing higher expected costs on behavior whose effect is to reduce economic efficiency. For example, the prospect of having to disgorge, with significant probability, some multiple of the unlawful gains from price fixing will deter some price fixing. The prospect that a proposed merger transaction will be challenged by the government upon review will prevent some inefficient transactions from being proposed.[18] Both of these desirable effects occur only if the behavior of the enforcement agency in reaction to a given business decision is reasonably predictable. Predictability by its nature constrains the discretion of the government and the courts, reducing their discretionary power acting alone.

4. CHINA'S ANTITRUST LAWS

4.1. Current Competition Policy

China already has a Law for Anti-Unfair Competition, promulgated in 1993.[19] For example, its article 12 prohibits tie-in sales against the wish of a buyer. Article 15 prohibits price fixing or bid rigging. But the Law also addresses many other issues, including bribery, deceptive advertising, coercive sales, appropriation of business secrets, etc. It is very common for new antitrust laws in developing countries to focus on such consumer protection issues. In the parlance of economics, relationships between buyers and sellers are sometimes beset by opportunistic behavior that may be difficult for the competitive market to correct, whether because of asymmetric information or because particular buyer/seller pairs do not expect to meet again. Similarly, certain contracts or contractual terms, even those that promote economic efficiency, may strike people as unfair. Examples include so-called 'victimless crimes,' unilateral refusals to deal and certain tying arrangements. Condemnations and restrictions of such market behavior may have great popular appeal. In societies that are skeptical of the legitimacy of markets, such practices often illustrate the popular or ideological basis for the skepticism. Monopolies and price fixing are but items on the list of potential market abuses, and it is not surprising to see consumer protection regulations incorporated into and even dominating so-called competition laws.[20] Also, advanced developed countries often have similar consumer protection regulations, but are more likely to have delegated their enforcement to specialized agencies.

China's 1993 law is too simplistic compared to the antitrust laws and competition policy guidelines in countries with more antitrust experience. It is hardly enough to deal with a broad range of competition issues. For example, it does not address antitrust issues related to mergers and acquisitions, which are an important part of antitrust policy in the developed countries.

Some antitrust elements are also seen in more specialized laws. For example, in the Commercial Banking Law passed in 1995, Article 9 stipulates that banks should not engage in improper competition. However, it is not clear what 'improper' means. The Price Law also has some provisions prohibiting price manipulations.

Because of the need to address some emerging competition issues in the absence of a full antitrust law, some administrative rules have been promulgated. Two recent such rules stand out.

The first is Provisions on Acquisitions of Domestic Enterprises by Foreign Investors (effective September, 2006).[21] These provisions apply only to foreign companies. Article 51 lays out the four conditions under which pre-merger notification is required: (1) one merging party's annual sales is above 1.5 billion RMB (approximately $180 million); (2) the foreign party has acquired more than ten other domestic companies in related industries in the past year; (3) one merging party's market share in China is above 20 percent; (4) post-merger market share is above 25 percent. Article 52 describes how a hearing is conducted when the authority thinks the merger will impede competition. Article 53 lays out five conditions relating to merging parties' assets, sales, and market shares inside China under which mergers outside China should be reported to China's Ministry of Commerce and the State Administration of Industry and Commerce. Article 53 is especially interesting because it allows China to intervene in mergers outside China.[22] The US and the EU commonly require review of mergers among foreign firms that trade within their respective jurisdictions.

The number of enterprises the foreign party has previously acquired in 'related industries' and the merging parties' 'market shares' specified in Articles 51 and 53 are too vague to be used as thresholds for merger notification. They depend on how the relevant market is defined in the antitrust sense. Because of their lack of objectiveness, these terms are not used as premerger notification thresholds in most jurisdictions that have established antitrust practice. Indeed, although market share appeared in some previous versions of China's draft Antimonopoly Law as a merger notification threshold, only the previous year's sales level is used as the threshold in the current version that was submitted to the NPC Standing Committee for review several months before the issuance of the Provisions on Acquisitions of Domestic Enterprises by Foreign Investors. It is puzzling why the learning in the antitrust legislative process was not reflected in the Provisions.

The other prior rule is Provisional Rules for Prevention of Monopoly Pricing (effective 11 November 2003), issued by the State Development and Reform Commission. The Rules prohibit the abuse of 'market dominance' and infers it through 'market share in the relevant market, substitutability of relevant goods, and ease of new entry.' However, it does not specify how relevant market is defined or how the inference of market dominance can be actually made. The Rules also prohibit price coordination, supply restriction and bid rigging. The Rules prohibit government agencies from illegally intervening in price determinations. However, what would be legal price intervention is not clear. The Rules are also unclear on prohibitions of below-cost pricing and price discrimination and could lead to excessive government intervention when there is not a competition issue.

The vagueness of China's preexisting law is hardly unusual. Most competition laws are written in general terms. Notably, the US Sherman Act contains the following fundamental provisions, which are incapable of being interpreted literally:

§ 1 Sherman Act, 15 U.S.C. § 1

Every contract, combination in the form of trust or otherwise, or conspiracy, in restraint of trade or commerce among the several States, or with foreign nations, is declared to be illegal. Every person who shall make any contract or engage in any combination or conspiracy hereby declared to be illegal shall be deemed guilty of a felony, and, on conviction thereof, shall be punished by fine not exceeding $10,000,000 if a corporation, or, if any other person, $350,000, or by imprisonment not exceeding three years, or by both said punishments, in the discretion of the court.

§ 2 Sherman Act, 15 U.S.C. § 2
Every person who shall monopolize, or attempt to monopolize, or combine or
conspire with any other person or persons, to monopolize any part of the trade
or commerce among the several States, or with foreign nations, shall be
deemed guilty of a felony, and, on conviction thereof, shall be punished by
fine not exceeding $10,000,000 if a corporation, or, if any other person,
$350,000, or by imprisonment not exceeding three years, or by both said
punishments, in the discretion of the court.

These clauses are no less vague than many provisions of China's draft
competition law. The details and the definitions are left to be developed by
courts and enforcement agencies. In the West, this permitted a revolution in
the accepted interpretation of competition law during the second half of the
last century, despite the absence of change in the statutes. This was
accomplished through the informal diffusion of economic learning through
the legal profession and the judiciary; arguably it could not have been
accomplished through formal legislation. The common law model is hardly
the only one that can be applied to the task of creating a system that is both
predictable and flexible, however. For example, an administrative agency
can develop policies and procedures which, if made public and followed
consistently, can provide guidance equivalent to case law, and in the case of
antitrust arguably more responsive to new learning and better-informed by
the progress of science. The role of the Department of Justice/Federal Trade
Commission Merger Guidelines serves such purposes in the US, even
though it has no binding force even on the behavior of prosecutors, much
less on courts.

4.2.   China's Proposed Antitrust Law

In this subsection, we offer some specific comments on China's draft
antitrust law.[23] At the outset it is necessary to observe that the proposed law
does not reflect adequately the current state of economic understanding of
the benefits that can arise from effective competition policy. On the other
hand, the proposed law clearly contemplates reliance on administrative
rather than judicial machinery as its primary enforcement mechanism, and
calls for the enforcement agency to issue detailed rules and regulations to
implement the law. In the end, given China's legal environment described
above, it is these rules and their enforcement that will matter most. It would
be inappropriate to evaluate the proposed law as if it were, as it would be in
the US, a set of instructions intended for the judiciary to interpret.

The ongoing policy debate on antitrust within the Chinese government is
not transparent, though sometimes there are media reports giving updates on
the status of the draft. Some earlier drafts were circulated within small

circles for comments at various stages. An unofficial draft of the proposed law was widely circulated outside China in 2003 and was the subject of a public commentary by the American Bar Association (ABA). A slightly revised draft was submitted for deliberation to the State Council in March 2004.[24] A subsequent 8 April 2005 revised draft received further comments by the ABA. Several more rounds of revisions were undertaken before a recent draft was submitted to the NPC's Standing Committee for its first review in June 2006.[25] These revisions appear to have incorporated some comments made by various parties including the ABA and the earlier published version of our chapter.[26] Our comments below are thus updated from our 2005 paper to reflect changes in the June 2006 draft ('the current draft').

4.2.1.   Efficiency objective

The objective of competition law, from an economic point of view, should be to improve continuously the economic welfare of society by increasing the output of goods and services that can be produced with available resources – in a word, to improve economic efficiency. The use of competitive market processes has proven an effective way to achieve this objective, both in China and elsewhere. Antitrust law seeks to promote the use of competitive markets (in place of, for example, SOEs or private monopolies) as a means to the end of improved efficiency. To be sure, virtually every country that has competition policy also has non-efficiency objectives, often objectives that would, if pursued, reduce social welfare. A society may very well decide to make such sacrifices as part of the political compromises necessary to maintain stability and consensus among its component interests.[27] But a decision to sacrifice economic welfare for some political objective probably should be made explicitly and narrowly at the legislative level, rather than delegated to enforcement agencies or courts. Otherwise, those in charge of enforcing the law will be faced, without adequate statutory guidance, with contradictory instructions, the practical effect of which may be to delegate too much discretion and legislative power to the bureaucracy.

4.2.2.   Definition of monopoly

Some previous drafts defined monopoly as activities that damage 'the legitimate interests of other business operators.' This definition was not only vague, but could also be (and often is, elsewhere) interpreted as an instruction to do the very opposite of seeking competition. The object of competitive behavior, from the point of view of firms that engage in it, is to take business away from competitors, and thus to harm them. Inefficient firms are thus driven from the market, or reduced to a more efficient size.

Competition policy cannot seek to preserve inefficient competitors, because to do so harms consumers. Thus, the law should not be interpreted to include the right of any business to be protected from competition.[28] The current draft has deleted the language related to other business operators from the definition of monopolistic behavior.

Also, a monopoly is perhaps better defined as a condition of a market than as a list of activities. (In the US, both monopolization and 'attempted' monopolization are statutory offences, but in practice only monopolies achieved through unlawful actions are held unlawful. Monopoly achieved through superior efficiency is not unlawful.) A monopoly that results from continued success in serving consumers should not be condemned, but rather encouraged.

Finally, the current draft includes price fixing in the definition of monopolization. While a price fixing agreement indeed seeks to establish an effective monopoly, there are substantial policy differences between the treatment of a single-firm monopolist and a cartel. In particular, price fixing agreements are almost always harmful to consumers, whereas single-firm monopolies are often beneficial or at least unavoidable. This definition may lead to unnecessary confusion of the two concepts, which most countries have found it useful to keep separate.

4.2.3.   Agreements among enterprises

The current draft has reflected various parties' comments, including ours, on the broad prohibitions of all agreements in earlier drafts and now outlaws agreements specifically among competitors. However, the current draft is not clear on how the vertical contracts will be analyzed. It is still important to note that contracts that are vertical (between firms and their suppliers or distributors) are seldom anticompetitive, and can be treated separately with less danger of deterring competitive behavior beneficial to consumers. The current draft still provides for exemptions that are permitted by the review process. As in earlier drafts, the provision exempting agreements among competitors to mitigate the effects of slow sales and large inventories during economic downturns is too broad, economically unsound and likely to hurt consumers.

4.2.4.   Presumption of lawfulness

The draft law, as noted above, contemplates a European-style competition regime wherein all competitive activity is automatically unlawful, except where specifically permitted by regulation (as with the EU 'block exemption' system, which is to be phased out) or exempted in a case-by-case review. In general, this is indistinguishable from a centrally-planned and controlled economy. Even if guided by a modern understanding of how markets and competition can serve the interests of consumers, this approach is likely to be unwieldy and to impose daunting delays and barriers in the path of competitive initiatives. A better approach may be to permit anything that is not specifically forbidden, with published guidelines for information and penalties for deterrence.

4.2.5.   Market definition

Some earlier versions of the draft law defined the term 'market' solely in geographic terms. Markets have important product dimensions as well as territorial dimensions, as described in the *United States Department of Justice/Federal Trade Commission 1994 Merger Guidelines*.[29] The current draft now has expanded the scope of the market to include the product dimension.

4.2.6.   Per se versus rule of reason

Use of the word 'monopoly' in the section concerned with 'agreements' may create unnecessary confusion. The distinction is between multi-firm behavior and unilateral behavior. Anticompetitive agreements generally require, as a necessary condition for causing consumer harm, that the parties create or attempt to create an economic monopoly. More substantively, monopolies and many agreements among competitors must be assessed individually, based on their effects on economic welfare, but some agreements among competitors can safely be proscribed 'per se.' These distinctions are especially useful because they permit fine tuning of the mechanism of deterrence. Unless antitrust enforcers are to attempt to examine every transaction in the economy, deterrence is the principal vector by which antitrust (and most other) laws achieve their effects on economic behavior. Deterrence of anticompetitive behavior, however, has a dark side: inadvertent deterrence of efficient behavior. The deterrent effect of a law or regulation is affected by the probability of detection and successful prosecution (itself a function of enforcement resources), the firm's understanding of the law, and the penalties expected to result from successful prosecution. Very effective deterrence of anticompetitive behavior will also deter procompetitive behavior if the law is unclear to private decision-makers or if private decision-makers anticipate frequent errors by prosecutors and judges.[30]

4.2.7.   Publication of decisions

An earlier draft states that 'the enforcement authority should publish its decisions,' a requirement that makes sense only if the published opinions are intended (as they should be) to influence future behavior of business firms, as discussed above in connection with deterrence. Publication of decisions and the reasoning behind them, however, is a necessary but not sufficient condition for effective deterrence. It is also necessary to have a rule that serves the purpose, in a common law system, of 'stare decisis.' That is, the enforcement authority must to some extent be bound by its prior decisions and reasoning. If prosecutors (or courts) can decide each case without regard to the ways in which similar facts have been analyzed and treated in the recent past, private firms have no basis to form expectations about the consequences of their actions. The effect of this is to increase the risks of doing business, thus discouraging investment by ruling out investment projects that do not have a sufficiently high expected return to compensate investors for taking on the risk of (erroneous) antitrust prosecution. The current draft has changed this language to that 'the enforcement authority may publish its decisions.' This subtle change seems to reflect a reluctance of the Chinese government to commit to full disclosure of its future antitrust decisions, which is not helpful for private firms attempting to form expectations about the antitrust authority's actions.

4.2.8.   Concentration thresholds
The current draft includes presumptive thresholds for holding a dominant market position, based on what economists call 'concentration ratios:' a single firm with more than 50 percent of the market, or the top two firms with more than two-thirds of the market, or three firms with more than three-quarters of the market. The specific thresholds are of course arbitrary, as are similar thresholds in other jurisdictions, but they may nevertheless be useful in the context of deterrence. In some earlier drafts, the rules are also ambiguous. If the largest three firms in a market have over three-quarters of the market, and individual shares of 70 percent, 3 percent and 2 percent, are all three regarded as dominant firms? Suppose each has 25 percent: is each a dominant firm? Neither result would make much sense. The current draft has added a provision that each firm's market share has to be at least 10 percent for it to be considered a dominant firm. This to some extent solved the problem in the first scenario, but not the second one. Most jurisdictions have adopted the HHI approach to measuring concentration, and most jurisdictions define dominance (or 'market power') in terms of a specific minimum market share, such as 35 percent, for the leading firm, plus the existence of barriers to entry.

4.2.9.   Monopoly pricing
The draft law forbids monopolistic pricing in the forms of 'unfairly high price in selling or unfairly low price in purchasing.' This is unlikely to be a useful provision for two reasons. First, every enterprise in a competitive market system should be encouraged to strive to achieve a monopoly or

dominant position through superior customer service, lower costs, and innovation. The primary incentive motivating such behavior is the prospect of earning higher profits. This provision, by denying the prospect of rewards from competitive effort, could act to reduce or eliminate the incentive to compete. Second, as a practical matter the calculation of the difference between an actual 'unfair' or monopolistic price and a hypothetical 'fair' or competitive price is daunting, and where it has been attempted in the West (e.g., in regulated industries), it has consumed vast resources and proved ineffective or worse. The current draft similarly proscribes 'predatory' pricing by a dominant firm, defined as pricing below 'cost.' The tendency in the academic literature has been to emphasize the difficulty of designing an appropriate and operational definition of 'cost' for this purpose, and to point out the possible incentive of enterprises to avoid vigorous price competition for fear of erroneous prosecution. US courts in recent years have emphasized the rarity of circumstances in which predatory pricing is likely to be profitable.

4.2.10. Price discrimination

The draft law proscribes price discrimination, by a dominant enterprise, between like customers. Economists generally view price discrimination as a device to extract additional surplus from customers, but not necessarily as harmful to economic efficiency. In some circumstances, as when demand in a market is too small to support even one firm charging a uniform price, price discrimination may be necessary to permit even a single firm to exist. Similar remarks apply to prohibitions in the draft law on tying, exclusive dealing, refusals to deal, and the like. Practices such as these that are either ambiguous in their effects, or legitimate competitive activity easily mistaken for the opposite, should be evaluated in terms of their effects on consumer welfare in particular cases, rather than condemned per se.

4.2.11. Mergers

The draft law provides for agency review of proposed mergers, acquisitions, and joint ventures, a very useful device to avoid anticompetitive concentration without the messy complication of ex post disassembly of a consummated transaction. Unfortunately, the current draft applies to all consolidations rather than just consolidations of competing firms. The effect could be to unnecessarily increase the delays associated with obtaining agency clearance for mergers with little or no potential for anticompetitive effects, including many beneficial mergers.

The current draft attempts to set out a list of the information required to be submitted by enterprises proposing to consolidate. The list is unduly vague and may preempt a more thoughtful and detailed information request from the enforcement agency, tailored to the circumstances of the particular transaction.

The current draft provides a limit on the time the agency can take to make a decision regarding a proposed transaction. This is a valuable provision. In some countries businesses complain that review periods are too long or even open-ended, and that opportunities for corruption are created by the process.

The factors for consideration of a proposed transaction include the effect on 'other business operators' and the effect on 'the development of the national economy and public interest.' These criteria are either subject to abuse by competitors or too vague to be useful in predicting which transactions will be disapproved. It will be very important for the enforcement agency to set out clearer and more specific criteria.

4.2.12.   Administrative monopoly

The current draft contains an entire chapter of prohibitions on anticompetitive activity by government agencies. For the reasons explained above, these may be the most important provisions in the law. However, the sweeping condemnation of monopolistic and anticompetitive behavior by government agencies provides no guidance to those decision makers who must decide whether necessary or otherwise legitimate functions of government, which incidentally have an anticompetitive effect, should nevertheless be permitted. An example is environmental regulations that have the effect of increasing the minimum efficient size of enterprises. It would be helpful to give decision makers some guidance, such as net improvements in consumer welfare, when such conflicts arise.

4.2.13.   Enforcement authority

Previous drafts proposed the establishment of an Enforcement Agency under the State Council. There had been speculations that such an Enforcement Agency would be created within an existing ministry, most likely the Ministry of Commerce. Many were concerned that such an agency would not have enough authority to investigate other government agencies suspected of abusing their administrative power to limit competition, especially if such agencies are ministries at a higher level in the government bureaucracy.

The current draft proposes another authority besides an Enforcement Agency proposed in earlier drafts: an Antimonopoly Commission at the cabinet level that conducts policy research, oversees the work of the Enforcement Agency, and coordinates work on major cases. A cabinet level Antimonopoly Commission will have more clout, which is much needed to combat administrative monopolies arising from other ministries acting as or for interest groups. However, it is not clear why the Enforcement Agency cannot be part of the Antimonopoly Commission, rather than part of an existing ministry. This proposed dual structure is strikingly reminiscent of the very unfortunate experience in Brazil, where three antitrust agencies were created, resulting in widespread complaints of delays and other impediments to commercial transactions for which antitrust review was required. Given the frequently observed turf wars among some Chinese government agencies and the waves of restructuring of government agencies in recent years aimed at reducing such inefficiencies, it would be unwise to create dual enforcement authorities.

The current draft makes the compromise that monopolistic activities subject to the antimonopoly law that are also within the scope of other regulatory agencies' investigative power based on other laws and administrative regulations shall be investigated by those other agencies and these other agencies report the results to the Antimonopoly Commission. The enforcement agency investigates such matters only when they are not investigated by other agencies. As a formal matter, this reflects US legal doctrine, which holds regulatory agencies responsible for including competition policy concerns among the factors to be considered in making regulatory decisions. That doctrine has seldom been useful in overcoming resistance to competition by regulated firms. If regulatory capture is a serious source of administrative monopoly in China, then such delegation is troubling.

4.2.14.   Penalties

The draft law provides for fines for enterprises that engage in agreements to limit competition and other offences. In earlier drafts, these fines were stated in terms of a fixed cash range, with no indexing for inflation and no criteria for determining the size of the fine within the specified range. Optimal deterrence requires fines that, on the margin, balance the gains to society from the deterrence of inefficient behavior against the loss to society from inadvertent deterrence of efficient behavior. While these calculations may often be impractical, the enforcement agency or the court should be instructed to be guided by such considerations. In the current draft, fines are stated in terms of a percentage of sales. The current draft also provides reduced penalty for voluntarily assisting the enforcement authority's investigation in monopolistic agreement cases, which is similar to the amnesty provision adopted by other jurisdictions in recent years, especially with respect to cartels. There are minor differences, though. For example, the lead antitrust offender is often not qualified for amnesty in most other jurisdictions.

Interestingly, the penalties for government agencies and officials who engage in anticompetitive behavior include not merely injunctive relief but demotion or termination for individuals and, where appropriate, criminal prosecution. It is quite unusual for competition laws to contain such provisions; more commonly government agencies and officials are held immune from antitrust prosecution. China obviously takes this problem very seriously.

Effective deterrence requires a penalty in excess of the anticipated gains from anticompetitive activity because the probability of a successful legal action by injured parties (especially customers) is far from certain. In some earlier drafts, private parties who are victims of anticompetitive activities are given a right to petition the People's Court for relief and damages. Damages include actual loss plus the defendant's profit, plus the plaintiff's legal expenses. This provision apparently permits recovery of damages in excess of actual loss, and thus serves the same purpose as the corresponding US treble damage provision. The correct multiple doubtlessly varies according to the circumstances. This provision has been reduced in the current draft to a mere statement that offenders shall take responsibility for civil liability. However, the amount of fines specified in the draft law may be sufficient to serve as a deterrent.

The current draft is unclear regarding structural remedies, such as dissolution of monopolies or divestiture of anticompetitive acquisitions. Such power exists in agencies and courts in the West, but is very rarely used. In China, where the structure of SOEs continues to present competitive problems, such remedies have been addressed in the past through legislation.

4.2.15.   Judicial review

Private parties are given the right to judicial review if they are not satisfied with the Enforcement Agency's decisions. In the context of China's current legal system, discussed above, it remains unclear whether this right increases or decreases the predictability of the process and therefore the potential for promotion of economic efficiency and growth. It is not clear what level of the Court will handle such appeals or whether the Court's decision will be final.

4.2.16.   Intellectual property rights and enforcement of guidelines

The draft law states clearly that an intellectual property right is not to be regarded as a per se unlawful monopoly. Beyond that useful provision, the current draft provides little guidance to officials who must decide whether a particular business practice constitutes an 'abuse' of an intellectual property right. As with mergers, this area must be the subject of detailed guidelines from the enforcement agency. And, indeed, the current draft does allow the enforcement agency to issue such guidelines, rules, and regulations covering not just intellectual property but its entire subject matter jurisdiction. It would be even more useful if the law required the enforcement agency and the People's Court to be bound by such regulations.

5. CONCLUSION

The salient feature of China's antitrust law is that it is designed to reduce the anticompetitive conduct of government agencies. Given China's present economic structure and its ambition to rely on competitive markets for future economic growth, this is a valuable feature of the proposed law. On the other hand, the draft law has two potentially serious flaws: a lack of focus on economic efficiency as the primary goal of competition, and therefore of competition law, and an apparent lack of awareness of the powerful economic effects of law-influenced expectations on private incentives. These flaws have the potential to leave on the table, unexploited, much of the long-term gain from adoption of a competition law. Both flaws can be remedied, however, by thoughtful and consistent enforcement of the law by an enforcement agency well-informed on matters of microeconomics and imbued with sufficient political clout to merit the attention of economic decision makers, both in the SOEs and in the domestic and foreign private sectors.

NOTES

1. We are grateful for comments from participants in the conference on China's Policy Reforms: Progress and Challenges, held at the Stanford Center for International Development (SCID) in October 2004, and for financial assistance from SCID. For an earlier version of this paper, see Owen, Sun and Zheng (2005).
2. For detailed analyses of China's economy in the recent decades, see Chow (2002).
3. See *Statistical Yearbook of China* (2004).
4. See State Bureau of Statistics (2003).
5. See Liu (2006).
6. See supra note 3.
7. See *People's Daily* (2004).
8. See Wang et al. (2003).
9. For example, faced with growing inventory and price drops, China's nine TV producers held a meeting in southern China in June 2000 to limit TV production and fix prices. The act was not successful and was widely criticized in the media.

10. See State Economic and Trade Commission (1998). Ironically, before its abolition in the most recent wave of government restructuring, SETC was one of a few government agencies in charge of drafting China's first antitrust law.

11. Anticompetitive behavior by state-owned enterprises is by no means a problem limited to China. SOE's can engage in certain anticompetitive acts, such as predatory pricing, without the discipline of having to recoup short-term losses with higher prices later. Thus, such behavior is more likely than in the private sector and can continue indefinitely. See Sappington and Sidak (2003).

12. It is increasingly likely that the antitrust enforcement agency will be housed in the Ministry of Commerce (MOFCOM). MOFCOM is the result of government restructuring that combined several cabinet level agencies in 2002, and is generally considered a powerful ministry, with jurisdiction over China's domestic and international trade. This may give the antitrust enforcement agency considerable power and legitimacy. In September, 2004, MOFCOM announced that it had established an Anti-Monopoly Investigation Office under its Division of Legal Affairs, at a time when the Anti-Monopoly Law was still being drafted.

13. The proposed Chinese antitrust law has gone through a series of drafts over the past several years. None of these drafts exists in a citable or official version. We comment here on what purports to be a June 2006 draft. It is clear that these drafts are released informally by officials seeking to stimulate comment and discussion.

14. Before 1994, China's telecommunication industry was monopolized by China Telecom, China's only telecommunication provider. In 1994, the Chinese government formed China Unicom, another telecommunication provider that competed with China Telecom in mobile phone and pager services. In 1999, China Telecom was broken up into two separate entities: China Mobile that provided mobile phone services and a new China Telecom that provided landline services. In the same year, the Chinese governments issued landline licenses to several other newly formed companies to compete with China Telecom. In the next round of restructuring in 2002, China Telecom was further divided and integrated with other telecommunication companies to form two 'competing' landline providers: China Netcom based in Northern China and China Telecom based in Southern China.

15. *The Wall Street Journal* reported, on the eve of China's then-expected enactment of the antitrust law, that many multinational corporations feared that they would become the law's first targets. See Buchman (2004).

16. However, the ban on discount air tickets was frequently ignored by the airlines, and the ban was finally lifted in early 2003.

17. Owen (2004) spells out this point in greater detail.

18. In its congressional submission for fiscal year 2001, the US Department of Justice Antitrust Division writes that the deterrence effect 'is perhaps the single most important outcome of the Division's work.' For detailed analysis, see Nelson and Sun (2002).

19. See Anti-Unfair Competition Law (1993).

20. See, e.g., Costa Rica, Law on Promotion of Competition and Effective Defense of Consumers (Law No. 7472) (1995); Jamaica, Fair Competition Act (1993), both in Organization of American States (2002).

21. A Provisional Rule that had essentially the same content on antitrust review was issued in 2003.

22. Mergers outside China that may impact China's market significantly are not unusual given that China has become a major market for many foreign companies. For example, in 1996, Germany's Mannesmann and Italy's Italimpianti, makers of specialized pipes for oil drilling, merged into a monopoly. The technology was suitable for developing countries only and China was the main buyer. Because the main market was outside Europe, merger notification was not required by the European Commission. See Fox (2003).

23. We are in agreement with much of the commentaries on the draft law undertaken by the American Bar Association (ABA), and we do not belabor points that we believe the ABA has covered adequately. See ABA (2003, 2005).

24. See China.com (2004) about comments from Shang Ming, Director of the newly established Antitrust Investigative Office in the Ministry of Commerce.
25. The NPC Standing Committee members have made a number of comments on this draft during their first review. See National People's Congress Standing Committee (2006).
26. See Owen et al., supra note 1.
27. But, for a defense of the proposition that economic efficiency should not be sacrificed to political or other non–deontological goals, see Kaplow and Shavell (2002).
28. See ABA (2003) discussion of definitions at 10–14.
29. See US Department of Justice and Federal Trade Commission (1997). Market definition is discussed in Section 1.
30. See Heyer (2004).

REFERENCES

ABA (2003), Joint Submission of the American Bar Association's Sections of Antitrust Law and International Law and Practice on the Proposed Anti-Monopoly Law of the People's Republic of China, www.abanet.org/antitrust/at-comments/2003/07-03/jointsubmission.pdf, 28 October, 2006,

ABA (2005), Joint Submission of the American Bar Association's Sections of Antitrust Law, Intellectual Property Law and International Law and Practice on the Proposed Anti-Monopoly Law of the People's Republic of China, www.abanet.org/antitrust/comments/2005/05-05/commentsprc2005woapp.pdf and the *Supplement*, www.abanet.org/antitrust/comments/2005/07-05/abaprcat2005-2fina l.pdf, 23 July, 2006.

Anti-Unfair Competition Law (1993), http://apecweb.apeccp.org.tw/doc/China/Com petition/cncom2.html, 20 November, 2006.

Buchman R. (2004), 'China hurries antitrust law', *Wall Street Journal*, 11 June, page A7.

China.com (2004), 'China's antimonopoly law is on the legislative agenda', http://big5.china.com.cn/chinese/law/661991.htm, 20 November, 2006.

Chow, G. (2002), *China's Economic Transformation,* London: Blackwell Publishers, Inc.

Fox, E.M. (2003), 'International antitrust and the Doha Dome', *Virginia Journal of International Law*, **43**, 911–22.

Heyer, K. (2004), 'A world of uncertainty: Economics and the globalization of antitrust', US Deptartment of Justice, EAG working paper 04-11.

Kaplow L. and S. Shavell (2002), *Fairness Versus Welfare*, Cambridge, MA: Harvard University Press.

Liu, Y.Q. (2006), 'The general trends and problems of China's private economic sectors', *Journal of China's Academy of Social Sciences*, June 2006, www.cpes.cass.cn/viewInfo.asp?id=351, 20 November 2006.

National People's Congress Standing Committee (2006), 'Selected comments on the draft antimonopoly law', http://www.npc.gov.cn/zgrdw/common/ zw.jsp?label= WXZLK&id=350218&pdmc=110106, 20 November, 2006.

Nelson P. and S. Sun (2002), 'Consumer savings from merger enforcement: A review of the antitrust agencies' estimates', *Antitrust Law Journal*, **69**, 921–60.

Organization of American States (2002), *Inventory of Domestic Laws and Regulations Relating to Competition Policy in the Western Hemisphere*, Washington, DC.

Owen B. (2004), 'Imported antitrust', *Yale Journal on Regulation*, **21**, 441–59.

Owen, B, S. Sun and W.T. Zheng (2005), 'Antitrust in China: The problem of incentive compatability', *Journal of Competition Law and Economics*, **1**(1), 123–48.

People's Daily (2004), 'Non-public economy blooming in China', 28 July, http://english.people.com.cn/200407/28/eng20040728_151132.html, 20 November 2006.

Sappington, D. and G. Sidak (2003), 'Competition law for state-owned enterprises', *Antitrust Law Journal*, **71**, 479–523.

State Bureau of Statistics (2003), 'Report on the second national census on basic economic entities', www.stats.gov.cn/tjgb/jbdwpcgb/qgjbdwpcgb/t20030117_61467.htm, 20 November 2006.

State Economic and Trade Commission (1998), 'Opinions on self-disciplinary prices adopted by some industries', 17 August, www.law999.net/law/doc/c001/1998/08/17/00107286.html, 20 November 2006.

Statistical Yearbook of China, www.cei.gov.cn, 28 October 2004.

US Department of Justice and Federal Trade Commission (1997), *Horizontal Merger Guidelines,* www.usdoj.gov/atr/public/guidelines/horiz_book/hmg1.html, 20 November 2006.

Wang, L., L.T. Shen and S.W. Zou (2003), 'Five comprehensive government restructures 1982–2003', *Xinhua News*, 6 March, www.people.com.cn/GB/shizheng/252/10434/10435/20030306/937651.html, 20 November 2006.

4. Property Rights and 'Original Sin' in China: Transaction Costs, Wealth Creation, and Property Rights Infrastructure

Andrew Sheng, Geng Xiao and Yuan Wang[1]

1. INTRODUCTION

This is one of a series of papers by the authors examining how China can reform its capital and financial markets by drawing lessons from the experiences of Hong Kong and other market economies. The first paper was presented in this conference series at Stanford last year and examined the development experiences in other economies.[2] The second paper, presented in Beijing and Shanghai looked at the need for a property rights infrastructure as a pre-condition for efficient capital market development and good corporate governance.[3] This chapter presents for the first time in English a Chinese version of a paper on property rights disputes in China presented in Beijing, Shanghai, and Hong Kong.[4] An overview of the role of property rights infrastructure (PRI) and the function of efficient markets was presented recently in Beijing.[5] There is a further paper, as yet unpublished, that examines the historical reasons why China did not evolve its own property rights infrastructure.[6]

China's economic reform has now advanced to a stage in which more attention should be turned to developing an integrated property rights infrastructure so as to derive lasting benefits to the economy. Hong Kong, which has a well functioning PRI including very effective regulatory and anti-corruption institutions, could serve as a live knowledge base for building and maintaining a modern PRI in China. The historical experiences of US and other matured economies could also provide useful lessons for China.

2.   WHAT IS A PROPERTY RIGHTS INFRASTRUCTURE?

A market is actually a property rights delineation, transfer and protection system. It depends on an infrastructure, comprising information and accounting services, legal and regulatory services and the judicial system, together with other supporting institutions, that gives legal protection of property rights. The concept, role and functions of PRI are discussed elsewhere in detail.[7] The PRI comprises three broad categories of institutions/ processes:

1. Institutions/processes for delineation of property rights:

- Central registry of property rights for land, property, shares, and other assets. The formal record of property rights is crucial in reducing the costs of enforcing property rights and of resolving property rights disputes.
- Accounting and legal process to define property rights in complicated forms of assets such as shares, bonds, options, and other ownership instruments.

2. Institutions/processes for exchange of property rights:

- Trading process such as retail and wholesale markets, auction houses, stock exchanges, futures markets, banks and insurance companies.
- Regulated intermediaries to facilitate complicated financial and non-financial transactions, including lawyers, accountants, auditors, credit rating agencies, credit bureaus, sponsors and other information service providers. These intermediaries are used for identifying, providing and verifying information about the value and quality of property rights, which is indispensable for due diligence when the property rights are traded.
- Clearing, settlement and payment systems to complete financial and non-financial transactions safely, timely, efficiently, and conveniently.

3. Institutions/processes for protection, enforcement, adjudication, and fine-tuning of property rights:

- The general rules of the game that forms the legal and economic system of a market economy: laws, regulations, standards, codes, and norms that protect property rights of all participants across space and time.

- Independent and transparent judiciary to adjudicate disputes over property rights and fine-tune property rights as necessary.
- Enforcement infrastructure including police, regulators, and armed forces that can enforce the judicial decisions and protect property rights firmly and fairly at a cost that is lower than the benefits to the society and the market.
- Mandatory disclosure regimes to ensure that important information about property rights, such as the financial statements of listed companies, are independently verified and accountable so as to facilitate self, regulatory and market disciplines on the corporate sector.
- Active and independent public watchdogs such as media, consumer councils, councillors/parliamentarians, and other civil society organizations to promote proper conduct and behaviour and accountability through public pressures and reputations.
- A well-functioning government with effective checks and balances that can provide basic political and social order.

A well-functioning PRI helps to build and maintain proper market behaviour and good credit culture and is the foundation for good governance in corporations, government agencies, market regulators and other market participants. The ultimate result of a strong PRI will be reflected in the quality of corporate decision-making and government policy-making that is essential for risk management at all levels. Specifically a good PRI leads to a good capital market, which then provides low-cost financing to good corporations.

3. 'ORIGINAL SIN' AND RELATIONSHIP WITH PROPERTY RIGHTS

Since its opening up strategy was implemented in 1979, China has enjoyed rapid growth and unprecedented wealth creation. China's economy has expanded at around 8 percent per annum for more than two decades. From a position where most property was owned by the state, the sale of state-owned enterprises to the private sector, the leasing of land use rights to individuals and foreign firms, as well as the establishment of the stock market have resulted in the emergence of private sector wealth. The private sector has expanded to a scale which is now as large as accounting for about three quarters of the employment, two thirds of GDP, one half of industrial and residential property value, one third of stock market capitalisation, and one fifth of bank loans. China's constitution now protects private property rights.

This rapid emergence of private sector wealth happened in China before the pre-conditions for a robust and efficient property rights infrastructure was firmly established. The resulting uncertainty about property rights has led to many disputes on the legitimacy and clarity of ownership. How did the private sector obtain this wealth? Was it through corrupt practices, tax evasion, smuggling, fraud or other illegal activities? The lack of clarity in ownership of property rights for the private sector is commonly called 'original sin' within China, as the entrepreneurs or owners of private business are unable to explain clearly the origin of such accumulated wealth.

The concern on 'original sin' has created huge moral and political debates. At one extreme, there is moral outrage; a belief that such illegally gotten wealth should be confiscated and those responsible charged criminally. At the other extreme, there are calls for amnesty in the same way that some Western countries give tax amnesties to enable past defaulters to start afresh. This chapter does not attempt to get into the moral or political issues, but uses a Coasian new institutional economics framework of transactions costs to examine the economic dimensions of 'original sin' and its possible resolution. It concludes that there is ample Western experience in dealing with this but all requires the pre-condition of a robust PRI.

One of the key difficulties in dealing with 'original sin' and the associated property rights disputes lies in the confusion about the substantive differences between two types of economic behaviour: criminal wealth transfer activities and non-criminal property rights disputes. The confusion of the two creates dilemmas in government policy-making, judicial decisions, and enforcement actions. To analyse the problem of 'original sin' in China objectively and find constructive solutions, some clear and useful principles to distinguish the two categories of behaviour are needed.

Applying new institutional economics,[8] this chapter develops an analytic framework to distinguish 'original sin' of criminal nature from non-criminal property rights disputes based on two principles: the transaction cost principle and the wealth creation principle. Our analysis suggests:

- When transaction costs are high and there is net wealth creation, the conflicts between the private businessmen and the state/public should be treated as property rights disputes and should be dealt with according to principles similar to the 'liability rule' as applied to the non-criminal cases in the western legal system. The persons inflicting harms or losses to others should pay damages but should not be punished.

- When transaction costs are low and there is no net wealth creation, the conflicts should be treated as criminal cases and should be dealt with according to principles similar to the 'property rule' as applied to the criminal cases in the western legal system. The persons inflicting harm or losses to others should be punished and pay damages.

The above economic and legal principles on dealing with 'original sin' and property rights disputes could be useful in guiding the design and implementation of reforms in China's judicial system, which is one of the key pillars for well-functioning PRI. These conceptual principles could also contribute to current debates in China on the issues of reform of state-owned enterprises and state asset management and the improvement of corporate governance.[9]

4. WEALTH CREATION, WEALTH TRANSFER AND SOCIAL COST

We need to define a few key concepts before developing the analytic framework for studying 'original sin' and property rights disputes. Let us separate conceptually the costs related to 'original sin' into two parts: Wealth Transfer (α) and Social Cost (β). Let us also separate conceptually the Private Sector Value Added (ε) from the 'original sin'-related Wealth Transfer (α).

> *Wealth Transfer* (α): Transfer of wealth and benefits related to private taking of state-owned assets or other stealing and rent-seeking activities.

> *Social Cost* (β): The money, time, and other resources spent on getting α. β is a social cost, or a waste of society's resources, from wealth transfer activities. It is a burden on the society and increases the cost of doing business.

> *Private Sector Value Added* (ε): The net creation of wealth from the legitimate business of the private sector.

In the above definition, α could involve both state-owned and privately owned enterprises and it can lead to quasi-fiscal costs such as non-performing loans in the state banks and unfunded pension liabilities for the government. This transfer is clearly inequitable and discourages legitimate wealth creation activities. But the wealth transfer itself is just redistribution and would not directly destroy wealth. It is difficult to avoid α when property rights are not defined clearly and when there is too much unnecessary regulation. α, if getting out of control, may become a threat to social stability.

Now let us look at a simplified national income account. We break national income into net state sector income and net private sector income.

Net State Sector Income = Tax Revenues + State Sector Value Added $- \alpha$;

Net Private Sector Income $= \varepsilon + \alpha - \beta$;

National Income = Tax Revenues + State Sector Value Added $+ \varepsilon - \beta$;

Since Wealth Transfer α is simply a transfer from the state sector to private sector, it does not appear in the consolidated National Income equation. In other words, the size of α does not affect directly the size of National Income.[10] To increase National Income, it is necessary to reduce social cost β.

But β is closely related to α. α is what motivates 'original sin'-related activities such as stealing, tunnelling, asset stripping and other rent-seeking. These activities then will generate Social Cost β. If there are no effective measures to stop people from rent-seeking, the competition among people who are trying to get Wealth Transfer α would increase Social Cost β to the extent that β could be greater than α.

Hence, to increase National Income, we need to minimize not only β but also α. If there are no state assets and no regulation-induced opportunities for wealth redistribution, α would be zero and β would also fall to zero automatically. One must recognize that 'original sin' involves two parties: the state sector and the private sector. Opportunities for committing 'original sin' exist because of discretionary authority by government officials. The greater the market distortion caused by laws and administrative rules, the greater the opportunity for wealth transfer (i.e. larger α).

The 'original sin' problem in China is complicated because wealth transfer-related criminal activities are often mixed up with non-criminal property rights disputes. Conceptually the total accumulated wealth of private businessmen in China can be represented by $\sum(\varepsilon + \alpha)$, which includes both $\sum\varepsilon$ and $\sum\alpha$. While $\sum\varepsilon$ is conceptually 'clean' of criminal activities, $\sum\alpha$ is often related to illegal or 'extra-legal' gains from private usage of state-owned assets, evasion of taxation, smuggling, gambling, vice, fraud in IPOs, and market manipulation etc.

However, in reality, it is difficult to measure $\sum \varepsilon$ and $\sum \alpha$ separately without a well-functioning PRI. A transparent and equitable 'due process' is needed to unravel the historical legacy of 'original sin' and this cannot be done purely by administrative or political means because of the moral issues and perceived inequities this brings. This is the dilemma in resolving the 'original sin' of private entrepreneurs in China. There is a national interest in promoting $\sum \varepsilon$ as it creates employment, growth, and tax revenues, but there is also public 'bad' with respect to $\sum \alpha$ as it is related to rent-seeking, unfair practices and corruption. Depending on which component of $\sum(\varepsilon + \alpha)$ is larger, you can have dramatically different views on the 'original sin' problem in China. The analytic framework we propose here however provides a more objective and constructive, and perhaps less emotional approach to look at the issue. We regard the 'original sin' in China as a problem of co-existence and conceptual confusion between criminal wealth transfer activities and non-criminal/civil property rights disputes.

Clearly China needs to develop institutions that are able to distinguish $\sum \varepsilon$ from $\sum \alpha$. Good systems for property rights registration and accounting would make it easier to measure $\sum \varepsilon$. Given the complexity of both criminally oriented 'original sin' and non-criminal property rights disputes, China needs a strong, independent, and transparent judicial system to resolve the two categories of conflicts through non-political, routine, and case-by-case processes. The judiciary in the western legal and economic system plays this function routinely without much interaction with its executive and legislative arms of government.

The lawyers and judges in the common law tradition have to identify which categories of the law would apply to each case (criminal or non-criminal laws such as tort). Facts have to be sorted out before they move to the next stage of adjudication. Hence, problems of original sin have to be resolved on a case-by-case basis, and cannot be resolved on the basis of 'broad principles'. This is where experienced lawyers and judges are needed to separate the criminal elements from civil cases. Clearly China can learn a lot from the development experiences of the legal and economic system in the mature Western market economies.

Putting aside the difficulties of developing PRI in general and a well-functioning judiciary in particular, we still need some clear principles on how to make proper distinctions between the 'original sin' of criminal nature and the non-criminal property rights disputes. Traditionally, we use the existing legal and regulatory rules as the only criteria when investigating corruption, criminal behaviour and property rights disputes. But this approach has a serious problem: the existing rules may be outdated and inconsistent with efficiency and equity principles. In fact, China's reform in the past decades is clearly a history of how the outdated rules inherited from the central planning era are changed gradually over time. To move from such a regime to a full market-based regime where property rights are clearly delineated and protected would require a clear institution-building path that involves a clear vision on how the PRI can and should be built.

5. PROPERTY RULE VERSUS LIABILITY RULE: THE TRANSATION COSTS PRINCIPLE

We need to distinguish the 'original sin' of criminal nature from non-criminal property rights disputes conceptually in order to differentiate the two categories of behaviour more effectively in practice. A problem with property rights enforcement in China is that historically the system is based on criminal sanctions, which is not necessarily the most appropriate in market-based property disputes.

The Western legal tradition distinguishes between civil and criminal cases, through what is now in economic terms called the property rule and liability rule. Swedish economist Lars Werin in his survey of law and economics literature provides the following definition on property rule and liability rule based on the concept of transaction costs.[11]

> *Property Rule*: If a person wants to expose someone else to the risk of harm or loss under circumstances where the transaction costs associated with a voluntary agreement are low, then he should buy the right to do so from the other person. If he inflicts a harm or loss without having bought this right, he will be punished, provided the court finds a sufficiently close connection between the harm or loss and his act. He may also have to pay damages to the victim.

> *Liability Rule*: If a person wants to expose someone else to the risk of harm or loss under circumstances where the transaction costs associated with a voluntary agreement are high, then he may do it. If he inflicts a harm or loss, he will have to pay damages to the victim, provided the court finds a sufficiently close connection between the harm or loss and his act. A court determines the size of the damages, in principle calculated so as to correspond to the harm or loss. The acting person will not be punished.

Many judges in the Western legal system apply the property rule and liability rule in their adjudication, without totally understanding the economic concept of transaction costs, as expounded by Nobel Laureate Ronald Coase.

In the context of transitional economies, where property rights need to move from state-dominated holdings to private holdings, it is important to understand that the lower the total transactions costs (including taxes and rent-seeking activity costs), the greater the ability of the market to function efficiently. In many emerging markets, such wealth transfers as theft, fraud, false accounting, corruption and the like result in huge unreported transaction costs. Accordingly, the move towards efficient market economies requires the building of PRI that reduces transaction costs.

The transaction costs principle being articulated explicitly in the property rule and liability rule can be abstracted from common sense practices through a simple example:

- A person stealing some medicine from a drugstore would face criminal charges of stealing. The reason is there is an open market with zero transaction costs for the person to buy the medicine, but he preferred to steal it for personal use at a loss to the drugstore.
- If, however, the person rushed into the drugstore and, without paying, took and used the medicine in order to save the life of some other person on the street, he may not only not be punished for stealing, but could be rewarded for being a public-spirited hero. The transaction costs of paying immediately for the medicine were high relative to the urgency of saving a human life.

6. THE WEALTH CREATION PRINCIPLE

The Western legal tradition, which operated on the basis of the need to protect individual property rights, including against interference from the state, has intuitively operated on the basis of lowering market transaction costs. When transaction costs are low, people would prefer to use the market to obtain the resources they want in order to minimize the total costs to the society. When transaction costs are high, using the market to obtain resources may be too costly, hence there may be an incentive to engage in criminal activities, i.e. steal or cheat. Hence, the transaction costs principle ultimately is consistent with the wealth creation principle. Lars Werin uses the wealth creation principle to describe the judge-made law in the common law tradition:[12]

- 'Property rights and rules on rights of transfer instituted by judge-made law tend systematically to produce incentives that promote efficiency, that is, encourage wealth-increasing acts and counteract wealth-decreasing acts, with no direct consideration of the consequences for the distribution of wealth.'

- 'Property rights and restrictions on rights of transfer instituted by politically-based law are of two kinds. They either concern "constitutional" and "night watch" matters, basic to any society and which require a purely political decision process; they then tend to be efficiency promoting. Or else they are framed so as to promote distributional objectives, with no regard to efficiency. The latter category dominates.'

The above analysis suggests that any market reforms, including the building of the PRI, would require a clear vision or social objective of reducing transaction costs and maximizing wealth-creation risk-taking by the private sector. This implies that the appropriate institutional framework, such as the judicial and regulatory structure (and in enforcement work), should be built with these objectives in mind.

What the above analysis suggests is that whilst economists can explain these conceptual issues, the resolution of these complex property rights disputes lies in the realm of law and regulation. This is why we conclude that China needs to focus on developing a well-functioning PRI and especially an effective judicial system that is specialized in handling these complicated cases. The function of PRI is not just to resolve 'original sin' and property rights disputes. As the historical issues are resolved, the gap between the actual practices and the existing laws and rules will be narrowed, reducing the probability of new 'original sin' from emerging. Each society has to go through this stage of development when it is modernizing its legal and economic system.

7. HISTORICAL LESSONS FROM US

Finally, it is important to point out that the presence of 'original sin' happens in all societies. Each dealt with this problem through its own evolving legal, economic and political systems. Entrepreneurs with 'original sin' will want to legitimize themselves in order to preserve their wealth. As Hernando de Soto correctly pointed out,[12] the United States confronted this problem in the 19th century. The US opened up new frontier territory, e.g., the Wild West, before proper title deeds were registered and law and order were imposed. As a result, most settlers became illegal squatters or miners. In this extra-legal situation, the lawlessness or extra-legality at the grass-root level conflicted with actual laws in the established society:

The crucial change had to do with adapting the law to the social and economic needs of the majority of the population. Gradually, Western nations became able to acknowledge that social contracts born outside the official law were a legitimate source of law and to find ways of absorbing these contracts.[14]

English common law, which the US law was originally based on, did not have means of handling transfers of dubious property titles, such as squatting rights. The common law protected established landlords against illegal squatters. However, in a situation of mass migration into new lands with unclear title and boundaries, the squatters in the US became the majority, and their rights had to be legitimised. This situation is not unlike the mass migration of rural labour into China's urban areas where the property title has not yet been made clear, since all land belonged to the state. It is also conceptually equivalent to the situation where entrepreneurial individuals created net wealth for society by using state-assets that were inefficiently managed under state-owned enterprises. If there are any disputes over such property rights, how should we deal with it?

In America's Wild West, attempts by the established landlords to enforce their rights created huge squatter/homestead owners' rebellion and disorder. When the squatters became the majority, new laws were passed to legalize their extra-legality. The legal device to legitimise their newly accumulated wealth $\sum(\varepsilon + \alpha)$ was the concept of 'pre-emption', which was an innovation to allow a squatter to buy the land that he had improved on (e.g. pay $\sum\alpha$ to the original landowner to legitimize $\sum\varepsilon$).[15] By legitimising extra-legal activities, the frontier states could then collect tax revenues and enforce property rights to land. This was a win–win situation for all concerned.

In other words, faced with the conflicts between the existing landowners and the extra-legal activities of the squatters, who became a strong political force by sheer numbers, 'American politicians thus had three choices. They could continue to try to thwart or ignore extra-legal activities, grudgingly make concessions, or become champions of extralegal rights.'[16] The US Congress gradually consolidated the diffuse and conflicting land laws that were out of touch with reality on the ground into a more consistent property rights system that recognized 'the two great principles of equity in [American] statutory law: The right of occupants ... to their improvements and the right of settlers on privately owned land, unchallenged for seven years and paying taxes thereon, to a firm and clear title to their land no matter what adverse titles may be outstanding.'[17]

Indeed, 'it took the [US] politicians some time before they awakened to the fact that alongside the official law, extralegal social contracts for property had taken shape and that they constituted an essential part of the nation's property rights system. To establish a comprehensive legal system that could be enforced throughout the nation, they would have to catch up with the way people were defining, using and distributing property rights.'[18] For example, in addressing illegal mining on state land, the US Mining Law of 1866, which legalized individual mining, was 'an explicit recognition that value added to assets was something the law needed to encourage and protect.'[19]

To sum up, 'the recognition and integration of extralegal property rights was a key element in the United States becoming the most important market economy and producer of capital in the world.'[20] 'The American experience is very much like what is going on in Third World and former communist countries. The official law has not been able to keep up with popular initiatives, and government has lost control.' For law to be obeyed, it must respond to the needs of the people. 'In the long and arduous process of integrating extralegal property rights [into a new formal property law system], American legislators and jurists created a system much more conducive to a productive and dynamic market economy.'[21]

Even today, the method to resolve 'original sin' in the US is evolving and innovating. The US courts use 'plea bargaining', or a legal settlement of their past sins by bargaining for a lower fine, to recognize and resolve economic misconduct quickly and efficiently. This is fiscally efficient because it takes considerable tax resources to investigate and determine the scale of 'original sin'. For example, in the investigation of securities analyst misconduct after the technology bubble, the US Courts settled for a US$1.4 billion fine on ten investment banks, which did not admit the liability involved but acknowledged that they had to pay for their misconduct. This was a legal device to settle economic issues of disputes over property rights that harmed society that is largely consistent with the liability rule.

The experience of other Asian economies shows that if corruption and market misconduct cannot be stopped, businesses will begin to legitimize themselves by taking over politics. The Asian experience is that business cartels may choose to 'backward integrate' into political parties in order to achieve 'regulatory capture'. This has created the unhealthy 'crony-capitalism' that was one of the causes of the Asian financial crisis.

Hernando de Soto sums up the situation very well:

> Today in many developing and former communist nations, property law is no longer relevant to how the majority of people live and work. How can a legal system aspire to legitimacy if it cuts out 80 percent of its people? The challenge is to correct this legal failure. The American experience shows that this is a threefold task: We must find the real social contracts on property, integrate them into the official law, and craft a political strategy that makes reform possible.[22]

The historical experiences of US are consistent with both the transaction costs principle and wealth creation principles. Outdated laws make property rights unclear and transaction costs high and they should not stop entrepreneurs from creating new wealth. China can learn from the US experience by focusing on resolving the historical conflicts with clear principles and practical reform action.

8. NEXT STEPS

Historian Ray Huang (1990) described the process of China's modernization and the establishment of a market economy in China as completing three parts of the Chinese word '立' (e.g. meaning 'standing up' in English), which consists of (1) the superstructure (the central bureaucracy), (2) the connecting networks and channels (property rights infrastructure), and (3) the grass-roots organizations and individuals.[23] According to Huang, China has already built up the upper and bottom parts but still needs to develop the middle part, e.g. the connecting networks and channels between the central bureaucracy and the grass-root organizations and individuals in order to make China mathematically manageable. Put in another way, China needs to build an effective property rights infrastructure to resolve property rights disputes and deter/reduce corruption and rent-seeking activities related to 'original sin'.

The concept of PRI can be likened to a highway. A PRI is an institutional highway for the flow of wealth and the creation and exchange of property rights. Recurring symptoms of economic and financial crisis, such as bad loans, corruption, commercial fraud, poor corporate governance, market manipulation and property rights disputes are rooted in the flaws of the PRI. When an accident happens in the institutional highway, the immediate reaction is to blame drivers or cars. Any investigation will look at the driver (the individual), the vehicle (the enterprise), the traffic rules (policies and regulations), and even whether traffic police were on the beat. But they often forget two fundamental factors: the quality of the highway (property rights infrastructure) and the brightness of street lamps (transparency), both of which are necessary conditions for a market economy. In other words, the design of the PRI is a pre-condition for a well-functioning market economy.

In 2000, China had one lawyer per 11 000 citizens, compared with one per 300 in the US, one per 700 in the UK, and one per 6300 in Japan. Similarly, China had one accountant per 9650 persons, compared with 412 in Hong Kong and 166 in US. In 2001, China had 28 percent employment in the service sector, considerably less than above 70 percent in the US,

France, UK, Singapore and Hong Kong. China today therefore has considerable way to go towards building capacity in its service (or property delineation, transfer and protection) sector.

The United States spends over US$1 trillion on regulatory activities, which is roughly 10 percent of GDP. Above-the-line transaction costs are expensive, since legal, accounting and regulatory costs are high. However, the market works, because below-the-line transaction costs are relative low compared to many emerging markets, where such costs are estimated at more than 10 percent of GDP, although they spend considerably less on regulatory activities. What is unseen is the 'lost opportunity' in wealth creation and growth, which is held back by costly wealth transfers or criminal activities.

The advantage of the judge-made common law system in a market economy is that this is a pragmatic and empirical system that is truly 'feeling the stones, as you cross the river.' The market place or social system throws up every day very special and complex situations of property disputes that are tested at different levels of courts. The written law requires objective interpretation. When new situations or knowledge arises, judges have to make a decision on the legal or social principles that define such issues. The accumulation of knowledge of cases and their judicial decisions forms an empirical base for society to resolve conflicts, build stable expectations and make decisions that have social legitimacy.

The robustness and durability of the common law system in resolving conflicts lies in its transparency and legitimacy. Every judge knows that he needs to know the law and the precedent decisions made by his predecessors. The opposing sides must present both the evidence and the legal principles for the judge to decide. If the judge makes an error of judgement, it can be appealed to a higher court, to clarify matters of legal principle.

The Chinese judiciary has made considerable progress in recent years in evolving case law precedents. However, considerable resources must be devoted to this area in order to match the urgent need to complement the rapid progress to a market system.

The National People's Congress has also made considerable progress in adapting new laws. But, copying law is easy. During the last two decades, China has copied considerable best-practice legislations from advanced economies, such as contract law, company law, securities law, and banking laws. The problem lies in enforcement. The current judicial system is not yet able to apply these laws efficiently and fairly since the judges have very limited independence from the local party and government bureaucracy. Some judges, who came from such a background as retired army officers or party officials, have little professional training in the legal principles. The

Chinese bureaucracy is efficient in providing basic social and economic order but it attempts to define and enforce property rights through administrative instruments. For a market economy to function efficiently, an independent judiciary and regulatory structure (key components of PRI) is vital.

China needs to review the development of the accounting profession to strengthen audit and disclosure quality. Areas such as a national credit reference agency, national network of property title registry, and market-based rating agencies, professional valuation agencies, and related infrastructure and services are all urgently needed to build the PRI.

After a quarter of century of reforms, China has reached the stage of economic development where the macroeconomic conditions provide a favourable opportunity for the next stage of reform: construction of a robust PRI to allow more efficient and orderly exchange and protection of property rights. China is no longer in shortage of savings and funds. Indeed, arguably it is suffering from an excess of savings. China's advantage as a latecomer to the market economy is that there is already enough experience and 'software' to bring in the people, processes and experiences, so that a sustainable and equitable market economy can be built to global standards.

Since Hong Kong is already an international financial centre with a PRI competitive and transparent by world standards, Hong Kong can bring in a wealth of market experience in building the PRI to facilitate China's transition to a fully competitive market economy that operates on global standards. Building PRI will take time and political will. China should not underuse and underestimate the value of the Hong Kong PRI in its reform efforts. How to build a modern and institutional property rights infrastructure is an important but complex task. Further research and discussion are needed before a clear action plan could be mapped out.

NOTES

1. The chapter reflects entirely the authors' personal view and does not represent the views of their employers. Xiao Geng would like to acknowledge the financial support for this research from Hong Kong's University Grants Committee (Project No: AOE/H-05/99) and the Stanford Center for International Development. The authors would like to thank Wu Jinglian, Gao Xiqing, Zhang Jun, Liang Zhiping, Zhou Qiren, Liang Hong, Gaik-Looi Tan and seminar participants in Beijing, Shanghai, Hong Kong, and Stanford University for helpful comments and discussions. This paper was presented at Stanford Center for International Development (SCID) conference 'China's Policy Reform: Progress and Challenges', Stanford University, 14–16 October 2004.
2. Sheng et al. (2003b).
3. Sheng et al. (2004a).
4. Sheng et al. (2003a).
5. Sheng (2004).

6. Sheng et al. (2004c).
7. Sheng et al. (2004b).
8. Werin (2003).
9. Sheng et al. (2004a).
10. For simplicity, we assume here there are no income effects.
11. Werin (2003), p. 204.
12. Werin (2003), p. 61.
13. This section draws heavily from de Soto (2000), Chapter 5, *The Missing History of US History.*
14. de Soto (2000), p. 106.
15. Op cit, p. 120.
16. Op cit, p. 130.
17. Op cit, p. 130.
18. Op cit, p. 136.
19. Op cit, p. 146
20. Op cit. p. 148.
21. Op cit. p. 150.
22. Op cit. p. 151.
23. Huang (1999), Chinese edition, page 3.

REFERENCES

De Soto, Hernando (2000), *The Mystery of Capital: Why Capitalism Triumphs in the West and Fails Everywhere Else,* New York: Basic Books.

Huang, Ray (1990), *China: A Macro History*, New York: M.E.Sharpe.

Huang, Ray (1999), *Broadening the Horizons of Chinese History*, Chinese edition, Taibei: New Century Publisher, English edition, New York: ME Sharpe.

Sheng, Andrew (2004), 'Optimal financial structure for economic growth: Lessons from other East Asian economies', Paper presented at Beijing University CCER Tenth Anniversary conference, 16–17 September.

Sheng, Andrew, Geng Xiao and Yuan Wang (2003a), 'China's financial reform: Property rights infrastructure and the resolution of "Original Sin", In Chinese, Presented Shanghai Institute of Law and Economics, Beijing, 13 December.

Sheng, Andrew, Geng Xiao and Yuan Wang (2003b), 'The future of capital markets in developing countries: Implications for China's equity markets', Paper presented at Stanford Center for International Development conference China's Market Reforms, Stanford, 19 September.

Sheng, Andrew, Geng Xiao and Yuan Wang (2004a), 'Corporate governance, capital market, and property rights infrastructure: The experiences of Hong Kong and lessons for China', Paper presented at Shanghai Academy of Social Science & 1990 Institute conference State-owned Enterprise Governance in China, Shanghai, 28–29 May.

Sheng, Andrew, Geng Xiao and Yuan Wang (2004b), 'China's financial reform and property rights infrastructure', Forthcoming in October 2004 issue of Perspectives, Property Rights and 'Original Sin' in China, **113**.

Sheng, Andrew, Geng Xiao and Yuan Wang (2004c), 'The property rights micro-foundations of macro-history: Ray Huang's analysis of market reform in China', Unpublished manuscript.

Werin, Lars (2003), Economic Behavior and Legal Institutions: An Introductory Survey, London: World Scientific.

5. Corporate Governance and Property Rights Infrastructure: The Experiences of Hong Kong and Lessons for China

Andrew Sheng, Geng Xiao and Yuan Wang[1]

1. INTRODUCTION

This is one of a series of papers by the authors examining how China can reform its financial markets by drawing lessons from the experiences of Hong Kong and other market economies. One of the papers analysed the property rights disputes in China from the perspectives of new institutional economics, emphasizing particularly the role of property rights infrastructure in resolving property rights disputes and commercial crimes and was included in this book in Chapter 4. This chapter reviews China's need for a property rights infrastructure as a pre-condition for efficient capital market development and good corporate governance, drawing particularly on lessons from Hong Kong's experience. An unpublished paper examines the historical reasons why China did not evolve its own property rights infrastructure (Sheng et al. 2004). An overview of the role of property rights infrastructure and the function of efficient markets was presented recently in Beijing (Sheng, 2004).

A major task of the transition from a planned economy to a market economy is to build a strong and well-functioning PRI. Good corporate governance and a competitive market economy can only be built upon a strong PRI. We argue that China's economic reform has now advanced to a stage in which more attention should be turned towards developing an integrated property rights infrastructure so as to derive lasting benefits to the economy. Hong Kong, which has a well functioning PRI, could serve as a live knowledge base for building and maintaining a modern PRI in China.

2. CORPORATE GOVERNANCE AS SELF, REGULATORY AND MARKET DISCIPLINES

Corporate governance is defined as 'the system of checks and balances that ensures that corporate management, including boards and board committees, senior corporate executives, auditors and corporate advisers, all carry out their fiduciary responsibilities owed to those they represent.' The checks and balances in the corporate governance can be summarized as comprising three disciplines: self discipline, regulatory discipline and market discipline. The three disciplines are usually implemented in three different institutional settings: ethics for self discipline, process for regulatory discipline and structure for market discipline.

Let us use Hong Kong's experiences to examine how these different dimensions of checks and balances work to ensure that enterprises follow the established ethics and rules as they compete for profits in the markets.

2.1. Self Discipline through Ethics

For self-discipline to work, the ethics of the persons involved in each level of corporate structure must act to protect the interests of the company as well as minority shareholders and the public interest. The ethics required for self discipline on the part of corporate insiders would bring rewards to them in the long run through reputation effects, but could diverge from their self interest in the short run. This is why self-discipline alone can rarely work to ensure good corporate governance. However, self-discipline is an essential ingredient in good corporate governance.

Under Hong Kong company law, the company is a legal entity with a unitary board that is responsible for its management. In other words, all directors, irrespective of whether they are executive or non-executive, are equally liable for the affairs of the company. By convention, the board appoints the senior managers, including the CEO and the auditors. It also sets and oversees the implementation of its agreed policies.

The board, through the CEO, is responsible for putting in place all the internal controls that prevent fraud and misconduct, including internal audits, dual controls and other checks and balances. The external audits are required by law, but paid for by the company. The board can also appoint external lawyers or specialists to advise the board on all major contracts and decisions. In general, the Company Secretary is the chief compliance officer, responsible to the board for ensuring that due diligence and compliance with the company law are achieved. Clearly, high ethical standards for the top executives are essential for good corporate governance because of their large discretionary power in running their company.

2.2. Regulatory Discipline through Processes

For the regulatory discipline to work well, it is necessary to develop good regulatory processes (or procedures), which could ensure that shareholders, management and staff perform in accordance with the ethical codes, rules, regulations and law. If any party violates the rules, the regulatory processes can be initiated. At the centre of the regulatory processes are the regulators, the judicial system and the police, which rely on the established regulatory processes to enforce the rules. To guard against abuses of regulatory, judicial and police power, the processes need to be transparent and cover mechanisms for resolving disputes not only among private parties but also between the private parties and the enforcers. In Hong Kong, such reviews are conducted by the Operations Review Committee of the Independent Commission Against Corruption, and the Process Review Panel of the Securities and Futures Commission.

Corporations in Hong Kong are subject to a considerable amount of regulatory checks and balances. Board members, who are ultimately responsible for the affairs of the enterprise, are subject to the Companies Ordinance and a variety of other legal responsibilities and duties. The first is the fiduciary duty to do their best. For negligence in their duties, they could be barred from holding future positions as directors of companies. They could be brought to court if they participated in any criminal or civil breaches of the law. Alternatively, according to the review of the Hong Kong company law that is being currently carried out, company directors could be sued by minority shareholders or by the regulators through derivative action suits.

If companies are listed, they are subject to a whole array of regulatory oversight by the stock exchange and other regulators through the listing rules, the securities law, and the taxation law and criminal legislation. Furthermore, the lending bankers to the companies have considerable influence on their financial discipline. The banks provide independent confirmation of the balances of the deposits and the credit position of the borrowers to their auditors, thus facilitating reliable auditing of the borrowers' accounts. If banks fail to fulfil their duties in exercising credit discipline over borrowers, they would not only be subject to their own internal audit, but also sanction by their regulators. Each part of the regulatory functions serves to reinforce the delineation, exchange and protection of property rights. In Hong Kong, good credit culture exercised by the banks helps reduce non-performing loans and prevents companies from weak credit and payment practices.

2.3.   Market Discipline through Structures

For market discipline to work, it is necessary to develop internal and external institutional structures that influence the behaviour of the corporations. The internal institutional structures include the arrangements for the board, the board committees, and various units for internal control, risk management and compliance. The external institutional structures cover not only the competitive environment for the traditional product, labour and equity markets, but also the more sophisticated markets for executives, corporate control and corporate information disclosure. These internal and external institutional structures define the competitive market pressures on the corporations. Under a competitive market environment with high transparency, it is difficult for poor corporate governance to perpetuate itself through state protection, monopolistic powers or poor access to information. Cases like Enron in the US demonstrate that poor corporate governance will be exposed sooner or later in a market environment.

Market discipline is enforced mainly through competition and transparency. But competition relies heavily on accurate, timely and readily accessible information for creditors, competitors, investors and analysts to assess risks and make decisions. The quality of information depends on the accounting standards used (e.g., International Accounting and Auditing Standards), the disclosure and transparency rules (such as disclosure requirements in Listing Rules), and the quality of audit. Having good information enables investors, creditors, regulators and other market participants to make crucial investment and investment protection decisions, such as buying, selling, holding or even engaging in legal suits to protect their interests. Moreover, good disclosure enhances accountability and checks and balances against abuses, such as misconduct or incompetence of corporate managers and corruption or incompetence of public officials.

Mandatory disclosure of information with enforcement by the regulators is important and useful in ensuring access to reliable and comparable information. However, a free and knowledgeable media is an important supplement to the costly regulatory disclosure. The market is able to generate and use information that is much richer than the mandatory disclosure. Hence a free market for information is indispensable for healthy capital market and good corporate governance. This is not to deny that the market occasionally produces misleading information through herding and mania. The analyst scandals that occurred during the tech bubble remind us that market discipline and regulatory discipline are complementary to each other and both are indispensable to enable a market to function efficiently.

With good information disclosure, market discipline on corporate behavior can be achieved through competition policy. Property rights would be corroded if economic rents were allocated through monopoly or oligopoly arrangements. The only way to reduce such economic rents is through open and transparent market competition. One of the lessons of the Asian crisis is that even though Asia relied significantly on self and regulatory disciplines on corporate behavior, the lack of market discipline due to heavy protection of certain industries weakened their capacity to compete under globalization and market liberalization. Protection creates vested interests that seek further rent-seeking behavior and also resist change. Consequently, the most important and complex market discipline is capital market discipline, which deserves more discussion.

3. CAPITAL MARKET DISCIPLINE CRITICAL FOR CORPORATE GOVERNANCE PERFORMANCE

In addition to the market for products, executive skills, labor and land, the capital market is critical in disciplining corporate behavior. Finance is a derivative of the real sector. A well-functioning financial system promotes efficient development of the real sectors. Defects in the financial sector tend to distort resource allocation and hold back economic development. Conversely, inefficiencies in the real sector will sooner or later be reflected in the weaknesses of the financial sector, through the emergence of chronic non-performing loans in the banking system.

The financial sector has essentially four major functions: resource allocation, price discovery, risk management and corporate governance. At the core of these functions is the capacity to distinguish good firms from bad firms. A well-functioning financial sector should reward good firms by reducing their cost of capital. Conversely, it should impose appropriately high costs of capital for bad firms either through credit rationing or risk provisioning. Through its lending and fund-raising function, the financial sector plays an important role in disciplining the corporate sector and hence is crucial to corporate governance performance.

In the early stages of economic development, strong banks can play a crucial role in developing strong financial discipline and good corporate credit culture. For example, enterprises in Hong Kong were subject to considerable credit discipline when the British trade banks insisted on independent auditing of financial statements and on providing high quality collateral in the form of warehouse receipts and letters of credit before lending to borrowers. Those firms that had poor accounting records and bad payment history were quickly cut off from bank credit and their costs of borrowing basically went up. On the other hand, the well-performing firms would enjoy relatively low costs of capital through flexible and easily accessible credit. Banks in Hong Kong played an important role of separating the good firms from the bad firms. When the bad firms were largely excluded from the credit markets, the banks in Hong Kong were able to use their interest spreads to cover the relatively low levels of non-performing loans arising mainly from business cycles and other business risks. Even during the recent Asian financial crisis, the ratio of non-performing loans in Hong Kong was very low. The stability of Hong Kong's banking sector was achieved without a deposit-insurance system and without any controls on capital mobility and interest rates.

Similarly, companies that seek public funds through listing in the stock exchanges in Hong Kong are subject to scrutiny by sponsors such as investment banks, vetting by exchanges, financial analysts and investor choices (as they have the options to shift their investment to other firms and other markets). Regulatory discipline also works through mandatory disclosure of their business transactions and performance and sanctioning on false and misleading disclosure. Like the banks in Hong Kong, the securities market in Hong Kong played an important role in selecting good firms. The costs of capital are made low for well-performing firms but very high for poor-performing firms. Firms that show signs of poor performance or misconduct will suffer higher price volatility, low liquidity and also attract tough investigations of individual and corporate misconducts by the regulatory agencies.

In the case of fraud and cheating, recent amendments in the Securities and Futures Ordinance and co-ordinated enforcement action by the SFC, Commercial Crime Bureau of the Police and ICAC have begun to sanction back such egregious behaviour.

In summary, a well-regulated and functioning financial system helps enterprises with good corporate governance and performance to raise funds efficiently and cheaply, while rejecting funding to firms with poor corporate governance and performance.

In recent years, information technology and globalization has also made the functions of financial system more transparent and more competitive. We now know much better how the financial systems define, exchange, and enforce property rights:

- First, a financial system comprises a set of hardware (networks of computers and other platforms) across which participants transact and exchange financial products (e.g., property rights), according to a set of agreed standards and rules of the game (i.e., software).
- Secondly, these financial products are transacted and then settled and cleared through various processes (such as trading software and

clearing, payment and settlement software), which used to be paper-based but are now increasingly digital.
- Third, global markets are a network of local market networks. The robustness and efficiency of global markets would depend on the robustness and efficiency of the weakest links in these local networks. In other words, financial systems are subject to local shocks and contagion, which could spread risks across the global networks.
- Fourth, increasingly, the standards and rules relating to operations in financial systems are being globalized and formalized given the competitive pressures on each local market. These include accounting, legal, operational and regulatory standards, such as International Accounting Standards, IOSCO Principles, and Basle Capital Accord Requirements etc.
- Fifth, property rights are described by information. Hence, disclosure and transparency is crucial in making good decisions and ensuring accountability (and hence right incentives) in market systems.

In other words, the institutional structure of financial markets is a complex system of participants trading property rights across a network made of both hardware and software. It is a dynamic system, because behaviour within the financial markets is determined and shaped by the passive rules and regulations as well as by the active behaviour of all participants, including in particular the regulators who carry out enforcement functions.

In the past, Asian economies focused on development through openness to trade and heavy investment in fixed capital goods or hardware. But as the Asian crisis has shown, the weaknesses in the financial system reflected overinvestment in hardware and underinvestment in software, or what this chapter calls the property rights infrastructure.

4.   THE ROLE OF PROPERTY RIGHTS INSTRASTRUCTURE IN A MARKET ECONOMY

Corporate governance and capital markets cannot function independently of their political, social, legal and economic environment. There is a growing literature on the close interaction between the legal and economic aspects of the integrated modern market system as reviewed in Lars Werin (2003). In this chapter, we try to make the key point that underlying corporate governance and capital market is the property rights infrastructure (PRI). The PRI comprises the system that delineates, registers, transfers and protects property rights within a legal jurisdiction. If any part of the PRI is defective, corporate governance cannot function effectively.

What most studies on corporate governance have not appreciated enough is that in the real world, an array of sub-systems of supporting institutions have been integrated over time and eventually formed what is collectively called PRI. If parts of the subsets do not function properly, the whole may not be effective. Hong Kong has a complete PRI arising from its history. As a free port, property rights were initially defined through foreign trade and exchange. Goods can be traded and exchanged more efficiently through hard currencies and a mutually accepted set of rules of trade and exchange. Primitive bartering systems are inefficient because of lack of transparency, standards and high transactions costs. The common law jurisdiction under which Hong Kong operated in came with a complete set of property rights infrastructure: land and stock registers, warehouse registers, accounting, commercial and financial law, courts, various specialized tribunals, arbitration centres, free media, stock exchanges, and commercial and financial intermediation services. All of these institutions operate together in an integrated system to transfer and protect property rights in Hong Kong. Property rights in Hong Kong can be transacted with great legal certainty, transparency and accountability and ultimately low transaction costs. The free media, credible judiciary and rule of law are built upon a solid property rights infrastructure. The integrated economic and legal system as a whole is the reason why Hong Kong is successful as an international financial and trade centre.

Each of the subsystems has evolved through its institutional history. An example is the governance structure of auditors. Accountants evolved like other professionals, through professional associations or self-regulated organisations (SRO). The SRO established its own code of ethics and professional standards of due diligence. If an auditor failed in his duties through negligence or by aiding and abetting corporate misconduct, the SRO would sanction the member. The same would happen in the case of lawyers, which are also subject to discipline by SROs. The conduct of professional bankers or investment bankers would be subject to supervision by respective banking or securities regulator.

The essential elements of a modern PRI include the following institutions grouped by three broad categories:

1. Institutions for delineation of property rights:

- Central Registry of property right (e.g., land registry, share registry) to officially record property rights. This is crucial in transparency of the property right and reducing the costs of enforcement.

- Accounting and legal process to define the property rights (annual audits and right to sue to protect property right).

2. Institutions for exchange of property rights:

- Trading process (such as stock exchange trading platform to enable transparent trading of property rights, and public auctions).
- Clearing, settlement and payment infrastructure (clearing house and payment system operated by banking system to enable transfers to be cleared and settled in final form through delivery of property right).
- Regulated intermediaries (intermediaries who help the transfer process should be sanctioned if they do not perform according to rules of the game).

3. Institutions for enforcement and fine-tuning of property rights:

- Rules of Game: norms, standards, codes, regulations and law that help protect the property rights of participants against abuses of the system.
- Enforcement infrastructure: there must exist regulators to enforce the rules but enforcement costs should not exceed benefits to markets.
- Independent and transparent judiciary to adjudicate disputes over property rights.
- Transparent media and disclosure regime to ensure that property right is independently verified and accountable (e.g., disclosure rules and mandatory publication of financial statements).

In a functioning market, the PRI essentially functions to vet the entry of market participants, ensure that they perform to market and ethical norms and those that damage public interest through inefficiency or misconduct (theft or fraud) exit the market. Each sector of the economy has different PRI, such as the trading, clearing and settlement system for the securities market. If the PRI is defective, then the property rights are not protected and indeed expropriated by players that are inefficient, loss making and in effect subsidized by the rest of the market.

In his path-breaking work, Hernando de Soto (2000) has uncovered six hidden benefits of private property (which is really what we call here property rights infrastructure):

- Fixing the economic potential of assets (efficient use of capital).
- Integrating dispersed information into one system (economy of scale in PRI and standards and low transaction costs).

- Making people accountable (private property as an ultimate guarantee on contract fulfilment or fulfilment of responsibility).
- Making assets fungible (allow convergence of risk-adjusted return on various assets).
- Networking people (increasing the extent of market and facilitate specialization).
- Protecting transactions (low enforcement costs when private property can be used as collateral and reduce transaction costs).

The Latin American experience shows that weaknesses in the PRI gives rise to a system that is not accountable, not fungible, with no network benefits, and little trading. Consequently, there is no credit culture. Ultimately, the poor are disadvantaged because the costs of entry into business are overwhelmingly high for small enterprises and poor people, while large enterprises can engage in regulatory capture to protect their vested interests against competition. When PRI is defective, transactions costs are high due to high risks or rent-seeking activities.

It should be pointed out that PRI is a public good that requires large investment to establish, but it can generate sustained benefits in the form of drastically reduced transaction costs in the economy. This is why the government has a responsibility in building a well-functioning PRI as soon as possible if the society wants a modern market economy. Since PRI is a system to delineate, exchange and protect property rights, the role of the government in the process of establishing PRI can be summarized as follows:

- Setting standards, rules, and legislations for a well functioning PRI;
- Defending property rights of citizens against non-citizens (national defence and foreign affairs functions);
- Enforce and protect private property rights by resolving disputes between citizens and citizens (adjudication and anti-crime functions);
- Creating mechanisms to constrain abuses of state power and resolve property rights disputes between citizens and the state (anti-corruption and human rights protection function).

In other words, the government's role is to build and maintain a well functioning PRI, across which participants can trade property rights.

Generally, people assume that regulation is efficiency promoting and serves public interest by addressing areas of market failure. But since the government is also an important part of the PRI, it is possible for government failure to generate high costs of operating PRI, which will affect the delineation, exchange, and enforcement of the private property rights of citizens. As the government is heavily involved in a number of the sub-systems of PRI, the coordination costs among these sub-systems could be very high when the government is weak or when politics dominates economics. Hence, an important and permanent function of the government is to create and maintain mechanisms to discipline itself and to maintain political and macroeconomic stability so as the citizens can have a stable political, social, legal and economic environment and a robust PRI.

Expressed in Coasian institutional economics, the role of government in a market economy is to reduce the total costs, including transaction costs and regulatory costs, of exchanging and protecting property rights. If property rights are subject to huge costs of exchange and protection, such as excessive taxation, corruption, risks of confiscation, theft and erosion through inflation, then capital flight and prevalence of mafia are likely.

After a quarter of century of reforms, China has reached the stage of economic development where the macroeconomic conditions provide a favourable opportunity for the next stage of reform: construction of a robust PRI to allow more efficient and orderly exchange and protection of property rights. China is no longer short of savings and funds. Indeed, it is arguably suffering from an excess of savings. Without a robust PRI, such savings could be dissipated through NPLs and corruption. What China needs now are experienced people with the right processes and governance structures to ensure that the PRI system is complete and is functioning effectively.

Indeed, the greatest benefit of allowing in FDI is to introduce competition and bring in people, processes and experiences so as the Chinese enterprises and skills could catch up and achieve global standards. Since Hong Kong is already an international financial centre with a PRI competitive and transparent by world standards, Hong Kong can bring in a wealth of market experience in building the PRI to facilitate the Mainland's transition to a fully competitive market economy that operates on global standards.

NOTE

1. This chapter reflects entirely the authors' personal views and does not represent the views of their employers. Xiao Geng would like to acknowledge the financial support for this research from the Hong Kong University Grants Committee (Project No. AOE/H-05/99).

REFERENCES

De Soto, Hernando (2000), *The Mystery of Capital: Why Capitalism Triumphs in the West and Fails Everywhere Else*, New York: Basic Books.

Sheng, Andrew (2004), 'Optimal financial structure for economic growth: Lessons from other East Asian economies', Paper presented at Beijing University CCER Tenth Anniversary conference, 16–17 September.

Sheng, Andrew, Geng Xiao and Yuan Wang (2004), 'The property rights microfoundations of macro-history: Ray Huang's analysis of market reform in China', Manuscript, July 2004, The University of Hong Kong,

Werin, Lars (2003), *Economic Behaviour and Legal Institutions: An Introductory Survey*, London: World Scientific.

6. China's Evolving Labor Market

Belton M. Fleisher and Dennis Tao Yang[1]

1. INTRODUCTION

In the nearly three decades since the inception of reforms, the structure of China's labor force has been fundamentally transformed. In 1978, an overwhelming majority of the labor force was either employed as agricultural workers in rural communes or as employees in urban state-owned enterprises (SOE), with virtually no labor flows between the rural and urban sectors. By 2004, however, over a third of the rural labor force had moved into non-farm activities (see Table 6.1), and about three-quarters of the urban labor force had found employment outside of the state sector, in urban collectives, joint ventures and private enterprises (see Table 6.2). Today, there are more than 100 million rural migrants working temporarily in cities, establishing a direct connection between the rural and urban labor markets.

Prior to reform, job changes were either prohibited or controlled by appropriate government agencies. The fundamental shifts in the distribution of employment across sectors and ownership categories that have occurred under reform require an allocative mechanism far more flexible and sensitive than nations have ever achieved with administrative controls. The emergence of a functioning labor market has been essential to this transformation, and this is recognized by the Government. A series of reform policies and deregulations have been instrumental in the emergence of labor markets in China, but due to the incomplete nature of reform, some existing policies and institutions still prevent the labor market from efficient operation. The uneven institutional evolution of labor markets and their regulation have profound social and political consequences. Dealing with this labor-market transformation is one of the most challenging tasks facing the Government and the Chinese Communist Party, and the way in which laws, regulations, and institutions evolve under this challenge raise a series of questions of great academic and policy interest. The goal of our chapter is to address some of these questions and to discuss and evaluate the ways in which answers are evolving.

Policy Reform and Chinese Markets

Table 6.1:   *Distribution of the Rural Labor Force among Economic Activities, 1978–2000 (millions)*

Year	Total rural laborers	Agricultural laborers	Non-agricultural laborers	
			Total	TVE workers
1978	306.4	284.6	21.8	22.2
1979	310.2	278.3	31.9	23.8
1980	318.4	298.1	20.3	25.4
1981	326.7	289.8	36.9	25.9
1982	338.7	300.6	38.1	27.7
1983	346.9	303.5	43.4	29.3
1984	359.7	300.8	58.9	49.2
1985	370.7	303.5	67.2	67.2
1986	379.9	304.7	75.2	77.0
1987	390.0	308.7	81.3	85.7
1988	400.7	314.6	86.1	93.0
1989	409.4	324.4	85.0	91.3
1990	420.1	333.4	86.7	90.2
1991	430.9	341.9	89.0	93.7
1992	438.0	340.4	97.6	103.3
1993	442.6	332.6	110.0	120.6
1994	446.5	326.9	119.6	117.6
1995	450.4	323.3	127.1	125.5
1996	452.9	322.6	130.3	131.7
1997	459.6	324.3	135.3	127.7
1998	464.3	326.3	138.0	122.7
1999	469.0	329.1	139.9	127.0
2000	479.6	328.0	151.6	128.2
2001	490.9	324.5	166.4	130.9
2002	489.6	319.9	169.7	132.9
2003	487.9	312.6	175.3	135.7
2004	487.2	306.0	181.2	138.7

Note: The number of TVE workers may exceed rural non-agricultural laborers because some TVEs engage in agricultural production.

Source: National Bureau of Statistics (NBS, various years).

We address two questions raised by China's ongoing economic reforms in the context of the labor force and labor markets: (1) What are the implications of economic reform in general for labor-market institutions? and (2) What are the current conditions of the labor markets and what are the major challenges for further reform? In dealing with these questions, we

Table 6.2: *Distribution of the Urban Labor Force by Types of Ownership,*
1978–2000 (millions)

Year	Total employed persons	SOE workers	Collective workers	Other types of ownership
1978	95.2	74.5	20.5	0.2
1979	100.0	76.9	22.7	0.4
1980	105.2	80.2	24.3	0.7
1981	110.5	83.7	25.7	1.1
1982	114.3	86.3	26.5	1.5
1983	117.5	87.7	27.4	2.4
1984	122.3	86.4	32.2	3.7
1985	128.1	90.0	33.2	4.9
1986	132.9	93.3	34.2	5.4
1987	137.8	96.5	34.9	6.4
1988	142.7	99.8	35.3	7.6
1989	143.9	101.1	35.0	7.8
1990	147.3	103.5	35.5	8.3
1991	152.6	106.6	36.3	9.7
1992	172.4	108.9	36.2	27.3
1993	175.9	109.2	33.9	32.8
1994	184.1	112.1	32.9	39.1
1995	190.9	112.6	31.5	46.9
1996	198.2	112.4	30.2	55.6
1997	202.1	110.4	28.8	62.8
1998	206.8	90.6	19.6	96.6
1999	210.1	85.7	17.1	107.3
2000	212.7	81.0	15.0	116.7
2001	239.4	76.4	12.9	150.1
2002	247.8	71.6	11.2	165.0
2003	256.4	68.8	10.0	177.6
2004	264.8	67.1	9.0	188.7

Source: NBS (various years).

treat the progress of economic reform to date and analyze how marketization of the Chinese economy has led to the need for radical changes in labor-market laws and regulations. Most importantly, we examine the applications of these laws and regulations and their implications for the allocation of labor. Our analysis will also reveal persistent labor-market problems and discuss the policy choices facing China's policymakers today.

Our treatment divides the discussion between rural and urban labor markets. The reason for this division lies in a fundamental characteristic of the Chinese economy under planning, namely, the formal segregation of the rural (agriculture-centered) and urban (manufacturing-centered) economies and labor forces. These two sectors were treated as critically related but separate entities during the entire period of central planning, starting in 1949, and this segregation remains at the center of Chinese labor-market problems and policies today, even as the two sectors are connected forcefully by the potential gains from trade and the major factor-market disequilibria between them.[2] Because basic economic forces are thwarted by segregation, major problems of incentives, mobility, wage differences, and social policy persist. The division between state/non-state ownership sectors, social security (including medical coverage and pensions) and unemployment (including unemployment insurance), and related topics of housing, education, and other social services are all related to drastically different policies and social problems that distinguish China's rural and urban economies.

In our discussion we measure the achievements of reform to date, as well as the need for further reform, with the metrics associated with economic efficiency and productivity. An irony worth noting is that this metric is based in part on formal analysis supporting the viability of government ownership under socialism (Lange and Taylor, 1966), and a major contributor to the reform movement has been the failure of both policy and practice to approach the frontier of efficiency and productivity in China. We treat the institutional factors underlying successes and failures of reform and we pay particular attention to policy issues, including the sequencing of reforms (e.g., provision of social security and implementation of labor contracts); coordination among various reforms (rural land arrangements and labor mobility, housing reforms and labor mobility); the political economy of reform (e.g., efficiency and protection of state-owned enterprises – SOEs); and other topics related to the conflicts and congruence of political and economic objectives.

In describing and analyzing China's labor-market reform it is essential to distinguish between laws and regulations as they are written ('on the books') and how they are applied (Ohnesorge, 2003). Evolution from a planned economy to freely operating markets involves governments at all levels relinquishing controls that they have long exercised, and governments reasonably fear the loss of political power and authority in so doing (Clarke, 2003). Nowhere is this connection between a move to free markets and loss of political power more closely related than in labor markets.

2. RURAL LABOR MARKETS

The segmentation of China's rural and urban labor markets can be traced to the heavy-industry-oriented development strategy pursued vigorously in the period of central planning.[3] The main mechanisms for enforcing this strategy consisted of the unified procurement and sale of agricultural commodities, the people's communes, and the household registration (*hukou*) system that designated the legal place of residency and work for the entire population. This development strategy resulted in massive distortions in the factor markets with excessive concentrations of capital in urban areas and of labor in rural areas. Prior to the reform in 1978, urban workers' productivity and earnings far exceeded those of their rural counterparts.

Within rural regions, the labor force was governed under the people's communes, which received production targets from the planning authorities and delivered procurements at state-dictated low prices. Ever since the tragic experience of the Great Leap famine of 1959–61, which resulted in 20 to 30 million excess deaths, national policies stressed agricultural production and local grain self-sufficiency. Rural industries were underdeveloped and remained subsidiary to agriculture (Findlay et al., 1994; Naughton, 1996). Thus from a labor-market perspective, there were two sets of problems with central planning on the eve of economic reform in 1978: (1) the pervasive labor-incentive problems due to the organization of work within communes; and (2) the severe misallocation of labor between rural and urban sectors, as well as between agricultural and nonagricultural activities within rural regions.

2.1. Reforms in Local Markets

Market-oriented development in rural China started with a package of three reforms: the replacement of production teams with households as basic production units (household responsibility system [HRS]); official increases in agricultural product prices; and the liberalization of markets for rural products. These reforms provided the necessary conditions for the boom in rural industries starting in the mid-1980s and were instrumental in the emergence of labor markets in rural China.

The change from communes to a household-based farming system began in 1979 in Anhui province and was essentially completed nationwide by 1983. This institutional change, which introduced marginal compensation for family work effort, solved the labor-incentive problems in the communes and resulted in dramatic increases in labor productivity and earnings. Consequently, the demand for workers declined on small Chinese farms. In the same period, the Government initiated planning reforms in which the state reduced the number of production targets (or categories). Of the remaining targets, few were mandatory and many were guided by complementary prices and incentive schemes (Sicular, 1988). Because the HRS increased families' command over their productive resources, including labor, farmers not only had incentives but also some freedom in seeking non-farm employment.

In 1979, the government also implemented large increases in state procurement prices for agricultural products, with a weighted increase in quota and above-quota prices of 22.1 percent.[4] As a result, large amounts of funds were injected into the rural economy, creating demand for industrial products and funds for capital investment, especially in non-farm production. Concurrently, the opening of rural markets not only accommodated the sale of non-farm products, but also facilitated the purchase of inputs for rural industries. Clearly, the three reforms were interrelated: each reinforced the impact of the others on the development of labor markets.

Hence, by the mid-1980s, the conditions for accelerated employment growth in China's rural industries were in place. Input and output markets had emerged, households were conscious of their alternative opportunities, and they had incentive to seek employment in the non-farm sector with higher earnings. There is little question that marginal productivity of labor in rural industries exceeded the levels in the cropping sector, indicating overallocation of labor to agriculture (Putterman, 1993; Yang, 2004).

Table 6.3 summarizes a series of government deregulations in the 1980s that became the catalyst for rapid expansion of rural enterprises. These well-coordinated policies reduced farmers' obligations in agriculture and loosened restrictions on labor mobility, prompting farm families to adjust their activities in accordance with relative profit margins. In 1985, grain-sown area at the national level fell by 4 percent, output by 7 percent, cotton-sown area by 26 percent, and cotton output by 34 percent (Sicular, 1988). In contrast, the number of township and village enterprises (TVEs) more than doubled in the same year, and their total labor force increased by 36.5 percent, following a year of strong growth in 1984 (see Table 6.1). These dramatic changes in policies and in farmers' responses marked the beginning of the sustained expansion in non-agricultural activities.

Indeed, the fundamental changes in the distribution of labor force shown in Table 6.1 have been the main feature of the rural labor market in China since the inception of reform (see, for example, de Brauw et al., 2002). Between 1978 and 2004, the rural labor force grew by 1.8 percent per annum, from 306.4 to 487.2 millions. However, the workers in rural non-agricultural activities increased by about 8.5 percent per annum, from 21.8

Table 6.3: Policies and Regulations on Rural Labor Mobility

Year	Policy initiatives
1983	Document No.1 of the Central Committee of the Chinese Communist Party (CCCCP): encouraged the emergence of specialized households in non-agricultural activities, including long-distance transport and marketing of commodities; permitted co-operative ventures and employment of labor (Ash, 1988).
1984	'Report on Creating a New Situation in Commune and Brigade-run Enterprises' by the CCCCP and the State Council: outlined a new development strategy targeting industries as the focus for future rural development; absorbing rural labor was one of the main objectives (Findlay et al., 1994).
1985	Document No.1 of the CCCCP: permitted farmers to work and establish businesses in nearby towns, conditional on financial capability and own provision of food grain. This deregulation officially permitted labor mobility in rural regimes.
1985	State announcement: the change from mandatory production plans and procurement quotas to purchasing contracts negotiable between the state and farmers (Lin, 1992). Implementations varied across regions and over time.

to 181.2 millions. Table 6.1 also shows how the incremental rural labor supply was absorbed during the entire period. The remarkable statistic is that approximately 88 percent of the increment found employment in the nonagricultural sector, with a majority finding jobs in TVEs. Empirical evidence shows that for 1986–95, the rapid expansion of non-farm activities contributed 43.6 percent of the total income growth of farm households for a large sample from Sichuan province (Yang, 2004).

Rural labor movements are not restricted to local jobs. In fact, rural-to-rural mobility, defined as employment of workers in rural villages other than their home villages, represents a rapidly growing component of the rural work force in recent years. According to the study by Lohmar and Rozelle (2001) based on a nationally representative survey of 215 villages, rural-to-rural migrant workers accounted for 1 percent of the rural labor force in 1988 (about 2 million), but grew quickly to 5 percent in 1995 (about 12.9 million). In 1995, the proportion of workers from other villages accounted for 62 percent in rural private enterprises and 46 percent of collective enterprises. Moreover, incoming labor from other villages did not negatively affect the non-farm employment opportunities of local residents or the wages they receive.

2.2. Rural–Urban Migration

The pursuit of the heavy-industry-oriented development strategy in the pre-reform era caused severe segmentation between the rural and urban sectors in China. The results were massive distortions in the factor markets with an excessive concentration of capital in urban areas and of labor in rural areas.[5] Accordingly, on the eve of economic reform in 1978, the urban–rural per capita income ratio reached 3.4 (see Table 6.4). The pressure for rural–urban migration was magnified by rural reform that reduced the demand for farm workers, and it could not be offset, even though it was ameliorated, by the burgeoning TVE sector. When rural reform abolished the communes in 1985 and reduced the role of central planning in agricultural production and sales, *hukou* became the most important legal barrier to rural–urban migration.

Table 6.4:   *Real per Capita Income for Rural and Urban Residents*
            (Units: nominal yuan per year; Ratio: rural=1)

Year	Urban per capita income (1)	Rural per capita income (2)	Ratio of urban to rural income (3)
1978	454	134	3.4
1979	523	160	3.3
1980	560	190	3.0
1981	567	219	2.6
1982	597	261	2.3
1983	620	296	2.1
1984	690	330	2.1
1985	692	358	1.9
1986	784	360	2.2
1987	801	369	2.2
1988	783	370	2.1
1989	778	343	2.3
1990	855	374	2.3
1991	916	378	2.4
1992	989	399	2.5
1993	1073	413	2.6
1994	1133	443	2.6
1995	1179	487	2.4
1996	1217	551	2.2
1997	1252	584	2.1

Source: NBS (various years) adjusted by methods described in Zhang et al. (1994) and sector-specific price deflators.

China has used a household registration system for tax collection and social control purposes for over 2000 years, but its current importance stems from its formal adoption by the Chinese government in 1958, with the issuing of *Regulations on Household Registration of the PRC*. According to the regulation, *hukou* designates a person's legal place of residence and work at the time of his or her birth based as the locality of the mother's registration (Chan and Zhang, 1999). Possession of the appropriate *hukou* (e.g., agricultural versus non-agricultural) also determines one's access to various amenities and social services such as health care, schooling and, until recently, rationed or subsidized food products, which were provided only to urban residents. Therefore, although rural workers had strong incentives to seek employment opportunities with better pay in cities, they had to overcome legal barriers to working in cities.

Because of the inefficiency and pressure for illegal migration associated with labor misallocation, the *hukou* system has been modified to permit more flexibility in reallocation of labor between rural and urban markets. The first major modification occurred in 1988, when the central government initiated a major policy reform that relaxed the controls over rural–urban migration – farmers were permitted to work and to carry on business in cities provided they could secure their own staples (Forbes and Linge, 1990). This regulation gave new opportunities for rural workers to work temporarily in cities, representing improvements over the old system in which college education – and not even marriage – provided the only legitimate access to urban registration (Chan and Zhang, 1999).

In the early 1990s, the end of food rationing made it easier for temporary rural migrants to live in cities because they no longer had to bring food with them from the countryside. They could purchase food directly without securing ration coupons. In 1998, the Ministry of Public Security issued another regulation loosening the control of *hukou* registration – those who moved to join their parents, spouses, and children in cities could also receive urban registration (Cai, 2003).

At of today, *hukou* reform remains incomplete and its progress varies across provinces and even cities. In general, local situations fall into one of three models (Cai, 2003): (1) in over 20 000 small towns, applicants may receive local registration if they have a permanent source of living and housing in the locality; (2) in many medium-size cities, including a few provincial capitals, requirements for gaining *hukou* status have been significantly reduced, some just requiring a long-term work contract; and (3) in a few megacities such as Beijing and Shanghai, obtaining *hukou* remains very difficult. Although the loss of the power to grant or withdraw *hukou* registration may be deemed a threat to the incumbent government's political power, popular pressure to relax *hukou* restrictions work in the opposite direction. In late 2005, the government announced an experimental plan for 11 provinces in which local governments would allow peasants to register, and have the same rights to social benenfits, as urban residents (Kahn, 2005). Another way in which urban–rural segmentation has diminished has been the expansion of existing cities into the surrounding countryside, serving to absorb agricultural surplus labor, and also the emergence of urban agglomerations, such as Shenzhen, from what had been countryside (French, 2004).

When restrictions on rural–urban migration were gradually lifted, the rural labor force responded to economic incentives by seeking employment in urban areas. The majority of rural workers who work temporarily in cities do not have the correct household registration or *hukou* status, and they are called the 'floating population.' Estimates of the size of the 'floating population' over the years vary with definitions based on length of temporary residence and geographic boundaries (across-townships or counties) (Cai, 2003). A research team at the Ministry of Agriculture (MOA, 2001) reported a summary of estimates based on their findings as well as survey results from the National Bureau of Statistics (NBS) and the Ministry of Labor and Social Security (MOLSS). In 1983, the total floating population was approximately 2 million. For the period between 1997 and 2000, the annual estimates for across-township migrants of whom the overwhelming majority were laborers were 38.9 million, 49.4 million, 52.0 million, and 61.4 million. Another independent survey by the MOA puts the estimate at 75.5 million for 2000. Based the 2000 census, Cai (2003) offered an estimates of 77 million rural-to-urban migrants for that year. An important message from these results is that the floating population is a significant component of China's labor force. In 2000, it accounted for about 11 percent of the total labor force in China.

Given the severe distortions at the inception of reform, the subsequent labor movements from the low productivity sector (agriculture) to the higher productivity sector (non-agricultural) became a major source of economic growth in China in the post-reform period. The estimates by the World Bank (1997) suggest that labor mobility contributed 1.5 percentage points to the annual GDP growth rate of 9.4 percent over the period 1978 to 1995; that is, 16 percent of the GDP growth of that period. This result is corroborated by Cai and Wang (1999) who concluded that labor reallocations, including labor transfers among regions, have accounted for 21 percent of annual GDP growth in the post-reform years.

2.3. Evidence of Remaining Distortions and Fragmentation

2.3.1. Problems within rural markets

Although substantial progress has been made in the development of a functioning rural labor market and farm families have enjoyed sustained income growth from diversified sources, several studies present evidence on continued distortions and market fragmentation. One puzzling observation based on available data is a persistent and widening wage gap between rural agricultural and non-agricultural sectors. Based on information from the NBS on the national average wage of TVE workers and estimated earnings per agricultural worker, Meng (2000) presents the wage gap for the period 1984–94. Inconsistent with the narrowing of the differences, the wage ratio of TVE workers to agricultural laborers actually increased from 1.52 in the beginning of the period to 1.94 at the end of the period. The existence of a wage gap may have resulted from multiple factors, such as differences in worker quality across the two sectors and higher costs of living and transportation costs accompanying employment in TVEs. But the widening gap is puzzling, suggesting the influence of significant institutional barriers to labor mobility.

Estimates of MPL between the agricultural and non-agricultural sectors corroborate the above evidence on wages. Using a production function approach, Wang (1997) estimated the MPL for agricultural and non-agricultural sectors, where the non-agricultural sector includes both TVEs and other types of rural industrial enterprises. The gap fell slightly during the period 1980–88 from a ratio of 2.55 in 1980 to 2.29 in 1988, but it started to widen again in 1989, reaching 3.68 in 1992. For the period 1987–92 using provincial level data, Yang and Zhou (1999) also found an increasing gap in agricultural and non-agricultural MPL, reaching 2.01 in 1992.

Gaps in wages and labor productivity across the sectors present indirect evidence of market imperfections in rural China, and direct tests corroborate these conclusions. In the analysis of the household, the separability result states that if factor markets are competitive, the labor actually used in production would be independent of the household size and composition (Bowles and Sicular, 2003). If the independence condition is rejected empirically, it implies non-competitive factor markets. A study by Bowles and Sicular, using panel data covering the years 1990–93 in Shangdong province, rejects the null hypothesis that family labor demand and supply are separable. They conclude that despite considerable progress in market reforms, in early 1990s rural households in China still faced difficulties transferring labor and land optimally given their household size and composition. In a separate study, using 1994 data from Zhejiang province,

Yao (1999) studies wage determination in TVEs and also tests the existence of competitive labor markets. His empirical analysis strongly rejects the competitive hypothesis, suggesting significant administrative controls on wages and employment.

2.3.2.   The two-tier labor markets

Micro empirical analysis has also shown that rural migrants in cities do not receive competitive job and wage offers. Meng and Zhang (2001) conducted a careful study of occupational segregation and wage differentials between urban residents and rural migrants in Shanghai based on two survey data sets containing individual information. They find that rural migrants are treated differently from their urban counterparts in terms of occupational attainment and wages, after controlling for productivity-related characteristics, such as education, gender, and work experience. With regard to occupational attainment, they show that around 22 percent of urban residents who would have been better suited for blue-collar jobs were given white-collar employment, while 6 percent of rural migrants who would have been suitable for white-collar jobs were relegated to blue-collar positions.[6] City residents also enjoyed a large wage premium. Lu and Song (2006) find similar evidence of *hukou*-based discrimination against rural migrants to Tianjin, based on a 2003 survey.

Urban residents as well as state and local governments are largely responsible for the existing situation. As Zhao (2000) points out, 'as urbanites enjoyed more and more government subsidies, better protection, and higher incomes, they also came to believe themselves as being superior to rural people. This became the historical and psychological basis for the discrimination toward rural people.' Arising from these prejudices and institutional factors, the segregation in the urban labor market causes losses of aggregate output and also worsens the economic position of those who are already poor, which in turn may contribute to social instability.

2.3.3.   Rural–urban income differences

Under efficient conditions, earnings for comparable labor across rural and urban areas should be about the same, corresponding to the equalization of marginal labor products across sectors. A key word, of course, is comparability. Rural and urban workers vary in many characteristics, not all observable, so that equality of wages across sectors is unlikely to be achieved in fact or even to be desirable from an efficiency perspective. In China, however, the ratio of urban to rural per capita income is very large indeed, considerably greater than in other developing and transitional economies. We believe that this results from severe barriers to efficient labor flows.

Table 6.4 presents urban and rural per capita total incomes and their ratios for the period 1978–97. The primary data sources are from the Rural and Urban Household Survey collected by China's National Bureau of Statistics with adjustments for (1) information on urban non-wage earnings, including provisions such as housing, health services, in-kind transfers, and various price subsidies, and (2) sector-specific inflation.[7] The earnings in urban areas have been about two to three times higher than the level in rural areas. The urban–rural ratio declined sharply as rural incomes responded to the spread of the Household Responsibility System after 1978 but tended to drift upward between 1985 and 1995 before beginning to decline slowly.[8]

Government policies that push for speedy industrialization by discriminating against agriculture may lead to rural–urban income disparity in developing countries. What should concern scholars and policy makers is the magnitude of the gap in China. Yang and Cai (2003) presents the ratio of non-agricultural to agricultural incomes for a standard worker across 36 countries. The ratios for the majority of the countries are below 1.5, contrasting sharply with the range for China, which generally fluctuates between 2 and 3. More specifically, in 1985, there were only four countries for which average urban earnings were more than twice average rural earnings. There were five countries in 1990 and three countries in 1995 that had ratios of 2 or more. Moreover, the countries with the ratio exceeding 3 were the poorest countries in the world, where market distortions were pervasive. They report that the ratio of non-agricultural to agricultural income in several Eastern European countries in 1995 varied between 1.19 in Poland to 2.01 in Bulgaria, the only country that approached the urban–rural income ratio in China in 1995.

There is evidence that barriers to migration diminished after the mid-1990s. As Poncet (2003b) reports, a major barrier to the integration of China's labor markets occurs at provincial borders. Her investigation on rural–urban migration flows use panel data on movement both within and between provinces extracted from the population censuses of 1990 and 1995. These data permit analysis of migration flows during two periods: 1985–90 and 1990–95. She estimates the 'border effects,' which is the additional cost of migration associated with crossing provincial borders. The study indicates substantial border effects that on average reduce interprovincial migration to less than 10 percent of what it would have been, given the effect of distance-related and other costs of rural–urban migration. The decline in interprovincial border barriers for the two periods, 1985–90 and 1990–95, helped reduce rural–urban income disparity.

Nevertheless, recent information indicates that China's rural–urban income divide is persistent. Sicular et al. (forthcoming) finds that in the year 2002, the mean household disposable per capita income differential was approximately 2.27 expressed as an urban/rural ratio; this is a measure that adjusts for spatial differences in the cost of living across regions. Although caution is required in making cross-country comparisons, these figures suggest that the fragmentation of China's rural–urban markets has been very serious indeed. Liu (2006) demonstrates that even when rural migrants manage to obtain an urban *hukou* direct and indirect effects persist, because the rural migrants still are affected by their lack of schooling and, equally serious, their lower return to schooling than that enjoyed by long-time urban *hukou* holders.

Despite the large absolute number of migrants in China, interregional movement is much smaller than might be expected in comparison to what it would be if relocation were unrestricted by existing legal and economic barriers. As Johnson (2003) reports, interprovincial migration in China between the 1990 and 2000 census was about one-fourth the magnitude of interstate migration in the United States. Given the immense regional labor-market disequilibrium that characterize today's China, a more telling benchmark is the United States during its period of greatest rural–urban population relocation, which was ten times the magnitude of China's migration flows today, relative to population.

Before going further, we address a possible objection to our focus on labor flows, namely, that capital flows are a substitute for human migration. In a perfectly homogeneous environment with no fixed geographical factors or agglomeration economies or diseconomies, equality of marginal products could be achieved by appropriate movement of either labor or capital. Moreover, it is well-known that in the classic Heckscher–Ohlin framework, interregional trade would substitute for interregional migration in equalizing marginal products. Poncet (2003b) considers this possibility for China and finds that the conditions under which migration and trade would substitute for each other do not hold. Indeed, Poncet finds that migration and trade are complementary and reducing interregional barriers to trade within China increase, rather than reduce, the potential gains from freer labor migration. In a related study, Au and Henderson (2002) model and estimate urban agglomeration economies in a production-function framework for 206 cities in China. Their estimates yield a familiar ∩-shaped relationship between city size and productivity, with the left-hand side being much steeper than the right-hand side. They find that barriers against migration to China's urban areas have resulted in a much higher proportion of cities being undersized, resulting in substantial productivity losses. The importance of 'under-urbanization' for rural–urban income gaps in China is confirmed in Chang and Brada (2006).

2.3.4. Rural–urban productivity differences

While income differences are indicators of the relative economic welfare of rural and urban residents, they may not accurately reflect the efficiency of resource allocation when wages are not determined through competitive mechanisms. Then, direct measurements of labor productivity are necessary. This is probably the case in China, so labor productivity estimates are needed to provide direct information on the sectoral misallocation of labor.

Several studies have found that the marginal productivity of labor (MPL) in state industries far exceeds the level in rural industries, and that the latter also far exceeds the level in agriculture. Yang and Zhou (1999) presents estimates of MPL for the three sectors using Chinese provincial data for the period between 1987 and 1992. They show that within this time period, the MPL in state industries was about 15 to 16 times of that in agriculture, and the MPL in rural industries was about 25 to 100 percent higher than in agriculture. These results are corroborated by other studies using more recent data. For instance, based on data covering the period 1987–98, Cai et al. (2002) present evidence that the ratio of agricultural labor productivity to industrial productivity ranges from 12 to 17 percent across the eastern, central and western regions in 1998. The productivity differences across the sectors are very large indeed.[9]

The evidence of large productivity differences across the sectors implies the existence of seriously fragmented factor in China. Consequently, as the model implies, if labor was reallocated from the low marginal productivity areas to the high marginal productivity areas, there would be gains in aggregate output without utilizing additional resources. A relevant policy question is: if more labor is transferred from agriculture to rural and state industries, how much would output increase?[10]

We have conducted a policy experiment based on partial equilibrium analysis of reallocating 1, 5, and 10 percent of the agricultural labor force to rural and state industries, with an equal percentage split of the total allocated to the two destination sectors. Each sector is given its own production function: rural and state industries use labor, capital and intermediate factors as inputs, while agriculture uses labor, land and machinery with weather also affecting its production. The production structures and parameter values are taken directly from the estimates made by Yang and Zhou (1999) and corresponding variable values for the Chinese provinces in 1992 are used in the policy experiment.[11] The policy experiment shows that improvements in the allocation of labor based on their productivity across sectors would realize substantial output gains. When labor leaves agriculture, output in that sector will fall, but by much less than the output in rural and state industries will increase. Thus, the experiments based on three hypothetical percentages of labor transfers would result in 0.66, 3.09, and 5.82 percent gains in aggregate output – substantial indeed. These results are supported in an independent study by Zhang and Tan (2003). In their framework consisting of four sectors (agriculture, urban industry, urban service, and rural non-farm production), the transfer of 1, 5, and 10 percent of labor out of agriculture and reallocating them to the other industries would result in 0.7, 3.3, and 6.4 percentage increases in the aggregate output. In a recent, unpublished paper, Fleisher, Li and Zhao (2006) show that if labor were reallocated among provinces to equate MPL in all provinces in the year 2003, per capita GDP would have increased approximately 7 percent.

However, these results do not necessarily imply that output gains can be realized instantly from labor reallocation, especially when there is unemployment and underemployment in the urban/state sector. Soft urban demand conditions for rural workers may affect the timing of realizing potential output gains. Moreover, our aggregate partial equilibrium analysis does not provide insights into the micro-level management of the urban/state sector. The ownership structure of urban enterprises, their incentive mechanisms, the substitutability of productive factors and the training of new employees all affect the capacity to absorb rural workers. The provision of city infrastructure could be another potential constraint.

2.4. Institutional Barriers and Policy Challenges

Despite major improvements in the institutional and policy environment, there still exist serious barriers to an efficient operation of labor markets in rural China. Although land rental markets have begun to emerge (e.g., Kung, 2002), under the HRS farm families have land-use rights but not rights of alienation. If they permanently leave agriculture, farmers must return the land to local authorities and consequently give up a stream of potential land earnings in the future (Yang, 1997). This pecuniary cost reduces labor mobility, as it raises the expected future wages that rural families require from their prospective destination when moving away from agriculture. As a result, Chinese farmers have less incentive to engage in family migration and are more willing to split family labor supply between farm and non-farm employment. This division of time is a second-best solution under the existing land arrangements that takes advantage of higher nonagricultural wages and avoids the loss in land values, as Yang (1997) argues. This is a factor that creates differential rural–urban labor earnings, as well as a wage–productivity gap between farming and nonfarming sectors, as documented earlier.

Moreover, China's farmland arrangements under the HRS obligate the farm household to deliver a part of its grain output to the state at quantities and prices specified by the government. Although there exist other land tenure systems, an overwhelming majority of the rural households have responsibility land (e.g., Brandt et al., 2002). When rental markets are restricted, the obligation of delivering procurement quota would reduce the flexibility of family labor allocation to alternative employment. In particular, the grain quota policies could create a wage gap between rural agricultural and nonagricultural sectors, as section 4.1 points out. Hence, further reforms in grain procurement systems and the property rights of rural land are needed.

Local protection is also a significant issue. For instance, a rural worker currently employed in the enterprise of another village does not receive an allocation of homestead or other housing arrangements, even if the job is permanent, thus imposing high costs on the migrants. In addition, workers from a village often earn much higher wages than outsiders after controlling for productivity-related characteristics (Yao, 1999). Serious segmentation still exists in rural labor markets (Fleisher and Wang, 2003a and 2003b). Recently, the Development Research Center of China's State Council conducted a nationwide survey of rural and urban enterprises on local protection (DRC, 2003). In regard to the forms of protection frequently used by local authorities, 'intervening in the labor market' tops the long list of 42 varieties. More specifically, this practice takes the form of 'giving priority to employing local citizens,' and 57.7 percent of the enterprises surveyed indicate that their local governments engage in such practices. The policy challenge lies in the design of incentive structures of local government in employment and wage determination that would lead to increased labor-market efficiency.

While reducing mobility barriers is important for factor market development, an alternative approach of raising rural labor productivity is to create non-farm job opportunities within commuting distance of village residents (Johnson, 2002). As Johnson suggests, the required capital investment of moving rural workers and their families to urban jobs is enormous – much higher than creating non-farm jobs in rural regions. This is because capital investment is required not only for the construction of housing but also the public costs of creating new urban communities, such as roads, public utilities and schools. In contrast, large savings are possible if jobs are created near the homes of rural workers. Johnson also points out that, in order to make villages attractive places to live, it is necessary to provide basic amenities to rural residents, including tap water, home toilets, affordable electricity and quality access to television signals. Other complementary policies include increasing educational investment and raising the quality of rural schools. Unraveling roles of schooling in the rural–urban nexus is an interesting challenge. For example de Brauw and Giles (2006) demonstrate that increased urban job opportunities feedback negatively to schooling attainment in rural communities, while Liu (forthcoming) shows that higher levels of community schooling attainment in rural communities increase the likelihood that individual rural residents will choose local non-farm employment over migration – evidence of a positive externality.

The lack of correct *hukou* subjects the 'floating population' not only to the risk of various arbitrary actions by local authorities carried out in the name of preserving social order and public safety, but also to significant economic costs in the form of fees, work permits, bribes and so on. Perhaps the most significant example is schooling. Although national and local laws require that the municipality of residence (whether or not one's *hukou* grants permanent residence rights) is responsible for providing nine years of primary schooling for each child, in practice this right is often denied. The result is that migrant families must pay fees ranging from 3000 to 30 000 yuan per year per child to have their children admitted to the regular school system or cooperate with other migrant families in providing their own schools and teachers. Even so, newspapers often contain reports of migrant schools being torn down by public authorities on grounds that they provide inferior schooling or are safety hazards (which are probably true claims; see e.g., Xie, 2003).

None of what we have said is meant to deny that there are in fact costs of providing public services for migrants, and these costs must be borne by the workers themselves, by their employers, by government, or some combination of them. The main problem at present appears to be that current laws and regulations frequently militate against the efficient allocation of labor, and where there are provisions to ensure the equitable treatment of migrants, they are often not incentive compatible with the goals of local governments.

3.   URBAN LABOR MARKETS

China's urban market reform began late and proceeded slowly relative to the sweeping rural reform. Within the urban sector commodity and goods markets were liberalized earlier and at a faster pace than labor markets.[12] On its face, the liberalization of commodity and goods markets would seem to have made ownership reform a simpler matter in urban areas than in rural areas, where procurement of essential inputs (e.g., electric power) militated in favor of enterprises retaining some relationship with local governments.

However, urban market reform involves complex structural change in ownership along with political sensitivity, which introduced their own complications (see Korzec, 1992).

Urban labor arrangements under central planning included labor allocation by labor bureaus; *hukou* (residence permit) required for housing, food subsidy, schooling, and health benefits; *dangan* (personal file) under the control of work unit or educational institution with its transfer required for a new job; incentives determined by permanent job tenure through retirement (the 'iron rice bowl'); and wage determination according to the 'wage grid' (Meng, 2000). All of these institutional arrangements imposed severe limitations on job mobility, and worker incentives to move were restricted further by provision of social security and even the education of children by the work units (SOEs or urban collectives).

3.1. The Need for Urban Labor-Market Reform

There is ample evidence that China's urban labor markets were inefficient under planning and continue to be so in the reform era (Korzec, 1992; Meng and Kidd, 1997). Big cities, coastal provinces, state enterprises, and production workers were favored over smaller urban areas, the interior, and non-traditional state enterprises well beyond the end of the Cultural Revolution. As a consequence, the benefits of China's exceptional growth have eluded large segments of the population, especially in the interior. Wage policies under planning in China (initially taken from the Soviet schemes, and also applied to much of Eastern Europe) aimed to promote income equality in the industrial sector by raising the wages of lower-skilled workers above their marginal products while severely restricting the pay of higher-skilled workers. Not only did these policies discourage individual enterprises from minimizing costs, they also seriously impeded rural–urban and interregional migration, preventing labor from flowing to its most productive use.

3.2. Urban Labor-Market Reform Policies

The gradualism has characterized almost all of China's transition from planning, also adequately describes the liberalization of urban labor markets. The labor contract system, which represents a relaxation of the job security provided under the 'iron rice bowl' arrangements, was first introduced in 1983 to cover new entrants to the state and collective enterprises. Incentive reform was at the heart of the transition to the HRS in agriculture that spread with a lag to rural enterprises and then to urban enterprises.

By 1995, 93 percent of SOE employees were under contract (Meng, 2000, pp. 81–2, Table 6.1). These reforms transferred some autonomy in hiring decisions from planners to enterprises, but left planners great scope to influence regional employment targets (Meng and Kidd, 1997). Wage reforms introducing various profit-sharing arrangements were introduced beginning in the late 1970s. However, the degree to which various bonus schemes actually provided better incentives to reduce shirking and increase worker productivity is open to question (Meng and Kidd, 1997). A managerial responsibility system was introduced later and described by Grove et al. (1995); subsequently, management acquired additional wage discretion (Xu, 2000). Fleisher and Wang (2001) and Knight and Li (2003) do find some evidence that wage-setting behavior goes beyond simple profit-sharing and incorporates some incentive-wage effects. Their data pertain to both rural and urban enterprises for the late 1980s and in the 1990s through 1999.

3.3.   Has Reform Been Effective?

There is ample evidence in published research to establish the inefficiency of labor allocation in China during the 1980s and into the early 1990s. At the firm level, Fleisher et al. (1996) provide evidence of gross discrepancies between wages and MPL in a major manufacturing industry. Fleisher and Wang (2003a and 2003b) corroborate this pattern in both rural and urban enterprises under various ownership forms through the early 1990s. These studies not only showed that college-trained workers were grossly underpaid relative to their marginal products, there is also considerable evidence from national surveys that the private returns to schooling in urban China were much smaller than in comparable transition and emerging economies as well as in advanced market economies. Since approximately 1995, however, returns to schooling have increased markedly in urban China (Zhang et al., 2005). Fleisher and Wang (2003c) also discuss this issue and cite numerous published and unpublished studies that corroborate the low return to schooling in China since reform. Fleisher, Hu and Li (2006) find significant underpayment of workers relative to their marginal contributions to production, and the degree of underpayment is greater for highly educated workers.

Although possession of an urban *hukou* makes it vastly easier for workers to move from job to job, mobility within the urban sector remains limited. Moreover, workers who have transferred from rural to urban *hukou* status are unable to entirely overcome the effects and stigma of their rural backgrounds (Liu, 2006). Generally, workers who are qualified for high-level technical and 'white-collar' jobs, particularly through schooling at the college level, are eligible for urban residence in most locations (Chan and Zhang, 1999). There is evidence that this greater potential mobility has begun to pay off for the better educated. Zhang et al. (2005) show that returns to schooling, particularly for college graduates, have risen sharply; and that, by 2001, returns in state-owned enterprises approached those in non-public enterprises (e.g., the private and jointly-owned sector), whereas, until the early 1990s, returns had been far higher in the non-public sector, albeit low by international standards (Zhou, 2000; Fleisher and Wang, 2003c).

Without barriers to movement, workers would seek jobs where pay is highest, other things equal, and firms would tend to locate their production where pay is lowest, and such adjustments would tend to reduce productivity and income differentials. There is evidence that even at the local level, interfirm worker mobility within China remains limited. Appleton et al. (2002) reports that by the end of 1999, *xia gang* workers laid off from SOEs, urban collectives, and local governments far outnumbered the 'official' (registered) unemployed, contributing to a de facto urban unemployment rate of more than 8 percent. Those most likely to be laid off and also to experience the longest spells of unemployment are the less educated, older workers, and female workers. The median spell of unemployment (including non-completed spells) was 10 months; the mean was 18 months. By comparison, in the United States from 1980 through 1993, the average annual completed duration of unemployment ranged from 10 to 14 weeks, while that in Canada ranged from 14 to 20 weeks (Baker et al., 1998). Giles et al. (2005) use data from the 2002 follow-up to the 2001 China Urban Labor Survey for five cities (Beijing, Wuhan, Shenyang, Fuzhou and Xian) to construct an internationally comparable measure of urban unemployment. They report an unemployment rate of 14.0 percent for the cities in their sample. They use their results to estimate the unemployment experience of permanent urban residents for the period 1996 through September 2002 and deduce an increase in unemployment from 6.1 percent to 11.1 percent, about 2.75 times larger than the official data suggest. They show that permanent residents have higher unemployment than migrants. They emphasize that official procedures for measuring unemployment lag far behind the liberalization of labor markets, and that there is need for statistical measures to catch up to market reality.

Further evidence of lack of urban labor mobility is provided by Knight and Li (2003). They use data relating to 1995 and 1999 from two urban household surveys conducted by the Chinese Academy of Social Sciences and the National Bureau of Statistics. The surveys contain worker-provided information on firm profitability and other characteristics. They find that interfirm wage differences increased during the period among all workers, more so among low-paid workers than among high-paid workers. They infer that interfirm mobility of workers was low. Employees of loss-making firms evidently preferred to retain their jobs, accepting wage cuts rather than seeking other employment. This behavior is eminently understandable in the context of China's poorly developed social safety net (Dong and Ye, 2003).

Evidence of inefficient distribution of human resources across regions abounds. Fleisher and Chen (1997) provide evidence of immense interregional productivity gaps among Chinese provinces in the 1980s. Moreover change seems to be working in the wrong direction. Jones et al. (2003) report that among 200 cities in China through 1999, policies that, a priori, are likely to raise productivity, such as openness to trade (e.g., special economic zones) and foreign direct investment, have also contributed to diverging income growth rates, thus raising income inequality. This contributes to pressures on the cities to absorb the millions of rural residents who seek urban jobs. Although there is evidence that regional segmentation has diminished since the mid-1990s (Poncet, 2003a and 2003b), it is still an important force limiting China's growth.

A comparison of China with the United States is instructive in regard to regional labor-market integration. Song et al. (2000) show that, in 1991, the coefficient of variation of per-capita GDP among 476 Chinese cities was 0.809, while the coefficient of variation of per-capita income was 0.259. In the late 1990s, the coefficient of variation of output per worker among 100 United States metropolitan statistical areas was 0.161 and the coefficient of variation of per capita income was 0.149 (Sprint, 2003). In 2001, the coefficient of variation of per capita personal income among 318 United States metropolitan statistical areas was 0.199 (authors' calculations from Newman, 2003). There are two remarkable features in this comparison of China with the United States. One is that urban per-capita GDP in China had four times as much variation relative to its mean as that in the US. The other is that urban per capita income in China indicates more regional inequality than in the US, albeit far less inequality of income than of production per capita.

3.4. Unemployment Insurance, Health Insurance, and Pensions

Enterprise reform in urban labor markets has outpaced social reform that would facilitate the reallocation of workers from declining to growing enterprises. As noted above, even such basics as the measurement of unemployment is very undeveloped in China (Giles et al., 2005). Labor resources released as SOEs and urban collectives seek to survive under increasingly hard budget constraints are wasted to society and suffer increasingly difficult economic hardships if they do not find new employment. These unemployed and disenfranchised workers are a major source of political unrest as is widely known. But perhaps an equally serious distortion results when employed workers, observing the risk in seeking to change jobs, remain employed in low-productivity firms when they could increase their productivity and potential earnings under alternative employment. For China to sustain its remarkable growth record, labor resources released as enterprise efficiency increases must be transferred, through markets, to productive employment. We next consider the remaining policy issues inherent in labor-market reform.

As emphasized by Appleton et al. (2002) and Giles et al. (2005), serious urban unemployment is a relatively recent phenomenon in China. While not directly comparable, the Great Depression of the 1930s created social disruption and unrest associated with mass layoffs and involuntary unemployment that was accommodated poorly under a variety of state programs. Federal legislation leading to the establishment of national coordination of state unemployment policies dates to that era in the United States. Similarly, the unemployment crisis in China is forcing the Government to formulate policies to deal with this explosive issue. The situation illustrates the 'crash-then-law' development of legislation emphasized by Chen (2003). Dong and Ye (2003) show clearly that unemployment insurance as a portable right available to all workers under clearly specified conditions does not exist in China. There is a hodgepodge of local and provincial arrangements that are proffered in varying fashions primarily to those holding *hukou* in the community providing the insurance. The principal burden of providing benefits falls on a combination of semi-private insurance companies funded by enterprise payments, the enterprises themselves, and local governments. Ironically, the Central Government opted out of guaranteeing unemployment benefits to most workers in the mid-1980s, as urban reform began to take off. China faces immense challenges in shouldering the fiscal burden of paying the government's share of unemployment benefits that result from the continued movement toward greater efficiency in government enterprises, and in dealing with the social unrest attributable to laid-off and retired workers whose nominal claims for unemployment compensation and pensions are eroded by financial inability and/or lack of will to fund them (Appleton et al., 2002).

Appleton et al. (2002) find no impact of the size of unemployment benefits on the length of unemployment. They interpret this empirical result (which is at odds with the estimated impact of unemployment compensation on unemployment duration in most studies) to be evidence of the purely involuntary nature of unemployment in China and also to the unattractiveness of the size of unemployment benefits relative to the wages of employed workers. They also find that government employment agencies and former work units remain by far the most important channels through which unemployed workers seek and find new jobs. Informal channels appear to be used much less frequently, and when they are, prove to be less effective. One reason for this appears to be that when a work unit or government agency bears some financial responsibility for unemployment compensation, there is greater incentive to aid in the job-search process. Perhaps a lesson can be drawn from this observation in designing improved incentives for the relocation and reemployment of workers who become unemployed through layoff or for other reasons.

Migrant workers without urban *hukou* face a different set of constraints. Many migrants face unemployment whether or not they leave their rural homes, given severe land constraints in much of China's countryside. In other words, even though rural 'employment' may be in principle the alternative for unemployed rural–urban migrants, the de facto alternative for those without either a regular job or urban *hukou* is likely to be subsistence on the urban fringe in migrant 'villages,' where residents make do as best they can, for example, as self-employed trash collectors and trash pickers in urban garbage dumps (Beja et al., 1999). Although such subsistence activity might theoretically be viewed as a 'solution' to the urban unemployment problem among migrant workers who literally find themselves between rocks and a hard place, there are genuine economic and social problems of external costs. Those costs manifest themselves in terms of health problems, schooling issues, and the social unrest that government officials know they cannot ignore without serious threat to social stability and their own survival. This is clearly an area in which rural land policies, provision of health care, and housing policy intersect.

4.   THE IMPACT OF THE WTO

China's accession to membership in the World Trade Organization will surely have important effects on the labor force and labor market as production of goods and services becomes more closely aligned with China's comparative advantages. Given that comparative advantages will be identified with a lag through market signals, we can only anticipate with uncertainty what labor force reallocations are likely to occur. Further uncertainty arises from the unknown course of the yuan. Will China accede to pressure to float its currency in relation to the dollar and euro? If some flexibility is allowed in foreign-exchange markets, in which direction will the yuan move? Although it may be 'common knowledge' that the yuan is grossly undervalued, some say by as much as 40 percent, how certain can we be that floating it will be sufficient for it to move toward purchasing-power parity with the world's major hard currencies? If China were to fully free up its foreign currency markets, might not 'capital flight' balance or even exceed the impact of net foreign investment? (Gunter, 2004).

Perhaps the most interesting and important question is the impact of foreign trade liberalization on the rural–urban disequilibrium, surely China's major deviation from optimal factor allocation. In the short run, China is viewed as labor-rich and land-poor, with both labor productivity and earnings in agriculture and rural areas in general being much lower than in urban areas. An implication of China's intensive labor endowment is that agricultural production should shift away from grain production toward labor-intensive crops; access to world markets should be favorable toward exports of commodities that benefit from intensive cultivation (Huang et al., 2000; Johnson, 2000; Lin, 2000). There is evidence that this shift has already taken place. China has displaced the United States as a major exporter of many fruits and vegetables not only to other Asian markets, but also to the United States itself. For example, garlic imports from Hong Kong and China grew from less than 1 million pounds in 2000 to 112 million pounds in 2005 (Barrionuevo, 2006). Moreover, while rising domestic income levels will reinforce the trend toward increased domestic consumption of luxury fruits and vegetables and dairy products, WTO will increase foreign competitive pressure on domestic producers in other areas.[13] Huang et al. (forthcoming) forecast that the net effect of these opposing forces on China's rural households will be positive, but unequally distributed. Households in the western region, where agricultural products have been more heavily protected from foreign competition, are most likely to suffer under WTO liberalization, for example. In a similar vein, Hertel and Zhai (2006) report simulation results based on a household-disaggregated, recursively dynamic CGE model to calculate the impact of current factor market distortions and WTO entry. They emphasize that foreign-trade liberalization will be generally beneficial to China's workers, but that for the benefits to be broadly shared, foreign-trade liberalization must be accompanied by factor market reforms. In particular, Hertel and Zhai show that without reform of rural land property rights, which would reduce the opportunity cost of rural–urban migration, and *hukou* regulation, China's rural workers will continue to lag behind urban, industrial workers in sharing the benefits of China's economic growth.

Within the services and manufacturing sectors, we may expect both direct and indirect effects. Direct effects come from competition with imports and from new firms opening within China. There will obviously be changes in the mix of ownership categories, with an increase in foreign-owned firms that provide further competition for the state-owned group.

Chen et al. (2003) corroborate the findings of Knight and Li (2003), that there exist significant barriers to interfirm mobility in China, particularly among firms of different ownerships types. This has important implications for the degree to which currently employed workers will easily transfer to new enterprises. Labor-market effects are likely to be concentrated within particular industries. For example, WTO accession is likely to put increasing pressure on major SOEs in the areas of financial services (e.g., Yeo, 2003). Direct effects will come as foreign-owned firms enter the financial services markets; demand will increase for domestic experts familiar with the language, local customs, and legislation. Some of these new employees may come from Chinese educated and currently working abroad, while others come from SOEs, which will be forced to meet the competition with higher pay or suffer loss of their most valuable workers, in turn forcing them to reduce their size and scope. Membership in the WTO will raise the presence of foreign-owned firms. If workers feel that taking jobs in foreign-invested enterprises risks the loss of traditional benefits available from SOEs, there will be less incentive to leave protected employment voluntarily.

Provision of an improved social safety net will permit labor markets to adjust more rapidly and the economy to reap greater benefits from the potential influx of new enterprises under WTO liberalization. Indirect effects will come, for example, from the lending policies of foreign-owned financial institutions. We may speculate that, if lending channels to township and village enterprises are enhanced both by the presence of more efficient financial institutions and/or that competitive pressure changes the performance of China's Rural Financial Cooperatives (Xie, 2003), rural non-agricultural employment opportunities will be enhanced.

In manufacturing, the entry of foreign-invested firms producing both for domestic consumption and for exports is predicted to expand sharply, e.g., in the automobile industry (Landler, 2003). To the extent that Volkswagen, General Motors, Daimler–Chrysler, Nissan, and others introduce their management skills and technology to China's low-cost labor, job opportunities and wages in urban manufacturing will increase. A recent example of projected export growth for China's auto industry is noted in an article, 'Daimler and Chery of China Planning Subcompact for US' (Bradsher, 2006). How these forces play out China's labor markets will depend largely on the remaining barriers, *hukou* and otherwise, to interfirm job changes and intercity and interregional labor mobility. To share in the benefits from greater employment opportunities, current employees of SOEs need to be able to take the new and better jobs without totally exposing themselves to the risk of unprotected unemployment, losing all health-insurance coverage, and so on.

5. CONCLUSIONS

We have sketched developments in labor-market reform over almost three decades in China. Although a fully functioning labor market approaching the flexibility of those of the major industrial nations remains to be achieved, there have been major successes. Among the most important accomplishments, there has been a gradual removal of the planning framework in the organization of labor within and among enterprises. The dominant role of rural communes in agriculture has disappeared, and state and collective enterprises in the urban sector are diminishing in their relative importance, both in terms of output and employment. Multiple forms of ownership and enterprise organization have emerged, and the role of private, foreign and joint-venture companies has been growing and accelerating with China's accession into the WTO. Moreover, there have been crucial and fundamental changes in work incentives for rural families, and for both managers and employees of enterprises. These include the removal of lifetime security for urban workers and the introduction of wage and managerial contract schemes more compatible with profit-maximization and cost-minimization. State-owned enterprises are increasingly subject to hard budget constraints. In addition, there has been gradual but incomplete movement toward integrated product and labor markets.

Nevertheless, there are still serious obstacles that stand in the way of smoothly functioning labor markets and often exacerbate the growing income inequality attributable to the movement toward a market economy. Most significant, *hukou* remains a critical barrier to rural–urban and inter-city integration. There is much evidence of village, city, and provincial border effects attributable both to *hukou* restrictions and to local protectionism along with the inability or unwillingness of the Central Government to enforce existing laws and regulations. In addition, there remain barriers to changing the ownership structure of firms, especially from state-owned and collective to private ownership, as well as acquisitions across city and regional boundaries, due to major weaknesses and incomplete reforms in the social safety net: in particular, unemployment insurance, health insurance, and the enterprise-based pension system. Another major deterrent is the inadequate development of complementary markets, particularly the housing market.

Given these perspectives, what are the key areas for further reform? We emphasize two that have high policy significance: local protection and coordination of reform. First, if local protectionism is to be reduced and ultimately eliminated, the Central Government must understand the incentives that local and provincial governments need to accept nationwide laws and regulations. In this regard, there is a serious need for research to identify relevant interest groups and the true objectives of local governments. We need to know who are the potential winners and losers from such specific reforms as the removal of mobility restrictions. Only by understanding the answers to these questions can incentive compatible rules be designed that will induce the desired responses from the involved parties. The Government should be prepared to compensate losers appropriately to overcome resistance to existing and new laws and regulations. The benefits derived from successful policy reform would provide incentives for all parties to implement the new rules and promote more efficient labor market institutions.

Second, labor market reform must be coordinated, because sensible deregulation in one area often creates the need for reform in other areas. An outstanding example is the need to coordinate reform of the social safety net with redeployment of SOE workers and reform of housing markets. In rural markets, procurement obligations and individuals' freedom to choose their place and type of job must be liberalized. Further, these policies affect, and are affected by, land tenure reform and will have important effects on urban labor markets through migration. The synergy created by coordinated reforms will amplify the benefits accruing to the labor sector and to the entire economy.

NOTES

1. This chapter was initially prepared for the Conference on 'China's Market Reforms' organized by Stanford Center for International Development, Stanford University. Subsequently, it was revised to include the up-to-date literature and anlaysis on recent changes in China's labor markets. We would like to thank Nicholas Hope, John Pencavel, Xiaojun Wang and the participants at the Stanford Conference as well as the Chinese Economists Society meetings for valuable comments and suggestions on earlier versions of this chapter. We are responsible for all remaining errors.
2. The analysis of rural labor markets presented here draws heavily from Fleisher and Yang (2006). However, this chapter extends the coverage to urban labor markets and explores the implications of China's accession to the WTO for the labor force.
3. The objective of this strategy was to achieve rapid industrialization by extracting agricultural surplus for capital accumulation in industries and for urban-based subsidies. See Knight and Song (1999) and Yang and Cai (2003) for up-to-date descriptions of the origin and evolution of China's rural–urban divide.
4. Quota prices for grain, oil crops, cotton, sugar crops, and pork were increased by an average of 17.1 percent. In addition, the premium paid for above-quota sale of grain and oil crops was raised from 30 percent to 50 percent of the quota prices. For details of these price changes and agricultural price adjustments in the following years of reforms, see Sicular (1988).
5. In 1978, the urban sector employed 95 million workers while the rural sector had a labor force of approximately 306 million. In contrast, the total value of fixed assets in the state-owned enterprises (primarily urban) counted for RMB 449 billion while the value of the fixed assets in agriculture was only about RMB 95 billion (NBS 1993; Perkins and Yusuf, 1984). These numbers indicate a capital/labor ratio of RMB 4726 per urban worker and a

ratio of RMB 310 per rural worker. The capital concentration in the urban sector is more than 15 times that of the rural sector.

6. In their study, white-collar jobs include professional, managerial and clerical employment, while blue-collar jobs include employment in wholesale trade, retail services, construction, production and other occupations. The percentage of rural migrants in white-collar jobs is 3.36, while the predicted value is 9.25; the corresponding percentages for urban residents are 36.69 and 14.49.

7. See Yang and Cai (2003) for detailed descriptions for making these adjustments. Three specific points are worth noting: (1) the methods used for computing urban non-wage incomes are based on a study by researchers at the NBS (Zhang et al., 1994). The lack of information on non-wage incomes in recent years makes the period end in 1997. On the rural side, incomes include value of products for own consumption. (2) In absence of area-specific deflators, aggregate consumer price indices for rural and urban sectors are applied to compute real incomes. (3) Per capita income differs from per worker earning. But because of limitations on data, we are not able to adjust for dependency ratios to compute per worker earning. Recent data (NBS, 2001) indicate that the number of dependants per rural laborer were 1.74, 1.64, 1.56 and 1.53 in years 1985, 1990, 1995 and 2000, which do not differ greatly from the comparable numbers of 1.81, 1.77, 1.73 and 1.86 for urban employee. Therefore the per capita income gap approximates sectoral per worker earning.

8. See Yang and Cai (2003) for analysis of policy factors that may have influenced the changes in rural–urban disparity over time.

9. These results are consistent with other empirical studies. See Nolan and White (1984) for estimates on output per worker in agriculture and state industries and Meng (2000) for productivity gap between rural agricultural and non-agricultural sectors.

10. In principle, one could carry out similar exercises of computing marginal productivity of capital, comparing their magnitudes across the sectors, and inferring output gains from optimally reallocating capital. But for empirical analysis this approach is not feasible because in Chinese official statistics different measures of capital are used across the sectors – number of tractors is a common measure of capital in agriculture, while fixed asset is used for industry. They are not directly comparable. Consequently we focus the attention to the consequences of labor reallocation.

11. As much as we would like to use more recent data for policy analysis, the choice of time period is constrained by multiple factors. Although the NBS has released input–output data for all three sectors since 1986, starting in 1993, the statistical yearbooks have changed the reports of several economic variables for rural enterprises, such as replacing gross sales information with value–added measures. Therefore, we conduct the policy experiment for 1992 because of the availability of parameter values from Yang and Zhou (1999) for that year and issues of data consistency.

12. Interregional integration of these markets across provincial boundaries remains incomplete (Poncet 2003a).

13. A quick Google search for two topics, 'China exports apples,' and 'China's dairy industry' yields on the first pages of results alone, references to reputable sources that emphasize both the effects of increased domestic demand, increased import competition, and increased exports due to changing agriculture specialization.

REFERENCES

Appleton, S., J. Knight, L. Song and Q. Xia (2002), 'Labor retrenchment in China: determinants and consequences', *China Economic Review*, **13** (2–3), 252–76.

Ash, R.F. (1988), 'The evolution of agricultural policy', *China Quarterly*, **116**, 529–55.

Au, Chun-Chung and J. Vernon Henderson (2003), 'Estimating net urban agglomeration economics with an application to China', manuscript, Providence, RI: Department of Economics, Brown University.

Baker, Michael, Miles Corak and Andrew Heisz (1998), 'The labour market dynamics of unemployment rates in Canada and the United States', *Canadian Public Policy*, **24**(s1), 72–89.

Barrionuevo, Alexei (2006), 'Imports spurring push to subsidize produce', *New York Times*, December 3.

Beja, Jean P., Michael Bonnin, Xiaoshuang Feng and Tang Can (1999), 'How social strata come to be formed: Social differentiation among the migrant peasants of Henan Village in Peking', *China Perspectives*, **23**(May–June).

Bowles, Audra J. and Terry Sicular (2003), 'Moving toward markets? Labor allcoation in rural China', *Journal of Development Economics*, **71**, 561–83.

Brandt, Loren, Jikun Huang, Guo Li and Scott Rozelle (2002), 'Land rights in China: A comparative review of the facts, fictions, and issues', *China Journal*, **47**, 67–97.

Bradsher, Keith (2006), 'Daimler and Chery of China planning subcompact for US', *New York Times*, 4 October.

Cai, Fang (2003), 'Removing the barriers to labor mobility: Labor market development and its attendant reforms', paper presented at the World Bank Workshop on National Market Integration in China, Beijing.

Cai, Fang and Dewen Wang (1999), 'Sustainability and labor contribution of economic growth in China', *Journal of Economic Research* (in Chinese), **10**, 62–8.

Cai, Fang, Dewen Wang and D.U. Yang (2002), 'Regional disparity and economic growth in China: The impact of labor market distortions', *China Economic Review*, **13**, 197–212.

Chan, Kam Wing and Li Zhang (1999), 'The *Hukou* system and rural–urban migration: Processes and changes', *The China Quarterly*, **160**(1), 818–55.

Chang, Gene Hsin and Josef C. Brada (2006), 'The paradox of China's growing under-urbanization', *Economic Systems*, **30**(1), 24–40.

Chen, Zhiwu (2003), 'Capital markets and legal development: The Chinese case', *China Economic Review*, **14**(4), 451–72.

Chen, Yi, S. Démurger and Martin Fournier (2003), 'Wage differentials and ownership structure in Chinese enterprises', manuscript, Clermont-Ferrand, France: CERDI, University of the Auvergne.

Clarke, Donald C. (2003), 'Corporate governance in China: An overview', *China Economic Review*, **14**(4), 494–507.

de Brauw, Alan and John Giles (2006), 'Migrant opportunity and the educational attainment of yourth in rural China', working paper, Michigan State University, http://www.msu.edu/~gilesj/adjg1final.pdf.

de Brauw, Alan, Jikun Huang, Scott Rozelle, Linxiu Zhang and Yigang Zhang (2002), 'The evolution of China's rural markets during the reforms', *Journal of Comparative Economics*, **30**, 329–53.

Dong, K. and X.F. Ye (2003), 'Social security reform in China', *China Economic Review*, **14**(4), 417–25.

DRC, Development Research Center, the State Council of China (2003), 'Research on measures, objects and degrees of local protection in Chinese markets: an analysis based on sample survey', paper presented at the World Bank Workshop on National Market Integration in China, Beijing.

Findlay, C., A. Watson and H.X.Wu (1994), *Rural Enterprises in China*, St. Martin's Press, New York.

Fleisher, Belton and Jian Chen (1997), 'The coast–non-coast income gap, productivity, and regional economic policy in China', *Journal of Comparative Economics*, **25**(2), 220–36.

Fleisher, Belton M. and Xiaojun Wang (2003a), 'Potential residual and relative wages in Chinese township and village enterprises', *Journal of Comparative Economics*, **31**(3), 429–43.

Fleisher, Belton M. and Xiaojun Wang (2003b), 'Skill differentials, returns to schooling, and market segmentation in a transitional economy: The case of Mainland China', *Journal of Development Economics*, **73**(1), 315–28.

Fleisher, Belton M. and Xiaojun Wang (2003c), 'Returns to schooling in China under planning and reform', working paper, Department of Economics, The Ohio State University.

Fleisher, Belton M. and Dennis T. Yang (2006), 'Problems of China's rural labor markets and rural–urban migration', *The Chinese Economy*, **39**(3), 6–25.

Fleisher, Belton, Keyong Dong and Yunhua Liu (1996), 'Education, enterprise organization, and productivity in the Chinese paper industry', *Economic Development and Cultural Change*, **44**(3), 571–87.

Fleisher, Belton M., Yifan Hu and Haizheng Li (2006), 'Economic transition, higher education and worker productivity in China', Unpublished manuscript, Department of Economics, Ohio State University, http://www.econ.ohio–state.edu/Fleisher/working_papers/Paper_Fleisher_Hu_Li_03_9_20061.pdf.

Fleisher, Belton M., Haizheng Li and Min Qiang Zhao (2006), 'Human capital, economic growth, and regional inequality in China', Unpublished manuscript, Department of Economics, Ohio State University, http://www.econ.ohio–state.edu/Fleisher/working_papers/DisparityPaper10_28_05.pdf.

Fleisher, Belton M. and Xiaojun Wang (2001), 'Efficiency wages and work incentives in urban and rural China', *Journal of Comparative Economics*, **29**(4), 645–62.

Forbes, D. and G. Linge (1990), 'China's spatial development: Issues and prospects', in G. Linge and D. Forbes (eds), *China's Spatial Economy – Recent Development and Reforms*, Hong Kong: Panther Press.

French, Howard W. (2004), 'New boomtowns change path of China's growth', *New York Times*, 28 July.

Giles, John, Albert Park and Juwei Zhang (2005), 'What is China's true unemployment rate?', *China Economic Review*, **16**(2), 149–70.

Grove, T., Y. Hong, J. McMillan and B. Naughton (1995), 'China's evolving managerial labor market', *Journal of Political Economy*, **103**(4), 873–92.

Gunter, Frank (2004), 'Capital flight from the People's Republic of China: 1984–1999', *China Economic Review*, **15**(1), in press.

Hertel, Thomas and Fan Zhai (2006), 'Labor market distortions, rural–urban inequality and the opening of China's economy', *Economic Modelling*, **23**(1), 76–109.

Huang, J., S. Rozelle and L. Zhang (2000), 'WTO and agriculture: Radical reforms or the continuatioin of gradual transition?' *China Economic Review*, **11**(4), 397–401.

Huang, J., Yang Jun, Zhigang Xu, Scott Rozelle and Ninghui Li (forthcoming), 'Agricultural trade liberalization and poverty in China', *China Economic Review*.

Johnson, D. Gale (2000), 'The WTO and agriculture in China', *China Economic Review*, 11(4), 402–4.

Johnson, D. Gale (2002), 'Can agricultural labour adjustment occur primarily through creation of rural non-farm jobs in China?', *Urban Studies*, 39(12), 2163–74.

Johnson, D. Gale (2003), 'Provincial migration in China in the 1990s', *China Economic Review*, 14(1), 22–31.

Jones, Derek C., Cheng Li and Ann L. Owen (2003), 'Growth and regional inequality in China during the Reform Era', *China Economic Review*, 14(2), 186–200.

Kahn, Joseph (2005), 'China to drop urbanite–peasant legal differences', *New York Times*, 2 November.

Knight, John and Shi Li (2003), 'Wages, firm profitability and labour market segmentation in urban China', manuscript, Oxford, UK: Department of Economics, Oxford University.

Knight, John and Lina Song (1999), *The Rural–Urban Divide: Economic Disparities and Interactions in China*, Oxford, UK: Oxford University Press.

Korzec, M. (1992), *Labor and the Failure of Reform in China*, London: Macmillan.

Kung, J.K. (2002), 'Off-farm labor markets and the emergence of land rental markets in rural China', *Journal of Comparative Economics*, 30, 395–414.

Landler, Mark (2003), 'Big hope for filling China's garages', *New York Times*, 12 September.

Lange, Oskar and Fred M. Taylor (1966), *On the Economic Theory of Socialism*, New York: McGraw-Hill.

Lin, Justin Y. (1992), 'Rural reforms and agricultural growth in China', *American Economic Review*, 82, 34–51.

Lin, Justin Y. (2000), 'WTO accession and China's agriculture', *China Economic Review,* 11(4), 405–8.

Liu, Zhiqiang (2006), 'Institution and inequality: The *hukou* system in China', *Journal of Comparative Economics*, 33(1), 135–57.

Liu, Zhiqiang (forthcoming), 'Human capital externalities and rural–urban migration: Evidence from rural China', *China Economic Review*.

Lohmar, Bryan and Scott Rozelle (2001), 'The rise of rural-to-rural labor markets in China', *Asian Geographer*, 20 (1–2), 101–23.

Lu, Zhigang and Shunfeng Song (2006), 'Rural–urban migration and wage determination: The case of Tianjin, China', *China Economic Review*, 17(3), 337–45.

MOA, Ministry of Agriculture (2001), 'A study on change of rural population and tenure system reform in China', Project Report, Beijing.

Meng, Xin (2000), *Labor Market Reform in China*, New York: Cambridge University Press.

Meng, Xin and M.P. Kidd (1997), 'Wage determination in China's state sector in the 1980s', *Journal of Comparative Economics*, 25(3), 403–42.

Meng Xin and Junsen Zhang (2001), 'The two-tier labor market in China – occupational segregation and wage differentials between urban residents and rural migrants in Shanghai', *Journal of Comparative Economics*, 29(3), 485–504.

Naughton, Barry (1996), *Growing out of Plan: Chinese Economic Reform 1978–1993*, Cambridge, UK: Cambridge University Press.

NBS, National Bureau of Statistics (1985–2001), *China Statistical Yearbook,* Beijing: China Statistical Publishing House.

Newman, Jeffrey L. (2003), 'Local area personal income', *United States Bureau of Economic Analysis*, http://www.bea.gov/bea/ARTICLES/2003/05May/0503LAP I.pdf.

Nolan, P. and G. White (1984), 'Urban bias, rural bias or state bias? Urban–rural relations in post-revolutionary China', *Journal of Development Studies*, **20**(3), 52–81.

Ohnesorge, John K.M. (2003), 'China's economic transition and the new legal origins literature', *China Economic Review,* **14**(4), 485–93.

Perkins, Dwight and Shahid Yusuf (1984), *Rural Development in China*, Baltimore: John's Hopkins University Press.

Poncet, Sandra (2003a), 'Domestic market fragmentation and economic growth in China', manuscript, Clermont-Ferrand, France: University of the Auvergne, CERDI.

Poncet, Sandra (2003b), 'Provincial migration dynamics in China: Borders, centripetal forces, and trade', manuscript, Clermont-Ferrand, France: University of the Auvergne, CERDI.

Putterman, Louis (1993), *Continuity and Change in China's Rural Development: Collective and Reform Eras in Perspective*, New York: Oxford University Press.

Sicular, Terry (1988), 'Agricultural planning and pricing in the post-Mao period', *China Quarterly*, **116**, 671–705.

Sicular, Terry, Yue Ximing, Bjorn Gustafsson and Shi Li (forthcoming), 'The urban–rural income gap and inequality in China', *The Review of Income and Wealth.*

Song, Shunfeng, George S.-F. Chu and Rongqing Cao (2000), 'Intercity regional disparity in China', *China Economic Review*, **11** (Fall), 246–61.

Sprint (2003), Online publication at: http://www3.sprint.com/PR/CDA/PR_CDA_Pr ess_Releases_Detail/0,3681,1048,00.html.

Wang, X.L. (1997), 'What contributed to China's rapid rural industrial growth during the reform period?', Ph.D. dissertation, Canberra: The Australian National University.

World Bank (1997), *China 2020: Development Challenges in the New Century*, Wahsington, DC: World Bank.

Xie, Ping (2003), 'Reform of China's rural credit cooperatives and policy options', *China Economic Review*, **14**(4), in press.

Xu, L.C. (2000), 'Control, incentives and competition: the impact of reform on Chinese state-owned enterprises', *Economics of Transition*, **8**(1), 151–73.

Yang, Dennis Tao (1997), 'China's land arrangements and rural labor mobility', *China Economic Review*, **18**(2), 101–15.

Yang, Dennis Tao (2004), 'Education and allocative efficiency: Household income growth during rural reforms in China', *Journal of Development Economics*, **74**(1), 137–62.

Yang, Dennis Tao and Fang Cai (2003), 'The political economy of China's rural–urban divide', in Nicholas C. Hope, Dennis Tao Yang and Mu Yang Li (eds), *How Far across the River? Chinese Policy Reform at the Millennium*, Stanford: Stanford University Press.

Yang, Dennis Tao and Hao Zhou (1999), 'Rural–urban disparity and sectoral labor allocation in China', *Journal of Development Studies*, **35**(3), 105–33.

Yao, Yang (1999), 'Rural industry and labor market integration in eastern China', *Journal of Development Economics*, **59**, 463–96.

Yeo, Steven (2003), 'The PRC qualified foreign institutional investors market', *China Economic Review*, **14**(4), 443–50.

Zhang, Junsen, Yaohui Zhao, Albert Park and Xiaoqing Song (2005), 'Economic returns to schooling in urban China, 1988–2001', *Journal of Comparative Economics*, **33**(4), 730–52.

Zhang, Xiaobao and Kong-Yam Tan (2003), 'Factor market integration across sectors and regions: Implications for economic growth in China', paper presented at the World Bank Workshop on National Market Integration in China, Beijing.

Zhang, Xinmin et al. (1994), 'The analysis of rural–urban income disparity', manuscript, National Bureau of Statistics of China.

Zhao, Yaohui (2000), 'Rural-to-urban labor migration in China: the past and the present', in Loraine West and Yaohui Zhao (eds), *Rural Labor Flows in China*, Berkeley: University of California Press, pp. 15–33.

Zhou, Xueguang (2000), 'Economic transformation and income inequality in urban China: Evidence from panel data', *American Journal of Sociology*, **105**, 1135–74.

7. China's Emerging Domestic Debt Markets

Pieter Bottelier[1]

1. THE CONTEXT: FINANCIAL SECTOR REFORM – A BRIEF OVERVIEW

The modernization and internationalization of China's financial system is perhaps the last and, in some ways, most difficult chapter in the country's economic transition from plan to market. Partly driven by China's WTO commitments, the speed of the financial sector reform has accelerated since the beginning of this century, especially since 2003. With the important exception of the Agricultural Bank of China, most commercial banks (state-owned and others) have been incorporated under China's Company Law, restructured and recapitalized. Many attracted foreign strategic minority partners. Four of the five central government-owned commercial banks (Bank of Communications, China Construction Bank, Bank of China, Industrial and Commercial Bank of China) listed successfully on the Hong Kong stock exchange and (in the case of ICBC) also on the Shanghai stock exchange. At the same time, efforts are being made to deepen and broaden domestic capital markets. Problems that seemed almost intractable only a few years ago, such as the massive overhang of non-performing loans (NPLs) and of non-tradable government shares in listed companies have been addressed and are gradually being resolved.

Popular confidence in domestic equity markets returned in 2006, a year that saw a record number of new domestic IPOs after a temporary suspension of new share issues. In the early part of 2007 authorities became very concerned about the development of potentially dangerous stock market 'bubbles'. An 8.9 percent drop of the Shanghai Composite Index on 27 February 2007 (after it had risen 130 percent in the preceding 12 months) triggered share price drops around the world the next day and much nervousness in financial markets. Shanghai's surprising global impact reflects growing awareness of (1) the significant extent to which China's economy has become 'globalized', (2) the fact that China is now the fourth (almost third) largest economy and third largest trader, and (3) the enormous appetite of foreign investors for Chinese equity in spite of the fact that China's currency remains unconvertible for most capital account transactions.

Primary and secondary debt markets – the subject of this chapter – are expanding rapidly, while the regulatory framework is being adjusted to reduce market segmentation, improve market liquidity and relax investment restrictions. The variety of tradable debt instruments has increased significantly in recent years. Apart from government bonds, policy bank bonds, non-financial corporate bonds and commercial drafts – debt instruments traded prior to 2003 – the market now also includes (1) central bank sterilization bills, (2) short-term corporate bills, (3) subordinated commercial bank debt, (4) bonds issued by other financial institutions, (5) RMB bonds issued by multilateral financial organizations (Panda Bonds) and (6) securitized bonds and various derivatives. Of these new instruments, central bank sterilization bills are unrelated to corporate funding, but they have become a very important component of domestic capital markets.

With the growing institutional investor base, market participation in both equity and debt markets has widened significantly. For example, the number of licensed participants in the interbank market – by far the largest and most important component of China's financial markets – now runs into the thousands, up from few hundred in the mid-1990s. Possible additional debt instruments, currently under consideration include: (1) RMB-denominated bonds that may be issued by China Development Bank in Hong Kong to take advantage of the growing RMB deposit base there, (2) bonds issued by qualifying lower-level governments for the financing of local infrastructure, (3) RMB-denominated bonds issued by foreign corporations operating in China (to reduce foreign exchange inflow and thus ease upward pressure on the exchange rate), and (4) foreign currency-denominated debt issued by domestic firms in the domestic market.

China's domestic bond market is already the second largest in Asia after Japan's. Most trading takes place on the interbank market which has become the backbone for downstream financial markets and also serves as medium for open market operations by the central bank. In early January 2007, China's central bank introduced the Shanghai Interbank Offer Rate (SHIBOR) as a benchmark money market rate. These factors, together with the ongoing liberalization of interest rates and a gradual relaxation of capital account restrictions contribute to the development of market-based pricing for bonds and loans of different maturities and facilitate market-oriented monetary policy, while setting the stage for a more flexible exchange rate policy. A few years ago, yield curves for government bonds were

Figure 7.1:   *Typical Yield Curves for Government Bonds on Two*
Arbitrary Dates: 7 October 2003 and 10 November 2006

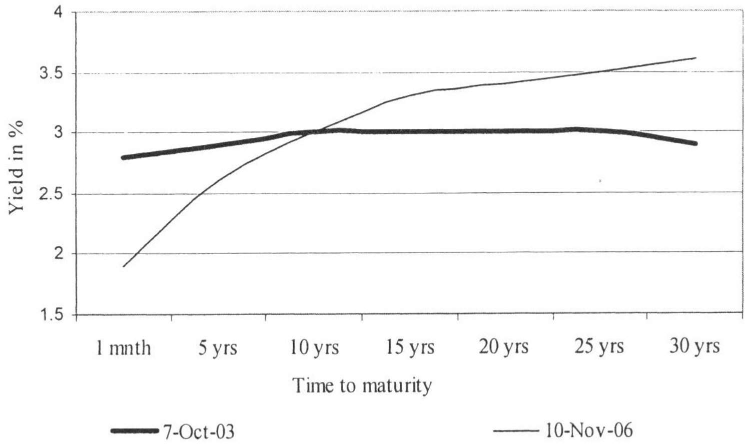

Sources: Ministry of Finance for yield curve of 7 October 2003 and Goldman Sachs (2006) for yield curve of 10 November 2006.

essentially flat, reflecting market-insensitive, administrative pricing and pervasive interest controls. A more meaningful reference yield curve is emerging (See Figure 7.1).

Reliance on the banking system for corporate financing has diminished somewhat in recent years due to high corporate profits and China's tradition to allow state-owned enterprises to reinvest profits without paying dividends. (This policy is now being changed – see below.) Corporate reliance on the banking system for *intermediated* funds, however, remains extremely high (close to 90 percent in recent years). China's financial markets remain bank-dominated, but the relative importance of equity funding is bound to increase and, as explained below, it is likely that corporate bonds will also become more important in the years ahead. The revival of China's stock markets and resumption of domestic IPOs in June 2006 (after a 12 months suspension of new issues, pending solutions for the non-tradable share problem) marks an important change. The non-financial corporate bond market has remained very small and restricted to a small number of large state-owned enterprises. This is likely to change in the years ahead as a result of the recent approval by the National People's Congress of a new Bankruptcy Law (2006), China's first ever Property Rights Law (March 2007) and the following two decisions by the National Financial Working Conference of January 2007 (namely (i) that state-owned corporations should start paying dividends to the state and (ii) to shift part of the responsibility for authorizing corporate bond issues from NDRC to CSRS), it seems likely that China's non-financial corporate bond market will widen and deepen significantly in the coming years.

Most recent measures aimed at developing China's capital markets are based on *Opinions of the State Council on Promoting the Reform, Opening and Steady Growth of Capital Markets*, a long-term perspective plan approved in January 2004. The least satisfactory aspects of China's financial markets at this time are: (1) highly speculative share buying practices on the stock exchanges, (2) inadequate access of private companies to state bank loans and capital markets, (3) a lack of transparency in the operations of the asset management companies that were created in 1998/9 to recycle NPLs, (4) excessive dependence of corporations on bank loans for domestically intermediated funds, (5) inadequate corporate governance standards, (6) still weak supervision by the regulatory agencies, and (7) overly restrictive investment regulations for pension funds and other institutional investors.

2. TRENDS IN FINANCIAL INTERMEDIATION

Banks continue to dominate financial intermediation in China (for a comparison with the US see Figure 7.2), but their relative importance is slowly diminishing, as the role of capital markets expands. The efficiency of domestic intermediation is improving, but too much capital is still allocated to low return or overly risky projects.[2] Part of China's abundant national savings continues to be intermediated through international capital markets at considerable cost to the national economy[3] – i.e. China attracts expensive FDI while investing in low-return foreign exchange reserves. The share of new corporate finance mobilized from capital markets – typically below 10 percent – rose to above 20 percent in 2006. This is mainly the result of the recent revival of China's domestic equity markets (boosted by reforms associated with the new Company Law and the new Securities Law which both became effective in 2006), large Chinese IPOs in Hong Kong, and the development of a rapidly growing market for short-term corporate debt since May 2005. A further opening of the domestic A-share market to qualified foreign institutional investors (QFII) and successful efforts to make non-tradable shares in listed companies tradable (after a lock-up period of up to three years) contributed to stock market revival.

After five years of malaise and anxiety about the future of non-tradable shares, China's stock exchanges seem to have entered a new phase of rapid

Figure 7.2: Structure of Financial System Assets: China and the US, end of 2005

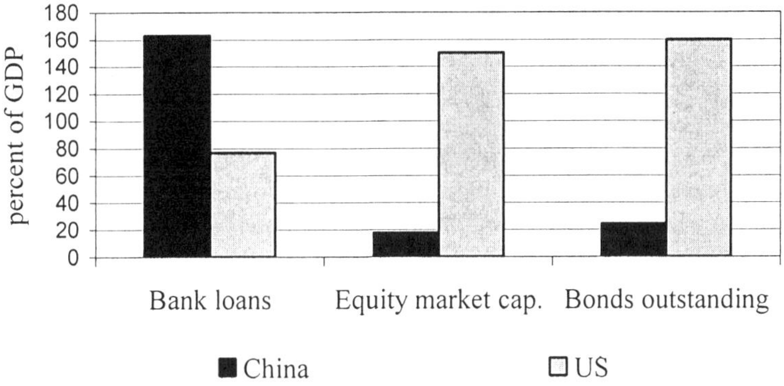

Source: IMF

expansion and institutional development which will eventually almost certainly include the integration of A and B share markets. Share prices recovered from their long slump since 2001 and there has been a veritable flood of domestic IPOs since the market was reopened for new share issues in June 2006. Speculative share purchases by individual shareholders[4] and public agencies, often irresponsibly financed, remain a major concern. It would be a major bonus for China's financial reforms if the short-term speculative behavior of numerous investors could be curbed and if domestic stock markets could begin to contribute to higher corporate governance standards through strict supervision of the markets and shareholder scrutiny of listed companies. This will require larger market participation by institutional investors (including qualified foreign institutional investors – QFIIs), mutual funds and the introduction of short selling and stock-index futures.[5]

3. GOVERNMENT RECOGNITION OF THE IMPORTANCE OF HEALTHY DEBT MARKETS

Especially since 2003, China's government has made great efforts to develop, integrate and better regulate domestic debt markets. Large, diversified and sound debt markets are needed to:

1. Reduce the dependence of corporations on banks for their funding needs.
2. Assist lower level governments in the financing of local infrastructure.

3. Satisfy the need of institutional investors for a broader range of financial instruments.
4. Permit market-oriented monetary policies by the central bank.
5. Facilitate the recycling and ultimate disposal of non-performing loans (NPLs) through capital markets.
6. Facilitate the gradual opening of China's capital account and flexibilization of the exchange rate.

In recent years the government has actively promoted the development of new debt instruments such as: (1) subordinated bonds issued by commercial banks (June 2004), (2) bonds issued by banks other than the three Policy Banks, e.g. Shanghai Pudong Development Bank, China Merchant Bank and Industrial Bank (the former Fujian Industrial Bank) (April 2005), (3) asset-backed securities, including mortgage loans and other financial assets such as NPLs (April 2005), (4) short-term corporate bills (May 2005) and (5) RMB-denominated 'Panda Bonds' issued by the Asian Development Bank and the International Finance Corporation (October 2005). Additional instruments planned or under consideration include: (1) RBM-denominated bonds issued by mainland banks (e.g., China Development Bank) in Hong Kong to take advantage of the rapidly growing RMB deposit base in the territory, (2) bonds issued by qualifying municipalities and provinces for the financing of local infrastructure and (3) RMB-denominated bonds issued by foreign corporations operating in China (to reduce foreign exchange inflows and upward pressure on the exchange rate), foreign currency-denominated debt issued by domestic firms in the domestic market.

Perhaps the most important recent development concerning domestic debt markets is a decision by the National Financial Working Commission meeting of 19–20 January 2007 to shift part of the responsibility for the regulation and supervision of non-financial corporate bonds from the National Development and Reform Commission (NDRC) to the China Securities Regulatory Commission (CSRC). Details of this decision remain to be worked out. It seems likely that NDRC will continue to handle bond issues by unincorporated state enterprises implementing state investment plans and that CSRC will be asked to develop a more conventional market-driven corporate bond market, essentially from scratch. Since 1993 the non-financial corporate bond market has been restricted to a few dozen large state-owned corporations (such as e.g., the Three Gorges Development Corporation, Baosteel, China Mobile, Petrochina and China Grid). The total amount of registered and tradable corporate bonds at the end of 2006 was only about US$31 billion. Each new issue had to be part of the national development plan and guaranteed by one of the large state commercial banks. Consequently, almost all non-financial corporate bonds were rated 'triple A' by China's domestic rating agencies. CSRC is expected to adopt a more market-oriented approach to the approval of corporate bonds issues and is unlikely to require special guarantees. China's non-financial corporate bond market may be expected to start expanding very rapidly in the near-term future and, since the quality of future corporate bonds is likely to vary greatly, China's rating agencies will face significant new challenges and responsibilities.

To improve risk management by traders and the liquidity of bond markets, the regulatory authority (PBoC) introduced new hedging tools such as outright repurchase agreements and forward bond transactions on the interbank market in April 2005 (Mu, 2006).

4. SIZE AND COMPOSITION OF CHINA'S DEBT MARKETS

China's domestic debt markets have expanded vary rapidly since the late 1990s in terms of new issues, amounts outstanding and market turnover. The amount of outstanding tradable debt (excluding central bank sterilization bills, NPLs and short-term drafts, but including short-term corporate bills) grew from only 5 percent of GDP in 1997 to 37 percent at the end of 2006. Comparable ratios for other Asian countries are: 24 percent for Indonesia, 43 percent for Philippines and 75 percent for South Korea (Goldman Sachs, 2006). The composition of both long- and short-term tradable domestic debt in China (excluding NPLs) at the end of 2006 was approximately as shown in Table 7.1.

At the end of 2006 the amount of all tradable domestic debt outstanding (excluding NPLs and AMC bonds[6]) was about double the market capitalization of tradable A and B shares, but only a little more than 50 percent of the amount of outstanding bank loans. These numbers illustrate the extent to which domestic financial intermediation in China remains dominated by bank loans in spite of the phenomenal growth of debt markets in recent years.

The largest component of domestic tradable debt at present consists of central bank sterilization bills. This is an unusual and potentially troublesome situation. It has nothing to do with the funding of corporations or government expenditures. It reflects central bank efforts to suppress domestic inflation that would otherwise result from foreign exchange purchases aimed at preventing or slowing exchange rate appreciation. When the central bank ran out of government bonds for open market operations aimed at the sterilization of excess money supply in the second half of

Table 7.1:   Volume of Tradable Long-Term and Short-Term Debt Outstanding, end of 2006

Debt instrument	Amount in US$ billion equivalent end 2006	Percent of tradable debt outstanding	Percent of 2006 GDP
Long-term maturities:		(long-term only)	
Government bonds	372	48	15
Policy bank bonds	293	38	12
Non-financial corporate bonds	31	4.2	3
Other bank bonds	30	4	1
Asset-backed securities	2.4	0.3	0.1
Panda bonds	0.4	0.04	0.01
Total long-term maturities	728.8		31
Short term maturities:		(short-term only)	
Central bank sterilization bills	414	45	17
Short-term corporate bills	225	24	9
Commercial paper (drafts)	280	30	11
Total short-term maturities	919		37
Total all tradable debt	1648		67

Sources: China Monetary Policy Report Q4 2006 and author estimated (for short-term corporate bills and drafts).

2003, it began to issue its own bills for that purpose. In the first half of 2006 the amount of outstanding central bank sterilization bills began to exceed the amount of outstanding government bonds. PBoC is now trying to reduce reserve accumulation through a variety of means and for a variety of reasons, including the wish to avoid the need for further large-scale sterilization though the sale of central bank bills.

5.   THE HISTORY OF DEBT MARKETS IN THE PEOPLE'S REPUBLIC OF CHINA

For students of China's market economic reforms, the emergence and development of domestic debt markets is of special interest. When the reforms started in the late 1970s, the financial system was essentially limited to one bank, the People's Bank of China (PBoC) which served as cash agent for the state, bank for state enterprises and the public, foreign exchange bank, and de-facto central bank. There was no need for insurance companies, institutional investors or financial markets. Financial system reform did not become a priority until the early 1990s when the liberalization of markets for goods and services had already advanced quite far. The first four state-owned commercial banks,[7] created in 1979 and 1984 (the year PBoC officially became China's central bank), continued to act as agents of the state, implementing the national development and credit plans, until the mid-1990s. The government's annual 'credit plan' was not officially abolished until 1998.

Some local, unofficial and unregulated markets for bonds and equity shares emerged spontaneously in the 1980s (Green 2003). It was not until after the opening of stock exchanges in Shanghai and Shenzhen (December 1990 and January 1991 respectively) that the Government began to pay serious attention to the regulation and supervision of such markets. By initially keeping the financial sector fully under state control and using state-owned commercial banks as fiscal agents, China was able to maintain fast growth with social stability and full (urban) employment during the initial phases of transition. In this way, China bought time so that people could adjust to market realities while new institutions developed. Delayed reform of state-owned enterprises and delayed liberalization of the financial sector were central to this cautious, gradualist approach.

Things began to change in the early 1990s when China once again experienced high inflation due to excessive credit expansion. This time, however, the economy was already semi-marketized. New policy instruments were needed to deal effectively with the macroeconomic instability of those days. The introduction of formal central government regulatory controls over the two stock exchanges[8] was combined with the beginning of financial market liberalization and state bank reform. The government also subjected itself to stronger market discipline by denying itself the option (from 1994) to borrow from the central bank for fiscal purposes. This measure was part of a complex set of financial sector reforms that included, *inter alia*, exchange rate unification, formal establishment and regulation of the interbank market for short-term loans and foreign exchange market, three specialized Policy Banks, and the start of open market operations by PBoC. A Central Bank Law and a Commercial Banking Law, under preparation since 1993, were passed by the National People's Congress and became effective in 1995.

Altogether, the measures of 1994–95 gave a powerful boost to the development of a domestic market for government bonds which was then still in its infancy. Government bonds were initially traded on the stock exchanges and later (from August 1997) also on the interbank market.

Financial sector reform moved center stage after the Asian financial crisis of 1997–98. The crisis in neighboring countries made China's leaders more keenly aware of the vulnerability of the country's financial system, in particular the state-owned commercial banks, which had accumulated huge volumes of (unrecognized) non-performing loans (NPLs) during the years they served primarily as fiscal agents of the state. Four state-owned asset management companies (AMCs) were established in 1998–99 to assist in the NPL clean up, which started in 1999. This marked the emergence of a market for non-bond debt, focused initially on NPLs. The AMCs were given a license for ten years, the same period as the maturity of bonds they issued to pay for (most of) the initial bunch of NPLs they acquired at face value.

Non-financial corporate bonds have been issued since the mid-1980s, initially without a regulatory framework. Since formal regulations were introduced in the early 1990s, the primary market for corporate bonds has been reserved for a few selected state-owned enterprises carrying out investment plans for the state. The primary and secondary markets for corporate bonds remained very small. As is recognized by the government, there is now an urgent need to broaden the domestic funding base of China's corporations, both state-owned and others, to reduce their current dependence on bank loans and reinvested profits. The rapidly growing ranks of institutional investors also need larger and more diversified debt markets for portfolio investment and balancing (Kim et al., 2003).

5.1. Government Bonds

In most market economies government bonds are the foundation for broader domestic debt markets. The government bond market offers pricing benchmarks for other types of debt instruments such as corporate and municipal bonds and it serves as the arena for open market operations by the central bank. Until the first quarter of 2006[9] government bonds dominated China's debt markets. In 2002 they still accounted for about 95 percent of all traded long-term debt (excluding NPLs). The total amount of government bonds issued and traded grew very rapidly since 1998 when China started a fiscal stimulus program aimed at preventing a sharp economic slow-down in response to the Asian financial crisis of 1997–98.

Domestic borrowing by the Chinese government between 1949 and 1979 was sporadic and the amounts involved were small. The aggregate amount borrowed during this 32-year period (in 1950, and during the period 1954–58) was only RMB3.85 billion (Lin, 2003). During the Mao period, the government typically borrowed from PBoC for fiscal purposes; there was no trading in government debt. Following the initiation of market reforms, the government issued bonds every year, beginning in 1981. In the 1980s, issues were small and in essence a form of taxation; they were part of the national credit plan. Government bonds were force-placed on the basis of administrative quotas, and payments for bonds were often deducted from payrolls or withdrawn from bank accounts (Kumar et al., 1997). State banks were not allowed to trade in government bonds, but individuals and non-bank agencies spontaneously began to trade government paper in unofficial curb markets. Thus, much like the informal equity markets of that time, largely unregulated secondary bond markets started in China in the 1980s.

In response to market pressures for government-led institutional development, bond markets were gradually legalized in the late 1980s and began to tailor new issues to market preferences; maturities were reduced and coupon rates increased to make bonds competitive with bank deposits. The secondary bond market developed more quickly after the opening of stock exchanges (which also listed bonds) in Shanghai and Shenzhen. The first voluntary placement of government bonds (through the stock exchanges) occurred in 1991. The now defunct Wuhan Securities Exchange Center, established in 1992, was for some years China's largest bond trading center, until the stock exchanges in Shanghai and Shenzhen absorbed this function. The next major development was the government's decision in 1993 to stop borrowing from PBoC for fiscal purposes. From 1994, the government funded all budget deficits through borrowing in capital markets. Domestic government bond issues jumped from RMB31.5 billion in 1993 to RMB102.9 billion in 1994 and rose steeply thereafter, especially during the period 1998–2002 when China applied fiscal stimulus policies. The rate of new government bond issues fell after 2002 when the economy no longer needed fiscal stimulus and the fiscal deficit shrank.

5.2. Policy Bank Bonds

The second largest issuer of tradable domestic bonds (other than central bank bills) is the China Development Bank (CDB), one of the three Policy Banks created in 1994[10] to facilitate the commercialization of state commercial banks. CDB specializes in the financing infrastructure projects with long gestation periods. Very large projects, such as e.g. the Three Gorges project, are financed directly by CDB or through the purchase by CDB of bonds issued by the Three Gorges Development Corporation. CDB also finances urban infrastructure through loans to local-government-owned corporations. According to CDB's annual report for 2005, the amount of CDB bonds outstanding at the end of that year was RMB 1541.5 (about $190 billion). Since the government does not formally guarantee CDB bonds, they are excluded from official government debt statistics.[11] For the analysis of China's public finances, however, CDB bonds should be regarded as semi-official government debt.[12]

Yield differences between comparable CDB and government bonds in the secondary market tend to be small, which suggests that the market expects CDB securities to be backed by the central government. CDB's published NPL ratio is currently below 1 percent and its capital adequacy ratio is above 9 percent. These favorable numbers mask the risk of default on unsecured CDB loans to municipal corporations for the financing of local infrastructure. An estimated 33 percent of CDB assets represents lending to corporations owned by lower-level governments and is potentially vulnerable to local financial problems. In September 2003, CDB successfully issued US$500 million worth of bonds in the domestic market. It was the first US$-denominated bond issued by a public agency in China. The only other Policy Bank that has issued bonds in the domestic market is the Eximbank. Its domestic bond debt outstanding at the end of September 2006 stood at the equivalent of about $60 billion.

5.3. Bonds Issued by Asset Management Companies to Pay for NPLs

The third largest issuer of domestic bonds (other than the central bank) is the group of four state-owned asset management companies (AMCs) established in 1998–99 to help recycle the NPLs they took over from state commercial banks and CDB. The estimated face value of AMC bonds issued is RMB 1162 billion yuan (about $150 billion at the January 2007 exchange rate). These bonds, which are held by the banks that sold NPLs to the AMCs, carry a below-market interest rate and are not officially guaranteed by the government.[13] They are not traded and not included in official statistics on government debt. Since AMC bonds held by state-owned commercial banks are counted as part of the banks' capital they carry an implicit government guarantee. Most AMC bonds will mature in the next few years. A conversion of some of the AMCs into multi-function profit-oriented financial institutions is under active consideration. Since it is impossible for the AMCs to break even (let alone earn a profit) on the recycling of NPLs they acquired at par (or above market value), the conversion of AMCs into commercial entities may reduce the ultimate burden on the Ministry of Finance as final (implicit) guarantor of the original AMC bonds.

5.4. Non-Financial Corporate Bonds

China's corporate bond market remains small and less developed than the markets for government bonds or stocks. At the end of 2006 the total amount of registered and tradable non-financial corporate bonds was only about US$31 billion (1.2 percent of tradable long-term debt). From 1984, selected non-financial state-owned enterprises were allowed to issue corporate bonds with the permission of PBoC. Initially the coupon rate was set 40 percent higher than the rate for 1-year deposits in state banks. Since the public regarded corporate bonds almost as secure as treasury bonds, this led to reduced demand for government bonds and a drain on saving deposits. To correct these problems, the government lowered the interest premium and set annual quotas for corporate bonds under the credit plan (Mehran et al., 1996). Like the informal equity markets that developed in the mid-1980s, local corporate bond markets remained largely unregulated and unsupervised until the early 1990s. After the opening of the Shanghai and Shenzhen stock exchanges new corporate bond issues soon began to decline relative to share issues. However, in 1992 the amount of funds raised through corporate bonds was still considerably larger than through share issues. After 1996, the balance shifted decisively in favor of share issues. Enterprises preferred to issue shares rather than bonds, as equity was perceived to be a less expensive way of raising funds in China.

The all time record amount of corporate bonds issued in 1992 (RMB69 billion) was part of the uncontrolled credit expansion of that time that contributed to high inflation. In 1993, as part of a package of macro-stabilization measures, the responsibility for controlling corporate bond issues was shifted from PBoC to the State Planning Commission (SPC) while the central bank governor (Li Guixian) was replaced. SPC introduced a quota system and reserved this instrument for large, central government-owned enterprises operating under the plan. The coupon rate, set by SPC at 150-250 basis points above the 1-year deposit rate, was unrelated to the maturity of the issue (ranging from 3 to 20 years). All issues had to be guaranteed by one of the large state-owned commercial banks. It is therefore not surprising that corporate bonds in China are typically rated AAA.[14] The challenges facing China's rating agencies will increase when non-guaranteed corporate bonds (and later municipal and provincial bonds) appear on the market.

In January 2007, the responsibility for authorizing corporate bond issues was split between the National Development and Reform Commission (NDRC, successor to SPC) to the China Securities Regulatory Commission (CSRC). Although the details remain to be worked out, this institutional change signals an important policy shift regarding corporate bond market development. Other factors that will help push the emergence of a more conventional, market-driven corporate bond market are: (1) the decision of January 2007 to require profit-making state-owned corporations to start paying dividends to their owner(s), (2) the new Bankruptcy Law of 2006, and (3) China's first ever Property Rights Law (approved by the NPC in March 2007). Since CSRC is unlikely to require bank guarantees for corporate bond issues authorized by it, the secondary market is also expected to become more diversified and more interesting for institutional investors. Trading in corporate bonds is largely concentrated on the Shanghai stock exchange, but some corporate bonds are also listed on the Shenzhen stock exchange. Turnover is very low.

5.5. Panda Bonds

The International Finance Corporation (the private sector financing arm of the World Bank) and the Asian Development Bank both issued RBM denominated 10-year bonds in China's interbank market in October 2005. The amounts and coupon rates were RMB1.13 billion, RMB1 billion and 3.40 percent, 3.34 percent respectively. Both issues were sold at par. This was the first time that multilateral agencies were permitted to issue local currency bonds in China. The proceeds were to be used for the financing of IFC- and ADB-financed projects in China. The Panda Bonds helped to soak up excess liquidity in the economy and contributed to a further diversification of bond instruments available for trading on the secondary market. It is likely that more Panda Bond issues will follow.

5.6. Asset-Backed Securities (ABS)

This is the newest category of debt instruments available in China (on an experimental basis). In April 2005 PBoC and China Banking Regulatory Commission (CBRC) jointly issued regulations on pilot credit asset-securitization, setting the stage for trial issues of mortgage-backed securities and other ABS. China Development Bank was the first Chinese bank to make use of this new facility by issuing (December 2005) RMB2.9 billion (about US$360 million equivalent) residential mortgage-backed securities and $4.2 billion (about US$525 million equivalent) non-secured infrastructure loans-backed securities in the interbank market on an experimental basis. This was followed by two issues for a total of RMB5.45 billion (almost US$700 million equivalent) of NPL-backed securities by two asset management companies (Cinda and China Orient) in December 2006 and January 2007.[15] All ABS issues so far were readily absorbed on the interbank markets and now trading on that market.

The development of mortgage-backed securities followed the privatization of urban housing that started around 1998[16] and the associated commercialization of urban housing construction. Since that time mortgage loans grew very rapidly as a share of state bank assets (to about 16 percent at the end of 2005, from less than 1 percent in 1997). Consumer loans, mostly for car financing, also expanded rapidly as a share of bank portfolios. Mortgage-backed securities have great potential in China as instruments to standardize mortgage contracts across financial institutions and to deepen domestic capital markets.

5.7. Central Bank Sterilization Bills

In the course of 2002 a significant, unexpected change occurred on the capital account of China's balance of payments. Before 2002 there had been annual capital outflows of US$15–30 billion per annum on the 'errors and omissions' account for many years. These unaccounted for capital outflows probably represented 'capital flight' from China. The flow reversed direction in the course of 2002 and turned into a large 'errors and omissions' inflow representing mostly speculative capital flows triggered by the expectation of a revaluation of the RMB and by rapidly rising real estate prices in Shanghai and other big cities. Given China's defacto fixed exchange rate policy, which had been in effect since 1995 (and was tightened in December 1997 in the wake of the Asian financial crisis), this structural balance of payments shift, amounting to some US$80–120 billion per annum between 2002 and 2006, triggered large purchases of foreign exchange by PBoC aimed at preventing currency appreciation. Irregular capital inflows, much more than the current account surplus, accounted for China's rapid build-up of foreign exchange reserves between 2002 and 2005.

A large part of the increased domestic money supply resulting from PBoC's foreign exchange purchases had to be sterilized to avoid excessive expansion of the domestic money supply. PBoC responded to this challenge by selling its stock of government bonds in open market operations on the interbank market and by introducing central bank bills for the same purpose when its stock of government bonds was depleted. From April 2003 PBoC has issued large amounts of central bank bills on the interbank market for sterilization purposes. These are short-term instruments with a maturity up to one year. The total amount outstanding at the end of 2006 was about US$414 billion equivalent, 45 percent of all short-term tradable debt at that time.[17] Since they only traded on the interbank market and owned exclusively operators on that market, central bank bills are sometimes (erroneously) excluded from debt market surveys. An interesting side effect of domestic sterilization efforts is the 'profit' earned by PBoC on account of the fact that the interest paid on domestic sterilization bills has generally been lower than the interest earned on foreign exchange reserves. PBoC is now trying to reduce the need for additional domestic sterilization through various efforts aimed at reducing foreign exchange reserve accumulation.

5.8. Short-Term Corporate Bills

This new instrument was introduced in May 2005 under the sponsorship of PBoC to compensate (in part) for the lack of access to the corporate bond market by the large majority of firms in China (Green, 2005). The maturity of these new corporate bills is usually one year. They quickly became popular and are actively traded in the secondary market. Since the discount rate tends to be well below the prime lending rate for bank loans, short-term corporate bills lower the cost of borrowing for the issuer. The total amount outstanding at the end of 2006 was about US$225 billion equivalent, representing about 24 percent of all tradable short-term domestic debt at that time.[18]

5.9. Commercial Paper (Drafts)

Commercial paper (commercial-accepted and bank-accepted drafts) have been issued and traded in China since the early 1980s (Green, 2006), but the relative importance of this instrument in short-term financial markets has greatly increased in recent years. Like short-term corporate bills, drafts are usually discounted below bank lending rates and even below PBoCs official discount rate for this instrument. Therefore, commercial paper represents another opportunity for firms in China to lower their cost of borrowing, provided, of course, the market is liquid enough to permit defacto roll-over of drafts. The total amount of drafts outstanding at the end of 2006 was about US$278 billion equivalent, representing about 30 percent of all tradable short-term domestic debt at that time.

Since both short term-term corporate bills and drafts are freely tradable at market-determined discounts, these instruments have contributed significantly to the liberalization of China's interest rate regime in recent years.

6. TRADING GOVERNMENT BONDS AND POLICY BANK BONDS

In the primary market, the government began to experiment with market-based distribution systems through specialized underwriters and primary dealers in 1994. This has gradually become the rule. An over-the-counter (OTC) market for bearer bonds has existed since the late 1980s.[19] There is another, more recently established interbank OTC market for the trade in book-entry bonds and Policy Bank bonds between banks, institutional investors and others licensed to trade on the interbank market.

About 95 percent of all domestic bond trading in China is conducted on the interbank market and the remainder takes place on the stock exchanges, mostly Shanghai (Mu, 2006). Until the end of 2002, almost all bond trading in China was in the form of repurchase (repo) transactions which is an indication of an 'illiquid' market. Since the beginning of 2003, the share of spot-transactions has gradually increased to about one-third of total turnover on the interbank bond market in 2006. The reduced share of repo transactions is an indication that China's domestic bond market has become more 'liquid'.

In August 1997, the market for government bonds was split between the interbank market and the stock market. This was the result of a PBoC decision to ban commercial bank trading on the stock exchanges and lending to securities firms (usually on the basis of repos) in an effort to curb speculative stock trading. Short selling by securities firms has been a recurrent problem in China. In February 1995, the futures market for government bonds essentially collapsed when Shanghai Wanguo, then a leading securities firm, sold short RMB211 billion worth of government bonds without collateral.[20] Short selling on the bond market was officially prohibited in June 1997.

A fourth market[21] for government bonds was created in February 2002 when PBoC allowed the trading of certificate bonds (also called savings bonds or saving certificates) held by individuals and institutions. Such bonds had been non-tradable until then and carried a higher interest rate than tradable bonds for that reason. They used to be held by the buyer until maturity. Certificate bonds issued prior to February 2002 are still not tradable, at least not officially. When newly issued certificate bonds were made tradable the premium interest over long-term deposit rates was removed.

The negative consequences for China's government bond market resulting from market fragmentation and unequal standards have been the subject of much government attention and corrective policy action in recent years. The World Bank Group has provided technical assistance to China in these matters. In summary, the development of China's government bond market and the parallel emergence of a regulatory framework occupied five distinct periods:

1981–86: The government issued all government bonds through mandatory placement with agencies of the state. All bonds had a zero-coupon structure and were non-tradable. The term was usually five years. Total annual issues were small; redemption started in 1986.

1986–93: The Ministry of Finance began to issue tradable bearer bonds, which gradually became accepted by the public and traded in the OTC market. Special financial agencies were set up in provinces to facilitate the initial sale and trading of government bonds throughout the country.

1993–97: After the introduction of a self-imposed ban on government borrowing for fiscal purposes from the central bank in 1994, the primary and secondary markets for government bonds took off while new bond instruments, including certificate bonds, were introduced. Book-entry bonds could be traded on the stock exchanges, but certificate bonds were non-tradable (until February 2002, when newly issued certificate bonds were made tradable for the first time). From 1993, underwriting syndicates and auctions were used to sell new issues at a market price.

1997–2002: Trading of government bonds among banks was shifted to the interbank market in an effort to curb harmful speculation on the stock exchanges by securities firms and others who obtained loans from the banks on the basis of repos. To reverse the negative effects of reduced liquidity and transparency resulting from market fragmentation, the government broadened access of non-bank financial institutions to the interbank market for government bonds. Between 1997 and 1999, the government did not issue any government bonds through the stock exchanges. During those two years, most issues were in the form of non-tradable certificate bonds. Issuance of tradable book-entry bonds was resumed in late 1999. Since that time, the government has typically sold about 25 percent of new issues though the stock market and the remainder through the interbank market. There were no bearer bond issues from 1998 through the first half of 2002. The total amount of new government bond issues increased rapidly after 1998 when China started a multi-year fiscal stimulus program.

2003–present: This period is marked by intensified financial market reforms, including the introduction of several new debt instruments, improved debt and equity market regulation, accelerated interest rate liberalization, efforts to improve the liquidity of bond markets and reduce market segmentation and some measures to reduce restrictions on capital account transactions. The introduction of short-term central bank bills in April 2003 and the increased availability of short-term government bonds (combined with gradual interest rate liberalization) have greatly improved the liquidity of bond markets and the usefulness of yield curves for government bonds for the pricing of other debt.[22] Guidelines laid down in the official document *Opinions of the State Council on Promoting the Reform, Opening and Steady Growth of Capital Markets* will provide the framework for capital market development in China for years to come.

7. OPEN MARKET OPERATIONS (OMO)

PBoC conducts OMO through primary dealers. It uses government bonds, bonds issued by Policy Banks and central bank bills for this purpose. Repos and reverse repo transactions (using securities as collateral) are an integral part of OMO and represented about two-thirds of a percent of interbank turnover in 2006. All OMO instruments used are tradable and transactions are voluntary. The range of government bond maturities has been gradually increased from 3 months to 30 years.[23] Until a few years ago, government bonds had long maturities only, which complicated the construction of a yield curve for such securities. Recently the Ministry of Finance introduced three-month and six-month bonds, which makes the range of maturities for official paper complete. The maturity of central bank bills is usually one year or less. PBoC has recently begun to experiment with the issue of somewhat longer maturity bills (up to 3 years). The maturities of repos and reverse repos range from seven days to a year, with a concentration around 14-day transactions.

8. BORROWING BY LOWER-LEVEL GOVERNMENTS

Lower-level governments in China are officially required to balance their budget without borrowing, except for selected, government-approved external bond issues (usually revenue-backed) for infrastructure financing, and for indirect borrowing (through the Ministry of Finance) from multinational development agencies such as the World Bank and the Asian Development Bank. However, many local governments also borrow elsewhere, usually indirectly, through corporations or agencies they own. Some of those corporations, such as for example the Shanghai City Construction & Investment Development Corporation, have placed infrastructure bonds in recent years. Mostly, however, local governments borrow (indirectly) from domestic banks, including China Development Bank. Some local governments borrow unofficially also from workers, pensioners and suppliers in the form of arrears in wages, pensions, and/or bill payments. There is no reliable information available on direct and indirect borrowing by lower level governments. The aggregate outstanding is believed to have grown very rapidly in recent years and part of the extraordinarily rapid domestic credit expansion from 2002–05 was due to borrowing by local governments, usually through their corporations.[24]

There is clearly a need for the development of (non-sovereign) municipal and provincial bonds. The current restriction on such instruments increasingly conflicts with the need of sub-national governments to finance infrastructure in transparent ways and with sound financial sector development. The introduction of municipal and provincial bonds will require a legal and regulatory environment, which does not exist at present. Local government access to domestic capital markets could be regulated such that the system promotes and rewards fiscal responsibility.[25] On the demand side, institutional investors need access to a broader range of bonds and yields than are currently available in the domestic market.

Once the bond market includes non-guaranteed corporate bonds and infrastructure bonds issued by local governments, the function of rating agencies in China will become more important and their task more challenging.

NOTES

1. The author is Sr. Adjunct Professor of China studies at Johns Hopkins School of Advanced International Studies (SAIS). He was head of the World Bank's resident mission in China from 1993 to 1997. Helpful comments from Nicholas Lardy and Tao Zhang are gratefully acknowledged.
2. See for example Dollar and Wei (2007).
3. A cost that may well be justified by benefits such as the transfer of technology, management experience and market access.
4. China is reported to have some 80 million individual shareholder accounts. A large, but unknown number of these are inactive and/or duplicative.
5. For a more detailed discussion of stock exchange reform needs see Fang (2007).
6. AMC bonds were issued to state-owned asset management companies at below market interest rates to pay for NPLs acquired from commercial banks at par. These bonds are kept on the balance sheet of the commercial banks as tier 2 capital and are not traded.
7. Bank of China, China Construction Bank, Agricultural Bank of China (all three in 1979), and Industrial and Commercial Bank of China (1984).
8. The China Securities Regulatory Commission (CSRC) was not established until late 1992, about two years after the stock exchanges of Shanghai and Shenzhen started operations under local government supervision, the former with the official blessing of the central government, the latter initially without (Green 2003).
9. This was the year when the volume of outstanding central bank sterilization bills began to exceed the volume of outstanding government bonds.
10. The other two are the Agricultural Development Bank of China and China Eximbank.
11. CDB was the first public bank in China to issue long-term floating rate debentures, subordinated debt, strip bonds, US$ denominated bonds for the domestic market and asset-backed securities. It is in many ways a pioneer development bank.
12. Before 1998, CDB bonds were guaranteed by the China International Trust and Investment Corporation (CITIC), another state-owned financial institution. No such

guarantees were extended in later years. The earlier CITIC guarantees appear to have been discontinued; they are no longer mentioned in official reports.

13. Under Chinese law, the state (represented by the Ministry of Finance) cannot guarantee debt issued by state corporations or agencies of the state since 1994.
14. Source: China Chengxin International Credit Rating Co., Ltd.
15. The Cinda issue of RMB4.75 billion was backed by RMB21 billion nominal value NPLs (a backing ratio of 4.4 to 1). The Orient issue of RMB700 million was backed by RMB9.16 billion nominal value NPLs (a backing ratio of 13 to 1).
16. The privatization of about 80 percent of China's urban housing stock, completed around 2003, was inspired, in part, by the wish to avoid a recession in the wake of the Asian financial crisis of 1997–98 and thus complemented the government's fiscal stimulus program. Because cash wages in the public sector were still very low, the transfer price of urban houses (almost all apartments) was on average only about one-third of market value. For that reason, resale rights of the new owners were restricted for the first five years. The total market value of urban housing privatized in the period 1998–2003 is estimated by this author at around US$2.5 trillion equivalent. The associated wealth transfer from public sector agencies to private owners was of the order of US$1.7 trillion. It was probably the largest privatization and wealth transfer program in history.
17. A small amount of central bank sterilization bills (about 2 percent of the amount outstanding at the end of September 2006) is not tradable; these represent forced bill purchases to compensate for insufficient reserve ratios at PBoC by some banks.
18. There are conflicting reports on the amount of short-term commercial bills outstanding at the end. Both Goldman Sachs (in its Global Economics Paper No. 149 of 20 November 2006) and Standard Chartered (in its Special Report on China's Bond Markets, 6 March 2007) put the amount below US$40 billion equivalent while PBoC's Quarterly Monetary Report put the amount at over US$200 billion equivalent.
19. For example, the Ministry of Finance announced on 18 August 2003 that it would issue RMB46 billion worth of book-entry bonds between August 20 and 26. Of this amount, RMB36 billion was to be sold through the interbank and the stock market, while RMB10 billion was reserved for OTC sales to individual investors through banks around the country.
20. This is referred to in China as 'Incident No. 327.'
21. The other three are the stock market (for bond trading), the interbank market and the OTC market.
22. The first four of these five periods are identified in Scott (2004).
23. Maturities offered by the Ministry of Finance now include 3-months, 6-months, 1, 2, 3, 5, 7, 10, 15, 20 and 30 years.
24. Lin (2003) estimates the non-arrears portion of unrecorded local government debt in 2001 at 2.3 percent of GDP. Lardy (2005) estimates that total local government debt at the end of 2003 amounted to about 19 percent of GDP.
25. Australia offers an interesting example of a well regulated and highly developed market for local government bonds that might be of interest for China.

REFERENCES

Dollar, D. and S.J. Wei (2007), 'Das (wasted) kapital: Firm ownership and investment efficiency in China', IMF Working Paper No. 07/9.

Fang, X. (2007), 'Taking stock in China', *Wall Street Journal*, 6 March 2007.

Goldman Sachs (2006), Global Economics Paper No. 149.

Green, S. (2003), 'China's stock market. A guide to its progress, players and prospects', *The Economist*.

Green, S. (2005), 'China's all new corporate paper market', *Standard Chartered, On The Ground (OTG)* – Asia.

Green, S. (2006), 'PBoC backs re-introduction of the draft', *Standard Chartered, On the Ground (OTG)* – Asia.

Kim Y. et al. (2003), 'Developing institutional investors in People's Republic of China', World Bank Country Study Paper.

Kumar, A. et al. (1997), *China's Emerging Capital Markets*, FT Financial Publishing Asia Pacific.

Lardy, N. (2005), 'China's banking reform', CLSA Speaker Series.

Lin S. (2003) 'China's government debt: How serious?', *China: An International Journal*, **1**, No. 1, March 2003

Mehran, H. et al. (1996), 'Monetary and exchange rate systems in China: An experiment in gradualism', IMF Occasional Paper, No. 141.

Mu, H. (2006), 'The development of China's bond market', Monetary Policy Analysis Group of PBoC (2006), China Monetary Policy Report Q3, 2006, BIS paper No. 26.

8. Incremental Reform and Distortions in China's Product and Factor Markets

Xiaobo Zhang and Kong-Yam Tan[1]

1. INTRODUCTION

Over the past 25 years China's transformation from a centrally planned to an increasingly market-driven economy has led to substantial efficiency gains and rapid economic growth (Maddison, 1998; Fan et al., 2003). However, as Young (2000) argues, the reforms may not have been sufficiently complete to improve domestic market integration. This could happen, for example, if increased interregional competition as a result of fiscal decentralization led local governments to impose trade protection measures against each other.

Young's work has stimulated a series of studies to investigate trends in market integration. A recent survey by the China State Council Development Research Center (2003) indicates that China's domestic product markets have become more rather than less integrated. Measures of regional protection have also declined significantly over the past decade. Wei and Fan (2004) show that output prices have become more integrated. Huang et al. (2004) use evidence from the rice market to argue that China's commodity markets are becoming increasingly integrated as a result of the reforms. Based on a panel data set of 32 industries at the two-digit level of aggregation in 29 provinces, Bai et al. (2004) find, after an initial decline, an increase in regional specialization of industrial production, suggesting diminishing impediments to regional trade flows. These findings appear to contradict Young's (2000) predictions about worsening market fragmentation.

Besides the final goods market it is also possible that distortions occur in factor markets. De Brauw et al. (2002) show that there has been a huge transfer of rural labor from the low-productivity farming sector to high-productivity non-farm sectors over the past two decades, suggesting a shift toward a more integrated rural labor market. Using the population censuses of 1990 and 1995 to examine labor flows across provinces, Poncet (2003) concludes that the interprovincial border barriers to labor migration have declined from the 1980s to the 1990s. Zhang et al. (2005) find that returns to education in nonpublic enterprises caught up with those in state-owned enterprises, indicating increasing labor mobility across sectors. Yet numerous studies suggest that there is still significant segmentation in the labor market (Meng, 2000; Knight and Li, 2005).

China has instituted several financial market reforms, such as the establishment of a stock market and regionalization of major banks. Yi (2003) argues that these reforms have made China's financial market more efficient. However, several empirical studies reach the opposite conclusion. Fan et al. (2003) find that the provincial marginal rates of return to capital in agriculture, urban industry, urban services, and rural enterprises have diverged since 1985. Boyreau-Debray and Wei (2003) use two methods to test the degree of capital market fragmentation based on provincial data for 1978–2000. The first approach is to examine the correlation of local savings and investment. In an integrated capital market the correlation should be low. The second approach, drawing from the risk-sharing literature, is to check the degree of consumption smoothing across time and space, which is an important indicator of capital mobility and asset market completeness. Both approaches show that the capital market has become more fragmented.[2]

In summary, the empirical literature on trends in market fragmentation and its extent is inconclusive. Most studies focus on either product or factor markets and over a short period only. The objective of this chapter is to document the evolution of both product and factor markets using a more integrated framework over a longer period covering the entire course of economic transition and reforms. To assess the degree of factor market fragmentation, the economy is divided into four sectors: urban industry, urban services, agriculture, and rural enterprises (all non-farm activities such as rural industry, construction, transportation, and commerce). The analysis is based on estimating production functions for each sector, using provincial time series data for 1978–2001. One side contribution of the analysis is the computation of a capital stock series by sector, using fixed investment data from the National Bureau of Statistics that are not yet fully available publicly. The estimated parameters from the regression equations are used to quantify the regional variation in the marginal products of capital and labor by sector. The results confirm that labor markets are becoming more integrated, but also show that capital markets have become more fragmented. As the reforms in the product markets have deepened, distortions seem to have shifted to the capital market. In this sense Young's (2000) argument is still valid: in a partially reformed economy distortions may beget more distortions. However, the distortions may not necessarily stay in the same sector.

The chapter first reviews the history of market development in China in the second half of the twentieth century. It then presents data on changes in labor and capital productivity across sectors and regions in the Chinese economy over recent decades and explores trends in product market integration. Regional variations in the marginal products of capital and labor are quantified and serve as good indicators of factor market integration. The efficiency gains for economic growth are simulated with the current barriers to factor flows across regions and sectors removed. A supplemental appendix, available at http://wber.oxfordjournals.org, provides additional details about the data.

2. MARKET DEVELOPMENT IN CHINA

This section briefly summarizes market development in China in the twentieth century.

2.1. Product Market

Market fragmentation has a long history in China. In the early 1950s China adopted a 'self-sufficient' agricultural and industrial policy at both national and provincial levels (Lin et al., 1996). Provinces were encouraged to develop their own industries and ensure enough grain production. However, the underlying economic structure was often inconsistent with a region's comparative advantage. Therefore, local governments had to impose various protections on local products. The planning system led to serious shortages in final goods, forcing the government to impose rationing on consumers as well.

Since the economic reforms of the late 1970s China has decentralized its fiscal system to provide more incentives for local governments to develop their economies (Zhang, 2006). Under the fierce competition that resulted from fiscal decentralization, interest groups in provinces and cities were eager to protect their local interests. Regional trade wars broke out in the 1980s and early 1990s (Young, 2000). In responding to the crises of regional trade blockades, the National People's Congress passed the 'Law on Unjust Competition' in 1993, and in 2001 the State Council issued order 303 'Stipulation of the State Council to Forbid Regional Blockade in Market Activities.'

2.2. Labor Market

In the 1950s the government established the *hukou* system of household registration, confining people to the village or city of their birth, to ensure enough agricultural labor to produce sufficient grain to support the industrial and urban sector. Rural and urban labor markets became totally segmented (Yang and Zhou, 1999).

Since the 1980s China has gradually reduced institutional barriers to migration (for more detail on China's labor market development, see Fleisher and Yang, 2003; and World Bank, 2005). In 1983 farmers were permitted to engage in transport and marketing of their products beyond local markets. In 1988 the central government permitted farmers to work in cities under the condition that they had to provide their own staples. Since the early 1990s various measures have been introduced to further relax the *hukou* system and encourage greater rural to urban labor mobility. Some cities have adopted a selective migration policy, issuing permanent residency to migrants who paid a fee, invested in local business, or bought expensive houses in the city. In addition, urban reforms of housing, employment policies, and the social security system; the lifting of rationing; and expansion of urban non-state sectors have made it easier for migrant workers to live in cities.

Despite progress in reducing institutional barriers to labor mobility, some obstacles still impede population movement across regions (Fleisher and Yang, 2003). For instance, most rural migrants in cities are unable to obtain legal residence permits and are treated as second-class citizens. They have to pay much higher fees for healthcare and schools than legal residents. Discriminatory treatment of rural migrant workers in employment and social services is commonplace, particularly in the formal sector.

2.3. Capital Market

In the central planning era banks were the dominant source of business financing (World Bank, 2005). They provided loans primarily to formal state enterprises within their locality. The central government exerted direct control over banks. Administrative rather than market forces determined capital movements. The major role of banks was to provide equity financing and to support national development strategies.

Since the late 1970s China has conducted a series of banking sector reforms. In 1983 the four state-owned commercial banks (Bank of China, Agricultural Bank of China, Industrial and Commercial Bank of China and Construction Bank of China) were reorganized to become more market oriented. In addition to direct vertical control within the bank, local governments were granted more horizontal controls over bank branches. As the economy developed rapidly, so did demand for credit. Local governments tightened their control over local bank branches by blocking saving deposits from moving elsewhere. Many local governments forced banks in their jurisdiction to extend credit to them, creating serious inflation in the early 1990s.

Since 1994 the central government has reasserted its control over the banks, ended local government control of bank branches, and set up regional banks to encourage capital mobility across provinces. However, loopholes remain in the system. In particular, local governments can use land to acquire loans to finance infrastructure (World Bank, 2005). Once land is acquired from farmers for public purposes, local governments and developers can use this 'state-owned' land as collateral for credit from the local branches of state banks. Land banking is a major driver of the rapid growth in infrastructure investment in China (Zhang, 2006).

Even after the establishment of the Shanghai and Shenzhen Stock Exchanges in December 1990, banks have retained a dominate role in financial markets. In 2000 the banking system accounted for about two-thirds of financial transactions, while the bond and stock market accounted for only 5 percent of financial flows (World Bank, 2005). There have been many abnormal phenomena in the development of the stock market (Lin, 2004). Most listed companies are state-owned enterprises and in general perform worse than non-public enterprises (Chen, 2003). Many listed companies performed well initially, but their performance deteriorated after the first year. The turnover rate has been much higher than in other countries. The scale of stock market activity is too small to contribute significantly to capital mobility across regions and sectors, something it should be able to do as it grows.

Despite the financial sector reforms rural small businesses still find it harder to obtain credit than do urban-based, state-owned enterprises. The recent arrest and release of millionaire entrepreneur Sun Dawu highlights the problem. Because of the difficulties in raising funds from state-owned banks and credit cooperatives, Mr Sun solicited deposits from his employees and local rural residents, which violated the state law (*The Economist*, 2004). Anecdotal evidence aside, more research is needed to quantify whether the capital market has become more integrated or more fragmented.

3.   CHANGES IN FACTOR PRODUCTIVITY

Driven largely by institutional reforms, the Chinese economy has experienced a dramatic transformation over recent decades.[3] The share of agricultural GDP in total GDP declined from more than half in 1952 to less than 20 percent in 2001, while the share of the rural nonfarm sector increased from almost zero to more than a quarter. Coupled with these structural changes was a massive shift of labor from the lower productivity agricultural sector to the higher productivity non-farm sector.

Table 8.1:   *Labor and Capital Productivity by Region*

Productivity	China	East	Central	Western	Northeast
Labor productivity					
1978	868	1073	707	619	1672
1984	1260	1655	1046	853	2072
1990	1841	2578	1471	1201	2912
1995	3356	5429	2567	1842	4409
2001	5949	9694	4468	3223	8063
Growth rate (%)	8.7	10.0	8.3	7.4	7.1
Capital productivity					
1978	36	41	38	25	45
1984	42	45	43	32	47
1990	41	42	42	36	43
1995	53	56	55	43	51
2001	52	52	54	47	57
Growth rate (%)	1.6	1.0	1.5	2.7	1.1

Note: The unit of labor productivity is 1978 yuan; the unit of capital productivity is 1978 yuan per 100 yuan capital stock. East includes the municipalities of Beijing, Shanghai, and Tianjin, and the provinces of Fujian, Guangdong, Hainan, Hebei, Jiangsu, Shangdong, and Zhejiang. Central includes Anhui, Henan, Hubei, Hunan, Jiangxi, and Shanxi Provinces. West includes the autonomous regions of Nei Mongol, Ningxia, Tibet, and Xinjiang, and the provinces of Gansu, Guangxi, Guizhou, Ningxia, Qinghai, Shanxi, Sichuan, and Yunnan. Northeast includes Heilongjiang, Jilin, and Liaoning Provinces.

Source: Calculated by the authors based on the data for 28 provinces, which are slightly different from those based on national data. For details on the data see supplemental appendix S.1, available at http://wber.oxfordjournals.org.

Table 8.2:   *Labor and Capital Productivity by Sector*

Productivity	China	Agriculture	Urban industry	Urban services	Rural nonfarm
Labor productivity					
1978	868	346	3 245	1 949	623
1984	1 260	509	3 783	2 883	856
1990	1 841	585	5 713	4 615	1 510
1995	3 356	761	8 597	6 275	4 917
2001	5 949	987	23 074	9 573	8 193
Growth rate (%)	8.7	4.7	8.9	7.2	11.9
Capital productivity					
1978	36	52	46	19	22
1984	42	74	45	26	30
1990	41	78	38	30	59
1995	53	74	45	33	121
2001	52	57	51	25	192
Growth rate (%)	1.6	0.4	0.5	1.1	9.8

Note: The unit of labor productivity is 1978 yuan; the unit of capital productivity is 1978 yuan per 100 yuan capital stock.

Source: Calculated by the authors based on provincial data. For details on the data see supplemental appendix S.1, available at http://wber.oxfordjournals.org.

Growth in labor and capital productivity by region and sector highlights the dramatic changes in factor markets and economic structure over the period 1978–2001 (Tables 8.1 and 8.2). Labor and capital productivities are calculated as the ratios of GDP to labor and capital; they are therefore measures of average not marginal productivity.

There are large regional variations in labor productivity, and they have widened over time. The northeast region had the highest labor productivity in 1978, but by 2001 it had fallen well behind the eastern region. The regional gap between the west and the rest of China has worsened over time. Compared with labor productivity, the regional disparities in capital productivity are much smaller, and they have narrowed over time.

Labor productivity grew fastest in the rural non-farm sector and slowest in the agricultural sector (see Table 8.2). Labor productivity began at a relatively low level in agriculture, and the gap with other sectors is now much wider. The transfer of rural labor from farm to non-farm activities will undoubtedly have enhanced overall economic growth and labor productivity. The rural nonfarm sector also experienced the most rapid growth in capital productivity and by 2001 had achieved the highest level of all sectors. These disparities highlight capital market imperfections and the hunger for credit and capital that remains within rural areas for non-farm activities. Broadening access to credit and investing more in the rural nonfarm sector would enhance economic efficiency and growth.

A comparison of the labor productivity of the industrial and service sectors relative to agriculture for China and several other Asian countries helps to put China's economic transformation in a broader international perspective (Table 8.3). The differences are stark. The labor productivity

Table 8.3: *Trends in the Labor Productivity of the Industry and Service Sectors as a Ratio of Agricultural Labor Productivity, China and Other Selected Asian Countries, Various Years*

Country/ year	Industry/ agriculture	Services/ agriculture	Country/ year	Industry/ agriculture	Services/ agriculture
China			Indonesia		
1978	7.0	4.9	1993	7.2	3.6
1988	4.6	3.8	1998	7.0	2.8
1995	5.4	3.2	2002	6.5	3.0
2001	7.5	4.0	Malaysia		
Philippines			1987	2.7	1.5
1989	4.4	2.1	1995	2.1	1.8
1995	4.5	2.1	2001	2.5	1.9
2002	4.2	1.8	Taiwan, China		
Korea, Rep.			1981	2.4	3.9
1987	2.5	2.6	1988	2.6	3.9
1995	2.4	1.9	1995	2.9	4.7
2002	3.1	1.7	2002	3.0	4.5
Japan			United States		
1990	3.2	3.0	1987	1.5	1.6
1995	3.1	3.4	1995	1.8	1.7
2001	3.3	3.4	2001	1.4	1.3

Source: World Bank, various years, World Development Indicators.

ratio of industry to agriculture is much higher in China than in other Asian countries. Moreover, while the ratios for other countries have generally remained stable or fallen, the ratio for China has risen substantially over the past 20 years. The same is true for the labor productivity ratio between services and agriculture. These extremely high ratios for China as well their increasing trends are symptomatic of major distortions in China's factor markets. There appears to be considerable potential for further economic growth simply by reallocating labor and capital among sectors.

4. TRENDS IN PRODUCT MARKET INTEGRATION

This section updates Young's (2000) analysis of the trends in product market integration. As in Young, the analysis uses the following sum of the squared deviations of the sectoral output shares of China's provinces from the group average to the degree of product market integration:

Unweighted measure: $\sum_i \sum_j (S_{ij} - \bar{S}_j)^2$ (8.1)

Weighted measure: $\sum_i \sum_j N * w_i (S_{ij} - \bar{S}_j)^2$ (8.2)

where S_{ij} denotes the share of sector j in province i's output; S_j is the group average S_{ij} across provinces; w_i denotes the province's share of total GDP of N provinces and $\bar{S}_j = \sum w_i S_{ij}$. In the absence of trade a region would return to an autarky type of Robinson economy, with a production structure diversified to cope with daily needs for food, clothes, shelter, and so on. Therefore, without trade, the likelihood of having a specialized production structure is much smaller than with trade integration. It is expected that the more barriers there are to interregional trade, the more similar the composition of output across provinces and the smaller the value of the measures.

Graphing the unweighted and weighted measures of the composition of output shares for 1978–2001 shows similar results – the composition of output converges up to the early 1990s and diverges thereafter (Figure 8.1). Product market development follows a U-shaped curve. An initial decline is followed by an upward trend that leads to a higher overall degree of regional specialization in 2001 than in 1978. The convergence between 1978 and the early 1990s replicates Young's (2000) finding that China's product market became more fragmented. However, the upward trend of the

Figure 8.1: Convergence in the Composition of Output

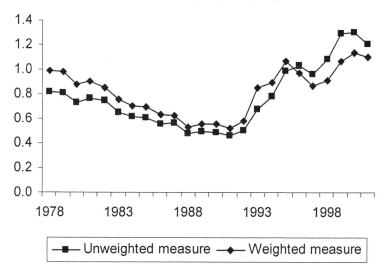

Note: The measures are the weighted and unweighted sum of squared deviations of the sectoral output shares of China's provinces from the national average.

Source: Authors' analysis based on data described in supplemental appendix S.1.

measures since the early 1990s indicates that product markets have become more integrated. The evolving pattern of regional integration reported here for a four-sector disaggregation of GDP also echoes the findings of Bai et al. (2004) based on a 36-industry breakdown. The turning-point coincides with the time when the central government took serious measures to remove interregional trade barriers. The initial market reforms may have brought about more distortions in the short run, but with deepening reform, the barriers in the product markets were broken down over time.

Figure 8.2 presents the standard deviation of the logarithmic provincial GDPs per capita of farming, urban industry, urban service, and rural non-farm activities. The variations in output per capita of urban industry and urban services are steady up to 1990 and then increase rapidly. The standard deviation of output per capita of farming increases by 81 percent from 1978 to 1994 and levels off thereafter, while the spatial distribution of rural nonfarm activity becomes increasingly uneven over the whole sample period. However, as Young (2000, p. 1111) notes: 'The imposition of trade barriers has clear implications for the interregional variation in output shares; it has no prediction regarding the variation in absolute output

Figure 8.2:   Standard Deviation of ln GDP per capita

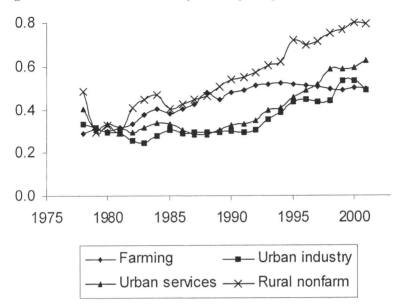

Source: Authors' analysis based on data described in supplemental appendix S.1.

levels.' Nonetheless, the variations of output per capita in the four sectors offer useful information on the evolution of spatial distribution of economic activities.

5.   VARIATIONS IN MARGINAL PRODUCTS OF CAPITAL AND LABOR

Following the analysis above of recent trends in product market integration, this section turns to an analysis of possible fragmentation in factor markets. Resource allocation is most efficient when the marginal product of each input is equalized across sectors and regions. Thus intersectoral and interregional variations in the marginal product of each factor can show the degree of factor market distortions and hence opportunities for achieving greater economic efficiency through improved factor allocation.[4]

Assume that real value added (GDP) by sector follows a well-behaved, neoclassical production function:

$$Y_{it} = f_{it}\left(X_{i1t},...,X_{ijt},...,X_{imt},T\right) \tag{8.3}$$

where X_{ijt} is input j for sector i in year t. A thornier question is what functional form of the production function to use. Considering both econometric estimation and theoretical consistency, the following Cobb-Douglas functional form can be specified:[5]

$$\ln\left(Y_{it}\right) = A_{it} + \sum_{j} b_{ij} \ln(X_{ijt}), \qquad (8.4)$$

where $A_{it} = a_{i0} + a_{it}t + a_{iit}t^2$

or $A_{it} = c_{i0} + \sum c_{it} D_t .$

D_t is a set of year dummy variables, and c_{it} is the corresponding coefficient. The parameters in equation (8.4) corresponding to labor and capital are their elasticities. The estimated function for agriculture includes arable land as a separate input in addition to capital and labor. Because arable land area does not change much and is location-specific, provincial dummy variables cannot be used to control for potential heteroscedasticity. As a compromise, dummy variables for the eastern, central, and western regions are added to the production functions. To capture technological change over time, the time trend and its square are included in one specification. In a second specification the fixed effects of year dummy variables are added.

To estimate production functions for each of the four sectors, data are used for 28 provinces for 24 years (1978–2001), providing a panel of 672 observations. Tibet is excluded mainly because of lack of data. For data consistency, Chongqing and Hainan Provinces are included in Guangdong and Sichuan Provinces, although they were separated in 1987 and 1997. A detailed description of the data used is provided in the supplemental appendix (available at http://wber.oxfordjournals.org/).

The results of the estimated production functions for the four sectors under two different specifications are presented in Table 8.4.[6] Because agricultural output is measured as value added, intermediate inputs such as fertilizer are excluded from output measures by definition. Including fertilizer and other intermediate inputs is more appropriate in estimating a production function for gross output. The results under the two different specifications are similar. The adjusted R^2s are high for all the regressions, indicating a good fit. The year dummy variables in the first specifications are jointly significant in all four regressions. Most coefficients for the time trend variables in the second specification are statistically significant.

The regression results for agriculture indicate that land still plays an important role in Chinese agricultural production. Among the regressions

Table 8.4: Estimated Production Functions by Sector, China

| | Specification I | | | |
	Agriculture	Urban industry	Urban service	Rural non-farm
Labor	0.430*	0.852*	0.708*	0.601*
	(0.026)	(0.037)	(0.036)	(0.026)
Capital	0.111*	0.256*	0.263*	0.364*
	(0.018)	(0.036)	(0.029)	(0.031)
Land	0.386*	–	–	–
	(0.031)			
Eastern region	0.081*	0.376*	0.373*	−0.325*
	(0.039)	(0.039)	(0.051)	(0.056)
Central region	−0.203*	−0.152*	0.107*	−0.391*
	(0.033)	(0.040)	(0.051)	(0.055)
Western region	−0.521*	0.044	0.018	−0.818*
	(0.035)	(0.047)	(0.048)	(0.057)
Year dummy variable	Yes*	Yes*	Yes*	Yes*
Adjusted R^2	0.951	0.928	0.917	0.958
	Specification II			
Labor	0.428*	0.819*	0.694*	0.565*
	(0.026)	(0.037)	(0.036)	(0.026)
Capital	0.114*	0.287*	0.273*	0.406*
	(0.018)	(0.038)	(0.029)	(0.032)
Land	0.386*	–	–	–
	(0.031)			
Eastern region	0.079*	0.373*	0.363*	−0.330*
	(0.039)	(0.040)	(0.051)	(0.058)
Central region	−0.203*	−0.156*	0.105*	−0.378*
	(0.032)	(0.040)	(0.043)	(0.058)
Western region	−0.522*	0.030	0.010	−0.791*
	(0.035)	(0.047)	(0.048)	(0.059)
T	0.071*	0.110	0.088*	0.037*
	(0.005)	(0.659)	(0.007)	(0.009)
$T^2/100$	0.112*	0.245*	−0.171*	0.323*
	(0.020)	(0.026)	(0.029)	(0.037)
Adjusted R^2	0.951	0.928	0.917	0.954

Note: Figures in parenthesis are standard errors. *Significant at the 10 percent level.

Source: Authors' analysis based on data described in supplemental appendix S.1, available at http://wber.oxfordjournals.org.

for all the sectors labor elasticity is larger than capital elasticity, indicating that China's comparative advantage lies in labor-intensive production.

Differences in estimated elasticities for the same input across sectors reflect differences in production technology, but on their own do not provide any indication of how efficiently resources are allocated. To obtain such insights it is necessary to calculate the marginal productivities of each factor. The marginal product of each factor is equal to the product of the estimated elasticity and the corresponding partial factor productivity:

$$\frac{\partial Y_{it}}{\partial X_{ijt}} = b_{ij}\frac{Y_{it}}{X_{ijt}}. \tag{8.5}$$

Figure 8.3 presents the marginal product of labor and capital by sector. The marginal product of labor is much higher in urban areas than in the farming and rural non-farm sector, indicating huge potential gains from rural to urban labor migrations. In 1990 the marginal product of labor in urban industry was about 19 times that of agriculture and the marginal product of labor of urban services was about 13 times that of agriculture. The results are comparable to the findings in Yang and Zhou (1999) that the ratios of the marginal product of labor in the state sector to the agricultural sector was about 15 and 16 between 1988 and 1992. The ratio of the marginal product of labor in the rural non-farm sector to the farming sector in 1990 was 3.6 in 1990, similar to the 3.7 in 1992 reported by Wang (1997). In 1993 the Company Law was passed to encourage privatization of town and village enterprises. As a result, their share in gross industrial output value jumped from 20 percent to 25 percent while that of state enterprises dropped from 43 percent to 34 percent from 1993 to 1995 (China National Bureau of Statistics, *China Statistical Yearbook*, various years). The large difference in marginal product of labor suggests potential gains in aggregate output from labor mobility across sectors.

The graph of the marginal product of capital by sector shows that the non-farm sector has grown much faster than other sectors and by 2001 has the highest value among the four sectors (see Figure 8.3). The marginal product of capital is lowest in the farming and urban service sectors.

Overall, the differences in marginal product of factors across sectors are quite large. A generalized entropy (GE) inequality measure was used to quantify the degree of variation in the marginal products of inputs across the 4 sectors and 28 provinces.[7] Because each province has four sectors, there are 2688 observations in all. Figures 8.4 and 8.5 graph the variations in the marginal products of labor and capital.

Figure 8.3:   *Marginal Products of Labor and Capital*

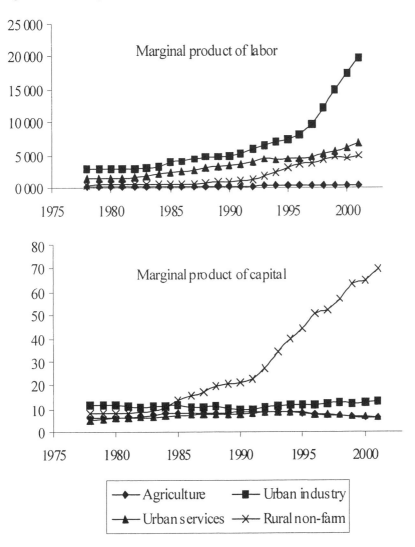

Source: Authors' analysis based on data described in supplemental appendix S.1, available at http://wber.oxfordjournals.org.

The marginal product of labor has shown some convergence over the reform period, except in the last five years of the analysis (which may be

Figure 8.4:   *Variations in Marginal Products of Labor and Capital by*
               Sector

Marginal product of labor

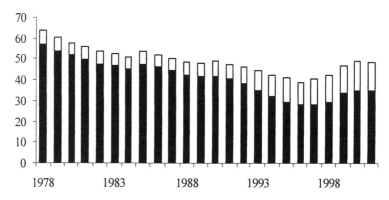

Marginal product of capital

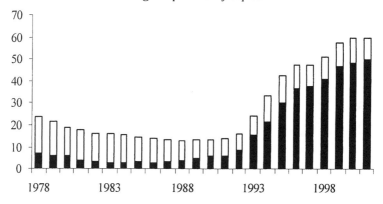

Note: The blank bars show the within-sector variation, while the solid bars show the
between-sector variation.

Source: Authors' analysis based on data described in supplemental appendix S.1.

the result of changes in the way the labor surveys were conducted during
those years; see supplemental appendix). Variation in the marginal product
of capital, by contrast, was steady between 1978 and the early 1990s before
rising substantially. The divergence in the marginal product of capital
during the 1990s indicates greater fragmentation of capital markets. This
finding is consistent with that of Boyrau-Debray and Wei (2003). These
results suggest that as competition intensified in product and labor markets,
distortions may have shifted to banking, real estate, and infrastructure

projects. In this sense the findings support Young's (2000) argument that partial reforms may lead to more distortions in the rest of the economy.

The GE family of inequality measures can be decomposed into the sum of within- and between-group components for any given partitioning of the population into mutually exclusive and exhaustive groups. Figure 8.4 graphs the within- and Figure 8.5 the between-group (region and sector) components of the variation in the marginal products of capital and labor. The ratio of the between-group component to overall inequality is called the polarization index (Kanbur and Zhang, 1999; Zhang and Kanbur, 2001).

Figure 8.5:   *Variations in Marginal Products of Labor and Capital by Region*

Marginal product of labor

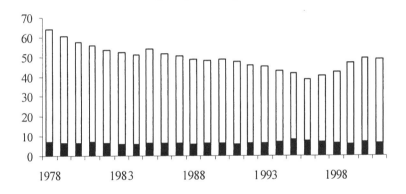

Marginal product of capital

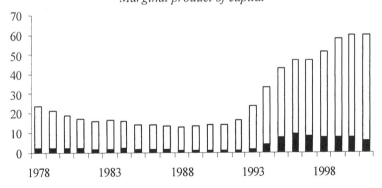

Note: The blank bars show the within-region variation, while the solid bars show the between-regiont variation.

Source: Authors' analysis based on data described in supplemental appendix S.1.

Intersectoral variations in the marginal products of labor and capital contribute far more to overall inequality than interregional variation. In particular, the sectoral polarization index on the marginal product of capital has increased. This provides further evidence that as the reform process has deepened in the product market, the capital market has become more distorted.

These results indicate that there is room to improve China's overall economic efficiency simply by reallocating factors among sectors and regions. Reversing the entrenched urban-biased investment policies and undertaking in-depth reforms within the financial sector would not only have the greatest impact on economic efficiency but would also promote greater equity as most poor people live and work in rural areas.

6.   POLICY SIMULATIONS

How large are the potential gains from improving factor market performance? To answer this question, estimated production functions from the first specification in Table 8.4 are used to calculate the potential increases in national GDP resulting from simulated factor reallocations.[8] Supplemental appendix S.2 reports the underlying models and baseline information. As a first step the models are calibrated to obtain the constant terms in the production functions of the four sectors based on the estimated elasticities on labor, capital, and GDP information for 2001. Doing that means that the production functions will predict the actual results for 2001. Next, the calibrated models are used in the four sectors to conduct policy simulations.

Considering the low level of labor productivity in the agricultural sector, the first experiment is to move additional labor out of that sector. With 2001 as a baseline three scenarios are evaluated: moving 1 percent, 5 percent, and 10 percent of the agricultural labor force out of agriculture and distributing it equally among the other three sectors (Table 8.5). Reallocating even 1 percent of the agricultural labor force could increase national GDP by 0.9 percent. Reallocating 5 percent or 10 percent increases national GDP by 4.4 percent or 8.8 percent. The results are supported by an independent early study by Yang and Zhou (1999), who find gains in aggregate output of 0.7 percent, 3.1 percent, and 5.8 percent based on the same three hypothetical percentage transfers of labor using 1992 as a baseline.

The second experiment simulates a change in the current urban-biased policies by shifting capital from cities to rural areas while keeping total capital constant. Reallocating 1 percent, 5 percent, and 10 percent of urban

Table 8.5: Impact of Alternative Policy Simulations on China's GDP

Experiment	Results		
Move x% of the agricultural labor force			
out of farming	1%	5%	10%
Change in GDP (%)	0.89	4.42	8.77
	(0.89)	(4.22)	(8.78)
Reallocate x% investment from cities to			
rural areas	1%	5%	10%
Change in GDP (%)	0.46	2.13	3.90
	(0.41)	(1.90)	(3.45)
Add x billion yuan of investment in rural			
areas	10	50	100
Change in GDP over 2001 (%)	0.03	0.15	0.29
	(0.03)	(0.14)	(0.27)
Change in GDP over 2001 (billion yuan)	3.66	18.26	32.31
Add x billion yuan of investment in urban			
areas	10	50	100
Change in GDP over 2001 (%)	0.01	0.04	0.07
	(0.01)	(0.04)	(0.08)
Change in GDP over 2001 (billion yuan)	0.92	4.58	9.16
	(1.03)	(5.16)	(10.30)
The ratio of returns to investment in	3.99	3.98	3.97
rural areas to urban areas	(3.60)	(3.59)	(3.58)

Note: The figures in the parentheses are the simulation results based on adjusted national GDP data.

Source: Authors' analysis based on data described in supplemental appendix S.1, available at http://wber.oxfordjournals.org.

capital to rural areas leads to gains in national GDP of 0.5 percent, 2.1 percent, and 3.9 percent.

The third experiment assumes that the government allocates all the additional investment in rural areas and distributes it equally between the agricultural and rural non-farm sectors. The investment is converted into capital stock using a discount rate of 4 percent and a national fixed asset price index.[9] An additional 10 billion yuan of investment in rural areas yields a 0.03 percent increase in national GDP, equivalent to 2.9 billion 2001 yuan. Considering that the farm and rural non-farm sectors are labor intensive, this scenario would likely also boost the incomes of many of the poorest people in China. When investment increases to 50 billion yuan, national GDP rises by 0.15 percent (14.3 billion yuan) and when it increases to 100 billion yuan GDP rises by 0.29 percent (28.4 billion yuan). Because the capital does not vanish immediately, the long-term impact is much higher. Assuming a 4 percent discount rate, the annual internal rate of returns to the investment in rural areas is more than 20 percent.

The next experiment considers a counterfactual scenario in which all the additional investment is distributed evenly in the two urban sectors. Under the three scenarios of investment of 10, 50, and 100 billion yuan, national GDP increases by 0.92, 4.58, and 9.16 billion yuan. As shown in the last row of the table, the rate of returns to rural investment is almost four times of that to urban investment.

The National Statistical Bureau adjusted national GDP figures based on the first economic census in 2004. To check the robustness of the results, the constant terms in the four production functions were recalibrated as shown in supplemental appendix S.2 using the adjusted 2001 GDP data by sector, and the same set of simulations was undertaken. The basic results are similar to those based on original GDP figures (see Table 8.5).

The policy simulation highlights the potential economic gains from reallocating factors from low- to high-productivity sectors. Removing barriers to labor movement, reversing the urban bias in government investment policies, and deepening reforms would significantly enhance overall economic growth. In addition, these policy changes could bring about favorable distributional effects by reducing regional and sectoral inequalities. Since large inequalities are a potential source of social conflict and instability, the far-reaching social impact of these policies could be equally important.

7.   CONCLUSIONS AND POLICY IMPLICATIONS

The aim of China's reforms is to reduce economic distortions and improve efficiency. This chapter has examined the changing patterns of distortions during the reform process, how past policies have contributed to these distortions, and the estimated cost to the economy through lower output and greater regional and sectoral disparity. The empirical findings indicate that product markets in China have become more integrated after a short period of increasing fragmentation in the early reform period. Labor markets also have become increasingly integrated due to a large shift in the labor force from the agricultural sector to non-farm sectors and relaxed constraints on migration. However, intersectoral differences in the marginal product of capital have grown during the reform period.

Local governments, which have been collecting rents in a partially reformed system, are the interim winners from reform. In the short run distortions might beget more distortions, as Young (2000) has shown. However, in response to the increasing fragmentation in product markets, the government has undertaken measures to remove local protections. Consequently, there are fewer and fewer rents to be collected in the product and labor markets over time, and the distortions have been increasingly squeezed into the financial and land markets (including infrastructure and real estate). For local governments these are the two last bastions for rent collection, as well as breeding grounds for corruption. Looking only at the product market suggests that the market might have become distorted in the short run. However, as the government responded to the problems with deepening reforms, the market became integrated. When all the sectors are considered, however, the results seem to support Young's argument that as some distortions in a partially reformed economy are removed, new distortions may be added. The key is whether the government can continue to add new reforms to squeeze out the distortions in the capital market as those in the product and labor markets were squeezed out before them.

The continuing large differences in labor and capital productivity across sectors suggests that China still has great potential for further efficiency gains through continued structural change. To realize this potential, however, restrictions on factor movement, in particular intersectoral capital movement, need to be removed. Efficient capital markets that can funnel new investment to sectors with higher returns still need to be developed. The higher capital returns in the rural non-farm sector suggest that more aggressive government policies should be sought to increase investment there or at least not hinder its movement. Such policies will not only improve overall economic performance, but will also narrow the development and inequality gaps between the rural and urban sectors. Similarly, the government should encourage labor movement from agriculture to rural enterprises, urban industry, and service sectors since labor productivity in these sectors continues to be much higher than in the agriculture sector.

While empirical estimates and policy simulations can provide rough order of magnitude estimates of structural problems, policy recommendations on gradual elimination of these distortions need to take into account complex issues of political feasibility, sequencing, implementation problems, downside risks of policy measures, nature of vested interests and how to overcome them, the need to minimize negative side effects, and the effects on equity, regional disparity, and rural–urban inequality. More research is needed to understand the political economy dimensions that have at times seriously constrained the pace of reform. Nonetheless, simulations of alternative policy proposals and their estimated effects could act as useful inputs to policymaking.

NOTES

1. Xiaobo Zhang is a senior research fellow at the International Food Policy Research Institute; his email address is x.zhang@cgiar.org. Kong-Yam Tan, formerly a senior economist at the World Bank Beijing Office, is a professor at Nanyang Technological University, Singapore; his email address is kytan@ntu.edu.sg. A supplemental appendix to this article is available at http://wber.oxfordjournals.org/.

2. Recent rent-seeking activities in the banking and real estate sectors include those of Yang Xiuzhu, vice chief of the construction department of Zhejiang Province, who extracted bribes from property developers and disappeared (*Caijing*, 23 July 2003); Shanghai real estate tycoon, Zhou Zhengyi, who was implicated in an array of illegal loans coupled with default on statutory compensations for relocatees whose homes were improperly demolished for redevelopment projects (*Shanghai Daily*, 6 September 2003); Chen Kai, a local government official of Fuzhou, Fujian Province, who borrowed an estimated $50 million from six state banks and provided kickbacks of around 5 percent of the loans to the lending officers (*Washington Post*, 17 December 2003); former chairman of China Everbright Group, Zhu Xiaohua, who was sentenced to 15 years in jail in November 2002 for taking bribes worth 4 million yuan (*Caijing*, 25 December 2002); and Zhu Yaoming, a stock speculator who was arrested in July 2003 for loan fraud involving 2 billion yuan, which he borrowed from securities firms and banks to speculate on stocks in the Shanghai and Shenzhen stock exchanges (*Caijing*, 25 December 2003). Numerous Communist Party officials have also been ousted for accepting bribes involving property and real estate projects. They include the former general secretary of Guizhou Province, Liu Fangren; former general secretary of Hebei Province, Cheng Weigao; former Minister of Land and Resources, Tian Fengshan; a former vice mayor of Shenzhen City; and a former mayor and a vice mayor of Shenyang City.

3. Lin (1992) provides a good reference for rural reforms; Groves et al. (1994) cover the reforms of state-owned enterprises; Lau et al. (2000) explain the rationale behind the successful price reforms.

4. Desai and Martin (1983) estimated the efficiency loss due to resource misallocation in industry in the former Soviet Union using a similar method. Syrquin (1988) conducted a similar exercise.

5. It is well known that the Cobb–Douglas form has caveats. It assumes constant returns to scale and strong separability among inputs. To test the robustness of the results on the first caveat, Zhang and Tan (2004) present an alternative specification using a varying coefficient model, and the basic findings are the same. Several flexible functional forms have been put forward to address the separability problem. However, their limitations have been increasingly recognized in the empirical literature (Chambers, 1988). For example, the multicollinearity problem inherent among the interactive terms and the fewer restrictions on the underlying production technology often lead to results that do not make much economic sense.

6. The calculations of variations in marginal products of factors are rather robust to various specifications in large part because marginal products are determined mainly by factor productivity across sectors rather than by the estimated elasticities. For simplicity, the inequality measures based on several alternative specifications are not reported here but are available on request.

7. Other measures are also used, and the results are similar. Following Shorrocks (1980), the GE measure in the marginal product of capital (k) can be written as:

$$
GE(c) = \begin{cases} \sum_{i,j} w_{ij} \left\{ \left(\dfrac{M_{ijk}}{\mu} \right)^{c} - 1 \right\} & c \neq 0,1 \\[2ex] \sum_{i,j} w_{ij} \left(\dfrac{M_{ijk}}{\mu} \right) \log \left(\dfrac{M_{ijk}}{\mu} \right) & c = 1 \\[2ex] \sum_{i,j} w_{ij} \log \left(\dfrac{\mu}{M_{ijk}} \right) & c = 0 \end{cases}
$$

where M_{ijk} denotes the marginal product of factor k for sector j in province i, μ is the arithmetic sample mean, and w_{ij} is the share of GDP of sector j for province i in total GDP. GE(0) is the mean logarithmic deviation, GE(1) is the Theil index, and GE(2) equals half the square of the coefficient of variation. In principle, the GE measures are sensitive to various parts of the distribution depending on the selected value of c. The simplest form of this equation was used in which $c = 0$. When $c = 0$, it is the mean logarithm deviation and more sensitive to the bottom part of the distribution. The results are similar for $c = 1$ and $c = 2$. The reason for using GE is its appealing property of decomposing overall inequality into between- and within-group subcomponents.

8. Policy simulations point out only the potential gains from reform. However, questions remain on the mapping from simulations to actual reforms. In addition, there are no standard errors. Therefore the precision cannot be assessed. It is likely that the simulations results depend on the underlying functional forms as well as the accuracy of the data. We are reassured in that simulations based on a varying coefficient model have led to similar findings (Zhang and Tan, 2004). In Table 8.5, we also check the robustness of the results by undertaking similar simulations with a baseline of higher labor productivity in the agriculture sector.

9. For the period 1991–2001 the national fixed asset price index is available from the *China Statistical Yearbook*. However, it was not published prior to 1991. Therefore, the national GDP deflator is used a proxy for the period 1978–91. For the whole period the calculated capital price index is 3.53, compared with the published GDP deflator of 3.33.

BIBLIOGRAPHY

Bai, C., Y. Duan, Z. Tao and S.T. Tong (2004), 'Local protectionism and regional specialization: Evidence from China's industries', *Journal of International Economics*, **63**(2), 397–417.

Boyreau-Debray, G. and S. Wei (2003), 'How fragmented is the capital market in China?', Paper presented at the Workshop on National Market Integration organized by the World Bank Beijing Office, 6 September, Beijing, Development Research Center of the State Council, Beijing.

Chambers, R. (1988), *Applied Production Analysis: A Dual Approach*, New York: Press Syndicate of the University of Cambridge.

Chen, Z. (2003), 'Capital markets and legal development: The China case', *China Economic Review*, **14**(4), 451–72.

China, National Bureau of Statistics (1990), *Historical Statistical Materials for Provinces, Autonomous Regions and Municipalities 1949–1989*, Beijing: China Statistical Publishing House.

China, National Bureau of Statistics (1996), *China Fixed Asset Investment Statistical Materials, 1950–95*, Beijing: China Statistical Publishing House.

China, National Bureau of Statistics (1997a), *Calculation Methods of China Annual GDP*, Beijing: China Statistical Publishing House.

China, National Bureau of Statistics (1997b), *The Gross Domestic Product of China, 1952–95*, Dalin, China: Dongbei University of Finance and Economics Press.

China, National Bureau of Statistics (Various years), *China Rural Statistical Yearbooks*, Beijing: China Statistical Publishing House.

China, National Bureau of Statistics (Various years), *China Statistical Yearbooks*, Beijing: China Statistical Publishing House.

China, National Bureau of Statistics (Various years), *China Township and Village Enterprise Statistical Yearbook*, Beijing: China Statistical Publishing House.

China State Council, Development Research Center (2003), 'Research on measures, objectives and degrees of local protection in Chinese market: An analysis based on sample survey', Paper presented at the Workshop on National Market Integration organized by the World Bank Beijing Office, 6 September, Beijing.

Chow, G. (1993), 'Capital formation and economic growth in China', *Quarterly Journal of Economics*, **108**(3), 809–42.

de Brauw, A., J. Huang, S. Rozelle, L. Zhang and Y. Zhang (2002), 'The evolution of China's rural labor markets during the reforms', *Journal of Comparative Economics*, **30**(2), 329–53.

Desai, P. and R. Martin (1983), 'Efficiency loss from resource misallocation in Soviet industry', *Quarterly Journal of Economics*, **98**(3), 441–56.

The Economist (2004), 'Wealth in Asia: China speaking out', 3 January, 26–7.

Fan, S., X. Zhang and S. Robinson (2003), 'Structure change and economic growth in China', *Review of Development Economics*, **7**(3), 360–77.

Fleisher, B. and D. Tao Yang (2003), 'China's labor market', Paper presented at the Stanford Center for International Development conference on 'China's Market Reforms', Stanford University, 19–20 September, Palo Alto, CA.

Groves, T., Y. Hong, J. McMillan and B. Naughton (1994), 'Autonomy and incentives in Chinese state enterprises', *Quarterly Journal of Economics*, **109**(1), 183–209.

Huang, J., S. Rozelle and M. Chang (2004), 'Tracking distortions in agriculture: China and its accession to the World Trade Organization', *World Bank Economic Review*, **18**(1), 59–84.

Kanbur, R. and X. Zhang (1999), 'Which regional inequality? The evolution of rural–urban and inland–coastal inequality in China (1983–1995)', *Journal of Comparative Economics*, **27**(4), 686–701.

Knight, J. and S. Li (2005), 'Wages, firm profitability and labor market segmentation in urban China', *China Economic Review*, **16**(3), 205–28.

Kohli, U. (1978), 'A gross national product function and the derived demand for imports and supply of exports', *Canadian Journal of Economics*, **11**(2), 167–82.

Lau, L., Y. Qian and G. Roland (2000), 'Reform without losers: An interpretation of China's dual-track approach to transition', *Journal of Political Economy*, **108**(1), 120–43.

Li, K. (2003), 'China's capital and productivity measurement using financial resources', Economic Growth Center Discussion Paper 851, Yale University, New Haven, CT.

Lin, J. (1992), 'Rural reforms and agricultural growth in China', *American Economic Review*, **82**(1), 34–51.

Lin, J. (2004), 'Viability and the development of China's capital markets', *China & World Economy*, **12**(6), 3–10.

Lin, J., F. Cai and Z. Li (1996), *The China Miracle: Development Strategy and Economic Reform*, Hong Kong: The Chinese University Press.

Maddison, A. (1998), *Chinese Economic Performance in the Long Run*, Paris: Organisation for Economic Co-operation and Development.

Meng, X. (2000), *Labor Market Reform in China*, New York: Cambridge University Press.

Ministry of Agriculture (1980–94), Various Issues, *China's Agricultural Yearbook*, Beijing: China's Agricultural Press.

Poncet, Sandra (2003), 'Domestic market fragmentation and economic growth in China', ERSA Conference Paper ersa03p117, European Regional Science Association.

Shorrocks, A. (1980), 'The class of additively decomposable inequality measures', *Econometrica*, **48**(3), 613–25.

Syrquin, M. (1988), 'Patterns of structural change', in Hollis B. Chenery and T.N. Srinivasan (eds), *Handbook of Development Economics*, Vol. I, Amsterdam: North-Holland.

Wang, X. (1997), 'What contributed to China's rapid rural industrial growth during the reform period?', Ph.D. dissertation, Department of Economics, The Australia National University, Canberra.

Wei, X. and C. Fan (2004), 'Converge to the law of one price in China', Paper presented at the Allied Social Sciences Annual Meeting, 3–5 January, San Diego, Calif.

World Bank (2005), *China: Integration of National Product and Factor Markets– Economic Benefits and Policy Recommendations*, Washington, DC.

World Bank (Various years), *World Development Indicators*, Washington, DC.

Yang, D. and H. Zhou (1999), 'Rural–urban disparity and sectoral labor allocation in China', *Journal of Development Studies*, **35**(3), 105–33.

Yi, Gang (2003), 'History of financial market', Paper presented at the Workshop on National Market Integration organized by the World Bank Beijing Office, 6 September, Beijing. Development Research Center of the State Council, Beijing.

Young, A. (2000), 'The razor's edge: Distortions and incremental reform in the People's Republic of China', *Quarterly Journal of Economics*, **115**(4), 1091– 135.

Zhang, J., Y. Zhao, A. Park and X. Song (2005), 'Economic returns to schooling in urban China, 1988 to 2001', *Journal of Comparative Economics*, **33**(4), 730–52.

Zhang, X. (2006), 'Fiscal decentralization and political centralization in China: Implications for regional inequality', *Journal of Comparative Economics*, **34**(4), 713–26.

Zhang, X. and R. Kanbur (2001), 'What difference do polarisation measures make? An application to China', *Journal of Development Studies*, **37**(3), 85–98.

Zhang, X. and T. Tan (2004), 'Blunt to sharpened razor: Incremental reform and distortions in the product and capital markets in China', Discussion Paper 13, International Food Policy Research Institute, Development Strategy and Governance Division, Washington, DC.

9. China's Emergence as the Workshop of the World

Will Martin and Vlad Manole

1. INTRODUCTION

Since the beginning of the reform era, China has become a manufacturing powerhouse. From desperate poverty and near autarchy, China has been able to grow rapidly and to greatly increase her openness with the world. Associated with this export growth has been a rapid shift in the export basket from natural resource-based products to manufactures. Further, the composition of these manufactures has shifted rapidly, from simple, labor-intensive products to a much more diversified basket of products, including many high-technology products. Producers in other countries are becoming concerned about the seemingly unstoppable momentum of this export machine, and policy attention has begun to focus on ways to restrain the competitiveness of Chinese exports – including the current campaign by the United States and Japan for a sizeable revaluation of the Chinese Yuan.

Not so well known is the fact that many other developing countries, including India, were able to make major changes in the structure of their trade over this period. While not experiencing anything like the rates of economic growth that China has, other countries that were also low-income in 1980 have fundamentally transformed the patterns of their trade. Agriculture and natural resources have declined sharply in importance as sources of export revenues, and the increasing share of manufactures has included a rising share of high-technology products. When evaluating the performance of China's export powerhouse, it seems important to compare it with developments in other countries at broadly similar levels of development.

A comparison of developments in the trade patterns of China and other members of the low-income class of 1980 seems likely to help highlight the factors that distinguish China's performance from other low income countries. We therefore begin by examining some of the key developments in the exports of China and other low-income countries. Because India, like

China, looms so large in this group, and because it has been extensively studied, we consider it separately throughout the chapter.

After examining the developments in export patterns, we turn to an analysis of the factors that have helped China to achieve its remarkable export performance. These clearly included the liberalization of trade and investment policies that were so central to the reforms, and the reforms of domestic enterprises and institutions needed to respond to the changes in incentives created by these reforms. Where possible, we contrast the developments in China with the corresponding changes in our 'control' group of low income countries.

We conclude with a short discussion of internal market barriers in China. While these barriers are clearly a problem for China's economic development, their impact on trade is less clear. Young (2000) even argues that they may have increased China's international trade by acting as a substitute for thwarted trade between regions within China.

2. DEVELOPMENTS IN THE EXPORT PATTERNS OF CHINA AND OTHER DEVELOPING COUNTRIES

In 1980, China had already moved far from the traditional stereotype of a developing country dependent solely on exports of primary commodities and dependent on imports of manufactures, a theme repeated even in recent textbooks on economic development (Todaro, 1994). At this stage, manufactures made up 50 percent of China's exports, as against 24 percent

Figure 9.1:   The Share of Manufactures in China's Exports

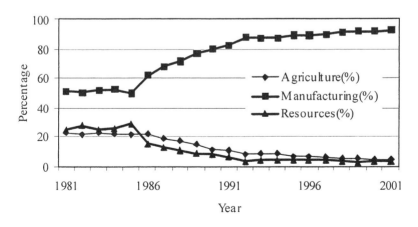

from resource-based products, and 26 percent from agriculture. As is shown in Figure 9.1, however, the share of manufactures in China's exports grew very rapidly from about 1995, rising to over 92 percent of total merchandise exports in 2001. The decline in the importance of resource-based products in China's exports has been dramatic, with agriculture accounting for only 5 percent of total exports in 2001, and natural resource-based products less than 3 percent. Part of this change was due to a sharp decline in China's exports of petroleum, a product that accounted for almost 22 percent of exports in 1980 and less than 1 percent in 2001.

The decline in the importance of agricultural and resource-based products in China's exports may not seem surprising, particularly given China's limited endowments of agricultural land and natural resources. However, similarly dramatic changes have been going on in other low-income countries. As is evident from Figure 9.2, the share of manufactures in the exports of low-income countries has risen sharply, from only 10 percent in 1981 to over 60 percent in 2001. To avoid selection bias, the group of low income countries presented in this and subsequent graphs was based on countries having income levels below $1000 in 1981, rather than at the end of the period.[1] Seen in the light of this 50 percentage point increase, the increase of 40 percentage points in the share of manufactures exports from China seems somewhat less remarkable.

The export pattern for India (Figure 9.3) also shows a strong shift over the period, although at a rate that is slower than for China or for the other

Figure 9.2:   *Export Structure of Low-Income Countries less China and India*

Figure 9.3:   Export Structure for India

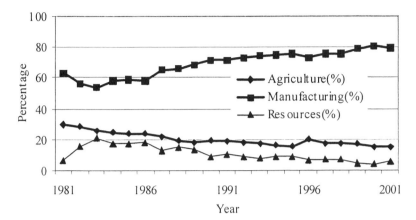

low income countries, and with a decline in the first few years of the sample. In India's case, agricultural exports remained relatively important, with over 15 percent of exports in 2001.

Over the period of analysis, the real price of oil and other energy products fell substantially. However, the decline in the share of natural resource exports is not greatly diminished by whether we deflate each series by a deflator in order to express them as quantity shares at base prices. When we do this for the low-income countries as a group, for whom exports of resources were important in 1981, we find relatively little change in the overall pattern. Most importantly, the rapid growth in the share of manufactured exports is an apparently robust result. To guard against the possibility that the results for the low-income group as a whole were driven by just a few countries, we also examined developments in the simple average of manufactured export shares, and found that this increased from 25 percent to more than 50 percent.

When we look beyond the product aggregates to obtain an indication of changes in the structure of developing country exports, and particularly in the technology level of their exports, we find that there have been substantial changes within each of these aggregates (see Figure 9.4).

China's export growth over the period was explosive, at 16 percent per year, more than double the world growth rate, and fast enough to double every four and a half years. Within China's exports, however, the rate of growth has varied considerably, with primary products growing at 6 percent per year and, at the other extreme, electronic products growing at 38 percent per year over the period. The results presented in Table 9.1 make clear that

Figure 9.4:   Export Structure of Low-Income Countries (deflated prices)

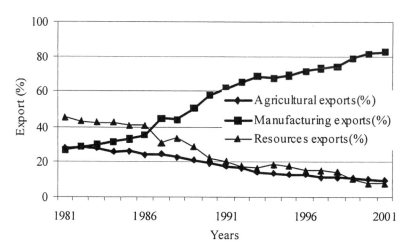

the expansion of manufactured exports from China and other low-income countries has not been simply an expansion of traditional low-technology products. Exports of low-technology manufactures such as textiles and garments did grow much more rapidly than world trade as a whole. However, the gap between the export growth rates of the low-income countries was generally greater for medium- and high-technology products than for the simpler manufactures. China's out-performance on electronic products was truly extraordinary, with export growth of 38 percent per year being almost three times the world average, and more than twice India's. However, the other low-income countries came much closer to China's performance in areas like automotives and components, and engineering products, and India outperformed China in process-industry products, and came close in the 'Other high-technology category'.

At the end of the period, the export pattern of each of our three groups looked entirely different from the situation in 1981. This is evident for each of our country groups (Table 9.2). For China, the most important export sector in 1981 was primary products, with a 36 percent share of exports – compared with just 5 percent two decades later. Resource-based manufactures declined too, so that the share of these two sectors had fallen from 54 percent to 12 percent. In 2001, the first place was taken by textiles with a share of 25 percent. A close second was electronics, within the high-technology sector, which increased from 1 to 22 percent. Electronics were also a big winner for the rest of low-income countries, going from 2 percent to 22 percent. Primary products still have the largest share for these

Table 9.1:   Export Growth by Sector and Technology Level, 1981–2001

Sector	China (%)	India (%)	Low-income less China and India (%)	World (%)
Primary products	6	6	1	2
Resource-based manufactures				
Agricultural	12	10	7	6
Other	10	11	4	5
Low-technology manufactures				
Textiles	16	10	14	8
Other	21	12	16	8
Medium-technology manufactures				
Automotive and components	23	12	22	8
Process industry products	12	17	14	7
Engineering products	26	11	21	8
High-technology manufactures				
Electronic	38	17	21	13
Other	20	18	10	9
Total	16	10	13	7

Note: Product definitions kindly supplied by WTO. Data analysis undertaken in the World Bank's WITS system using partner trade data from UN COMTRADE.

countries although they declined from 74 percent to 27 percent. We also notice an increase in share of textiles, from 4 percent in 1981 to 19 percent in 2001. For the low-income countries less China and India and especially for China we observe a dynamic change in the pattern of exports, a significant increase in the share of exports in sectors with more complex technologies. For India we see a decrease in the share of primary products, from 29 percent to 14 percent, compensated mainly by an increase in the share of non-agricultural resource-based manufactures, from 22 percent to 27 percent. Compared with China, the pattern of Indian exports seems to be stable, with the weight on low-technology and resource-based manufactures and primary products.[2]

Such broad, sweeping changes across the developing world require explanations that go substantially beyond the changes in any one country.

Table 9.2:   *Export Share by Sector and Technology Level, 1981–2001 for
China, India and Low-Income Countries Less China and India*

Sector	China		India		Low-income countries less China and India	
	1981	2001	1981	2001	1981	2001
Primary products	36	5	29	14	74	27
Resource-based manufactures						
Agricultural	6	3	3	3	8	8
Other	12	4	22	27	9	6
Low-technology manufactures						
Textiles	25	25	31	29	4	19
Other	9	20	6	8	1	5
Medium-technology manufactures						
Automotive and components	0	1	1	1	0	1
Process industry products	6	2	2	5	1	3
Engineering products	3	14	4	4	0	6
High-technology manufactures						
Electronic	1	22	1	3	2	22
Other	1	2	1	3	0	1

Note: Product definitions kindly supplied by WTO. Data analysis undertaken in the World
Bank's WITS system using partner trade data from UN COMTRADE.

3.   WHY DID SUCH RAPID INCREASES IN MANUFACTURING EXPORTS OCCUR?

A number of factors were clearly involved in the observed rapid increases in
the importance of manufactured exports from low-income countries. Some
of these factors have reflected changes in national policies, but for such a
sweeping change to have occurred, there must surely also have been some
changes in the global environment for exports from developing countries.
One key development has surely been improvements in transport and
communications that, in conjunction with developing-country reforms,
allowed the production chain to be broken up into components, with
developing countries playing a key role in global production sharing.
Another has surely been the ability of countries to enter new product lines,

and so avoid the declines in the terms of trade so feared by many earlier thinkers on development.

3.1. Global Production is Creating New Opportunities ...

Much of the change in developing-country export patterns, and particularly the rise in high-technology exports, is associated with the phenomenon of global production sharing (Deardorff, 2001; Hummels et al., 2001). Production sharing requires reliable transportation, communication, and other services to break production down into discrete stages, each undertaken in the countries best suited to it. Labor-intensive stages of production, for example, are done in labor-abundant countries. Potentially, production sharing can greatly expand the range of activities in which developing countries can participate – holding out the promise of increasing employment and reducing poverty.

Of course, breaking the once-rigid linkages between stages in the production process makes it more difficult to interpret the implications of the shift to manufactures – particularly high-technology products. In many cases, developing countries undertake only those production activities that require low-skilled labor – a low-tech part of the production of products such as textiles and clothing, and of high-tech commodities. However, the buoyant demand for such commodities helps offset the relatively stagnant demand for some traditional agricultural commodities.

The move to global production sharing heightens the importance of timely, efficient, and low-cost transportation. Even quite small differences in transport costs and the timeliness of transportation services can have quite dramatic consequences for incomes in countries. Hummels (2001) estimates that an increase of one day in the time taken to deliver a good is equivalent to an increase of 0.8 percent in the cost not just of transportation, but also of the good itself. Redding and Venables (2004) conclude that differences in transport costs in a world of global production sharing may account for a large proportion of the observed differences in incomes between countries. In a world of global production sharing, countries must pay transport costs to get their inputs, and to market their outputs. If value added is a small share of output value, then transport costs have enormous leverage on the residual returns available to pay workers and owners of capital. If value added is 20 percent of the gross output value in the absence of trade costs, then a transport cost of 10 percent of output to ship products out, and an equal cost to bring in components, would essentially wipe out all returns to productive factors.

To gain an idea of the potential impact of global production sharing on China and India,[3] we have calculated indexes of vertical specialization of the type developed by Hummels et al. (2001).[4] These indexes show the share of imported inputs embodied in each unit of goods exported – either directly or after indirect use of imported inputs is taken into account. Although imperfect – they do not allow for differences between export- and domestically-oriented sectors in their use of intermediate inputs – these measures provide a structured assessment of the extent and trend in production sharing. Two sets of results are presented in each figure. The lower bars estimate direct use of imported intermediates in exports, while the higher bars represent direct plus indirect use.

Production sharing in India increased by more than 50 percent between 1980 and 1998 (Figure 9.5). In China, even though production sharing

Figure 9.5:   Vertical Specialization – India

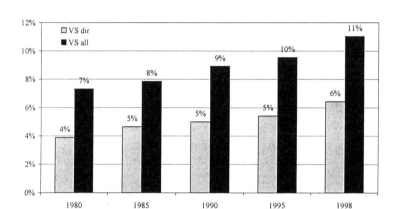

Figure 9.6:   Vertical Specialization – China

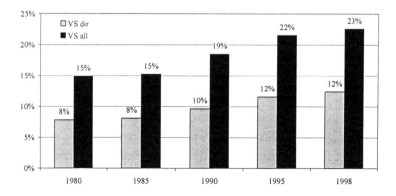

began from a considerably higher level than in India, it also increased by almost 50 percent over the period to 23 percent (Figure 9.6). Even so, the estimates understate the importance of global production sharing in China, where policy has strongly favored the use of imported inputs in labor-intensive production of manufactures (Ianchovichina, 2003), and where exports based on the processing of imported intermediates account for more than half of total exports. However, they highlight the substantial increase in the importance of the phenomenon in China over the period – particularly since 1987, when duty-free access was extended to a wide range of imported intermediates used in the production of exports.

3.2.   ...And Developing Countries Have Expanded the Range of Products that They Produce

An important new strand of literature has focused attention on extensive margin growth in countries whose exports are growing rapidly. Kehoe and Ruhl (2002) find that a large part of the expansion in exports in countries undergoing liberalization and successful trade expansion comes from products that were not traded prior to liberalization. Hummels and Klenow (2005) point out that such growth may have the important advantage of allowing countries to escape the deterioration in the terms of trade that would be predicted by standard Armington-type trade models.

To gain some indication of whether this phenomenon has been an important feature of the export growth experience of China and India, we examined the extent to which expansion in the range of products produced has played an important role in the expansion of their exports. To do this, we followed the Kehoe–Ruhl approach of ranking commodities in descending order of export value (using 3 digit SITC commodities in our case), and focusing on the commodities at the bottom of the ranking, which collectively accounted for 10 percent of initial export value. As Kehoe and Ruhl note, this approach ensures that the export levels of these commodities are individually insignificant without introducing the arbitrary – and inherently discriminatory across countries – cutoffs that are required when an absolute dollar value is used to define zero exports in the initial situation.[5]

When we examine the export performance of the least exported products from China in 1980, we find very rapid growth in these products during the following 20 years. Figure 9.6 shows just how rapid was the growth in these exports, with their share rising from 10 percent of total exports to 45 percent. This aligns quite strongly with Kehoe and Ruhl's result that countries undergoing major liberalizations see the share of the bottom 10 percent of their exports rise to as high as 40 percent of their exports – and suggests that China's liberalization in this period must have been quite profound. If we consider the growth in the first ten years, we find that the export share of these products rose from 10 percent to just over 25 percent in 1990. Much of this overall growth can be explained by just three categories of products: telecommunication equipment (SITC 764), automatic data processing machines (SITC 752) and accessories for automatic data machines (SITC 759). In 1981, the sum of their share of total exports was less than a tenth of a percent (0.096 percent). In 2001, the sum of their share of total exports was almost 15 percent.

The growth of the products that were new after 1980 continued after 1990, with the share of these products in China's exports growing from 25 to 45 percent in 2001 (see Figure 9.7). However, the pace of innovation through the introduction of further new products appears to have slowed. If we focus on the products effectively not exported in 1990, we see that the share of these products rose from 10 percent to 14 percent in 2001 (see Figure 9.8). This suggests that the policy reforms undertaken in the 1980s may have been more influential in facilitating the introduction of new export products than the far-reaching reforms to non-tariff barriers, tariffs and exchange rate distortions (see Ianchovichina and Martin, 2004) undertaken in the 1990s.

The introduction of new products in India's export basket proceeded much less smoothly than in China. After an initial surge in the early 1980s, the share of exports from products effectively not exported in 1980 fell back to its initial level (see Figure 9.9). It appears that this growth was largely the result of special factors such as the export of oil products, and not based on comparative advantage being acquired or unleashed as a result of reforms.

Figure 9.7:   *Growth in Export of New Products in China Since 1981*

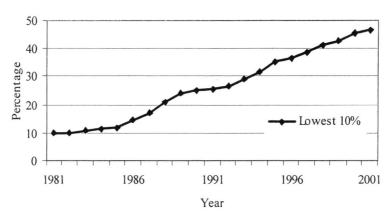

Figure 9.8:   *Growth in Exports of New Products in China after 1990*

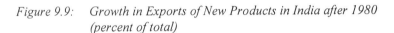

Figure 9.9:   *Growth in Exports of New Products in India after 1980*
                                  (percent of total)

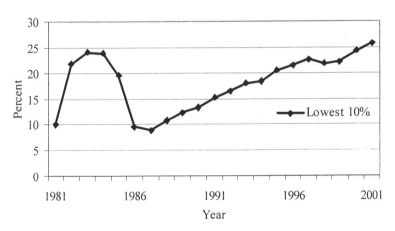

After 1990, the growth in exports of new products from India was much more rapid (see Figure 9.10). In this period, the share of exports accounted for by new products rose very steadily, from 10 percent in 1990, to almost 20 percent by 2001. Further, the most important of these products in terms of market share in 2001 were products such as chemicals (SITC 514, 515) and accessories for automatic data machines (SITC 759) which acquired a market share of almost 4 percent compared with a quarter percent in 1981. Given the well-known difficulties involved in inferring the restrictiveness

Figure 9.10:   *Growth in Exports of New Products in India after 1991*
                  (percent of total)

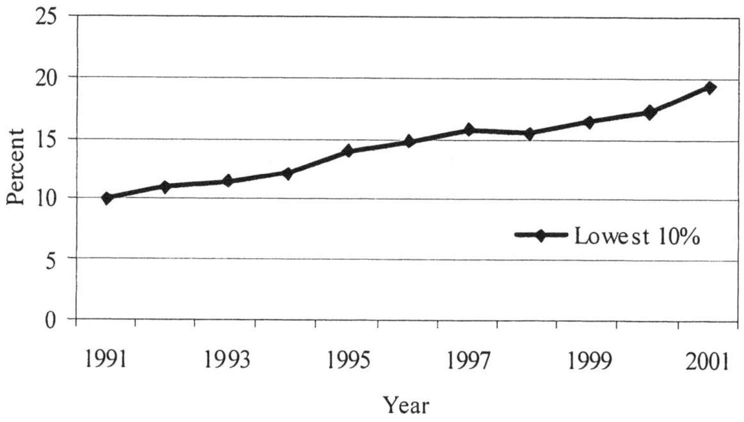

of trade policies, the evidence on emergence of new products from India provides a tentative indication that true liberalization of the trade regime in India began after 1990, rather than 1980.

4.   WHAT CONTRIBUTED TO THESE LARGE CHANGES IN TRADE PATTERNS?

Many factors have contributed to the large changes in the volumes, composition and value of exports from China, India and other low-income countries. One important factor has almost certainly been the dramatic changes in trade and foreign exchange policies in low-income countries, although it is frequently difficult to identify the turning points in trade regimes given the multiple, overlapping trade policy instruments wishing to restrict trade.

4.1.   Trade Policy Reforms

The wave of trade policy reforms that have swept the developing world since the mid-1980s seems likely to have been an important influence on developing countries' increase in participation in world manufactures trade. As is well known, trade barriers bear ultimately on the sectors that cannot pass on the resulting costs, and particularly on exports, and there is every reason to expect that they will bear more heavily on manufactures, which are frequently more dependent on purchased intermediates than are agricultural or resource producers.

The extent and pattern of the tariff reductions in China, India and the other low-income countries of 1980 show some considerable divergences. The data on simple average tariffs presented in Table 9.3 show that China, India and the other low-income countries had very high tariffs in the mid 1980s.

As is clear from Table 9.3, China made relatively little progress in reducing tariffs during the 1980s, and the incidence of NTBs actually rose over part of the period. Lardy (1991) estimated that the coverage of NTBs was considerably higher in the late 1980s than in the numbers reported by UNCTAD, and that the coverage of import licenses alone was approximately two-thirds of all imports in the late 1980s.

Table 9.3: Tariff Rates and NTM Frequency, 1981–2001

| Year | China | | India | | Low-income | |
	Simple Average Tariff (%)	NTM Freq. (%)	Simple Average Tariff (%)	NTM Freq. (%)	Simple Average Tariff (%)	NTM Freq. (%)
1981	49.5	NA	74	NA	36	–
1985	39.5	10.6	99	81	36	–
1989	40.3	23.2	79	65	31	–
1992	42.9	11.3	94	63	35	–
1993	39.9	–	71*	99	27	31
1994	36.3	–	55*	–	27	–
1996	23.6	–	38.6*	–	19	–
1997	17.6	–	34.4*	–	19	–
1998	17.5	–	40.2*	93.8	19	16.2
1999	17.2	–	39.6*	–	16	–
2000	17.0	–	NA	–	15	–
2001	16.6	10	32.3	–	15	–
Post-Accession	9.8	6.8	NA	NA	NA	NA

Notes: * denotes including surcharges.

Sources: Ianchovichina and Martín (2003); UNCTAD (1994); UNCTAD TRAINS database, Srinivasan (2001).

To conclude that there was limited progress on trade reform in China during the 1980s would, however, be ignoring the nature of the trade regime prior to the reforms, and of the reform process. The pre-reform Chinese trade regime was dominated by between 10 and 16 Foreign Trade Corporations (FTCs) with effective monopolies in the import and export of their specified product ranges (Lardy, 1991). Planned import volumes were determined by the projected difference between domestic demand and supply for particular goods, with export volumes set at levels necessary to finance planned imports.

Conventional trade policy instruments such as tariffs, quotas and licenses were of very limited importance in China's pre-reform system. Price-based measures such as tariffs were obviously unimportant since the planning system was based on quantity decisions rather than behavioral responses to prices. There was little need for quotas or licenses since the quantities to be imported could be controlled through the monopoly trading corporations.

Reform of China's trade regime had four major dimensions: increasing the number and type of enterprises eligible to trade beyond the initial handful of centrally controlled foreign trade corporations; developing the indirect trade policy instruments, such as tariffs, licenses, quotas, and duty exemption schemes, that were absent or unimportant under the planning system; reducing and ultimately removing the exchange rate distortion; and reforming prices so that they could play a role in guiding resource allocation. These reforms of the trading system were inextricably linked with reform of the enterprise sector to allow indirect regulation through market-determined prices to replace direct regulation of enterprise outputs.

The number of FTCs with trading rights was progressively expanded, with trading rights provided to branches of the FTCs controlled by the central government, and to those controlled by regions and localities, until there were thousands of these firms. Since 1984, these trading enterprises have been legally independent economic entities (Kueh, 1987) and state-owned trading enterprises of this type now appear to operate very strongly along commercial lines (Rozelle et al., 1996). Joint ventures between domestic and foreign firms, and firms located in the special economic zones were also allowed to trade their own products relatively early during the reform process. At a later stage, large producing firms began to gain direct foreign trade rights.

An important feature of the reforms was the introduction of special arrangements for processing trade, such as duty exemptions and rebates of Value Added Tax payments. Imports of intermediate inputs for use in the production of exports were almost completely liberalized, as were capital goods inputs for use in joint ventures with foreign enterprises. These categories of imports came to represent a very large share of total imports, with intermediate inputs into exports accounting for almost 44 percent of total imports in 1999.[6]

The primary transitional device used to reduce, and ultimately remove, the distortions in both commodity prices and exchange rates was the two- (or more) tier pricing system. Under the two-tier pricing system for commodities, the plan price continued to operate for the quantity of the commodity that producers were contracted to supply. However, to stimulate output, producers were allowed to supply additional output at a secondary market price. The two-tier system for foreign exchange involved an overvalued official exchange rate and a higher secondary-market rate, and distorted trade by discouraging both exports and imports (Martin, 1993; World Bank, 1994). Over time, the gaps between official and secondary market prices were narrowed or eliminated, and the two-tier system for foreign exchange was abolished with unification of the exchange rate in 1994.

Trade policy reform in India began in what was largely a market economy, and so did not require the complex transition to a market economy involved in China. However, the reforms required were enormous. A quarter of GDP was produced in public enterprises, and expansion of any firm involving over 50 workers required a licence (Joshi and Little, 1996). Certain sectors were reserved for small-scale production. As in China, major domestic policy reforms were required before the enterprise sector could fully respond to world price incentives transmitted through the trade regime.

Bulk imports of many commodities were canalized through state enterprises similar in many respects to China's pre-reform Foreign Trade Corporations, and all imports were subject to licensing or were prohibited during the 1980s. Imports of consumer goods were subject to an effective ban for long periods.

Srinivasan (2001) traces the process of reforming India's trade regime from the initial, major reforms in 1991. As in China, it involved removing the overvaluation of the currency, a process completed in 1993, and the abolition of the government monopoly on imports of commodities other than petroleum and agricultural products. Tariffs have been reduced but – without the impetus provided by WTO accession – not by nearly as much as in China. However, Pursell (2003) notes that WTO rules did require a substantial reduction of protection in India when India lost its attempt to maintain quantitative restrictions for balance-of-payments purposes. Average tariffs in India are roughly twice as high as in China, and are likely to be three times as high after China's accession commitments are phased in.

4.2.   Trade Liberalization and Incentives for Manufacturing Exports

One important consequence of trade liberalization is a differential reduction in the burden imposed by protection on the manufacturing sector. The burden on exports of tariffs through intermediate input costs is illustrated by the cases of China and India in 1986, when estimated rates of average protection were first available for each country, and 1997, following large reductions in protection (Figures 9.11 and 9.12). The impact of protection on exports differs considerably from country to country, but two key features are evident. First, agricultural processing and manufacturing (whether labor- or capital-intensive) for export are much more heavily taxed than are agricultural and resource commodities. Second, the rate of taxation has generally declined substantially since the mid 1980s, while remaining substantial for industrial products.

At the levels of protection prevailing in 1986, export activities in agricultural processing and in capital- or labor-intensive manufactures were taxed at essentially prohibitive levels in both India and China.

In India, the taxes directly imposed by protection on agricultural processing and capital-intensive manufacturing averaged more than 60 percent. (Non-tariff measures, domestic licensing requirements, and exchange-rate distortions, if computed, would have further increased the effective tax rate.)

In China, the direct impacts of protection appear to have been on the same order of magnitude, with agricultural processing facing taxes of more than 70 percent and labor-intensive manufactures close to 60 percent. These problems were compounded by strong obstacles to the expansion of domestic state-run firms, which were overcome in part by the emergence of an entirely new class of firms – the township and village enterprises – not subject to the constraints of the state-run firms.

Although a very few agricultural processing and manufacturing activities that depended less on intermediate inputs might have been able to survive at average tariff rates of 100 percent (as in India), it seems highly likely that reductions in tariffs – and non-tariff barriers – of the type observed around the world between 1986 and 2001 (World Bank, 2001) must have contributed to the great expansion of developing countries' manufacturing exports.

Reductions in average tariffs were complemented by the introduction of duty-exemption or drawback arrangements under which export producers obtained access to duty-free inputs for use in export production. These arrangements offer one way, legal under GATT, to reduce the burdens imposed by import duties. China has used them successfully to develop

Figure 9.11:   Tariffs Tax Exports in India

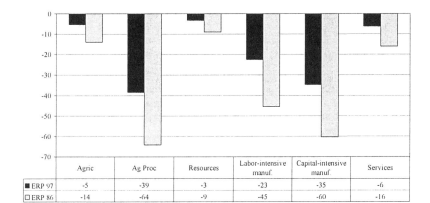

	Agric	Ag Proc	Resources	Labor-intensive manuf.	Capital-intensive manuf.	Services
■ ERP 97	-5	-39	-3	-23	-35	-6
□ ERP 86	-14	-64	-9	-45	-60	-16

Figure 9.12:   Tariffs Tax Exports in China

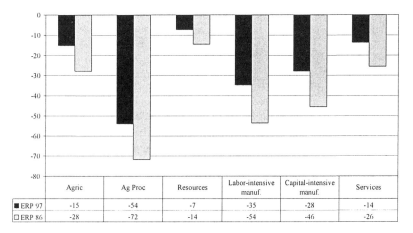

	Agric	Ag Proc	Resources	Labor-intensive manuf.	Capital-intensive manuf.	Services
■ ERP 97	-15	-54	-7	-35	-28	-14
□ ERP 86	-28	-72	-14	-54	-46	-26

labor-intensive exports (Ianchovichina, 2003; Ianchovichina and Martin, 2004).

They are an imperfect solution to the problems created by protection, however. Whether introduced throughout the economy or in specific free-trade zones, such arrangements are administratively demanding. In many cases, particularly in Africa, they have failed to operate successfully (Madani, 1999). Further, they tend to encourage firms to concentrate on production activities that add a small amount of value to imported inputs, rather than on activities more closely integrated with domestic production. Ianchovichina (2003) found that exporting activities had become much more import-intensive than other industries as a result of the incentives created by duty exemptions Since one of the key lessons of the new economic geography is that there may be substantial gains from activities that encourage the development of backward – as well as forward – linkages (Amiti, 2003), incentives toward shallow processing activities may cause highly protected economies to miss many opportunities for growth. Reductions in overall tariffs are a much better alternative than duty exemption. Not only do they remove the incentive for unnecessarily shallow specialization, but they also reduce the price of nontraded goods and factor inputs (Corden, 1997), and further increase the stimulus to production for export.

Another problem with relying on duty exemptions rather than relatively low and uniform tariff rates is that their introduction reduces the pressure for more general reductions in protection, since exporters – a potentially powerful source of pressure for reduction – no longer suffer the direct impact of protection (Cadotet al., 2002).

4.3.   Accumulation of Human and Physical Factors

The changes in the trade structure and in the technological complexity of the exports suggest significant transformation in the capacity of production for China, India and other low-income countries. Such an increase in competitive exports might be expected to require changes in the exporting countries' endowments of physical and human capital per worker. While we are cognizant of the possibility that accumulation does not necessarily lead to their productive use (Pritchett, 2000; 2001), it seems difficult to envisage a shift in the production structure to more capital- and skill-intensive factors without adequate supplies of the resources needed to produce them.[7]

We look at the variation of investment as a percentage of GDP as a measure of change in physical capital (Table 9.4). In 1981 China had a high level of investment, 26 percent of GDP. In the next 20 years we see an almost continuous increase in the investment rate, to 38 percent of GDP. This high, and increasing, rate of investment, and the resulting rapid accumulation of capital is reflected in exports by the increase in importance of capital-intensive industries like electronics and machinery. This presumably contributed to the much more rapid growth of more capital-intensive industries, and the relative decline of simpler activities in the primary sector. From Table 9.2 we see that in 2001 the electronic industry had almost caught up with the textile industry in share of exports (22 percent versus 25 percent).

Table 9.4:   Investment as a Share of GDP (percent)

Year	China	India	Low-income less China and India
1981	26	19	20
1982	28	19	20
1983	29	19	18
1984	30	20	17
1985	29	21	17
1986	30	21	17
1987	31	21	18
1988	31	22	18
1989	26	22	18
1990	26	23	19
1991	27	22	20
1992	31	22	20
1993	37	21	20
1994	36	22	22
1995	35	24	22
1996	34	23	22
1997	34	22	20
1998	35	22	21
1999	36	22	20
2000	36	22	20
2001	38	22	20

Note: Simple average across countries

For India, the investment rate was lower, and rose by much less – from 19 to 22 percent of GDP. The low-income countries started with investment of 20 percent of GDP in 1981 and ended with the same share in 2001. The decrease in investment in the 1980s is compensated by a surge in the 1990s. The shift toward more capital-intensive exports illustrated by Table 9.2 does not seem to be supported by investment data. From the experience of the low-income countries as a group it is likely that reforms that freed up domestic capital and allowed effective utilization of foreign capital were more important than investment per se.

We considered two indicators for human capital per worker, the average school years (Table 9.5) in the total population older than 15 years and declines in the illiteracy rate (Table 9.6). The illiteracy rate in China was 32 percent in 1981 and fell to 14 percent in 2001. In the same period, the

Table 9.5: *Average Schooling Years in the Total Population (>15 years)*

Year	China	India	Low-income countries less China and India
1980	4.8	3.3	2.7
1985	4.9	3.7	3.0
1990	5.9	4.1	3.4

Table 9.6: *Illiteracy Rate, Adult Total (percent of people 15+)*

Year	China	India	Low-income countries
1981	32	58	52
1982	30	57	52
1983	29	56	51
1984	28	56	50
1985	27	55	49
1986	26	54	48
1987	25	53	48
1988	24	52	47
1989	23	51	46
1990	22	51	45
1991	21	50	45
1992	20	49	44
1993	20	48	43
1994	19	48	42
1995	18	47	41
1996	17	46	41
1997	17	45	40
1998	16	44	39
1999	16	44	38
2000	15	43	38
2001	14	42	37

average schooling years increase from 4.8 years to 5.9 years. This suggests an increase in human capital that is reflected in the shift in export structure toward more technologically complex exports. In India we see a slower decrease in illiteracy from 58 percent to 42 percent. The average years of schooling rose from 3.3 years in 1981 and to 4.1 years in 2001. The low-income countries started from a relatively high level of illiteracy, 52 percent, in 1981 and reached 37 percent in 2001. In the same period, the average schooling years increased from 2.7 years to 3.4 years. It seems difficult to explain the increase in the technology intensity of exports from this group in terms of increased human capital. This suggests that changes in policies were probably more influential that accumulation of human capital in the growth of high-technology exports from developing countries.

5. TEXTILES AND CLOTHING

Textiles and clothing trade warrants particular attention because it is such an important export for China, because of the peculiar structure of protection policies that have restricted the growth of China's exports of these goods, and because drastic reform of these policies has taken place with the abolition of the quotas in January 2005. As is well known, exports of textiles and clothing to the industrial countries (and frequently to developing countries as well) are subject to particularly high tariffs, and also to a system of bilateral quotas that developed under the Multi-Fiber Arrangement.

While agreement was reached in the Uruguay Round to phase out the MFA quotas against developing country exports of textiles and clothing, this agreement (the Uruguay Round Agreement on Textiles and Clothing or ATC) did not apply to China until it acceded to the WTO. Following accession, China became eligible for the benefits of the gradual phase-in of textile products to GATT disciplines under the first three tranches of the ATC, and for the abolition of all remaining quotas on 1 January 2005. Although 51 percent of textile and clothing products had been integrated into GATT in accordance with the ATC by January 2002, this resulted in the abolition of only a small number of quotas, since the industrial countries were free to choose the products to integrate and typically chose products for which developing countries were not important producers.

Thus, the key turning point in the abolition of the textile and clothing quotas for China, and for other developing countries, was 1 January 2005, when all textile and clothing products were integrated under GATT rules. Other WTO members retained the option of trying to restrict China's exports using a range of provisions under China's WTO Accession agreement (see Bhattasali et al., 2004) including the special textile safeguard or the Product Specific Safeguard in China's WTO Accession agreement. In addition, they can target Chinese exports under antidumping actions (to which China is particularly vulnerable because of the non-market economy provisions, see Messerlin, 2004) or exports in general under the WTO provisions on safeguards or countervailing duties.

One indication of the extent to which China's exports were restricted by the textile quota arrangements is provided by the export tax equivalents of the export quotas that apply against China's exports. To gain an indication of the restrictiveness of the quotas, we obtained data on the transaction prices of the quotas in China, and on the unit value of the exports of these goods from China (which includes the price of the quota).[8] Since quotas are legally transacted in China, these quota prices should give a good indication of the extent to which the quotas restrict trade and act like an export tax. To put the restrictive effects of the quota into comparable units, we expressed their prices relative to the unit value of the exports net of the quota price, to obtain an estimate of their export tax equivalents.

The average measured export tax equivalents of the quotas are about 10 percent for textiles, and 22 percent for clothing. The export tax equivalents for clothing were generally much higher in 2002, despite the abolition of some of these quotas from the beginning of 2002. While the average rates

Table 9.7:   Textile and Clothing Export Tax Equivalents (percent)

Category	Description	2001	2002
336	Cotton dresses	15	191
340	Non-knit shirts, men and boys	20	143
641	Non-knit blouses, women	25	130
239	Baby garments and accessories	27	113
648	Slacks, etc., women and girls	16	121
360	Pillowcases	4	133
647	Trousers, men's synthetic	19	114
326	Sateen fabric	0	132
342	Cotton skirts	28	94
345	Cotton sweaters	41	77
339	Knit blouses	49	69
640	Non-knit shirts, mens and boys	30	85
635	Coats, women and girls	32	79
840	Synthetic woven shirts	15	94
315	Printcloth fabric.	22	76
	Simple average all items	10	25
	Standard deviation	13	37
	Average all textiles	10	9
	Average all clothing and apparel	15	29

of these quotas might not seem alarmingly high, the extent of their variation from product to product and from year to year is extraordinary. As shown by Francois and Martin (2004) and Martin et al. (2003), such large variations in protection over time and across closely-related commodities are likely to greatly increase the cost of protection[9] If the industrial countries were attempting to provide technical assistance in the design of a costly form of protection, it would be difficult indeed to surpass the textile and clothing quotas as a case study.

There were strong reasons to expect China to gain substantially from the removal of the MFA quotas. One reason for this was the apparently high export tax equivalents of the quotas. Where pairwise comparisons are possible – as they are for Hong Kong, India and Pakistan – the export tax equivalents of China's quotas generally appeared to be higher than for its competitors.[10] Another, much simpler, index of the restrictiveness of each exporter – the share of that supplier's exports shipped to non-quota markets – also suggests that China's exports were strongly restricted by the quota regime. COMTRADE numbers for 2001 suggested that a staggering 80 percent of China's exports of WTO textiles and clothing goods were to markets other than the EU, the US and Canada. While this number is probably considerably overstated because of the well-known problem of goods transshipped through Hong Kong being identified as exports from China to Hong Kong, it is very much higher than for other exporters such as Hong Kong (27 percent), India (14 percent) and Thailand (22 percent).

Simulation analyses of the effects of abolishing the MFA quotas invariably show China as gaining, even though such analyses for developing countries frequently return mixed results (see, for example, Yang et al., 1997) For many countries, the efficiency gains they receive in production, and the gains from higher prices on world markets are outweighed by the loss of quota rents.

One important feature of the adjustment of China's manufacturing sector to the abolition of the quotas that appears to have received little attention to date is the likely shift of resources in China into textiles and clothing relative to other manufacturing activities. To investigate this question, we analyzed the impact of abolishing the textile and clothing quotas with a model that takes into account the duty exemption arrangements that are so important for China's manufacturing export sector (see Ianchovichina, 2003 and Ianchovichina and Martin, 2004). The results, reported in Table 9.8, suggested that China's exports of a range of commodities would likely fall as her exports of apparel and textiles rise sharply. These divergent trends in exports highlight the importance for policy makers in other countries of ensuring that their policies allow exporters to diversify into as wide a range

Table 9.8:   *Quota Abolition in China will Reduce Exports of some other Commodities*

Sector	Aniticipated change (%)
Apparel	125.7
Automobiles and parts	−22.8
Cotton	−8.6
Electronics	−10.6
Leather and shoes	−5.0
Metal products	−11.9
Textiles	41.9
Other manufactures	−14.1

of products as possible. Policy frameworks specialized to allow production of textiles and clothing under, for instance, duty exemption arrangements will expose their economies to great risks.

The actual experience following quota abolition was somewhat different. Partly this was because the EU, the US, and several other countries imposed transitional safeguards on China's exports of these items. However, these quotas proved less binding than expected by many, partly because they were considerably bigger than those previously applying, and partly because the recent evolution of China's exports has shifted rapidly away from textiles and clothing towards electronic products (Dimaranan et al., 2007).

6. INTERNAL MARKETS FOR MANUFACTURES IN CHINA

A key element of the early economic reforms in China was the development of secondary markets for the exchange of materials between firms. A frequent characterization of the Chinese economy addresses the gap between the economic performances of coastal and inland provinces. More generally, a vast literature examines the variation in economic performance of China's provinces and the trade between them. It is an open debate on the level of protection for the inter-provincial trade and the scarcity and the low quality of the relevant data fuels the discussions.

The changes in economic policy that started in 1978 reflect a decentralization of the economic decision power in favor of provinces and localities. At the same time, significant rigidities in the price structure (low prices for raw materials, high prices for finite products) provided incentives for provincial authorities to restrict trade so as to capture the associated rents (Young, 2000). An entire strand of literature (reviewed in Young, 2000 and Naughton, 2000) describes the protective barriers erected by local governments in favor of local industries in the 1980s. Young (2000) argues that market fragmentation induced by rent seeking activity continues even after the removal of rents and supported this claim with price and agricultural data mainly from *China Statistical Yearbook.*

Naughton (2000) disputed Young's results, arguing 'it is extremely difficult to make robust conclusion about inter-regional trade ... from structural data alone'. He used new data, the input–output tables compiled by China's provinces in 1987 and 1992, and found that in the 1990s, inter-provincial trade was large, and, comparing China with multinational entities like EU or ASEAN, he found that 'China's provinces did not stand out as clearly autarchic economic units.'

Poncet (2003) used provincial input–output tables from 1987, 1992 and 1997. She found that average provincial absorption of goods from other provinces decreased from 34 percent in 1987 to 20 percent in 1997. Poncet used a border-effect method for Chinese data and found an increase in the impediments to inter-provincial trade in China reflected by tariff equivalents from 37 percent in 1987 to 51 percent in 1997, comparable with results from EU, OECD and Canada–US integration. Her results suggested an increase in market fragmentation in China.

A major new World Bank study of national market integration in China (World Bank, 2004) concludes that local protectionism continues despite laws and exhortations at the national level, and requirements for an integrated market included in China's WTO commitments. These problems are seen as a consequence of structural features of the economy such as fiscal decentralization and dependence of local governments on local firms for their tax. The study concludes that the protectionist practices continue to play an important role in judicial independence, government procurement and intervention in the labor market. There are problems for manufactured goods such as automobiles, and in monopolized sectors such as alcohol production, but these barriers seem less important than in government procurement and particularly in the labor market. Survey results suggest that barriers to market integration have declined during the past decade.

7. CONCLUSIONS

China's emergence as a major exporter of manufactures is well known. Less well known perhaps is the rapid transformation towards manufactures of other countries that were poor in 1980. The rapidity of this transformation suggests that common factors, such as vertical specialization in production, may have played an important role. We examine the transformation of China's exports relative to those of India and other low-income exporters. We find that the share of manufactures rose rapidly in each case, and that the most rapid growth was in relatively skill-intensive manufactures. A key part of China's export growth came from the emergence of new exports, which occurred rapidly in the 1980s, and less rapidly in the 1990s. In India, by contrast, this process did not begin until the 1990s. Reductions in protection in China and India disproportionately reduced the cost burden on manufactures and agricultural processing. Despite their rapid growth, China's exports of textiles and clothing appear to have been considerably retarded by protection imposed under the Multi-Fiber Arrangement, implying that the expansion of China's exports of these products after 2005 is likely to be rapid.

APPENDIX

Table 9.9:   Low-Income Countries less China and India

Code	Country	Code	Country
BGD	Bangladesh	MLI	Mali
BEN	Benin	MRT	Mauritania
BTN	Bhutan	MAR	Morocco
BOL	Bolivia	MMR	Myanmar
BFA	Burkina Faso(Upper Volta)	NPL	Nepal
KHM	Cambodia	NER	Niger
CMR	Cameroon	NGA	Nigeria
CAF	Central African Republic	PAK	Pakistan
TCD	Chad	PNG	Papua New Guinea
EGY	Egypt, Arab Rep.	PHL	Philippines
GHA	Ghana	SEN	Senegal
GIN	Guinea	LKA	Sri Lanka
HND	Honduras	SDN	Sudan
IDN	Indonesia	TZA	Tanzania
KEN	Kenya	THA	Thailand
LAO	Lao PDR	TGO	Togo
LSO	Lesotho	VNM	Vietnam
MDG	Madagascar	ZMB	Zambia
MWI	Malawi	ZWE	Zimbabwe

The classification of countries by income is based on the *World Development Report 1982*, World Bank, with $1000 (dollars 1981) as the limit between low-income countries and middle-income countries. In the group there are countries with no significant conflict in 1981–2001.

NOTES

1. The classification of countries by income is based on *World Development Report 1982*, World Bank, with $1000 (dollars 1981) as the limit between low-income countries and middle-income countries. The industrialized countries are considered a separate group (World Bank, 2003). For a list of countries, see Appendix.
2. We analyze the export of non-service products. One of the most dynamic sectors for India was the exports of software and related services, that has experienced average annual growth of 22 percent (1990–2000) or 47 percent (1995–2000) and has a share of more than 16 percent of India's total exports (UNCTAD, 2002).
3. Such an index is probably not very meaningful for a composite group such as the low-income countries.
4. Following Hummels et al. (2001) we use the VS (Vertical Specialization) index. For direct effects for the country k: $VS_k = (\mathbf{uA^M X})/X_k$ where u is a $1 \times n$ vector of 1's, $\mathbf{A}^M$ is the $n \times n$ imported coefficient matrix, $\mathbf{X}$ is an $n \times 1$ vector of exports, n is the number of sectors, and X_k is the sum of exports across the n sectors. We may add the indirect effects to the index: $VS_k = [\mathbf{uA^M(I - A^D)}^{-1} \mathbf{X}]/X_k$, where $\mathbf{I}$ is the identity matrix and $\mathbf{A}^D$ is the $n \times n$ domestic coefficient matrix.
5. As Kehoe and Ruhl (2002) note, a cutoff of $50 000 means something very different for China and for Nepal.
6. Source: Customs General Administration, People's Republic of China.
7. Martin and Warr (1992), for example, show that the decline of agriculture in Indonesia can be explained better as a consequence of Rybczynski effects resulting from greater accumulation of capital than by the price change factors emphasized in the partial equilibrium literature.
8. Data on quota prices were obtained from www.chinaquota.com and data on import prices and conversion factors from the US Office of Textile Administration. The lowest accepted quota price bids for each month were used in the analysis on the grounds that the marginal bid should be the best indicator of the ruling market price. If average or peak bids are used, the export tax equivalents are frequently much higher.
9. Francois and Martin (2004) show that the squared mean of protection and the variance over time can be added to estimate the cost of intertemporal variation of protection. Martin et al. (2003) show that the cost of the highly variable protection under the CAP is two and a half times what would be estimated using a standard, highly-aggregated model.
10. These competitors can take some comfort from the fact that the composition of their exports is very different from China's.

REFERENCES

Bhattasali, D., Shantong Li and W. Martin (2004), 'WTO accession, policy reform and poverty reduction, an overview', in D. Bhattasali, Shantong Li and W. Martin (eds), *China and the WTO: WTO Accession, Policy Reform and Poverty Reduction Strategies*, Washington DC: Oxford University Press and the World Bank.

Cadot, O., J. de Melo and M. Olarreaga (2003), 'The protectionist bias of duty drawbacks: evidence from Mercosur', *Journal of Development Economics*, **59**(1), 161–82.

Corden, M. (1997), *Trade Policy and Economic Welfare*, 2nd edition, Oxford: Oxford University Press.

Deardorff, A. (2001), 'International provision of trade services, trade and fragmentation', *Review of International Economics*, 9(2), 233–48.

Dimaranan, B., E. Ianchovichina and W. Martin (2007), 'Competing with giants: who wins, who loses?', Ch 3 in L.A. Wintersand and S. Yusuf (eds), *Dancing with Giants: China, India, and the Global Economy*, Washington DC: World Bank.

Francois, J.F. and W. Martin (2004), 'Commercial policy variability, bindings, and market access', *European Economic Review*, **48**, 665–79.

Hummels, D. (2001), 'Time as a trade barrier', Mimeo, Krannert School of Management, Purdue University, West Lafayette.

Hummels, D. and P. Klenow (2005), 'The variety and quality of a nation's exports', *American Economic Review*, **95**(3), 704–23.

Hummels, D., J. Ishii and K.M. Yi (2001), 'The nature and growth of vertical specialization in world trade', *Journal of International Economics*, **54**, 75–96.

Ianchovichina, E. (2003), 'GTAP-DD: A model for analyzing trade reforms in the presence of duty drawbacks', GTAP Technical Paper No 21, www.gtap.org.

Ianchovichina, E. and W. Martin (2004), 'Impacts of China's accession to the World Trade Organization', *World Bank Economic Review*, **18**(1), 3–27.

Joshi, V. and I.M.D. Little (1996), *India's Economic Reforms 1991–2001*, Bombay: Oxford University Press.

Kehoe, T. and K. Ruhl (2002), 'How important is the new goods margin in international trade?', Mimeo, University of Minnesota, Minnesota.

Kueh, Y. (1987), 'Economic decentralization and foreign trade expansion in China', in J. Chai and C.K. Leung (eds), *China's Economic Reforms*, Hong Kong: University of Hong Kong.

Lardy, N. (1991), *Foreign Trade and Economic Reform in China, 1978–1990*, Cambridge: Cambridge University Press.

Madani, D. (1999), 'A review of the role and impact of export processing zones', Policy Research Working Paper 2238, World Bank, Washington DC.

Martin, W. (1993), 'Modeling the post-reform Chinese economy', *Journal of Policy Modeling*, **15**(5 and 6), 545–79.

Martin, W. and P. Warr (1993), 'Explaining the relative decline of agriculture: A supply-side analysis for Indonesia', *World Bank Economic Review*, **7**(3), 381–401.

Martin, W., D. van der Mensbrugghe and V. Manole (2003), 'Is the devil in the details?: Assessing the welfare implications of agricultural and non-agricultural trade reform', World Bank Working Paper, World Bank, Washington DC.

Messerlin, P. (2004), 'China in the WTO: Antidumping and safeguards', in D. Bhattasali, Shantong Li and W. Martin (eds), *China and the WTO: WTO Accession, Policy Reform and Poverty Reduction Strategies*, Washington DC: Oxford University Press and the World Bank.

Naughton, B. (2000), 'How much can regional integration do to unify China's markets?', CREDPR Working Paper No. 58, Stanford University, August.

Poncet, S. (2003), 'Measuring Chinese domestic and international integration', *China Economic Review*, **14**, 1–21.

Pritchett, L. (2000), 'The tyranny of concepts: CUDIE (Cumulated, depreciated investment effort) is not capital', *Journal of Economic Growth*, **5**, 361–84.

Pritchett, L. (2001), 'Where has all the education gone?', *World Bank Economic Review*, **15**(3), 367–91.

Pursell, G. (2003), 'Trade policies in South Asia', Mimeo, World Bank, Washington DC.

Redding, S. and A. Venables (2004), 'Economic geography and international inequality', *Journal of International Economics*, **62**, 53–82.

Rozelle, S., A. Park, Jikun Huang and Jin Hehui (1996), 'Bureaucrat to entrepreneur: The changing role of the state in China's transitional commodity economy', Mimeo, Stanford University.

Srinivasan, T.N. (2001), 'Integrating India with the world economy', Mimeo, Yale University, 7 November.

Todaro, M. (1994), *Economic Development*, New York: Longman.

World Bank (1982), *World Development Report*, Washington DC: World Bank.

World Bank (1994), *China: Foreign Trade Reform*, Washington DC: World Bank.

World Bank (2001), *Global Economic Prospects 2001*, Washington DC: World Bank.

World Bank (2004), 'Fragmentation of national product and factor markets: Economic costs and policy recommendations', Mimeo, World Bank, Beijing.

Yang, Y., W. Martin and K. Yanagishima (1997), 'Evaluating the benefits of abolishing the MFA in the Uruguay Round package', in T.W. Hertel (ed.), *Global Trade Analysis: Modeling and Applications*, Cambridge: Cambridge University Press, 253–79.

Young, Alwyn, (2000), 'The razor's edge: Distortions and incremental reform in the People's Republic of China', *The Quarterly Journal of Economics*, **115**(4), 1091–135.

10. China's Emergence, Real Exchange Rates and Implications for East Asian Regional Trade and Growth

David Roland-Holst[1]

1. INTRODUCTION

Over the last decade, a new landscape of economic relations has begun to emerge in the Pacific Basin. In this region as much as anywhere else, the agenda of globalization has advanced, more countries are embracing outward economic orientation and open multilateralism as a means of accelerating domestic economic growth. Most prominent of the later entrants in the regional arena is China, whose economic reforms have led it to record growth rates, dramatically accelerating export expansion and sharply improving material living standards.

China's global economic emergence is one of the defining characteristics of modern globalization. This most populous economy has also, over the last two decades, been the fastest growing, and a significant part of this growth has been leverage by external demand. While satisfying millions of foreign consumers, however, Chinese exports have engendered ambivalent and even hostile sentiments among other producers, both in the markets they penetrate and among other export competing nations. The latter group is concentrated in East and Southeast Asia, and this region is facing significant adjustments as a result of China's dramatic emergence.

Preoccupation with China's opening has also drawn new attention to East and Southeast Asian trade blocs. Many of the more established regional agreements (e.g. ASEAN) are being re-examined in light of China's WTO accession and are in some cases moving to include China. At the same time, adoption of the WTO agenda by this most populous of formerly non-aligned countries has given special impetus to globalization as the prevailing standard for multilateral trade relations, calling into question the central tenets of regionalism. For these reasons, East Asia's existing trade arrangements will undergo searching examination and, in all likelihood, significant change in the coming years.

In addition to export competitiveness, another symptom of China's external success has emerged in the global trade debate, unprecedented reserve accumulation. As a combined result of sustained trade surpluses and managed exchange rate policies, China now holds the world's largest expatriate dollar reserves. This financial 'overhang' now exceeds $1 trillion and represents a complex adjustment risk for the global trading system. In fact, a number of East Asian economies have pursued stable exchange rate policies while the real landscape of regional trade has changed dramatically around them. The monetary implications of this divergence, including nominal rates of exchange, prices, and interest rates have been very widely discussed and remain controversial, but the Chinese situation has attracted particular attention because of its rapid emergence.

Presumably, sensitivity of these monetary issues relates to the real side of the economy. Despite this, very little evidence exists on actual structural adjustments that might ensue from more flexible exchange rates in East Asia. This chapter aims to support more complete policy dialogue by showing how patterns of East Asian trade and domestic economic activity could shift with adjustments in one salient real exchange rate, that of China. Using a global simulation model, we forecast changing trade and economic structure over the next two decades, considering scenarios for status quo growth and alternatives where structural imbalances are constrained to induce real exchange rate adjustment. Our results suggest a mixed verdict on the efficacy of exchange rate intervention, revealing relatively intricate shifts in the regional activity matrix when the Pacific Basin's most dynamic economy experiences shifts in its aggregate terms of trade.

2.   ASIAN REGIONAL TRADE PATTERNS AND THE TRADE TRIANGLE

Before examining scenarios for alternative trade and exchange rate regimes, it is instructive to examine a baseline scenario covering the forecast period 2007–20. The general baseline calibration procedure and more detailed information about the model and data are given in a companion paper, and only essential features are summarized. The present dynamic forecasting model was constructed according to generally accepted standards, implemented in the GAMS programming language, and calibrated to the GTAP global database.[2] The result is an 18-country/region, 18-sector global CGE model, calibrated over a 24- year time path from 2001 to 2020.

To set the dynamic baseline, the model was calibrated to annualized real GDP growth rates obtained from consensus independent estimates displayed in the first column of Table 10.1.

Table 10.1:   *Selected Macroeconomic Indicators, Baseline Scenario*
              (percentage annualized growth rates, 2000–2020)

	Real GDP	Absorption	Exports	Imports	Exp. PI	Imp. PI	Real ER
China	7.10	6.94	6.27	5.85	−0.22	−0.18	−0.04
Japan	2.20	2.12	2.37	3.15	0.22	−0.13	0.35
NIE	4.34	4.42	4.01	4.21	−0.09	−0.08	−0.01
ASEAN	4.75	4.55	4.46	4.25	−0.26	−0.13	−0.13
USA	2.62	2.61	3.07	2.94	0.12	−0.09	0.21
EU	2.52	2.63	2.37	2.60	0.13	0.01	0.13
ROW	3.65	3.65	3.69	3.40	−0.19	−0.09	−0.11

Sources: DRI, IMF, Cambridge Econometrics.

These baseline results have also been discussed extensively in Roland-Holst (2002), but a few salient points are worthy of re-emphasis. Growth rates for China are moderate in historical context, and China in 2020 will still lag behind the United States, EU, and Japan in aggregate real GDP. However, its share of total world trade (exports + imports), will nearly equal the US and significantly exceed Japan. Moreover, by about 2008 China will be Asia's largest individual importer and by about 2010 its largest exporter. China's exports by destination will be directed primarily at the US and EU. For more than half of its imports, China will rely on East and Southeast Asia. Korea and Taipei, China combined (NIE) will be the largest regional source of these, followed by Japan and ASEAN. Finally, China will become Japan's largest trading partner in terms of both imports and exports.

One of the most arresting and important results of this investigation, however, is the estimated emergence of a trade triangle that will leverage regional trade via China's expanding exports and induced domestic growth. This result offers an important inference for regional policy: China's expansion may represent a challenge to traditional Asian exporters, but it also offers unprecedented opportunities for new export expansion. Contrary to the view that China's exports will stifle competitiveness and growth among its neighbors, these results show that China's expansion, particularly when accelerated by WTO accession, constitute a windfall opportunity for regional exporters.

Consider global trade patterns partitioned into three geographic spheres, China, the Rest of East and Southeast Asia, and the rest of the world (ROW). Because the OECD countries account for 75 percent of world trade,

Figure 10.1: Asian Trade Triangle, 2005

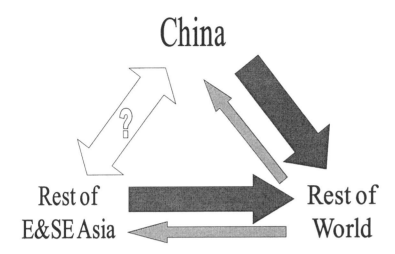

they will dominate the third group. With this in mind, the schematic in Figure 10.1 represents trade among these groups in the year 2005, indicating export flows by dark gray arrows and import flows in lighter gray. The general message here is one of head-to-head export competition by Asian economies in ROW markets. Both of the former are currently running substantial surpluses on trade in that direction, and their bilateral trade (China–ROEA) is indeterminate for the moment.

Now contrast this with a schematic rendering of the results obtained for the baseline in 2020. Even without China fulfilling its WTO commitments, trade patterns have shifted dramatically. In particular, China sustains and even increases its structural trade surplus with the (mainly western OECD) ROW, while at the same time developing a structural deficit of about equal magnitude with the rest of East and Southeast Asia. Yes, China appears to have displaced other Asian exports to third region markets, but the relentless growth of its domestic absorption has offset this and created dramatic new export opportunities for its regional neighbors.

The logic behind this transitive mechanism is straightforward. Apart from a prodigious endowment of human capital, China is a very resource-constrained economy. To sustain its baseline growth rates, this economy must sharply increase absorption of external resources, intermediates, and capital goods. This is true for export sectors, where the needs for capacity expansion to meet external demand are very substantial. Moreover, income

Figure 10.2:   Asian Trade Triangle, 2020

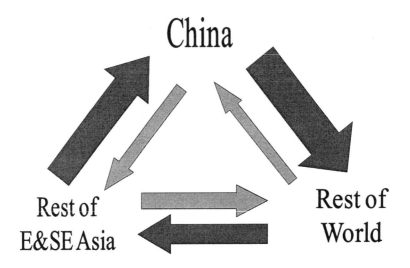

Table 10.2:   Bilateral Trade Balances, Baseline Scenario
              (year 2020 in billions of 2001 USD)

				Importer				
Exporter	China	Japan	NIE	ASEAN	USA	EU	ROW	Total
China	0	−5	−135	−41	166	66	71	122
Japan	5	0	39	20	23	−15	−50	21
NIE	135	−39	0	19	−32	−32	−12	40
ASEAN	41	−20	−19	0	18	8	12	41
USA	−166	−23	32	−18	0	48	−40	−168
EU	−66	15	32	−8	−48	0	34	−41
ROW	−71	50	12	−12	40	−34	0	−16
Total	−122	−21	−40	−41	168	41	16	0

growth in China will inexorably change demand patterns, accelerating import demand for agricultural products (meat and/or animal feed) and energy in particular.

In any case, the schematic representation is only intended to motivate the triangle concept. Table 10.2 presents the actual bilateral balances for 2020 as forecast by the model. Here the triangle is delineated within a matrix of component trade relationships, each generally consistent with the intuition arising from the schematic.

Note in the first row how China registers surpluses with the USA, EU, and ROW, while running bilateral deficits with Japan, NIE, and ASEAN. In the closure of this model, aggregate foreign savings for each country are held constant in real terms, essentially fixing aggregate trade balances in this reference case. The constituent bilateral balances are endogenous, however, and evolve in the indicated triangular relationship because of the underlying comparative advantages of the trade partners.

3.   SIMULATION RESULTS

Using the multi-country model and baseline information discussed above, we conducted a series of policy experiments reflecting more liberal East and Southeast Asian trade regimes at the global, regional, and national levels. In particular, we compared global tariff abolition with three East Asian regional arrangements that resemble Free Trade Areas presently being discussed. The results obtained make more apparent both the potential rewards of further liberalization and the very complex incentives facing East Asian participants in regional and global negotiations. Four general results are worthy of emphasis:

1. Global trade liberalization (GTL) confers greater aggregate gains, not only on the world but on a decisive majority of individual countries and every East Asian regional grouping considered.
2. The regional Free Trade Areas considered here would, in the absence of other negotiating initiatives, benefit most FTA member countries, but less so than globalization.
3. China's role in all these scenarios is unique and appears to be governed by complex incentives. China gains much less in relative terms than either ASEAN in the AFTA or the rest of East and Southeast Asia under GTL. The reason for this is that China can realize most of its export growth by eliminating its own protection unilaterally, while a large part of the export gain to East and Southeast Asia comes from Chinese market access.
4. The trade triangle enables China to 'deliver globalization' to its regional neighbors by its accession to the WTO, i.e. East and Southeast Asia can capture most of the absolute export growth expected from full globalization by just forming an ASEAN+3 FTA. Put differently, our results indicate that, in the wake of China's WTO accession, the best strategy for East and Southeast Asia is to pursue globalism through more comprehensive regionalism.

Building on the baseline forecasts, a variety of trade liberalization scenarios for East and Southeast Asia were examined with reference to China's WTO accession. In particular, unilateral Chinese liberalization was compared with several examples of East and Southeast Asian regionalism and a reference global trade liberalization scenario (GTL) that abolishes all tariffs. The results are consistent with some conventional intuition and in other ways indicate the complexity of the regional negotiating environment.

At the national level, unilateral liberalization is also evaluated for a number of larger East Asian economies. The results are then compared to a reference scenario where bilateral partners reciprocate, conferring free market access on the country removing all its tariff barriers. Not surprisingly, these two alternatives can differ significantly, depending upon prior protection patterns and domestic resource constraints. Although there are important characteristics of the individual country scenarios, these results suggest that the choice between unilateral and negotiated tariff removal should be made on a case by case basis. Indeed, unilateral removal would rarely be preferable, but negotiated liberalization should be informed by more detailed analysis of partner-specific and sector-specific considerations.

3.1. Adjustments in Trade Patterns

Before presenting more detailed results, aggregate effects of seven counterfactuals for regional trade liberalization are evaluated. Each scenario includes the first one as a new baseline including China's accession to the WTO:

1. CNWTO: China joins the WTO, status quo policies elsewhere
2. AFTA: ASEAN Free Trade Area
3. AFTAPC: AFTA plus China
4. NEAFTA: Northeast Asian Free Trade Area (China, Japan and Korea)
5. ASEAN+3: AFTA plus China, Japan and Korea
6. PAC3: Pacific Trilateralism – China, Japan, USA
7. GTL: Global trade liberalization

The first of these represents realization of China's commitments to the WTO, assuming other countries simply continue with status quo policies. This then forms a revised baseline for the other scenarios, which are then contrasted with five East Asian regional scenarios reflecting different kinds of Free Trade Area. Scenario 2 considers the conventional notion of an ASEAN Free Trade Area (AFTA), including abolition of trade taxes between all countries in the region, with maintenance of prior individual protection against the rest of the world. Scenario 3 extends AFTA to include China, as was agreed in principal last year in Cambodia. The fourth scenario captures another idea discussed recently, a Northeast Asian Free Trade Area, liberalizing trade between China, Japan, and Korea. The FTA for Scenario 5, ASEAN+3, is the most inclusive, bringing together the principal economies of East and Southeast Asia. Finally, a scenario with as much geopolitical as economic significance is included, a trilateral FTA between the world's two largest economies, the US and Japan, and China. If China's growth rate proves sustainable, it will ultimately have to be accommodated into trade and capital flow patterns that have more profound global implications. Many other scenarios could be studied with the same methodology, but these five are adequate to support initial discussion of the salient issues regarding globalization and East Asian regionalism. Finally, Scenario 7 is a reference case representing the hypothetical culmination of the WTO process, global trade liberalization (GTL). This may be an ephemeral goal, but the results given here at least help to calibrate expectations about the potential gains from truly open multilateralism.

A general indication of the results for these FTA scenarios is given (in terms of total export effects) in Figure 10.3.

As intuition would dictate, we find that GTL yields the largest and most widespread gains, both for the region and for the rest of the world. The AFTA plus China regional arrangement is beneficial to all members and expands their trade within the region and with the rest of the world, but more detailed results indicate that it induces significant trade diversion away from non-members.[3] Despite these effects, ASEAN's ability to

Figure 10.3:   Real Exports in 2020 (percent change from baseline)

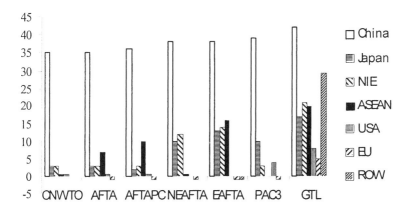

leverage China's growth would appear to make this arrangement quite attractive to them.

China's role in all these scenarios is a unique one, however, and appears to be governed by complex incentives. China gains much less in relative terms than either ASEAN in the AFTA or the rest of East and Southeast Asia under GTL. The reason for this is that China can realize most of its export growth by eliminating its own protection unilaterally, while a large part of the export gain to East and Southeast Asia comes from Chinese market access.

China may have other reservations about regionalism that limit its willingness to take detours from the path to globalization. In particular, our detailed results indicate that China might experience adverse terms of trade effects by diverting its trade into smaller zones delineated by Southeast Asian regional preferences. In addition to this, it appears that most regional arrangements would reinforce China's neo-mercantilist position vis-à-vis economies outside the region. In each scenario, China is estimated to increase ex-Asian exports more than it increases ex-Asian imports, while doing the opposite for East and Southeast Asia.

These two issues could make it difficult to recruit China into East and/or Southeast Asian regional agreements, yet our results indicate its membership is essential to the gains realized by others. Barring China's participation, most regional pacts would yield only small gains and other regional economies would probably be better off going directly toward the goal of GTL. Thus, China's current orientation, i.e. GTL as reflected in its assertive WTO commitments, is the primary goal for this country and may ultimately be the best route for other East and Southeast Asian economies.

Regional gains indicate the trade triangle at work. As emphasized in the last section, our results predict emergence of a systematic pattern of triangular trade for East and Southeast Asia. The trade triangle reveals that China's export expansion offers significant growth leverage to its neighbors. Strategic responses to China's emergence must take account of this, exploiting the triangle to translate regionalism into globalism. The extent to which East and Southeast Asian economies can facilitate access to the triangle through FTAs will of course depend upon negotiations involving China itself.

In particular, economies of the region need to negotiate relatively inclusive FTAs with China to avoid being crowded out of regional and extra-regional markets. The regional incidence of global export gains from the triangle depends critically on this. Our results indicate that significant trade diversion could occur among regional exporters, at the expense of those countries who opt out of an FTA including China.

Finally, China's situation in the East and Southeast Asian trading region appears to be unique in other important respects. Because of the sheer size and growth momentum of this economy, it apparently is in a position to 'go it alone' on the path to globalization, i.e. most of its own benefits from multilateralism can be captured by unilateral liberalization. This fact not only strengthens its resolve to follow that path, but could limit any incentive to be drawn into preferential, trade diverting regional agreements.

Because of these complex incentives, China possesses two carrots and one stick in regional negotiations. The carrots are access to its own domestic market and, by joining China in an FTA, greater indirect market access to the rest of the world (the triangle-induced export effect). The stick, obviously, is one of the carrots, used instead as a club: denial of market access and, worse, trade diversion arising from direct export competition by China and its partners. Clearly, the mercantile view of China is too simplistic, but this country still holds a special position in the regional negotiating environment, and other East Asian and Southeast Asian economies must take account of this fact. Overall, our results support a view that China's global emergence represents both challenges and enormous opportunities for East Asian regional economies. The effectiveness of today's policy makers in this context will be judged by their ability to identify both, facilitating timely adjustment to the former and proactive development of the latter.

China's importance to the regional adjustment process is undeniable, with Chinese goods and services representing one-third to one-half of all East Asian trade growth across the four scenarios. However, a rather upbeat interpretation arises from the estimates for Chinese trade within the East Asian region. In every scenario except 2 (where it is excluded from AFTA), Chinese imports from East Asia grow faster than its regional exports.

At the same time, however, it should be noted that China's exports to the ROW more than offset its East Asian imports. This happens because China presents higher prior protection than it faces within each of the trade groupings considered, and thus the Chinese real exchange rate depreciates in every liberalization scenario it joins. The rest of East Asia, on the other hand, faces higher protection than it presents, driving up its real exchange rate and sending real imports above exports in every scenario. Note that these are essentially macro responses to the prior burdens of trade distortion, and tell us very little about underlying patterns of comparative advantage. The latter are only revealed in more detailed country and sector analysis.

The following tables present bilateral trade adjustments arising from some of the FTA scenarios we considered. The differences between these are revealing, and help to elucidate the incentives facing regional negotiators. The first results, in Table 10.3, could be captioned 'The China Threat Scenario,' since it reflects China's unilateral WTO initiative with passive responses on the part of its neighbors. This represents a worst case scenario, where other East and Southeast Asian economies take no action to enhance the leverage offered by the trade triangle. In such a situation, our results indicate that China's regional partners would experience serious trade diversion, crowded out Chinese export competition in both their own region and in ROW markets.

The biggest losers are Korea and Taipei, China (NIE) who experience losses in bilateral exports of −10 percent (to Japan), −11 percent (ASEAN), and −13 percent (USA), −10 percent (RU and ROW), and even −7 percent of their own bilateral trade because they have missed the opportunity to enter a more liberal expansionary partnership. Japan and ASEAN are also crowded out of Asian and other ROW markets significantly, but in smaller relatively amounts. Note that trade with China itself, via the triangle, more than offsets these losses in every case, but the foregone exports to third markets are still sacrificed.

Contrasting these results with the recently negotiated, but still relatively limited ASEAN plus China (AFTAPC) scenario, it is apparent in Table 10.3 that partnership with China has two prominent advantages.[4] Firstly, it actually increases trade with China over the CNWTO scenario, as would be expected given the new partnership. Secondly, however, it also enables ASEAN to expand its triangle benefits and even increase exports to third markets. On the obverse, however, ASEAN significantly reduces imports

Table 10.3: *Bilateral Trade Flows – CNWTO (percent changes in 2020 with respect to baseline)*

| | Importer | | | | | | | |
Exporter	China	Japan	NIE	ASEAN	USA	EU	ROW	Total
China	0	37	43	36	31	35	32	34
Japan	38	0	−4	−6	−7	−5	−5	3
NIE	32	−10	−7	−11	−13	−10	−10	3
ASEAN	28	−4	−1	−2	−5	−3	−4	1
USA	24	−1	1	−1	0	−1	−1	1
EU	22	0	1	−1	−2	−1	−2	0
ROW	13	0	2	2	−2	−1	−1	0
Total	26	5	6	2	2	0	1	3

Notes: As the subtitles indicate, rows of this and following tables refer to export supply, while columns refer to import demand. This input–output layout is used here to capture bilateral trade flows, here in terms of percent change in ther terminal year.

Table 10.4:   Bilateral Trade Flows – AFTAPC (percent changes in 2020 with respect to CNWTO)

				Importer				
Exporter	China	Japan	NIE	ASEAN	USA	EU	ROW	Total
China	0	−4	−4	47	−3	−4	−3	1
Japan	2	0	1	−10	1	1	1	0
NIE	2	0	0	−12	1	1	1	0
ASEAN	2	4	3	33	3	3	1	9
USA	1	0	0	−6	0	0	0	0
EU	1	0	0	−5	0	0	0	0
ROW	2	0	0	−7	0	0	0	0
Total	2	0	0	9	0	0	0	1

from third partners, an important diversion effect. Moreover, China reduces exports to third markets, as these goods are diverted to ASEAN markets. As usual, the members of a trade conclave benefit from two components of trade expansion, new growth and diversion. Clearly, this relatively exclusive FTA may be a step in the right direction, but it cannot realize to full potential of regional trade expansion, nor carry ASEAN very far along toward globalization.

The most inclusive scenario considered is ASEAN+3, the results for which are given in Table 10.4. Here the benefits of a more expansive and diversified liberal market are very apparent. Including two OECD economies in particular leads to a more 'North–South' FTA, with economic diversity needed to expand the basis for regional specialization and scale economies in export production. The benefits for members are quite dramatic. Indeed, their trade expansion within the region now mirrors that of China itself (compare Table 10.1), indicating the leverage of the trade triangle is working more effectively once the FTA can facilitate market access across the region. Interestingly, however, the main percentage gains for Asian economies come not from direct exports to China, but from intra-regional trade expansion. Asian exports to China expand only moderated over the CNWTO base, since China's WTO accession already confers market access to Asia. What remains for this scenario to achieve is the opening of trade elsewhere in the region, facilitating multilateral linkages to complete the market growth instigated by China. These can be expected to take the form mainly of intermediate links running between China's direct partners and its upstream and downstream counterparts, running through the complex web of regional supply chains.[5]

*Table 10.5:   Bilateral Trade Flows – ASEAN+3 (percent changes in 2020
             with respect to CNWTO)*

Exporter	Importer							
	China	Japan	NIE	ASEAN	USA	EU	ROW	Total
China	0	21	33	27	−8	−9	−8	3
Japan	2	0	39	40	−2	−2	−2	10
NIE	3	50	31	43	0	−1	−2	11
ASEAN	4	49	35	26	5	4	0	14
USA	5	−4	−11	−9	1	1	1	−1
EU	4	−2	−10	−11	1	0	0	0
ROW	5	−9	−10	−8	1	0	1	−1
Total	4	12	10	13	−1	0	−1	2

*Table 10.6:   Bilateral Trade Flows – GTL (percent changes in 2020
             with respect to CNWTO)*

Exporter	Importer							
	China	Japan	NIE	ASEAN	USA	EU	ROW	Total
China	0	−1	5	12	−4	4	25	6
Japan	4	0	19	23	5	15	29	13
NIE	7	28	16	37	10	17	36	18
ASEAN	8	25	18	21	16	23	26	19
USA	7	11	17	8	0	9	3	7
EU	13	14	32	17	15	−7	30	6
ROW	14	31	18	15	6	42	49	30
Total	9	15	18	18	7	7	27	14

Turning to country-specific results, Table 10.6 presents bilateral trade flow adjustments in response to global trade liberalization (GTL), expressed as percentage changes with respect to the CNWTO levels forecast for 2020. This is clearly a very expansionary scenario, indicating annual export growth over the base year of between of between 6 and 30 percent for the trading countries/regions selected, and with bilateral growth often much higher. Trade within the residual ROW group expands by 40 percent above CNWTO 2020 levels, for example.

While the general impression is one of trade growth, with the overwhelming majority of flows expanding, some bilateral ties will remain fairly constant or even contract. Net changes in bilateral trade are the result of shifting relative real exchange rates, which in turn result from differences in prior protection levels. Thus it is worth noting that, even in the case of multilateral tariff abolition, trade diversion still results because of asymmetries in prior protection patterns. Fortunately, the diversionary effects are relatively small in this global free trade scenario, and they are far outweighed by trade creation at each national level and, therefore, in the aggregate.

Now we compare the globalization results with those in the most inclusive Asian FTA, ASEAN+3 (Table 10.5). As we noted above, one of the most striking features of the ASEAN+3 results is the scope and magnitude of trade diversion. As one would expect with a regional agreement, trade expands within the East and Southeast Asian bloc, but at a significant expense to trade with and within the rest of the world. There is dramatic (if uneven) expansion of bilateral trade ties across East and Southeast Asia, and many individual bilateral flows expand much more than under globalization. Despite this, however, all the E&SE regions considered experience more total trade growth under GTL.

Thus it is reasonable to ask why an ASEAN+3 would be preferable to the first scenario. The most obvious answer has to do with uncertainty and risk aversion, two salient features of the multilateral negotiating environment that have sustained regionalism in this era of globalization. In particular, many countries view a smaller, more certain (and perhaps more expedient) payoff from regional liberalization as preferable to a more hypothetical future prospect of global free trade. The relative transparency and tractability of regional accords alone might make them preferable to global ones, but of course they need not even be perceived as mutually exclusive.[6] On the contrary, some advocates of regionalism, particularly of the North–South variety, argue that they offer important precedence for more comprehensive global negotiations, both in terms of negotiating standards and domestic adjustments arising from conformity.

Apart from many issues related to uncertainty, impetus for a regional agreement comes from two very practical considerations. First, for every East Asian economy considered, the ASEAN+3 FTA confers most of the total import and export growth they would experience under global free trade (the average is 73 percent). Thus a regional agreement, in many ways easier and more certain to negotiate, gives it members most of the total trade gain that globalization might offer. An essential caveat, however, is that the composition of this trade might be different, and much of this expansion seems to be bought at the expense of relations with partners outside the region. Thus we can see from these results that regionalism is substantially beneficial, but not how it constitutes a path to globalization or, ultimately, the two can be reconciled.

Patterns of adjustment outside the region are complex, with both trade creation and diversion. The removal of an extensive set of tariffs within one region creates a new set of (*de facto*) trade preferences within the rest of the world, and we see modest offsetting ex-East Asia trade growth in most cases. Occasionally, however, small reductions in bilateral trade outside the region are probably induced by trade contraction with respect to East Asia (see e.g. ROW). Generally speaking, economies outside East Asia stand by and watch regional trade expand in the region and contract with respect to them, with only negligible adjustments to their other bilateral ties. Thus much of the trade growth within the East Asia region is offset by diversion.

Returning to the sub-regional arrangements, it appears there would be little enthusiasm for an AFTAPC arrangement outside East Asia since, like the other East Asian pacts, it actually reduces ROW trade. The more detailed results in Table 10.1 also reveal unwelcome trade diversion with respect to East Asian neighbors, driving down total exports and imports for Japan, Korea, and Taiwan. For the world as a whole, trade grows by less than 10 percent of what would arise from GTL, and for Asia total trade growth is less than half what it would be under ASEAN+3. More seriously, the biggest partner to this arrangement would obtain less than a third of the ASEAN+3 gains and about a fifth of the GTL gains from joining this discriminatory arrangement. Worse, China would be forced into a neo-mercantilist position of trying to expand ROW exports (against contracting ROW exports from East and Southeast Asia) while substantially cutting ROW imports. In addition, Chinese import demand would be diverted away from important regional allies such as Japan and Korea. All in all, it is unclear why China would sustain such an arrangement against more inclusive ones, particularly given its assertive prior commitment to the WTO process.

Before moving on to examine unilateralism, we summarize results from two other FTA scenarios. The first of these represents a hypothesis about northern regionalism in the Asian Pacific, referred to as a Northeast Asian Free Trade Area (NEAFTA). We examined this prospect in Scenario 5, where China, Japan, and Korea remove all tariff barriers among themselves. Given the size of the economies being considered, both the net and compositional trade effects of this arrangement are more dramatic, as can be seen in Table 10.4. Still, total trade grows only by about half of what an ASEAN+3 agreement would yield, and only a fraction of GTL's trade gains are realized. Total intra-regional trade grows by almost the same amount as under GTL, but significant ROW trade diversion offsets these gains and the region only enjoys about half the export and import growth it would under GTL. The same reasoning generally holds for China's trade. Again, however, China is in the difficult position of trying to expand exports to ROW while reducing corresponding imports.

As a final scenario, we examine the PAC3 arrangement including Japan, China, and the US, an idea that is more grounded in regional strategic thinking. Still, given the scale and diversity of the economies considered here, these results could be interesting. Given that this arrangement also draws in an extra-regional economy, and the world's largest, it might make an interesting comparison case with respect to GTL and the Asia-only scenarios. In reality, however, this scenario is less than compelling for two of the three countries. Japan experiences most of the trade growth because of relatively high prior protection, but significantly less than it would under ASEAN+3. Otherwise, trade diversion outweighs most of the potential export gains for both China and the US. The US does appear to alter its trade patterns in important ways, but would presumably antagonize many trading partners in the process. While this might serve as an inducement to bring the latter into a larger regional or even global agreement, it is difficult to see the PAC3 FTA as a stable coalition in the region.

Table 10.7: *Bilateral Trade Flows – NEAFTA3 (percent changes in 2020 with respect to CNWTO)*

				Importer				
Exporter	China	Japan	NIE	ASEAN	USA	EU	ROW	Total
China	0	30	38	−7	−6	−6	−6	2
Japan	4	0	44	1	1	1	1	7
NIE	4	63	37	1	3	2	2	8
ASEAN	3	−8	−9	0	1	1	1	0
USA	3	−5	−11	0	0	1	1	0
EU	2	−3	−10	0	0	0	0	0
ROW	4	−9	−10	1	1	0	0	0
Total	4	8	8	−1	−1	0	0	1

Table 10.8: *Bilateral Trade Flows – PAC3 (percent changes in 2020 with respect to CNWTO)*

				Importer				
Exporter	China	Japan	NIE	ASEAN	USA	EU	ROW	Total
China	0	21	−8	−8	15	−8	−4	3
Japan	6	0	3	2	19	2	7	7
NIE	3	−5	0	−1	−5	0	−1	0
ASEAN	4	−9	1	1	−6	1	0	0
USA	5	28	1	1	0	1	0	3
EU	3	−3	0	0	−3	0	0	0
ROW	6	−5	1	1	−2	1	0	0
Total	4	7	−1	−1	2	0	0	1

3.2. Incentive Compatibility

Since the seminal work of Viner on this subject over 50 years ago, there has been sustained debate about the incentive properties of regional arrangements, both with respect to larger universes of liberalization and, especially, in comparison with unilateral trade liberalization (UTL).[7] Using theoretical models with two or three goods and three countries, a number of authors have argued that regional arrangements are strategically dominated, for individual countries, by unilateral liberalization, and that incentives must therefore be devised to effect voluntary participation in FTA.[8] In this section, we present results that challenge the generality of this conclusion, indicating that the East Asian FTA can dominate or be dominated by unilateralism, depending upon the economy under consideration. On the basis of this and other evidence presented in this chapter, we recommend that the efficacy of trade agreements be decided empirically rather than with rules-of-thumb inferred from simplified theoretical models.[9]

To better understand the incentives facing of a prospective FTA member, we ran a series of policy simulations to estimate the effects of two kinds of unilateralism. In the first case, the country[10] under consideration abolishes tariffs unilaterally and without negotiated or other concessions from trading partners. This scenario we refer to simply as UTL. In the second case, we look at an extreme (and admittedly artificial) reference for negotiated liberalization, where the country abolishes its own tariffs and each of its trading partners reciprocates bilaterally while maintaining their other external tariffs at baseline levels (called UTLR for UTL reciprocated). We see these two cases as bracketing the potential outcomes of unilateral tariff abolition for the country in question. For present discussion, we disaggregated the larger regional economies in the data set but then confined ourselves to a subset for this detailed analysis.

4. RMB APPRECIATION AND STRUCTURAL ADJUSTMENT

Most outside observers see China's burgeoning foreign exchange reserves as evidence of exchange rate management. In particular, it appears that the RMB is currently below an internationally weighted equilibrium rate that would bring reserves within a more conventional range as a percentage of other macro aggregates. Within China, there may be strongly held opinions about exchange rate management. These include, among others, influential stakeholders with neo-mercantilist views regarding export competitiveness and import protection. In light of this, and relatively intense differences on this subject with some trade prominent partners, it has been difficult for China to achieve rapid RMB adjustment, even in the presence of massive reserve accumulation. This situation contributes to complex redistributive forces within Chinese society, both across social groups and generations, yet there is relatively little independent empirical analysis to elucidate this or the implications of alternative policies.

4.1. Scenarios for Real Exchange Rate Appreciation

To examine the implications of greater RMB flexibility, we examine a scenario where the Pacific regional economies maintain constant ratios of net foreign saving to real GDP. The adjusting variable in this case is the domestic GDP price index, a proxy for the real exchange rate (RER).

Figure 10.4 (details in Table 10.9) depicts the aggregate results of this alternative macro closure rule, including significant RER for China. Because of sustained export surpluses, all the Asian economies experience RER appreciation in varying degrees. China is in the lead for analogous reasons, yet the total adjustment is less than might be expected because China is also experiencing bilateral deficits with respect to its neighbors. Appreciation with respect to the US RER, by contrast, is over 20 percent over the period under consideration, a figure generally in line with current public discussion.

Figure 10.4:   Real Exchange Rate Adjustments

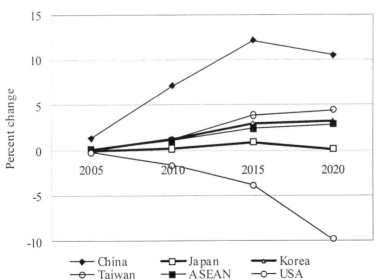

Table 10.9:   Real Exchange Rate Adjustments

	2005	2010	2015	2020
China	1.29	7.23	12.09	10.52
Japan	0.00	0.26	0.88	0.14
Korea	0.13	1.28	3.04	3.27
Taiwan	−0.01	1.28	3.85	4.43
ASEAN	0.15	1.10	2.45	2.93
USA	−0.21	−1.62	−3.78	−9.78

4.2. Trade Adjustments

More detailed structural adjustments can improve understanding of the policy setting for exchange rate management. In the context of trade adjustment, a few salient effects emerge in the RER appreciation scenario. On the export side Chinese exports are adversely affected with respect to the WTO scenario, but still rise above steady growth in baseline values. Growth of exports is slower than is non-Japanese trading partners, largely because China's RER 'opening' has sharply stimulated their export opportunities.

On the other side of regional trade flows, we see the converse effect of exchange rates, with China experiencing dramatic import expansion while its neighbors lag behind. All countries expand trade, but this important (multilateral) component of China's absorption nearly triples across the decade 2010 to 2020. To this extent, we are seeing China and the US exchanging places from the Asian regional perspective. Indeed, in light of these dynamics it is reasonable to ask if a Strong RMB Consensus might emerge in the wake of the long-held Strong Dollar Consensus. Certainly, trade reorientation on the part of China's neighbors give them two important growth advantages. Export expansion toward China offers important diversification away from traditional, North–South patterns of trade. It also represents a commitment to the world's most dynamic consumer market.

Beneath the veneer of macro shifts, dramatic patterns of trade diversion emerge, both between countries and within sectors. The simulation model we use has a significant amount of sector detail, but space constraints prevent detailed discussion of these in this chapter. Even so, a few salient features merit emphasis:

1. China's import dependence accelerates across a wide spectrum of products, but especially energy and food.

2. Asian exports to China will reflect traditional comparative advantages, with high income Asia exporting technology and education intensive products and capital goods, while the rest of Asia ships more diverse consumer goods, intermediates, and raw materials.
3. Other Asian exports accelerate despite RER appreciation (because China is experiencing significantly higher appreciation), increasing their domestic purchasing power sharply.

Figure 10.5:   Asian Export Trends

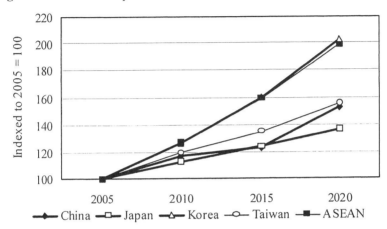

Figure 10.6:   Asian Import Trends

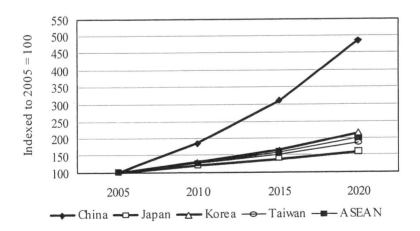

4.3. Domestic Growth

Perhaps the most interesting result of the RER experiment is that, contrary to neo-mercantile or other protectionist arguments, China's aggregate real economic growth accelerates with currency appreciation. In particular, the attenuation of export growth is more than offset by domestic demand expansion, implying that historic exchange rate rigidity may have actually retarded domestic structural transition as well as aggregate growth.

Figure 10.7 shows how China's growth (well above the baseline trend) accelerates ahead of other regional economies. The primary driver of this is increased domestic purchasing power, in particular for essential components of the national balance sheet like raw materials, basic consumer goods, and a wide spectrum of intermediate and capital goods. The result is a dramatic shift from external to domestic demand as the engine of real economic growth. In this context, consumer final demand has higher tertiary and employment intensive content and thus longer multiplier chains across the domestic economy.

Figure 10.7:   Real GDP Trends

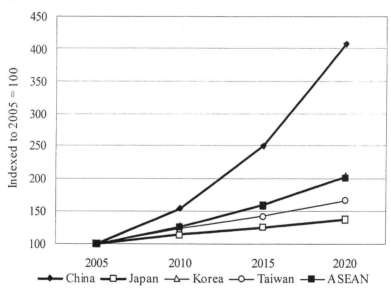

4.4. Capital Market Implications

Obviously, all these current account adjustments will be reflected in the capital account, especially at the bilateral level. Such shifts are notoriously difficult to generalize, yet a few observations are relevant. Under the assumed macroeconomic closure, foreign savings are constrained by real GDP and growth of the trade surplus is slowing. This means FDI is increasing in both absolute and relative terms, with two main effects. First, to the extent that foreign investors are more selective and able to add value to domestic assets, China will experience rising average quality of domestic investment and asset holding. This has important implications for productivity growth and competitive discipline, particularly as export discipline recedes. Secondly, RER appreciation will induce accelerated (and discounted) technology transfer. The cost of embodied foreign technology is falling, which will also contribute to accelerated substitution/adoption/ modernization.

As the RER appreciates and FDI accelerates, an extensive sectoral rotation will be set in motion across the economy. Non-tradable prices will rise relative to tradables, and domestic resources will be drawn toward these activities. This can be very beneficial to development of the internal market, but there are two potential pitfalls. The first is a variant of classic Dutch disease, disengagement from external competitive discipline.

A second source of risk comes from labor intensity of emergent demand. The net employment characteristics of the sector rotation will be very important to long-term employment levels and composition. If, for example property leads the growth of non-tradable demand rather than services, it could be difficult to maintain employment rates or limit the growth of inequality.

4.5. Labor Markets

We have assumed full employment across all scenarios. Clearly, however, compositional features of the employment question will determine how much economic potential is realized and how the benefits of higher growth rates are distributed across each economy. For the Asian region, detailed analysis of sectoral adjustments is needed to assess this question. For China, elastic supplies of unskilled workers are probably less of an issue than recruitment of skilled labor. In any case, observations from three perspectives on labor markets are relevant:

1. How high?
   a. Skilled labor demand may be rising faster than supply. This trend is being accelerated by FDI, for which skilled labor appears to be a complement.

    b. What is the real capacity of formal and informal education/training to deliver higher productivity?

2. How long?
    a. Demographic transition and rising dependency. Aging and family policy may intensify the pressure on the working labor force.
    b. The only way out is ever-increasing labor productivity.

3. How wide?
    a. Migratory pressure will continue as the opportunity cost of labor in the rural sector declines monotonically.
    b. Actual migration must continue to be demand-driven.
    c. Regional growth rates will increasingly determine aggregate growth (median vs. average growth).

4.6. Regional Issues

On the current account, tempering China's export competitiveness and accelerating absorption looks good to regional neighbors. However, there will certainly be intensified regional competition for primary products and intermediate goods. This will squeeze regional balance sheets as a broad shift from export competition to competition for imports ensues. RER appreciation will help China in this purchasing power competition, but intensify the underlying regional (and global) challenges of resource sustainability. Under such conditions, major trends that are already in evidence can be expected to persist and even intensify.

Firstly, there will an expansion of resource-seeking multilateral partnerships. China is already heavily engaged in this, including mining in South America, energy in Central Asia and Africa, etc. On the private sector side of the same trend, China and perhaps others will have strong incentives to pursue global vertical integration, investing to secure sources of upstream products and factor services. This will have the secondary effect of strengthening downstream market power and will probably accelerate downstream consolidation. Within more highly articulated international supply chains, there will be strong incentives to shift value by bargaining and technology diffusion across national boundaries. Who benefits from this process of supply chain integration nationally is today a matter of pure speculation. Looking to Japanese experience, with its extensive networks of overlapping foreign ownership, overseas facilities and equity listings, it is apparent that the benefits of 'network' globalization are widely dispersed, serving the interests of parent company shareholders but many others as well.

5. CONCLUSIONS

China's remarkable growth experience has inspired both admiration and apprehension on the part of its neighbors. By establishing new standards for efficient international division of labor and using this to sustain unprecedented growth in the world's most populous economy, China has redefined the landscape of regional and global competition. This research uses an empirical simulation model to examine the implications of these events for the Asian region generally and for China in particular.

Among other findings, this research predicts that China will be the largest trading economy in East Asia by about 2010. It will be the region's largest exporter by this time, but its largest *importer* by 2008 at the latest. A decade ago, China was seen by its neighbors as a relentless threat to their export-driven prosperity. Now it appears that Chinese absorption will be a primary driver of sustained Asian regional growth. China's internal market, animated by both domestic demand and export requirements, will accelerate other East Asian export growth significantly and create historic opportunities for regional investors. Provided Asian economies do not isolate themselves from the process of Chinese trade liberalization, the net effect of China's growth can be hugely positive.

As part of this process, an East Asian trade triangle will emerge, where China develops a sustained trade deficit with East Asia and a surplus with Western OECD economies of nearly equal magnitude. The trade triangle enables China to 'deliver globalization' to the region as a by-product of its own WTO accession. In this sense, East Asia can capture many of the benefits of full globalization just by forming an inclusive FTA like ASEAN+3. In negotiations with China, Asian countries should be mindful of these broader objectives.

Our results indicate that, in the wake of China's WTO accession, the best strategy for East Asia is to pursue globalism through more comprehensive regionalism. In other words, a substantial portion of China's OECD trade surplus will ultimately accrue to its regional neighbors. This has profound implications for patterns of both North–South and regional capital accumulation, an important area of future research and financial policy dialogue.

If regional balances over the next two decades were to be stabilized with real exchange rate appreciation, a complex set of adjustments would ensue. Most of these are consistent with prior intuition, but the magnitudes are important for policy reasons. For China, the overall RER would adjust only moderately, but bilateral adjustments could be larger (11 percent globally, against 20 percent vis-à-vis the US).

As a part of a sustained appreciation, China's trade would move in the expected direction. Total export growth would slow but continue, while imports would accelerate rapidly. Aggregate regional trade would not change in trend, but the composition would shift dramatically with export switching from Western OECD markets to China. As part of this geographic shift, a 'strong RMB' could be expected to assume part of the burden of global demand sustainability long carried by a 'strong dollar.' Indeed, it is an interesting open question as to how the policy environment and financial markets might adapt to this.

Perhaps most importantly, this research indicates that the Chinese economy would experience significant additional growth with RER appreciation, mainly due to accelerated growth of the internal economy. It is apparent from this research that undervaluation of the exchange rate is restricting China's access to essential resources, commodities, and intermediate goods, undermining enterprise expansion and household real incomes. Like most distortionary policies, managed exchange rate regimes entail welfare transfers between social groups (and generations). These results suggest there is also an aggregate (growth) opportunity cost to foreign exchange accumulation.

Among other findings, it appears that RER appreciation will induce significant sectoral rotation of both final demand and investment in China. The employment implications of this could be favorable, since non-tradables are generally more labor-intensive, but some categories like property will contribute less to employment growth and more to inequality trends.

NOTES

1. Thanks to colleagues at the Asian Development Bank Institute and seminar participants at Stanford and UC Berkeley for valuable comments.
2. GTAP is a 66 country/region, 57 sector global database with detailed domestic industry and bilateral trade accounts. See Hertel et al. (2002) for complete documentation.
3. Throughout this chapter, we use the term trade diversion to mean a redirection of export supply from one trade partner to another, and by trade creation we mean an increase in total exports. These concepts differ from those used in the classical theory of customs unions, where comparative costs of production are the defining characteristics.
4. Note for the sake of interpretation that these and other results that follow are defined as changes with respect to the CNWTO scenario (rather than the baseline discussed earlier).
5. The multilateral chains in such Asian supply networks often represent the majority of value creation for final goods in the region, whether produced for export or domestic consumption. For a more detailed discussion of such networks and empirical estimates of their significance, see Roland-Holst (2003a).
6. See, e.g. World Bank (2000) for extensive discussion of the incentive properties of regional and multilateral agreements.
7. See e.g. Viner (1950), or a more modern statement in Kemp and Wan (1976).

8. For recent writing in this vein, see e.g. de Melo et al. (1993), Hoekman and Leidy (1993), and Whalley (1996).
9. Roland-Holst and van der Mensbrugghe (2002) reached analogous conclusions in a Latin American context.
10. Among the latter, for example, are powerful advocates of China's food self-sufficiency, who perceive RMB appreciation opening the country to an avalanche of farm products, including those from subsidized OECD producers.

BIBLIOGRAPHY

Anderson, Kym, Joe Francois, Tom Hertel, Bernard Hoekman and Will Martin (2000), 'Potential gains from trade reform in the new millennium', Paper presented at the Third Annual Conference on Global Economic Analysis, held at Monash University, 27–30 June.

Brown, Drusilla K., Alan V. Deardorff and Robert M. Stern (1992), 'A North American Free Trade Agreement: Analytical issues and a computational assessment', *The World Economy*, **15**, 15–29.

de Melo, Jamie, Arvind Panagariya and Dani Rodrik (1993), 'The new regionalism: A country perspecitve', in J. de Melo and A. Panagariya (eds), *New Dimensions in Regional Integration*, New York: Cambridge University Press.

Francois, Joseph and Kenneth Reinert (1997), *Applied Methods for Trade Policy Analysis: A Handbook*, New York, NY: Cambridge University Press.

Hertel, Thomas W. (ed.) (1997), *Global Trade Analysis: Modeling and Applications*, New York, NY: Cambridge University Press.

Hoekman, B. and M. Leidy (1993), 'Holes and loopholes in integration Agreements: History and prospects', in K. Anderson and R. Blackhurst (eds), *Regional Integration and the Global Trading System*, London: Harvester Wheatsheaf.

Hoekman, B. and M. Kostecki (1995), *The Political Economy of the World Trading System: From GATT to WTO*, New York/Oxford: Oxford University Press.

Lee, Hiro, David Roland-Holst and Dominique van der Mensbrugghe (1999), 'APEC trade liberalization and structural adjustment: Policy assumptions', APEC Discussion Paper Series, APEC Study Center, Graduate School of International Development, Nagoya University, March.

Kemp, M.C. and H.Y. Wan (1976), 'An elementary proposition concerning the foundation of customs unions', *Journal of International Economics*, **6**, 95–7.

OECD (1998), 'Economic modelling of climate change', OECD Workshop Report, 17–18 September, Paris. (Summary at http://www.oecd.org/dev/news/ Environment/ summary.pdf.)

Roland-Holst, David (2002), 'An overview of China's emergence and East Asian trade patterns to 2020', Research Paper No. 44, Asian Development Bank Institute, Tokyo.

Roland-Holst, David (2003a), 'Global supply networks and multilateral trade linkages: A structural analysis of East Asia', Research Paper, Asian Development Bank Institute, Tokyo.

Roland-Holst, David (2003b), 'East Asian patterns of comparative advantage', Research Paper, Asian Development Bank Institute, Tokyo.

Roland-Holst, David and Dominique van der Mensbrugghe (2002), 'Regionalism versus globalization in the Americas: Empirical evidence on opportunities and challenges', published jointly in *Integration and Trade and Économie Internationale*, Institute for the Integration of Latin America and the *Caribbean/Inter-American Development Bank and Centre d'Études Perspectives et d'Informations Internationales*, Washington and Paris, forthcoming.

Viner, J. (1950), *The Customs Union Issue*, New York: Carnegie Endowment for International Peace.

Whalley, J. (1996), 'Why do countries seek regional trade agreements?', NBER Working Paper No. 5552, April.

World Bank (2000), *Trade Blocs*, Policy Research Report, World Bank/Oxford UP.

World Bank (2002), *Global Economic Prospects and the Developing Countries: Making Trade Work for the World's Poor*, Washington: The World Bank.

11. The Chinese Approach to Capital Inflows: Patterns and Possible Explanations

Eswar S. Prasad and Shang-Jin Wei[1]

1. INTRODUCTION

China has in many ways taken the world by storm. In addition to its swiftly rising prominence in the global trading system, where it now accounts for over 6 percent of total world trade, it has also become a magnet for foreign direct investment (FDI), overtaking the United States (in 2003) as the number one destination for FDI.

It was not always thus. China's integration with the global economy began in earnest only after the market-oriented reforms that were instituted in 1978. Capital inflows, in particular, were minimal in the 1970s and 1980s, impeded by capital controls and the reluctance of international investors to undertake investment in a socialist economy with weak institutions and limited exposure to international trade. All of this changed in the early 1990s, when FDI inflows surged dramatically on account of the selective opening of China's capital account as well as the rapid trade expansion that, in conjunction with China's large labor pool, created opportunities for foreign investors. These inflows have remained strong ever since, even during the Asian crisis of the late 1990s.

Given China's status as a global economic power, characterizing the nature and determinants of China's capital inflows is of considerable interest for analytical reasons as well as for understanding the implications for the regional and global allocation of capital. Our primary objective in this chapter is to provide a detailed descriptive analysis of the main aspects of capital inflows into China. Given the degree of interest in China and the relative paucity of data, we aim to provide a benchmark reference tool for other researchers, including by providing some critical perspectives on the numbers that we report.

Section 11.2 presents a detailed picture of the evolution of China's capital inflows. A feature of particular interest is that China's capital inflows have generally been dominated by FDI, which, for an emerging market, constitutes a preferred form of inflows since FDI tends to be stable and associated with other benefits such as transfers of technological and managerial expertise. An interesting aspect of these inflows is that, contrary to some popular perceptions, they come mainly from other advanced Asian countries that have net trade surpluses with China, rather than from the United States and Europe, which constitute China's main export markets. As for other types of inflows, China has limited its external debt to low levels, and non-FDI private capital inflows have typically been quite limited, until recently.

In Section 11.3, we examine the evolution of the balance of payments and dissect the recent surge in the pace of accumulation of international reserves. A key finding is that, while current account surpluses and FDI have remained important contributors to reserve accumulation, the dramatic surge in the pace of reserve accumulation during 2001–04 is largely attributable to non-FDI capital inflows. We provide some analytical perspectives on the costs and benefits of holding a large (and growing) stock of reserves. There has also been considerable international attention focused recently on the issue of the currency composition of China's massive stock of international reserves (which is now second only to that of Japan). Despite data constraints, we attempt to shed what little light we can on this issue, both by carefully examining a popular source of data for China's holding of US securities and by calculating the potential balance of payments implications of reserve valuation effects associated with the depreciation of the US dollar in recent years.

Section 11.4 discusses the broader composition of China's capital inflows in the context of the burgeoning literature on financial globalization. Notwithstanding the recent surge of non-FDI inflows, FDI remains historically the dominant source of inflows into China. The literature on the benefits and risks of financial globalization suggests that China may have benefited greatly in terms of improving the risk–return trade-offs by having its inflows tilted so much toward FDI.

Whether this composition of inflows is a result of enlightened policies, the structure of institutions or plain luck is an intriguing question. In Section 11.5, we examine various hypotheses that have been put forward to explain why China has its inflows so heavily tilted toward FDI. In this context, we provide a detailed description of China's capital account restrictions and how these have evolved over time. While controls on non-FDI inflows as well as tax and other incentives appear to be proximate factors for explaining the FDI-heavy composition of inflows, other factors may also have contributed to this outcome. It is not straightforward to disentangle the quantitative relevance of alternative hypotheses. We argue, nonetheless, that at least a few of the hypotheses – including some mercantilist-type arguments that have been advanced recently – are not consistent with the facts.

2. THE CHINESE PATTERN OF INFLOWS AND SOME INTERNATIONAL COMPARISONS

2.1. The Evolution of Capital Inflows

Gross capital inflows into China were minuscule before the early 1980s. After 1984, the 'other investment' category, which includes bank lending, increased significantly and accounted for the largest share of total inflows during the 1980s (Figure 11.1). FDI rose gradually from the early 1980s to early 1991 and then rose dramatically through the mid-1990s. During the 1990s, FDI has accounted for the lion's share of inflows. It is interesting to note that FDI inflows were only marginally affected during the Asian crisis. Figure 11.2 provides some more detail on the evolutions of the main components of the capital account, both in terms of gross outflows and inflows. Note that all components other than FDI show sharp increases in outflows in the period immediately after the Asian crisis, with the subsequent recovery in net inflows of these components taking two to three years to materialize. Recent data indicate that, after remaining in a range of

Figure 11.1:   *Level and Composition of Gross Capital Inflows, 1982–2005 (in billions of US dollars)*

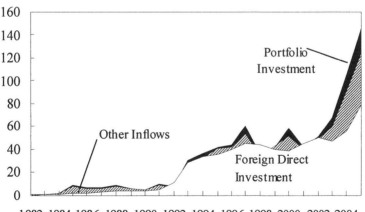

Figure 11.2:   *Gross Capital Flows by Component, 1982–2005*
                  (in billions of US dollars)

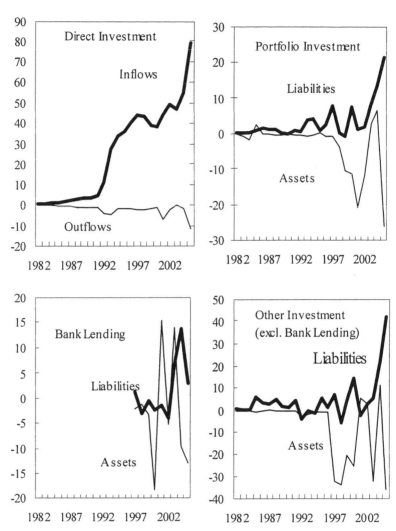

Note: Scales differ across the four panels of this figure.

Source: CEIC database.

Figure 11.3:   Asian Economies and Emerging Markets: Net Capital Flows, 1990–2005 (in percent of GDP)

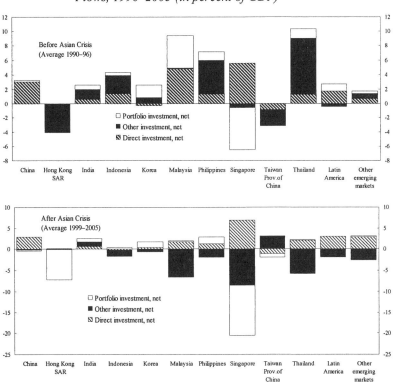

Note: Average for other emerging markets in EMBI+ index, excluding Latin America and Asian countries.

Source: World Economic Outlook database.

around $50 billion during 2002–03, gross FDI inflows increased to almost $68 billion in 2005.

From a cross-country perspective, China's net capital inflows are of course large in absolute magnitude but hardly remarkable relative to the size of the economy. Before the Asian crisis, many of the other 'Asian tigers' had significantly larger inflows relative to their GDP (Figure 11.3, top panel). What is striking, however, is that, except for Singapore, the share of FDI in total inflows is clearly the highest for China. Its total net inflows as a share of GDP rank among the highest across all emerging markets after the Asian crisis, especially since many of the Asian tigers were no longer the darlings of international investors (Figure 11.3, lower panel). While the net inflows dropped sharply across all emerging markets after the late 1990s, the interesting thing to note is that most of the inflows that did come into the emerging markets after 1999 took the form of FDI.

China's average net inflows, and the share of FDI in those inflows, look quite similar during the periods 1990–96 and 1999–2005. Since FDI is clearly the main story in the context of China's capital inflows, we now turn to a more detailed examination of these flows.

2.2. Foreign Direct Investment

Over the past decade, China has accounted for about one-third of gross FDI flows to all emerging markets and about 60 percent of these flows to Asian emerging markets (Figure 11.4, top panel). Even excluding flows from Hong Kong SAR to China from these calculations (on the extreme assumption that all of these flows represent 'round-tripping' of funds originating in China – this point is discussed further below), China's share in these flows to emerging markets is substantial (Figure 11.4, lower panel). The shares spike upward during the Asian crisis and, more recently, in 2002, when weaknesses in the global economy resulted in a slowdown in flows from industrial countries to most emerging markets other than China. With the pickup in flows to emerging markets in 2003, there has been a corresponding decline in China's share, even though flows to China remained essentially unchanged.

Where are China's FDI inflows coming from? Table 11.1 shows the share of utilized FDI by source country. Some aspects of the results are worth noting. First of all, the share of Hong Kong SAR has declined steadily over the past decade, from 58 percent in 1994 to 30 percent in 2005. One of the concerns in interpreting FDI data for China is that a significant portion of these flows could potentially represent round-tripping to take advantage of preferential tax treatment of foreign investment relative to domestic investment. Much of this round-tripping is believed to take place through Hong Kong SAR. While it is difficult to estimate the extent of round-tripping, the declining share of Hong Kong SAR in total inflows at least suggests that the magnitude of round-tripping as a share of total FDI inflows may have been declining over time. On the other hand, the shares of small economies like the Virgin Islands and Western Samoa, which have risen over the past few years, could now be accounting for some of these round-tripping flows.[2]

Asian economies account for a substantial fraction of China's FDI inflows. For instance, over the period 2001–05, five Asian economies – Hong Kong SAR, Japan, Korea, Taiwan Province of China, and Singapore – together account for about 60 percent of FDI inflows. That a lot of

China's FDI comes from these relatively advanced Asian economies suggests that these flows do bring the usual benefits associated with FDI,

Figure 11.4: *China's Share of Foreign Direct Investment Inflows to Emerging Markets, 1994–2005*

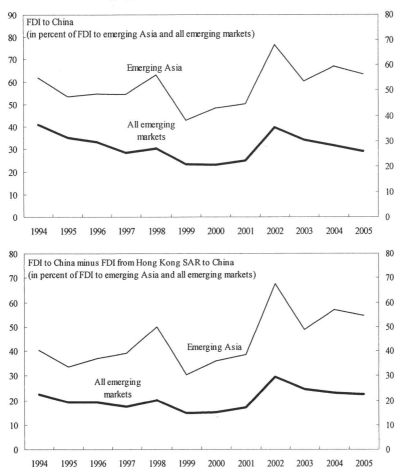

Notes: This figure uses data on gross FDI flows. The bottom panel excludes gross FDI flows to China originating from Hong Kong SAR from both the numerator and denominator of the two ratios shown.

Sources: World Economic Outlook database, CEIC database, and authors' calculations.

Table 11.1: FDI Inflows by Source Country (percent share)

	1994	1995	1996	1997	1998	1999	2000	2001	2002	2003	2004	2005
Hong Kong SAR	58.2	53.4	49.6	45.6	40.7	40.6	38.1	35.7	33.9	33.1	31.3	29.8
Virgin Islands	–	–	–	–	8.9	6.6	9.4	10.8	11.6	10.8	11.1	15.0
Japan	6.1	8.2	8.8	9.6	7.5	7.4	7.2	9.3	7.9	9.4	9.0	10.8
Korea	2.1	2.8	3.3	4.7	4.0	3.2	3.7	4.6	5.2	8.4	10.3	8.6
United States	7.4	8.2	8.2	7.2	8.6	10.5	10.8	9.5	10.3	7.8	6.5	5.1
European Union – 15	–	–	–	–	–	11.1	11.0	8.9	7.0	7.3	7.0	8.6
Taiwan Province of China	10.0	8.4	8.3	7.3	6.4	6.4	5.6	6.4	7.5	6.3	5.1	3.6
Singapore	3.5	4.9	5.4	5.8	7.5	6.6	5.3	4.6	4.4	3.8	3.3	3.7
Australia*	0.6	0.6	0.5	0.7	0.6	0.0	0.8	0.7	0.7	1.1	1.1	1.1
Western Samoa	–	–	–	–	0.3	0.5	0.7	1.1	1.7	1.8	1.9	2.2
Macao SAR*	–	–	–	–	0.9	0.8	0.9	0.7	0.9	0.8	0.8	0.8
Others	12.0	13.4	16.0	19.3	14.7	6.5	6.7	7.9	8.9	9.2	12.6	10.9
Total	100	100	100	100	100	100	100	100	100	100	100	100

Notes: Data for the regions denoted with * for 2004 and 2005 are not available, so the same share has been assumed as in 2003. This table is based upon data for utilized (rather than contracted) FDI.

Sources: CEIC database and CEIC China database.

including transfers of technological and managerial expertise. The other interesting point to note is that – contrary to the widespread perception of large direct investment flows from western industrial economies to China – the United States and the European Union (EU) economies together accounted for only 14 percent of total inflows in 2005, and even that is down from a share of 22 percent in 1999–2000. Even if one were to assume that half of the reported FDI inflows from Hong Kong SAR are accounted for by round-tripping and that all of the share of the Virgin Islands in fact represents flows originating in the United States, the share of the United States and the EU in China's total FDI inflows would be about 30 percent, a large but hardly dominant share.

To which parts and regions of China's economy are FDI inflows being directed? Table 11.2 shows that about two-thirds of these flows have been going into manufacturing, with real estate accounting for about another 10 percent. Within manufacturing, the largest identifiable share has consistently gone to electronics and communication equipment. The share of manufacturing has risen by 15 percentage points since 1998, largely at the expense of the shares of utilities, construction, transport and telecommunication services, and real estate. Since the industries with declining FDI shares are largely focused on non-traded goods, the evolution of this pattern of FDI seems to be consistent with the notion that these inflows have been stimulated by China's increasing access (both actual and anticipated) to world export markets following its accession to the World Trade Organization (WTO).

The regional distribution within China of utilized FDI inflows has shown some changes over time (Table 11.3). Guangdong Province has typically accounted for about one-quarter of FDI inflows, consistent with its proximity to Hong Kong SAR and its reputation as an exporting powerhouse, but its share fell by 10 percentage points from 1995–97 to 2004. The big winner over the past few years has been Jiangsu Province (next to Shanghai), which increased its share from 12 percent in 1995–97 to 25 percent in 2003, thereby displacing Guangdong from the lead position.[3] However, Jiangsu's share fell back to 15 percent in 2004. This has come at the expense of the relative shares of provinces such as Fujian, Tianjin, Hebei, and Hainan. Except for Fujian, however, the other provinces did not have large shares to begin with.

Another phenomenon of some interest is the increase in FDI outflows from China. As China intensifies its trade linkages with other Asian economies, anecdotal evidence suggests that its FDI outflows have increased significantly in recent years. This phenomenon has been actively encouraged by the Chinese government as part of its policy of gradual

Table 11.2:   Utilized FDI by Sector (percent share)

	1998	1999	2000	2001	2002	2003	2004	2005[a]
Primary sector	1.4	1.8	1.7	1.9	1.9	1.9	1.8	1.2
Extraction industries	1.3	1.4	1.4	1.7	1.1	0.6	0.9	0.5
Manufacturing	56.3	56.1	63.5	65.9	69.8	69.0	71.0	71.1
Textile	3.4	3.4	3.4	4.1	5.6	4.1	3.3	3.4
Chemicals/ raw materials	4.3	4.8	4.4	4.7	6.0	4.9	4.9	5.4
Medicine	0.8	1.7	1.3	1.3	1.7	1.4	1.1	0.8
Ordinary mach.	2.1	2.4	2.6	2.8	3.2	2.9	3.0	3.3
Special use equip.		1.3	1.3	1.7	2.5	2.3	3.0	3.0
Electronics/ comm. equip.	5.3	7.8	11.3	15.1	20.0	11.9	13.7	14.1
Utilities	6.8	9.2	5.5	4.8	2.6	2.4	1.9	3.2
Construction	4.5	2.3	2.2	1.7	1.3	1.1	1.3	0.7
Transport/ telecom. services	3.6	3.8	2.5	1.9	1.7	1.6	2.1	2.1
Distribution industries	2.6	2.4	2.1	2.5	1.8	2.1	1.2	1.5
Banking/ finance		0.2	0.2	0.1	0.2	0.4	0.4	0.5
Real estate	14.1	13.9	11.4	11.0	10.7	9.8	9.8	8.8
Development/ operations	12.0	11.7	10.7	10.2	9.9	9.5	8.2	8.4
Social services[b]	6.5	6.3	5.4	5.5	5.6	5.9	5.9	5.9
Hotels	1.1	1.8	1.1	1.0	0.9	0.9	0.6	0.4
Health care, sports and social welfare	0.2	0.4	0.3	0.3	0.2	0.2	0.1	0.0
Media/ broadcasting	0.2	0.2	0.1	0.1	0.1	0.1	1.6	1.4
Scientific research services	0.1	0.3	0.1	0.3	0.4	0.5	0.5	0.6
Other	2.4	1.9	3.6	2.3	2.5	4.2	1.5	2.5
Total	100	100	100	100	100	100	100	100

Notes:
[a]   Through June 2005.
[b]   Assumed the same share as in 2003 as the definition of this category has changed.

Source: CEIC database.

Table 11.3: *Foreign Direct Investment Inflows into China by Region (in percent of total FDI inflows)*

	1995–2004	1995–97	2000–2004	2004
Guangdong	24.2	27.0	21.2	16.5
Jiangsu	15.2	12.8	16.9	14.8
Shanghai	8.7	8.8	9.1	10.4
Fujian	8.1	9.9	6.4	3.2
Shandong	7.8	6.2	9.9	14.3
Beijing	3.9	3.4	3.9	4.2
Zhejiang	5.0	3.4	6.7	9.5
Tianjin	4.0	4.8	3.2	2.8
Liaoning	5.1	4.3	6.2	8.9
Hebei	1.9	2.0	1.5	1.2
Guangxi	1.3	1.8	0.8	0.5
Hubei	2.3	1.7	2.7	2.9
Hainan	1.3	2.1	0.8	0.2
Hunan	1.8	1.7	1.9	2.3
Jiangxi	1.4	0.8	2.0	3.4
Henan	1.2	1.4	1.0	0.7
Anhui	0.8	1.2	0.7	0.7
Sichuan	0.9	1.0	0.9	0.6
Heilongjiang	0.9	1.4	0.7	0.6
Jilin	0.7	1.0	0.5	0.3
Shaanxi	0.7	1.0	0.6	0.2
Chongqing	0.6	0.9	0.5	0.4
Shanxi	0.5	0.4	0.4	0.1
Inner Mongolia	0.5	0.2	0.7	0.6
Yunnan	0.3	0.3	0.2	0.2
Quizhou	0.1	0.1	0.1	0.1
Gansu	0.1	0.2	0.1	–
Qinghai	–	–	0.1	–
Ningxia	–	–	0.0	–
Xinjiang	–	0.0	0.0	–
Guangdong	24.2	27.0	21.2	16.5
Jiangsu	15.2	12.8	16.9	14.8
Shanghai	8.7	8.8	9.1	10.4
Fujian	8.1	9.9	6.4	3.2
Shandong	7.8	6.2	9.9	14.3
Beijing	3.9	3.4	3.9	4.2
Zhejiang	5.0	3.4	6.7	9.5
Tianjin	4.0	4.8	3.2	2.8
Liaoning	5.1	4.3	6.2	8.9
Hebei	1.9	2.0	1.5	1.2

Source: CEIC database.

capital account liberalization. Since 2001, some steps have been taken each year to ease restrictions on FDI outflows. However, while it is true that FDI outflows have risen sharply from the mid-1990s to 2005, the total outflows are still modest, amounting to only about $7 billion in 2005 (Table 11.4). Much of these outflows have indeed gone to other Asian economies, especially Hong Kong SAR. The United States has, over the past decade, accounted for about 8 percent of China's FDI outflows. More recently, the Chinese government has encouraged FDI outflows to countries in Asia and Latin America in order to ensure more reliable sources of raw materials (for instance, by purchasing mining operations) and upstream products for processing in China.[4]

2.3. External Debt

Unlike some other emerging markets, China has been quite cautious about taking on external debt (Figure 11.5). There has been little sovereign borrowing until very recently and, as a matter of policy, enterprises have been discouraged from taking on external debt. As a consequence, notwithstanding the significant increase in the absolute amount of external debt since the mid-1980s, the ratio of external debt to GDP has remained relatively stable at around 15 percent since the early 1990s.

However, it is not just the level of external debt but also the maturity structure of this debt that has been shown to be associated with currency and financial crises. As discussed earlier, countries that have more short-term debt relative to long-term debt tend to be more susceptible to such crises. On this score, one noteworthy development is that the share of short-term debt in China's total external debt has risen significantly, from 9 percent in 2000 to 56 percent in 2005 (Figure 11.6 and Table 11.5).[5] This level is close to the threshold that some studies have identified as posing a high risk of crises. However, this increase could appear more dramatic than warranted since this ratio appears to have bottomed in 2000. Furthermore, a significant part of the increase in the relative importance of short-term debt since 2001 can be accounted for by the surge in trade credits. Trade credits constituted 32 percent of total external debt in 2003, up from 13 percent in 2001 (Table 11.5).[6] While trade credits often have short maturities, they do not pose the same type of risks as other short-term borrowing since they tend to be closely linked to subsequent export receipts.

In short, while the stock of debt is in itself not a source of concern, the maturity structure and composition of this debt bears careful observation.[7]

Table 11.4: Total Outward Foreign Direct Investment (top ten countries with the highest average percent share between 2001 and 2004)

	1995	1996	1997	1998	1999	2000	2001	2002	2003	2004	2005	1995–2000*	2001–2004*
Total amount (USD mn)	110.0	290.0	200.0	260.0	590.0	551.0	785.0	2701.0	2850.0	5500.0	6920.0	—	—
Hong Kong SAR	18.9	39.9	4.0	4.9	4.1	3.2	25.6	13.2	9.3	17.4	—	12.5	16.4
United States	22.0	2.0	0.0	9.9	13.7	4.2	6.8	5.6	4.0	2.6	—	8.6	4.7
Thailand	60.7	1.7	0.0	0.3	0.3	0.6	15.5	0.1	1.7	0.5	—	10.6	4.5
Republic of Korea	3.5	0.1	0.0	0.4	0.0	0.8	0.1	3.1	6.8	11.0	—	0.8	5.3
Vietnam	1.8	0.7	0.3	0.9	1.1	3.2	3.4	1.0	0.3	0.4	—	1.3	1.3
Australia	0.9	0.3	0.0	-0.1	0.3	1.8	1.3	1.8	1.2	4.2	—	0.5	2.1
Cambodia	0.0	7.9	6.1	2.3	5.6	3.1	4.4	0.2	1.2	1.8	—	4.2	1.9
Brazil	0.5	0.6	13.7	0.6	0.1	3.8	4.0	0.3	0.0	0.1	—	3.2	1.1
Russia	0.1	0.0	0.8	1.0	0.6	2.5	1.6	1.3	11.9	2.0	—	0.8	4.2
Yemen	0.0	0.0	0.0	0.0	0.0	2.0	2.7	0.0	0.0	0.4	—	0.3	0.8

Note: * Denotes averaged over years.

Source: CEIC China database.

275

Table 11.5: External Debt

	1995	1996	1997	1998	1999	2000	2001	2002	2003	2004	2005
Total (billions of US dollars)	106.6	116.3	131.0	146.0	151.8	145.7	170.1	168.5	193.6	247.5	281.0
(percent of GDP)	14.6	13.6	13.7	14.3	14.0	12.2	12.8	11.6	11.8	12.8	12.6
By Maturity (percent of total debt)											
Short-term[a]	11.2	12.2	13.8	11.9	10.0	9.0	29.7	32.5	39.8	45.6	55.6
Medium- and long-term debt	88.8	87.8	86.2	88.1	90.0	91.0	74.2	72.0	62.3	54.4	44.4
By Type (percent of total debt)											
Registered external debt	–	–	–	–	–	–	87.3	84.6	81.1	79.7	67.7
Trade credit	–	–	–	–	–	–	12.7	15.4	18.9	20.3	32.3
Registered External Debt by Debtor[b] (percent of registered external debt)											
Public and publicly-guaranteed	29.2	28.8	27.5	28.5	31.2	33.6	33.5	34.8	–	18.4	17.3
Chinese-funded enterprises	11.0	10.6	10.2	10.6	9.7	9.3	7.6	6.9	4.9	3.3	2.4
Chinese-funded financial institutions	33.5	29.6	25.3	23.3	22.7	20.5	20.2	22.0	21.2	36.2	33.8
Chinese-funded non-financial institutions	10.8	9.7	8.5	6.6	5.3	3.9	2.9	3.0	2.7	–	–
Foreign-funded enterprises	2.1	3.2	5.3	6.3	–	–	23.7	22.9	24.1	24.5	26.6
Foreign-funded financial institutions	–	–	–	–	–	–	11.5	10.4	13.3	17.4	[c]19.3
Other	13.5	18.1	23.2	24.6	31.2	32.7	0.5	0.0	0.2	0.1	53.7

Notes: Maturity structure is based on classification by residual maturity of outstanding debt.

[a] Assumes original maturity through 2000 and remaining maturity from 2001 onwards.

[b] Effective June 2004, loans from foreign governments that are assumed by policy banks were reclassified under debt of Chinese-funded financial institutions (rather than debt of government departments). Furthermore, in 2004, the outstanding external debt of government departments decreased but that of Chinese-funded financial institutions increased by US$18.7 billion. This accounts for the sharp shift in the shares of these two categories in 2004.

[c] As of September 2005.

Sources: CEIC, Chinese authorities, and author's calculations.

Figure 11.5:   External Debt: Cross-Country Comparison, 1990–2004 (in percent of GDP)

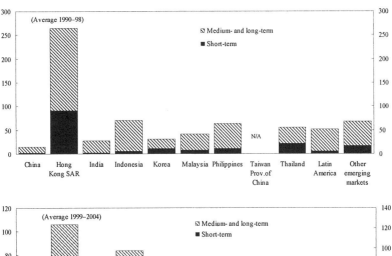

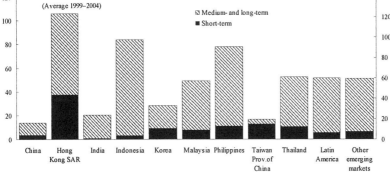

Note: In the top panel, the average for Hong Kong SAR consists of data between 1996 and 1998, and the average for Korea consists of data between 1994 and 1998. The average for emerging markets in EMBI+ index, excluding Latin America and Asian countries.

Sources: World Economic Outlook database, CEIC database, and joint BIS–OECD–IMF–WB statistics on external debt. Includes private sector debt.

3.   INTERNATIONAL RESERVES[8]

3.1. Recent Developments

A different perspective on China's capital inflows is provided by examining the evolution of the balance of payments and the stock of international

Figure 11.6:   External Debt, 1985–2005 (in percent of GDP)

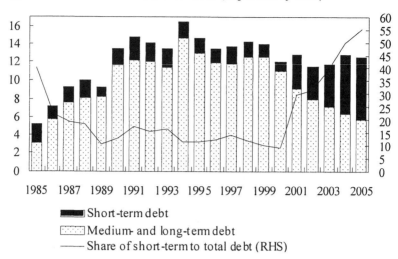

■■■ Short-term debt
▒▒▒ Medium- and long-term debt
——— Share of short-term to total debt (RHS)

Source: CEIC.

reserves. Table 11.6 shows that China's gross international reserves have risen sharply over the past decade, from well below $50 billion during 1990–93 to $897 billion at the end of 2005.[9]

In 2004, gross reserves rose at an even faster pace than in previous years, reaching $619 billion at the end of the year, according to official figures. However, it is necessary to add in the $45 billion used for bank recapitalization at the end of 2003 to this stock in order to allow for comparability of the stock levels in 2003 and 2004 (these adjusted figures are reported in Table 11.6). Thus, we arrive at an increase of $206 billion, or an average of about $17.2 billion a month, during 2004 (compared to $162 billion, or about $13.5 billion a month, during 2003). Similarly, in 2005, adjusting official figures for bank recapitalization, yields a reserve accumulation figure of $233 billion for the year, or about $19.5 billion a month.

It is instructive to examine the factors underlying changes in the pace of reserve accumulation over time. After registering relatively small changes over the period 1985–93, reserve accumulation rose sharply and averaged $30 billion a year over the period 1994–97. This was largely due to a strong capital account, which in turn reflected robust FDI inflows in the order of $30–40 billion a year. Interestingly, the errors and omissions category was significantly negative over this period (averaging about minus $15 billion a

Table 11.6:   The Balance of Payments (in billions of US dollars)

	1997	1998	1999	2000	2001	2002	2003	2004	2005
Gross International Reserves	143.4	149.8	158.3	168.9	218.7	295.2	[a]457.2	[a]663.9	[b]896.9
Increase in international reserves	35.7	6.4	8.5	10.5	47.3	75.5	[a]162.0	206.7	[b]233.0
Current account balance	29.7	29.3	21.1	20.5	17.4	35.4	45.9	68.7	160.8
Merchandise trade balance	46.2	46.6	36.0	34.5	34.0	44.2	44.7	59.0	134.2
Capital account balance	23.0	−6.3	5.2	2.0	34.8	32.3	97.8	110.8	89.0
FDI, net	41.7	41.1	37.0	37.5	37.4	46.8	47.2	53.1	67.8
Errors and omissions, net	−17.0	−16.6	−17.8	−11.9	−4.9	7.8	18.4	27.0	−16.8
Non-FDI capital account balance (including errors and omissions)	−35.6	−64.0	−49.6	−47.4	−7.4	−6.7	69.0	84.9	4.4

Notes:
[a]   Reserves data for 2003–2004 include the $45 billion used for bank recapitalization at the end of 2003. This amount is added to non-FDI capital inflows.
[b]   Reserves data for 2005 include the $45 billion used for bank recapitalization at the end of 2003, as well as additional $15 billion recapitalization in April 2005, $5 billion in Sept 2005 recap, and $6 billion fx swap. These amounts are added to non-FDI capital inflows.

Sources: CEIC, PBC, SAFE, and authors' calculations.

Table 11.7:   A Decomposition of the Recent Reserve Build-up (in billions of US dollars)

	1998– 2000 (1)	2001– 2004 (2)	Change (2) – (1)	2001– 2005 (3)	Change (3) – (1)
Foreign reserve increase	8.5	80.0	71.5	122.9	114.4
Current account balance	23.7	32.9	9.2	41.8	18.2
Capital account balance	0.3	40.0	39.7	68.9	68.6
FDI, net	38.5	43.8	5.3	46.1	7.6
Errors and omissions, net	−15.4	7.1	22.5	12.1	27.5
Non-FDI capital account balance (including errors and omissions)	−53.6	3.3	57.0	35.0	88.6

Note: The values are the averages across the time period.

Sources: CEIC, PBC and authors' calculations.

year), suggesting that unofficial capital outflows were occurring at the same time that significant FDI inflows were coming in through official channels.

Reserve accumulation then tapered off during 1998–2000, the years right after the Asian crisis. A sharp rise in outflows on other investment and large negative errors and omissions together offset much of the effects of continued robust FDI inflows and a strong current account, the latter reflecting an increase in the trade surplus.

The subsequent sharp increase in reserves since 2001 is noteworthy, particularly because it was accompanied by a sustained export boom and the possibility – according to a number of observers and analysts – that the renminbi may have become significantly undervalued over this period.[10] It is instructive to compare the factors underlying the accumulation of reserves in 2001–04 relative to 1998–2000.

Table 11.7 shows that the average annual increase in foreign exchange reserves during 2001–04 was an order of magnitude higher than during 1998–2000. The current account surplus was on average larger in the latter period, but it does not account for much of the increase in the pace of reserve accumulation since 2001. Similarly, while FDI inflows are an important contributor to reserve accumulation, there is little evidence of a major increase in the pace of these inflows in the latter period. The most significant increase is in non-FDI capital inflows (including errors and omissions), which swung from an average of minus $53.6 billion in 1998–2000 to $35.0 billion in 2001–04, a turnaround of $89 billion on an annual basis. Errors and omissions, in particular, changed from an average of minus $15.4 billion in the first period to $12.1 billion in the second.

This decomposition is significant as it shows that much of the increase in the pace of reserve accumulation during 2001–04 is potentially related to 'hot money' rather than a rising trade surplus or capital flows such as FDI that are viewed as being driven by fundamentals. The large turnaround in the errors and omissions category could potentially be indicative of unrecorded capital flows into China, stimulated by the prospect of an appreciation of the renminbi against the US dollar. The trade balance has shot up since then, rising to $134 billion in 2005 (see Table 11.6). The decomposition in Table 11.7 (last two columns) shows that the trade balance played a much bigger role in the reserve accumulation for 2001–05 relative to 1998–2000.

It is worth trying to investigate in more detail where the unrecorded flows (in the errors and omissions category) are coming from, how much larger could they be in the absence of capital controls, and how much money may try to find its way around the capital controls. Anecdotal evidence suggests that the money flowing in is primarily accounted for by a reversal of outflows from Chinese households and corporates that took place during the 1990s to evade taxes or to avoid losses associated with a possible depreciation of the renminbi. It is difficult to answer precisely the question of how much such money is outside of China and could potentially come back into the country.

We take a simple and admittedly naive approach of adding up errors and omissions and portfolio flows and labeling the total as 'hot money' that could potentially switch directions within a short time horizon. Figure 11.7 shows the amount of such hot money flows over the past two decades.[11] The lower panel shows that the cumulative amount of errors and omissions since the early 1990s is quite large, peaking at about $150 billion, and the recent swing has reversed at best a small part of this flow. Under this interpretation, there could potentially be significant amounts of further inflows if there continues to be a strong expectation of an appreciation of the renminbi.

An alternative, and more benign, possibility is that the errors and omissions category may in part reflect an accounting issue.[12] China's officially reported holdings of foreign bonds are not marked to market in terms of exchange rate valuations while the stock of international reserves on the People's Bank of China's (PBC's) balance sheet do reflect these currency valuation effects. This implies, for instance, that any changes in the dollar value of reserve holdings could end up in the balance of payments under the errors and omissions category.[13] In the absence of published data

Figure 11.7:   Errors and Omissions and Portfolio Investment, net for 1982–2005 (in billions of US dollars)

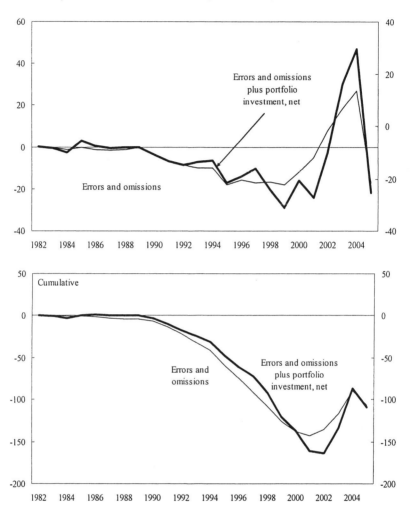

Source: CEIC and World Economic Outlook database.

on the currency composition of foreign exchange reserves, it is widely believed that a substantial fraction of China's foreign exchange reserve holdings is in US treasury bonds, with the remainder in government bonds denominated in euros and other currencies.[14] Given the recent large swings in the value of the US dollar, however, even modest holdings of reserves in instruments denominated in other major currencies could have a significant quantitative impact on the dollar value of gross reserves.

3.2. Implications of the Recent Reserve Build-up

The fact that China's capital inflows over the past decade have been dominated by FDI is a positive outcome. As documented above, however, non-FDI capital inflows have accounted for much of the recent surge in the pace of reserve accumulation. This raises a question about whether, from China's domestic perspective, the continued rapid build-up of reserves is desirable.

The literature on the optimal level of reserves (see, e.g., Aizenman and Marion, 2004, and references therein) does not provide a clear-cut way of answering this question. The usefulness of a large stock of reserves is essentially that, especially for a country with a fixed exchange rate system, it can be useful to stave off downward pressures on the exchange rate. The trade-off results from the fact that developing country reserves are typically held in treasury bonds denominated in hard currencies. The rate of return on these instruments is presumably lower than that which could be earned by physical capital investment within the developing country, which would typically have a scarcity of capital. In addition, the capital inflows that are reflected in reserve accumulation could increase liquidity in the banking system, creating potential problems in a weakly supervised banking system as banks have an incentive to relax their prudential standards in order to increase lending. Sterilization of capital inflows to avoid this outcome could generate fiscal costs as the rate of return on domestic sterilization instruments is typically higher than that earned on reserve holdings.

China, however, appears to be a special case in some respects. China's low (controlled) interest rates imply that, since its reserve holdings are believed to be held primarily in medium- and long-term industrial country treasury instruments and government agency bonds, there are in fact net marginal benefits to sterilization. This is of course enabled by domestic financial repression – with no effective competition for the state-owned banking sector – and capital controls.[15] Furthermore, with domestic investment rates of around 40 percent (supported mainly by domestic saving, which is an order of magnitude larger than FDI inflows), capital scarcity is apparently not a concern, and it is not obvious that the marginal return on investment is higher than the rate of return on reserve holdings, particularly in the likely scenario in which the allocation of capital remains the sole prerogative of an improving but still inefficient state banking system.[16]

Commonly used reserve adequacy indicators provide one way of assessing the insurance value provided by reserve holdings (Figure 11.8). China's reserve holdings provide comfortable coverage of its imports, more

Figure 11.8:   Reserve Adequacy Indicators, 1995–2005

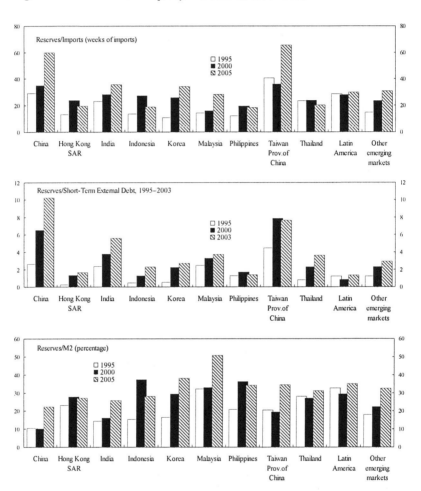

Notes: In the top panel, end-of-year reserves are shown as a ratio to the number of weeks' worth of imports in that year. Data for remaining panels are also based on end-of-year figures. The average for emerging markets in EMBI+ index, excluding Latin America and Asian countries.

Sources: IFS, DOT, WEO, and Joint BIS–IMF–OECD–World Bank Statistics of External Debt.

so than most other emerging markets. The stock of reserves at the end of 2005 accounted for about 60 weeks worth of imports in that year, significantly above the corresponding figures for most other emerging markets. In terms of reserve coverage of short-term external debt, China outperforms virtually every other emerging market, with its reserves amounting to more than ten times short-term external debt (in 2003).[17] One aspect where China's position looks less favorable relative to other emerging markets is the reserve coverage of the monetary base, which is a useful indicator of reserve adequacy in the context of a currency peg. Reflecting the high degree of monetization of the Chinese economy (the ratio of M2 to GDP at end-2004 was about 1.9), reserves cover only about 20 percent of M2.

As a related matter, in addition to providing a buffer to stave off any future downward pressures on the fixed exchange rate, the high level of reserves has in fact been cited as necessary to cushion the financial sector from external shocks. Reported non-performing loans (NPLs) in the banking system amounted to about 30 percent of GDP in 2003 (see Prasad et al., 2004), similar in magnitude to the stock of reserves, suggesting that the present level of reserves could be used to finance a bailout of the banking system if the need should arise. Indeed, the recapitalizations of three of the major state commercial banks using reserves is indicative of the intention of the Chinese authorities to use reserve holdings to help strengthen the books of state banks. However, there are concerns that deficiencies in accounting practices and the reporting of non-performing loans (NPLs) could mean that their true level is higher than the reported numbers. Furthermore, the rapid expansion of credit in recent years has contributed to an investment boom could result in a new wave of problem loans in the future if the surge in investment results in excess capacity being built up in some sectors (Goldstein and Lardy, 2004). This could justify maintaining a high level of reserves.[18]

One risk associated with maintaining a high level of reserves, however, is the vulnerability of the balance sheet of the PBC to changes in the industrial country treasury yield curve. An upward shift in the yield curve could significantly reduce the mark-to-market value of Chinese holdings of industrial country treasury instruments.[19] Similarly, an appreciation of the currency relative to, e.g., the US dollar could lead to a fall in the renminbi value of dollar-denominated treasury bond holdings. Since the primary sterilization instrument in China – central bank bills – is denominated in renminbi, this would lead to a net capital loss in domestic currency terms. Interestingly, this suggests that, at least on this dimension, the costs of a move toward greater exchange rate flexibility (which, under present circumstances, is expected to lead to some appreciation of the renminbi in the short run) could increase as the stock of reserves rises.[20] It could also increase the incentive to diversify out of dollar assets and into other hard currencies.

To summarize, there is no clear evidence that the build-up of reserves in China has significant direct sterilization costs, although it could have some efficiency costs and also expose the balance sheet of the PBC to some exchange rate and capital risks, at least on a mark-to-market basis.

4.   VIEWING CHINA'S CAPITAL INFLOWS THROUGH THE PRISM OF THE LITERATURE ON FINANCIAL GLOBALIZATION[21]

It has long been an article of faith among most economists that international capital flows allow for a more efficient global allocation of capital. For capital-poor developing countries in particular, financial integration (with world capital markets) was seen as a key to moving onto a high growth path. In addition, financial integration in theory provides enhanced possibilities for consumption smoothing through better sharing of income risk across countries. Those developing countries that subscribed to this logic by liberalizing their capital accounts starting in the mid-1980s – a group that has come to be known as the emerging markets – captured a lion's share of the net capital flows from industrial to developing economies that took place over the subsequent decade. Capital account liberalization proved, however, to be a mixed blessing, with many emerging markets suffering debilitating financial and balance of payments crises in the late 1990s. But do the crises by themselves imply that financial integration is not advisable for developing countries? A closer look at the evidence is in order.

4.1.   Financial Integration and Growth

In theory, there are a number of channels through which capital inflows can help to raise economic growth in developing countries. These include direct channels such as augmentation of domestic savings, lower cost of capital, transfer of technology, and development of the domestic financial sector. Indirect channels include the inducements for better domestic policies offered by capital account openness and the promotion of specialization of production. Theory drives one inexorably to the conclusion that financial integration must be good for growth.

The empirical evidence, however, paints a far more sobering picture. It is true that emerging markets as a group have posted much higher growth on average than other developing economies over the past two decades. Notwithstanding the painful crises that many of them experienced, these countries have done far better overall in terms of raising per capita incomes. However, this does not by itself imply a causal relationship. Indeed, while there is a considerable divergence of results among different studies, the weight of the evidence seems to tilt toward the conclusion that it is difficult to find a strong and robust causal link once one controls for other factors that could affect growth (Prasad et al., 2003, provide an extensive survey of this literature). There is of course an element of endogeneity here – financial integration could induce countries to have better macroeconomic policies and improve their institutions, but this effect would not be picked up in a regression framework. However, there is at best mixed evidence that financial integration induces a country to pursue better macroeconomic policies (Tytell and Wei, 2004). More research is needed on this question, but the bottom line is that it is difficult to make a prima facie case that financial integration provides a strong boost to growth in emerging markets.

4.2. Financial Integration and Volatility

As for volatility, economic theory has the strong implication that access to financial markets – either at the household or national level – must be welfare enhancing from a consumption-smoothing perspective. So long as aggregate shocks (at the relevant level of aggregation) are not dominant in explaining variations in household or national income growth, financial markets should improve welfare by providing a mechanism that allows individual economic units to share their idiosyncratic income risk. The reason countries (and households) like to do this, of course, is to smooth their consumption growth and reduce the otherwise necessarily close linkage of national consumption growth to national income growth and its intrinsic volatility. While some countries may not be able to take full advantage of such risk-sharing opportunities (e.g., due to problems of monitoring and moral hazard), access to international financial markets should improve their welfare – in terms of reducing consumption volatility – at least marginally.

The reality for emerging markets is starkly different. Recent research suggests that, for these countries, the ratio of consumption growth volatility to output growth volatility in fact increased on average in the 1990s, precisely during the key period of financial globalization (Kose et al., 2003). Note that this result cannot simply be ascribed to the fact that some of these countries experienced crises during this period. In principle, a country should be able to do no worse than having its consumption growth be as volatile as its income growth. Formal regression analysis controlling for a variety of other determinants of volatility and growth suggests the existence of a nonlinearity in the relationship between the degree of financial integration and the relative volatility of consumption growth.[22]

An increase in financial integration from a low to a medium level tends to be associated with a rise in the relative volatility of consumption growth. At one end of the spectrum, for countries with very limited access to international financial markets, consumption growth tends to be about as volatile as income growth.[23] At the other end, industrial countries, which tend to be highly integrated into global financial markets, appear to be able to take advantage of financial openness to effectively reduce their relative consumption growth volatility. For emerging markets, the problem of course is that international investors are willing to provide capital when times are good. These countries often lose access to international capital markets precisely when times are bad (see, e.g., Kaminsky et al., 2004). Thus, sadly, it is precisely those countries that dip their toes into the waters of financial globalization that appear to be penalized by the procyclical nature of their access to world capital markets.

The situation appears bleak. Developing countries need external capital to grow. But is financial integration just 'snake oil' – delivering at best weak growth effects and exposing countries to higher volatility? The answer, it turns out, depends.

4.3. The Composition of Captial Inflows Matters

A large literature shows that it is not just the degree of financial openness, but the composition of capital inflows, that determine the quality of a developing country's experiences with globalization (see Prasad et al., 2003, for a survey and additional references for the points made below). For instance, FDI inflows tend to be far less volatile than other types of inflows. In particular, FDI appears to be less subject to sharp reversals than other types of inflows, particularly bank lending.[24] External debt, on the other hand, clearly increases vulnerability to the risks of financial globalization. In particular, debt crises are more likely to occur in countries where external debt is of relatively short maturity (see, e.g., Frankel and Rose, 1996; and Detragiache and Spilimbergo, 2001).

The problem, of course, is that the composition of inflows as well as related matters such as the maturity structure of external debt are not entirely under the control of developing country governments. Countries with weak macroeconomic fundamentals are often forced to rely more on external debt and end up having little choice but to borrow at short maturities. Financial integration can in fact aggravate the risks associated with weak macroeconomic policies. Access to world capital markets could lead to excessive borrowing that is channeled into unproductive government spending, ultimately increasing vulnerability to external shocks or changes in investor sentiment. In addition, lack of transparency has been shown to be associated with more herding behavior by international investors, which can destabilize financial markets in an emerging market economy. Furthermore, a high degree of corruption tends to adversely affect the composition of a country's inflows, making it more vulnerable to the risks of speculative attacks and contagion effects.

Thus, the apparently negative effects of globalization appear to be related to a particular kind of threshold effect. Only countries with good institutions and sound macroeconomic policies tend to have lower vulnerability to the risks associated with the initial phase of financial integration and are able to realize its full benefits.

4.4. The Right Composition of Inflows for China

From a number of different perspectives, China is a prototypical developing country that is best served by FDI rather than other types of inflows. In the context of the above discussion on the benefits and potential risks of financial globalization, the dominance of FDI in China's capital inflows implies that it has been able to control the risks and get more of the promised benefits of financial integration than many other emerging markets that have taken a less cautious approach to capital account liberalization.

FDI may have served China well in other ways also. Given the low level of human capital and technical expertise in China, FDI could serve as a useful conduit for importing technical and managerial know how (Borensztein et al., 1998). Furthermore, the state-owned banking system is inefficient at allocating credit. This system has improved over time, particularly with the much-heralded end of the directed policy lending that these banks were forced to undertake until the late 1990s. However, most bank credit still goes to the public sector, especially since, with the controls on lending rates that existed until end-October 2004, banks were not able to price-in the higher risk of lending to new and/or small firms in the private sector (see Dunaway and Prasad, 2004). As the experiences of some of the Asian crisis countries have shown, a weakly supervised banking system that is allowed to raise funds abroad and channel them into the domestic economy can generate serious imbalances. Thus, restrictions on bank borrowing from abroad can serve a useful purpose.

With a fixed exchange rate, openness to other types of financial flows, which tend to be less stable and are subject to sudden stops or reversals, would be less advisable. For instance, external borrowing by banks could cause instability in exchange markets and would have at best dubious effects on growth. Substantial opening of the capital account would also be inadvisable in this context, suggesting that the sort of selective opening that China has pursued may have some advantages (see Prasad et al., 2004).

5. WHAT EXPLAINS THE COMPOSITION OF CHINA'S CAPITAL INFLOWS?

China appears to have benefited from a pattern of capital inflows heavily tilted toward FDI. A key question is how China has attained such a composition of its inflows, one that many emerging markets aspire to but that few achieve. Some context is important before addressing this question. Earlier work by Wei (2000 a, b and c) suggests that the size of FDI inflows into China relative to its GDP size and other 'natural' determinants is not unusually high. If anything, China seems to be an underperformer as a host of FDI from the world's five major source countries. In more recent years, with the continued rise in FDI, China may have become a 'normal' country in terms of its attractiveness as a destination for FDI.

One explanation for the composition of China's capital inflows is that it is the result of a pragmatic strategy that has been adjusted over time through trial and error. The pattern in the 1980s and early 1990s could well have reflected a combination of inertia and luck, with the post-1997 pattern reflecting the scare of the Asian financial crisis. Indeed, at the beginning of the reform period in the late 1970s and early 1980s, there were few capital inflows of any kind.

The early stage of reform sought to import only the type of foreign capital that was thought to help transmit technical and marketing know-how, thus the policy enunciated as 'welcome to FDI, but no thank-you to foreign debt and portfolio flows.' Export performance and foreign exchange balance requirements were initially imposed even on foreign-invested firms. The restrictions on FDI were relaxed step by step, together with certain 'super-national treatment' (of incentives) for foreign-owned enterprises and joint ventures. Over time, the government also started to relax restrictions on foreign borrowing by corporations (and taken steps to expand the B-, H-, and N-shares markets). The government declared in the mid-1990s that it intended to implement capital account convertibility by 2000.

The psychological impact of the subsequent Asian financial crisis may have been profound. Several countries that China had regarded as role models for its own development process (especially Korea) went into deep crises in a very short period of time. It was a common perception among policymakers in China that the swings in the non-FDI part of the international capital flows had played a crucial role in the process. In this sense, the Asian financial crisis caused a rethinking in the Chinese approach to capital inflows. The idea of capital account liberalization by 2000 disappeared and in its place rose the notion that the higher the level of foreign exchange reserves the better in order to avoid painful crises.

5.1. Incentives and Distortions Affecting FDI

A more traditional explanation for the composition of China's capital inflows is that the unusually high share of FDI could reflect a simultaneous policy mix of discouraging foreign debt and foreign portfolio inflows as well as providing incentives for FDI.[25] Indeed, the existence of tax benefits for FDI has meant that, until recently, the playing field was in fact tilted in favor of foreign-funded firms. This was conceivably a part of an enlightened policy choice, which included restricting other types of inflows using capital controls.

Since China promulgated laws governing foreign investment at the start of the reform, the government has offered generous tax treatment to foreign firms. In the first two years that a foreign-invested firm makes a profit, it is exempt from corporate income tax. In subsequent years, foreign companies are subject to an average corporate income of 15 percent, less than half the normal rate of 33 percent paid by Chinese companies.

Tax exemptions and reductions constitute only one aspect of government incentives favoring FDI. To capture these incentives more comprehensively and to place the Chinese FDI regime in a cross-country comparative context, we now make use of the description of the legal FDI regimes for 49 countries in 2000 constructed by Wei (2000b), who in turn relied on detailed, textual descriptions prepared by PricewaterhouseCoopers (PwC) in a series of country reports entitled 'Doing Business and Investing in China' (or in whichever country that may be the subject of the report). The 'Doing Business and Investing in ...' series is written for multinational firms intending to do business in a particular country. They are collected in one CD-ROM titled 'Doing Business and Investing Worldwide' (PwC, 2000). For each country, the relevant PwC country report covers a variety of legal and regulatory issues of interest to foreign investors, including 'Restrictions on foreign investment and investors' (typically Chapter 5), 'Investment incentives' (typically Chapter 4), and 'Taxation of foreign corporations' (typically Chapter 16).

To convert the textual information in these reports into numerical codes, we read through the relevant chapters for all countries that the PwC series covers. PwC (2000) contains information on incentives for FDI in the following four categories:

(a) Existence of special incentives to invest in certain industries or certain geographic areas;
(b) Tax concessions specific to foreign firms (including tax holidays and tax rebates, but excluding tax concessions specifically designed for export promotion, which is in a separate category);
(c) Cash grants, subsidized loans, reduced rent for land use, or other nontax concessions, specific to foreign firms; and
(d) Special promotion for exports (including existence of export processing zones, special economic zones, etc).

For each category of incentives, we then created a dummy variable, which takes the value 1 if a particular type of incentive is present. An overall 'FDI incentives' variable can then be constructed as the sum of the above four dummies. This variable takes a value of zero if there is no incentive in any of the categories, and 4 if there are incentives in all of them.

Of the 49 countries for which one can obtain information, none has incentives in all four categories. The median number of incentives is 1 (mean = 1.65). China is one of the only three countries that have incentives for FDI in three categories – the other two countries being Israel and Egypt. Therefore, based on this information, we might conclude that China offers more incentives to attract FDI than most countries in the world.

Of course, legal incentives are not the only things that matter for international investors. To obtain a more complete picture, one also has to look at legal restrictions. The same PwC source also offers information, in a standardized format, on the presence or absence of restrictions in four areas:

(a) Existence of foreign exchange control (this may interfere with foreign firms' ability to import intermediate inputs or repatriate profits abroad);
(b) Exclusion of foreign firms from certain strategic sectors (particularly national defense and mass media);
(c) Exclusion of foreign firms from additional sectors that would otherwise be open in most developed countries;
(d) Restrictions on foreign ownership (e.g., they may not per permitted 100 percent ownership).

We generated dummy variables for each category of restrictions and created an overall 'FDI restriction' variable that is equal to the sum of those four dummies. This variable takes the value of zero if there is no restriction in any category, and 4 if there are restrictions in all of them.

The median number of restrictions is 1 (mean = 1.69). Interestingly, China is one of only five countries in the sample that place restrictions on FDI in all four categories. Different restrictions and incentives may have different effects on FDI, so they cannot be assigned equal weights. Notwithstanding this caveat, in terms of the overall legal regime, it is not obvious that China makes for a particularly attractive FDI destination (as of 2000).[26]

So far, we have been discussing explicit incentives and restrictions that are written into laws and regulations. Of course, there can be many other implicit incentives or restrictions that are nonetheless an important part of the overall investment climate in the mind of potential investors. For example, corruption and bureaucratic red tape raise business costs and are part of the implicit disincentives for investment. Statistical analyses by Wei (2000a, b, c) suggest that these costs are economically as well as statistically significant.

To sum up, while the Chinese laws and regulations offer many legal incentives to attract FDI, they should be placed in context along with many implicit disincentives as well as explicit legal restrictions in order to form a more complete assessment of the overall investment climate.

5.2. A Mercantilist Story

Another hypothesis for explaining China's pattern of capital inflows is that the encouragement of FDI inflows is part of a mercantilist strategy to foster export-led growth, abetted by the maintenance of an undervalued exchange rate (see papers by Dooley et al., 2004a, b; henceforth, DFG). The basic idea here is that, with a large pool of surplus labor and a banking system that is assumed to be irremediably inefficient, a more appropriate growth strategy for China is to use FDI to spur 'good' investment in the export sector and to maintain an undervalued exchange rate in order to maintain export competitiveness. To support this equilibrium, China allows manufacturers in its export markets (the US market in particular) to bring in FDI and take advantage of the cheap labor to reap substantial profits, thereby building a constituency in the United States to inhibit any action to force China to change its exchange rate regime. In addition, China's purchases of US government securities as a part of its reserve holdings acts as a 'collateral' or insurance policy for foreign firms that invest in China.

While this is an intriguing story, the facts do not support it. For instance, most of the FDI inflows into China have come from countries that are exporting to China rather than importing from it (see Section 2). Furthermore, it is worth noting that (i) China chose not to devalue in 1997–98, even though that would have increased its exports; (ii) the massive build-up of foreign exchange reserves is a relatively recent phenomenon; and (iii) for much of the past two decades up to 2001, the Chinese currency was likely to be overvalued rather than undervalued according to the black market premium. Even if one were to accept the DFG approach as a sustainable one, there is a conceptual question of whether it is the right approach. To take just one aspect, the sheer size of domestic saving (more than $500 billion a year) eclipses FDI (at about $45–50 billion a year, an order of magnitude smaller). Hence, writing off the domestic banking sector and focusing solely on FDI-led growth can hardly be regarded as a reasonable strategy. In short, while the DFG story is a seductive one and has many plausible elements, it does not appear to be a viable overall approach to fostering sustainable growth in China.[27]

5.3. Institutions and Governance

A different possibility, suggested by the work of Yasheng Huang (2003), is that the dominant share of FDI in China's inflows over the past decade reflects deficiencies in domestic capital markets. In particular, private firms have faced discrimination relative to state-owned enterprises, both from the banking system (in terms of loan decisions by state-owned banks) and the equity market (in terms of approval of stock listings). As a result, private firms have taken advantage of pro-FDI policies in an unexpected way and used foreign joint ventures as a way to acquire needed capital in order to undertake investment. Foreign investors have presumably been willing to go along because they are appropriately compensated by their Chinese partners in the form of profit shares, even in cases where the foreign investors may have no particular technological, managerial, or marketing know-how to offer. If the Chinese financial system had no such discrimination in place, much of the foreign investment in the form of joint ventures might not have taken place. In this sense, the deficiency of the domestic financial system may have artificially raised the level of inward FDI.

This is an interesting hypothesis and may well explain part of the inward FDI in the 1980s. However, there is some mismatch between this hypothesis and the data, especially in terms of the time-series patterns of FDI inflows. On the one hand, inward FDI has been increasing at a rapid rate – indeed more than half of the cumulative stock of inward FDI can be accounted for by recent inflows over the period 1998–2003. This hypothesis would require a financial system ever more discriminatory of private firms. On the other hand, domestic banks have become increasingly willing to make loans to non-state firms. Similarly, in the equity market, both the absolute number and the relative share of the non-state-owned firms in the two stock exchanges have been rising. Therefore, it seems to us that

Huang's hypothesis is unlikely to be a major part of the explanation for the rapid rise in inward FDI in recent years.

Governance, which includes various aspects of public administration, is another potentially important determinant of the composition of inflows. Unlike other types of inflows, FDI that is used to build plants with joint ownership by Chinese entrepreneurs provides foreign investors with the best possibility of being able to successfully negotiate the bureaucratic maze in China. However, this is somewhat at odds with recent literature that has examined the role of weak institutions (high level of corruption, lack of transparency, weak judicial system, etc.) in affecting the volume and patterns of capital inflows. Low levels of transparency typically tend to discourage international portfolio investment (Gelos and Wei, 2004). Weak public governance – especially rampant insider trading – tends to exacerbate stock market volatility, further discouraging foreign portfolio inflows (Du and Wei, 2004). High corruption also tends to discourage FDI (Wei, 2000). However, taken together, these factors are unlikely to explain the particular composition of the Chinese capital inflows, since weak public governance by itself should tend to tilt the composition away from FDI and toward foreign debt (Wei and Wu, 2002).

It is not straightforward to empirically disentangle the various hypotheses that we have reviewed above for explaining why China gets more FDI than other types of inflows. In our view, the nature of the capital controls regime and the incentives for FDI appear to have played a big part in encouraging FDI inflows. But the story is not quite that straightforward, since one would expect a counteracting effect from factors such as weak governance, legal restrictions on investment by foreigners and poor legal infrastructure and property rights. Furthermore, it is useful to keep in mind that FDI inflow figures may have been artificially inflated by the incentives for disguising other forms of inflows as FDI in order to get around capital account restrictions and to take advantage of tax and other policies favoring FDI.

6. CONCLUDING REMARKS

In this chapter, we have provided an overview of developments in China's capital inflows and analyzed the composition of these inflows in the context of a rapidly burgeoning literature on financial globalization. We have also examined a number of hypotheses for explaining China's success in attracting FDI inflows. Further research will be needed to disentangle the competing explanations for this phenomenon, but there is little evidence that mercantilist stories are the right answer. Understanding the reasons for China's success in tilting inflows toward FDI is important, especially as

China continues its integration into world financial market and becomes more exposed to the vagaries of these markets. China has done well so far in managing the risks associated with financial globalization, but major challenges remain to ensure that continued integration with financial markets does not worsen the risk-return trade-off.

NOTES

1. We are grateful to Jahangir Aziz, Ray Brooks, Michael Dooley, Sebastian Edwards, Mark Wright, and participants at the NBER Capital Flows Conference, the Stanford China Conference, a conference at the Graduate School for International Studies (Geneva), and a seminar at the China Center for Economic Research for helpful comments and suggestions. We are indebted to members of the IMF's China team, from whose work we have drawn extensively. We owe a particular debt to Qing Wang, who provided many useful suggestions and comments. Ioana Hussiada provided excellent research assistance. This is a revised and updated version of a paper that is forthcoming in an NBER volume on Capital Flows edited by Sebastian Edwards.
2. A more likely possibility is that those could be flows from sources such as Japan, Taiwan Province of China, and the United States that are channeled through such offshore financial centers in order to evade taxes in the source countries.
3. In the early 1980s, Guangdong was heavily promoted as a leading experimental lab for market-oriented reforms, in part due to its proximity to Hong Kong SAR. By contrast, the reform of the Yangtze River Delta region (especially Jiangsu, Shanghai, and Zhejiang) was held back in the 1980s. Shanghai was a key provider of revenue to the central government and, since the experiment with a market economy was considered as being risky, central planning features were largely retained there until the late 1980s. Once it was clear that the market economy experiment was working well, reforms in Shanghai went into full swing.
4. Official reports note that the cumulative amount of outward FDI as of the end of 2004 was $37 billion, which does not seem to match the annual data shown in this table. Based on anecdotal and other evidence, however, the upward trend in FDI outflows is incontrovertible even if the magnitudes may be suspect.
5. The ratio of short-term external debt to GDP has risen from 1.2 percent to 7.0 percent over this period.
6. One cautionary note about the trade credit data in the external debt statistics is that they are partly estimated from data on imports. Consequently, they do not always match the balance of payments data on trade credits (discussed below), which are based on sample surveys. But the broad trends revealed by these two sources are similar.
7. The World Bank's 2003 Global Development Finance Report (pp. 136–39) indicates that, in recent years, about 70 percent of China's outstanding long-term external debt has been denominated in US dollars, and about 15 percent has been denominated in Japanese yen. Data on the currency composition of short-term external debt are not available in this report.
8. Some of the analysis in this section draws upon work done by members of the IMF's China team.
9. These figures include the $45 billion used to recapitalize two state commercial banks in 2003, the additional recapitalization in 2005, and foreign exchange swaps in 2005. To understand the evolution of the capital account, it is relevant to include that figure in the calculations.
10. There is a considerable range of opinions about the degree of undervaluation of the renminbi. IMF (2004) and Funke and Rahn (2004) conclude that there is no strong

    evidence that the renminbi is substantially undervalued. Goldstein (2004) and Frankel (2004), on the other hand, argue that the renminbi may be undervalued by at least 25–30 percent. Market analysts have a similar broad range of views.

11. Capital flight through underinvoicing of exports or overinvoicing of imports may not show up in the errors and omissions or any other part of the balance of payments statistics. Net errors and omissions may also understate unrecorded capital flows to the extent that there are offsetting unrecorded flows on current and capital account transactions, or even among transactions within each of these categories. Gunter (2004) estimates that capital flight during the 1990s may have been greater than suggested by such crude estimates.

12. The calculations below are based upon unpublished work by Ray Brooks.

13. China does not report its international investment position, which would clarify this matter.

14. There has been a great deal of recent interest in the share of Chinese official reserve holdings accounted for by US dollar-denominated instruments, particularly treasury bonds. The recent depreciation of the US dollar has fueled speculation that China has been diversifying away from US dollar bonds into other currencies.

15. This suggests that there are implicit costs to these sterilization efforts. However, determining the incidence of these costs is not straightforward; much of these costs are presumably borne by depositors in the state banks in the form of low real returns on their deposits.

16. See Boyreau-Debray and Wei (2004) for evidence of low returns to lending by state banks.

17. Figure 11.8 uses Bank for International Settlements (BIS) data on external debt that are, in principle, comparable across countries. Based on official Chinese data, reserves amount to about six times the stock of short-term external debt, still above comparable ratios in almost all other emerging markets.

18. Preliminary indications are that the reported ratio of NPLs to GDP has declined in 2004, but this may partly be attributable to the transfer of some NPLs off the books of state commercial banks.

19. One could argue that these notional capital losses in mark-to-market terms should not be of concern if the Chinese authorities' intention is to hold the bonds to maturity. This argument has validity only so long as the reserves do not need to be liquidated before maturity.

20. A related point is that if the accumulation of reserves continues apace, the potential capital loss from any appreciation would grow over time, suggesting that an earlier move toward exchange rate flexibility would be preferable from this narrow perspective (if such a move was regarded as being inevitable). In any event, we doubt if this factor will play a significant role in influencing the timing of a move toward greater flexibility.

21. The discussion in this section draws on Prasad et al. (2003).

22. In this subsection, the term 'relative' volatility of consumption growth should always be taken to mean its volatility relative to that of income growth.

23. Even in a closed economy, of course, the existence of investment opportunities should allow for some degree of intertemporal smoothing of national consumption.

24. See Wei (2001). The evidence that net FDI flows to emerging markets are less volatile than portfolio flows is weaker (see Dooley et al., 1995; Wei, 2001).

25. Tseng and Zebregs (2002) discuss other factors that may have helped to attract FDI, such as market size, infrastructure, and the establishment of open economic zones, which have more liberal investment and trade regimes than other areas.

26. The regression analysis in Wei (2000b and 2001) suggests that these FDI incentives and restrictions variables explain a part of the cross-country variation in inward FDI.

27. Roubini (2004) and Goldstein and Lardy (2005) present broader arguments against the DFG story.

REFERENCES

Aizenman, J. and N. Marion (2004), 'International reserve holdings with sovereign risk and costly tax collection', *The Economic Journal*, **114**, 569–91.

Borensztein, E., J. De Gregorio and J.-W. Lee (1998), 'How does foreign direct investment affect growth?', *Journal of International Economics*, **45**, 115–35.

Boyreau-Debray, G. and S.-J. Wei (2004), 'Pitfalls of a state-dominated financial system: Evidence from China', CEPR Discussion Paper No. 4471, United Kingdom: Centre for Economic Policy Research.

Detragiache, E. and A. Spilimbergo (2001), 'Crises and liquidity: Evidence and interpretation', IMF Working Paper 01/2, Washington: International Monetary Fund.

Dooley, M.P., S. Claessens and A. Warner (1995), 'Portfolio capital flows: Hot or cold?', *World Bank Economic Review*, 9(1), 53–174.

Dooley, M.P., D. Folkerts-Landau and P. Garber (2004a), 'The revived Bretton Woods system: The effects of periphery intervention and reserve management on interest rates and exchange rates in center countries', NBER Working Paper 10332, Cambridge, MA: National Bureau of Economic Research.

Dooley, M.P., D. Folkerts-Landau and P. Garber (2004b), 'Direct investment, rising real wages and the absorption of excess labor in the periphery', NBER Working Paper 10626, Cambridge, MA: National Bureau of Economic Research.

Du, J. and S.-J. Wei (2004), 'Does insider trading raise market volatility?', *The Economic Journal*, **114**(498), 916–42.

Dunaway, S. and E. Prasad (2004), 'Interest rate liberalization in China', www.iht.com/articles/2004/12/04/edprasad_ed3_0.php, 04 December.

Frankel, J.A. and A.K. Rose (1996), 'Currency crashes in emerging markets: An empirical treatment', *Journal of International Economics*, **41**, 351–66.

Frankel, J.A. (2004), 'On the Renminbi: The choice between adjustment under a fixed exchange rate and adjustment under a flexible rate', Manuscript, Kennedy School of Government, Cambridge, MA: Harvard University.

Funke, M. and J. Rahn (2005), 'Just how undervalued is the Chinese Renminbi?', *The World Economy*, 28, 465–89.

Gelos, G.R. and S. Wei (2005), 'Transparency and international portfolio holdings', *Journal of Finance*, **60**, 2987–3020.

Goldstein, M. (2004), 'Adjusting China's exchange rate policies', Institute for International Economics Working Paper 04/126, Washington: Institute for International Economics.

Goldstein, M. and N.R. Lardy (2004), 'What kind of landing for the Chinese economy?', Policy Briefs in International Economics, No. PB04-7, Washington: Institute for International Economics.

Goldstein, M. and N.R. Lardy (2005), 'China's role in the revived Bretton Woods system: A case of mistaken identity', manuscript, Washington: Institute for International Economics.

Gunter, F.R. (2004), 'Capital flight from China', *China Economic Review*, **15**, 63–85.

Huang, Y. (2003), *Selling China: Foreign Direct Investment During the Reform Era*, Cambridge: Cambridge University Press.

IMF (2004) 'People's Republic of China: Article IV Consultation – staff report', www.imf.org/external/pubs/ft/scr/2004/cr04351.pdf, 05 November.

Kaminsky, G., C. Reinhart and C. Végh (2004), 'When it rains, it pours: Procyclical capital flows and macroeconomic policies', in M. Gertler and K. Rogoff (eds), *NBER Macro Annual 2004*, Cambridge, MA: National Bureau of Economic Research.

Kose, M.A., E.S. Prasad and M.E. Terrones (2003), 'Financial integration and macroeconomic volatility', IMF Staff Papers, **50**, 119–42.

Prasad, E. (ed.), S. Barnett, N. Blancher, R. Brooks, A. Fedelino, T. Feyzioglu, T. Rumbaugh, R.J. Singh and T. Wang (2004), 'China's growth and integration into the world economy: Prospects and challenges', IMF Occasional Paper No. 232, Washington: International Monetary Fund.

Prasad, E., K. Rogoff, S. Wei and M.A. Kose (2003), 'The effects of financial globalization on developing countries: Some empirical evidence', IMF Occasional Paper No. 220, Washington: International Monetary Fund.

Prasad, E., T. Rumbaugh and Q. Wang (2005), 'Putting the cart before the horse? Capital account liberalization and exchange rate flexibility in China', IMF Policy Discussion Paper 05/1, Washington: International Monetary Fund.

PricewaterhouseCoopers (2000), 'Doing business and investing worldwide' (CD-Rom).

Roubini, N. (2004), 'BW2: Are we back to a new stable Bretton Woods regime of global fixed exchange rates?', www.roubiniglobal.com/archives/2004/10/are _we_back_to.html 08 October.

Tseng, W. and H. Zebregs (2002), 'FDI in China: Lessons for other countries', IMF Policy Discussion Paper 02/3, Washington: International Monetary Fund.

Tytell, I. and S.Wei (2004), 'Does financial globalization induce better macroeconomic policies', unpublished manuscript, Washington: International Monetary Fund.

Wei, S. (2000a), 'How taxing is corruption on international investors?', *Review of Economics and Statistics*, **82**(1), 1–11.

Wei, S. (2000b), 'Local corruption and global capital flows', *Brookings Papers on Economic Activity*, **2**, 303–54.

Wei, S. (2000c), 'Why does China attract so little foreign direct investment?', in Takatoshi Ito and Anne O. Krueger (eds), *The Role of Foreign Direct Investment in East Asian Economic Development*, pp. 239–61, Chicago: University of Chicago Press.

Wei, S. (2001), 'Domestic crony capitalism and international fickle capital: Is there a connection?', *International Finance*, **4**(1), 15–45.

Wei, S. and Y. Wu (2002), 'Negative alchemy? Corruption, composition of capital flows, and currency crises', in Sebastian Edwards and Jeffrey Frankel (eds), *Preventing Currency Crises in Emerging Markets*, pp. 461–501, Chicago: University of Chicago Press.

12. Foreign Direct Investment in China and East Asia

Busakorn Chantasasawat, K.C. Fung, Hitomi Iizaka and Alan Siu

1. INTRODUCTION

In recent years, China has become a favorite destination for foreign direct investment (FDI). Despite the problems associated with SARS (Severe Acute Respiratory Syndrome) in 2003, China received US$53.5 billion worth of FDI (UNCTAD 2004). In 2004, China further received US$60.6 billion.

The success of China in attracting FDI is no accident. One of the earliest strategic policy reforms of China was to open up its Southeastern part to attract foreign investment. China's attempts to introduce markets into its economy go hand in hand with the liberalization of its FDI regime. In some ways, FDI reforms can be seen as the vanguard of domestic market reforms.

While increases in FDI from the outside world are complementary to China's efforts to modernize its economy, most of China's Asian neighbors are concerned about the prospects of a rising China that absorbs more and more of the investment from major multinationals. Several Asian governments have publicly noted that the emergence of China has diverted FDI away from their economies. Policymakers throughout the region are convinced that the rise of China has contributed to the 'hollowing out' phenomenon, a situation where investors choose China over other countries as a destination for their investment. This in turn has led to a continued loss of manufacturing industries and jobs, further weakening the vitality of these economies.

In this chapter, we examine empirically the question of whether China's successful FDI policy has diverted FDI away from a group of Asian economies. The economies of our interest are Hong Kong, Taiwan, Republic of Korea, Singapore, Malaysia, Indonesia, Philippines and Thailand. Our research strategy is to control for standard determinants of

FDI and then add a proxy to represent the 'China effect'. We next investigate sign, significance and magnitude of the China effect.

The organization of this chapter is as follows. In the next section, we survey relevant policy issues and current literature. In section 3, we set up the empirical model to be estimated. In section 4, we present and discuss our results. Section 5 concludes.

2. RECENT POLICY CONCERNS

Many analysts, commentators and policymakers in Asia have voiced concerns about the economic rise of China and its possible adverse effect on FDI inflows into their countries. In November 2002, Singaporean Deputy Prime Minister Lee Hsien Loong (who has since become the Prime Minister of Singapore) commented that 'Southeast Asian countries are under intense competitive pressure, as their former activities, especially labor-intensive manufacturing, migrate to China. One indicator of this massive shift is the fact that Southeast Asia used to attract twice as much FDI as Northeast Asia, but the ratio is reversed.'[1] According to KOTRA, the state-run trade and investment promotion agency of the Republic of Korea, the rate of FDI in most Asian countries is falling as global investors are being drawn to invest in China.[2] World Economic Forum director for Asia, Frank J. Richter, said if the Asian countries do not take prudent and pragmatic steps to be as competitive as China, the FDI flows into these economies would be adversely affected.[3] Furthermore, Taiwan's Vice Premier Lin Hsin-I said that facing the rapid rise of the Mainland Chinese economy, Taiwan would have to take effective measures to increase its competitiveness. Taiwan has to implement the 'go south' policy to encourage Taiwan to switch their investments from the Mainland to Southeast Asian countries.[4]

Is China's FDI policy a *friend* or an *enemy* to its Asian neighbors? What determines FDI inflows into the Asian and other economies? Is there a 'China effect'? To get some insights as to what methodology we should pursue, we briefly review some relevant academic literature.

Brainard (1997) empirically examines the determinants of the ratio of US export sales to total foreign sales (the sum of export sales by sales by foreign affiliates) by industry. She uses a framework to focus on factors that favor concentration of production (i.e. favoring exports) vs. proximity to overseas customers (i.e. factors that favor sales by foreign affiliates). The explanatory variables include freight costs to the export market, tariffs of the host country, per capita gross domestic product, corporate tax rates, measures of trade and FDI openness, measures of plant scale economies and corporate scale economies. She also adds a dummy representing whether a country has had a political coup in the last decade. In her random effects estimation, almost all the variables have the right signs and are significant. The major exception is the corporate tax rates, which has the opposite sign as predicted.

Gastanaga et al. (1998) focus on policy reforms in developing countries as determinants of FDI inflows. They employ both ordinary least squares as well as panel estimations. Expected rates of growth, corporate tax rates, degree of corruption and degree of openness to FDI are all important determinants of FDI flows into these economies. Hines (1995) and Wei (1997) both examine impact of institutional factors on FDI. By employing a corruption index, Hines shows that after 1977, US FDI grew faster in less corrupted countries. Wei (1997) uses OECD FDI data and shows that both corruption and tax rates have negative effects on FDI flows. Wei's estimations are cross-sectional.[5]

3. THE EMPIRICAL MODEL

In this section we provide an empirical model used in estimating the impact of China on inward FDI of various Asian economies. The economies we examine include Hong Kong, Singapore, Taiwan, the Republic of Korea, Thailand, Malaysia, Philippines and Indonesia.[6] The years examined in this analysis are from 1985 to 2001. The strategy here is to control for all the standard explanatory variables of FDI in the Asian economies. We then add an additional variable to capture the effect of China. To proxy for the China effect, we choose the level of the inflows of China's FDI. Obviously, Chinese inward FDI can also be dependent on the inward FDI of these Asian economies as well as other standard determinants. In order to capture such a reciprocal relationship between the inflows of FDI to China and that to other Asian economies, the FDI equations for both the Asian economies and China are estimated simultaneously.

The basic regression model for inward FDI to Asian countries and to China are written as a linear specification of the following form:

$$\ln(AFDI_{i,t}) = \alpha_0 + \alpha_1\ln(CLNFDI_t) + \beta_1\ln(AGROWTH_{i,t}) +$$

$$\beta_2\ln(ACORRUPT_{i,t}) + \beta_3\ln(ADUTY_{i,t}) + \beta_4\ln(AGOV_{i,t}) +$$

$$\beta_5\ln(AWAGE_{i,t}) + \beta_6\ln(AOPEN_{i,t}) + \beta_7\ln(AILLIT_{i,t}) +$$

$$\beta_8\ln(ACPTAX_{i,t}) + \beta_9\ln(ATEL_{i,t}) + \beta_{10}\ln(AINCOME_{i,t}) +$$

$$\beta_{11}\ln(OUTFLOW_t) \tag{12.1}$$

$$\ln(CLNFDI_t) = \gamma_0 + \delta_1\ln(AFDI_{i,t}) + \rho_1\ln(CGROWTH_t) +$$

$$\rho_2\ln(CCORRUPT_t) + \rho_3\ln(CDUTY_t) + \rho_4\ln(CGOV_t) +$$

$$\rho_5\ln(CWAGE_t) + \rho_6\ln(COPEN_t) + \rho_7\ln(CINCOME_t) \tag{12.2}$$

where the subscript 'i' stands for country i and 't' for period t. Variables beginning with the letter 'A' denote variables that belong to the Asian countries and those beginning with the letter 'C' denote China variables.[7]

The independent variables examined in the analysis are believed to exert an influence on inward FDI in each country of Asia and China by changing the investment environment through institutional and policy changes as well as the relevant economic conditions.

The main variable in this chapter is the proxy for the China effect *CLNFDI*. Two important aspects are examined in our analysis. First is the terms of location of an export platform – a multinational may choose between investing in China and another Asian country. In this case, the multinational takes into account all factors of the host country, including wage rates, political risks, infrastructure, etc. that comprise a suitable site for low-cost production. As a result, investing in China leads to a reduction of FDI inflows in another Asian economy. The sign of *CLNFDI*, according to this argument is negative. We shall call this the '*investment-diversion effect*'.

The second aspect is the production and resource linkages between a growing China and the rest of Asia. In manufacturing, this takes a form of further specialization and growing fragmentation of production processes. For instance, an investor sets up factories in both China and Thailand to take advantage of their respective comparative advantages in different stages of productions. Through production linkages components and parts are traded among China and other Asian economies. An increase in China's FDI is then positively related to an increase in Thailand's FDI. Therefore a different but complementary argument is that as China grows, its market size increases and its appetite for minerals and resources also rises. Subsequently, foreign firms rush to establish production base in China to serve the local market and/or to export to other countries. At the same time, other multinationals also invest in other parts of Asia to extract minerals and resources to export to China whose demand for raw materials is soaring. This line of reasoning leads us to predict that the sign of *CLNFDI* is positive. We call this effect the '*investment-creation effect*'. Theoretically we cannot determine a priori the net effect of investment-creation and investment-diversion for China. It is thus important to examine this issue empirically, as we attempt to do in this chapter.

A substantial literature confirms empirically the importance of size of host market and growth factors as measured by GDP per capita and GDP growth, respectively. Foreign investors who target local markets are assumed to be more attracted to a country with higher GDP growth rate as it indicates larger potential demand for their products. The effect of this variable on investment incentive is therefore expected to be larger than the effect on those who are not market-seekers. Furthermore, for foreign investors who operate in industries characterized by relatively large economies of scale, the importance of market size and its growth is magnified, because they can exploit scale economies after the market size attains a certain threshold. The signs of GDP growth and per capita GDP are expected to be positive.

Since labor cost is a major component of the cost function, various versions of wage variables are frequently tested in the literature. A high wage, other things being equal, deters FDI. This must be particularly true for firms that engage in labor-intensive production activities. Therefore, conventionally, the expected sign for this variable is negative. However, there are no consistent empirical results for the effect of labor cost on investment incentives. While some studies show that there is no significant role of labor costs, others indicate a positive relationship between labor costs and FDI. The latter result is often attributed to advanced levels of labor productivity or quality of human capital that may be reflected in the wage variables.

Level of human capital is demonstrated to be another important determinant for marginal productivity of capital. It has been shown in various studies that skill-related variables are host country specific. When a host country is more appealing to labor-intensive foreign investment that requires a relatively lower level of skills, the importance of the human capital variable tends to be small. On the other hand, labor skill is more significant as a factor for a host country, in which more capital- and technology-intensive investment projects are concentrated. In this analysis, we utilize illiteracy rates as a proxy for the level of human capital.

A hypothesis that better developed regions with a superior quality of infrastructure are more attractive to foreign firms relative to others is also examined by utilizing number of telephone mainlines per 1000 people as a proxy in our regressions.

In addition, we examine the significance of institutional factors in determining FDI by incorporating level of corruption and level of government stability. Corruption can discourage FDI by inducing higher costs of doing business. Hines (1995) shows that FDI from the United

States grew more rapidly in less corrupted countries than in more corrupted countries after 1977. Wei (1997) presents an alternative explanation where the effect of corruption on FDI is large, negative and significant. Unlike taxes, corruption is not transparent and involves many factors that are more arbitrary in nature. An agreement between a briber and a corrupt official is hard to enforce and creates more uncertainty over the total questionable payments or final outcome. Wei demonstrates that this type of uncertainty induced by corruption leads to a reduction in FDI. Political stability of a government is another important factor that has an influence on FDI inflows. Uncertain political climate and its related risks can impede FDI inflows in spite of other favorable economic conditions. Since the indices of corruption and instability assign higher scores to a less corrupt or more stable country, the expected signs of the variables, *ACORRUPT* and *AGOV*, are positive.

Corporate tax rates, openness to foreign trade and import duty, a proxy of tariff barriers, are included in the analysis as policy-related variables. The effect of tariffs on behavior of multinational enterprises (MNEs) is methodologically demonstrated by Horst (1971). He predicts that in the face of higher tariffs imposed by host countries, other things being equal, MNEs will increase its production abroad and decrease its exports. More recent models highlight the effect of tariffs on FDI within the context of vertical and horizontal specialization within MNEs. An MNE engaged in vertical FDI is characterized by individual affiliates that specialize in different stages of production. Semi-finished products are then exported to other affiliates for further processing. By fragmenting the production process, parents and affiliates take advantage of factor price differentials across countries. Horizontal specialization on the other hand, involves affiliates' engagement in similar types of production. An MNE engaged in horizontal FDI is generally associated with marketing-seeking behavior; its motivation is to avoid trade costs.

MNEs that engage in vertical production networks may find it beneficial to invest in countries with relatively low tariff barriers. This means their imported intermediate goods will be cheaper. Therefore, the expected sign of *ADUTY* is negative. In contrast, high tariff barriers induce firms to engage in horizontal FDI to replace exports with production abroad by foreign affiliates (Brainard, 1997; Carr et al., 2001). Such tariff jumping implies a positive relationship between *ADUTY* and FDI.

AOPEN is included to examine the importance of openness to international trade in an economy. The variable measures degree of general trade restrictions of each country. Following the same line of reasoning above, a negative relationship between openness and market-seeking FDI is expected, and a positive relationship is expected for export-oriented FDI.

Another policy-related variable that can influence the host country's location advantage is the host country's corporate or other tax rates. MNEs, as global profit maximizers, can be assumed to be sensitive to tax factors, since they have a direct effect on their profits. Evidence of significant negative influences of corporate tax rates is reported in previous studies by Wei (1997), Gastanaga et al. (1998), and Hsiao (2001).

Finally, to control for the supply side of FDI, we include *OUTFLOW* – total global outflows of FDI – for each year.[8] All variables are transformed into logarithms. Data sources and additional explanations of variables are provided in Appendix A.

In our estimations, we assume for each FDI equation that there is a collection of factors that are omitted from the regression, and these factors are specific to each individual country. Therefore, we estimate equations that take the following form:

$$y_{it} = \alpha + \beta' x_{it} + u_i + \varepsilon_{it},$$

where the disturbance term, ε_{it}, is associated with both time and cross-sectional units; and u_i is a random disturbance that associates with the ith country and is assumed to be constant through time. In other words, the country-specific constant terms are assumed to be randomly distributed across the cross-sectional units. The formulation of the model is specified as follows.

$$\ln(AFDI_{i,t}) = a_0 + a_1 \ln(CLNFD_{i,t}) + \ln X_{i,t} b_i + u_i + e_{i,t} \qquad (12.3)$$

$$\ln(CLNFD_{i,t}) = \gamma_0 + \gamma_1 \ln(AFDI_{i,t}) + \ln Z_{i,t} \rho_i + v_i + w_{i,t} \qquad (12.4)$$

where X and Z are vectors of explanatory variables from equation (12.1) and (12.2), respectively; $e_{i,t}$ and $w_{i,t}$ are disturbance terms; and u_i and v_i are individual country effect. The above simultaneous equation system is estimated by a two-stage least-squares regression (2SLS).

4. RESULTS

4.1. Regressions using Levels of FDI inflows

Table 12.1 shows results from the first set of panel simultaneous regressions using level of FDI inflows as the dependent variables. To avoid multicollinearity problem, variables that are highly correlated are not

Table 12.1:   *Panel Regression Results with Levels of FDI*

Independent Variables	(1)	(2)	(3)	(4)	(5)
CLNFDI	0.2979	0.2957	0.2184	0.1960	0.2024
	(2.690)***	(2.628)***	(1.842)*	(1.911)*	(1.866)*
AGROWTH	0.5820	0.6575	0.4322	0.5072	0.4413
	(0.773)	(0.881)	(0.545)	(0.680)	(0.571)
ACORRUPT	0.3713	0.4375	0.8022	0.3801	0.6258
	(1.503)	(1.716)*	(3.126)***	(1.553)	(2.686)***
ADUTY	0.0606	0.0867	−0.3388	0.0707	−0.1188
	(0.304)	(0.438)	(1.843)*	(0.347)	(0.592)
AGOV	0.0726	0.1183	0.0506	0.0707	0.0288
	(0.456)	(0.712)	(0.287)	(0.445)	(0.174)
AWAGE	−0.1168	–	–	–	–
	(1.044)	–	–	–	–
AOPEN	0.7905	0.8705	–	0.5858	–
	(4.302)***	(4.405)***	–	(3.043)***	–
AILLIT	0.2334	0.2021	0.5542	0.4112	0.6551
	(1.330)	(1.168)	(3.387)***	(2.405)**	(4.118)***
ACPTAX	−1.2000	−1.3238	−0.5793	−1.0496	−0.5823
	(3.321)***	(3.532)***	(1.625)	(2.875)***	(1.685)*
ATEL	–	−0.1282	0.1077	–	–
	–	(1.423)	(1.392)	–	–
AINCOME	–	–	–	0.0656	0.2720
	–	–	–	(0.579)	(2.816)***
OUTFLOW	0.4623	0.4482	0.7083	0.6260	0.7264
	(2.521)**	(2.460)**	(3.860)***	(3.581)***	(4.236)***
Constant	−1.6157	−1.6647	−4.3587	−3.8717	−6.3133
	(0.743)	(0.827)	(2.133)**	(1.713)*	(2.975)***
R-square	0.7206	0.7222	0.6819	0.7212	0.6975
F-test: p-value	0.0000	0.0000	0.0000	0.0000	0.0000
Observations	130	131	131	131	131

Notes: Absolute value of t statistics in parentheses, * significant at 10%; ** significant at 5%; *** significant at 1%.

included simultaneously. For each of the dependent variables, there are five specifications. The first specification in column (1) includes *AWAGE* but not *ATEL* and *AINCOME*. In column (2), we look at the effect of *ATEL* and leave out *AWAGE*, and *AINCOME*. Column (3) examines *ATEL* by additionally excluding *AOPEN* due to its moderate correlation with *ATEL*. The effect of *AINCOME* is studied in columns (4) and (5).

Our main variable of interest *CLNFDI* is positive and highly significant in all specifications. A 10 percent increase in the FDI inflows to China would raise the level of FDI inflows to the East Asian countries by about 2 to 3 percent depending on the specifications. Despite considerable concerns in policy circles that an increase in FDI flow to China is at the expense of other regional economies, this study shows otherwise; those economies can actually benefit from it. This result may be explained by production-networking activities among Asian countries as well as increasing demand for raw materials and resources by China.[9]

Many of the countries examined here are involved in vertical specialization, particularly in electric and electronics industries. This is evident in shares of the two-way trade in the same industry in the total volume of trade among the nations (Table 12.2). Economic ties among these nations have deepened rapidly in the 1990s. The significance of the China effect in level of FDI inflows to our group of Asian countries may reflect such interdependence. Our central result is that the *investment-enhancing effect dominates the investment-diversion effect.* Overall China is a positive force for FDI inflows into other Asian economies.

The effect of openness, denoted by the variable *AOPEN*, has an expected positive sign and is always significant in its inclusion. Openness captures degree of both tariff and non-tariff measures including trade impediments.

Table 12.2:   China's Two-Way Trade of Electric Equipment with its Neighbors, 2004

	Exports of electrical equipment to China (US$1000)	Rank in exports to China	Imports of electrical equipment from China (US$1000)	Rank in imports from China
Taiwan	23 851 636	1	3 513 061	1
Rep. of Korea	18 571 820	1	6 638 518	1
Singapore	4 992 460	1	5 275 117	1
Thailand	2 917 693	1	1 258 441	2
Malaysia	9 987 515	1	2 175 148	2
Philippines	6 314 601	1	1 479 093	1
Indonesia	602 847	5	948 541	1

Source: China's Custom Statistics Monthly, 2004, December.

In contrast to the effect of tariff barriers proxied by *ADUTY*, the impact of openness to trade on inflows of FDI is substantial. The results in Table 12.1 suggest that, other things being equal, the marginal effect of trade liberalization of the Asian countries on their FDI inflows is approximately twice as large as that of the China effect. Trade impediments can take various forms such as local content requirements, technology transfer requirements, domestic sales and export requirements, and so on. Our results imply that reductions in these types of trade barriers can play a vital role in promoting FDI to the Asian countries.

Corporate tax is another variable that is found to exert a large influence on level of the FDI inflows in this analysis. Although many countries offer various forms of tax incentives to foreign investors, corporate tax rates can be considered as one of the most influential tools that promote investment since it has a direct impact on profitability of investment projects.

Unlike many of the previous studies, the growth rate of GDP does not appear to play an important role in attracting FDI in this analysis. On the other hand, per capita income is found to be a significant factor only in equation (12.5). This suggests that foreign investors' decision to invest in Asia is more sensitive to current market size than market potential for their products.

Degree of government stability and index of corruption are found to be positively associated with the level of FDI. In particular, corruption index variables in columns 3 and 5 are significant and have coefficients much larger than those of the corresponding China effect. Finally, the *OUTFLOW* variables are all positive and significant. *OUTFLOW* represents the impact of an overall supply effect on the inflows of FDI to these Asian economies.

4.2.   Regressions of Individual Countries' Share in FDI to Asia

The model in this section uses individual countries' share in FDI inflows to Asia as the dependent variable in equation (12.3). Note that the dependent variable in the China equation (12.4) is still the level of China's FDI. We can also use China's share in FDI inflows to Asia instead of the level of China's FDI. However, between the years 1985 and 2001, China and these East Asian countries accounted for 89 percent of total FDI inflows to Asia. Consequently, an increase in the share of FDI inflows to China will almost certainly ensure a reduction in the shares of FDI inflows to those eight economies. To avoid this, we continue to use the level of China's FDI inflows.

Given that FDI inflows into China and our eight Asian economies already constitute a bulk of FDI that goes to Asia, it will not be surprising to

Table 12.3:   *Panel Regression Results with Individual Countries' Shares in Asian FDI*

Independent Variables	(1)	(2)	(3)	(4)	(5)
CLNFDI	−0.3189	−0.3446	−0.3968	−0.3241	−0.4066
	(3.405)***	(3.553)***	(3.722)***	(3.394)***	(4.146)***
AGROWTH	0.4276	0.4864	0.2907	0.4738	0.3032
	(0.601)	(0.690)	(0.383)	(0.665)	(0.408)
ACORRUPT	0.3985	0.4876	0.8250	0.3373	0.6612
	(1.729)*	(2.055)**	(3.386)***	(1.446)	(2.958)***
ADUTY	−0.0058	0.0186	−0.3965	0.0130	−0.2012
	(0.031)	(0.100)	(2.250)**	(0.066)	(1.040)
AGOV	0.2122	0.2737	0.1955	0.1824	0.1727
	(1.418)	(1.756)*	(1.164)	(1.201)	(1.086)
AWAGE	−0.1328	–	–	–	–
	(1.252)	–	–	–	–
AOPEN	0.7715	0.8552	–	0.6427	–
	(4.471)***	(4.584)***	–	(3.499)***	–
AILLIT	0.1756	0.1370	0.4891	0.3264	0.5811
	(1.056)	(0.837)	(3.123)***	(1.998)**	(3.792)***
ACPTAX	−1.1052	−1.2374	−0.5006	−1.0009	−0.5009
	(3.228)***	(3.489)***	(1.464)	(2.869)***	(1.504)
ATEL	–	−0.1460	0.0906	–	–
	–	(1.716)*	(1.229)	–	–
AINCOME	–	–	–	0.0210	0.2379
	–	–	–	(0.194)	(2.558)**
OUTFLOW	0.1403	0.1563	0.3817	0.1684	0.3920
	(0.869)	(0.963)	(2.263)**	(1.025)	(2.470)**
Constant	2.0938	1.8492	−0.6611	0.8398	−2.3597
	(1.032)	(0.981)	(0.340)	(0.390)	(1.160)
R-square	0.5715	0.5795	0.5055	0.5694	0.5250
F-test: p-value	0.0000	0.0000	0.0000	0.0000	0.0000
Observations	130	131	131	131	131

Notes: Absolute value of t statistics in parentheses, * significant at 10%; ** significant at 5%; *** significant at 1%.

find that an increase in FDI to China reduces individual countries' share. Nonetheless it is still useful to estimate the impact. It is evident from our regressions that an incremental increase in FDI to China will decrease a proportion of FDI that each country receives. A 10 percent increase in

China's FDI causes the East Asian individual country's share in FDI to Asia to decrease by about 3 to 4 percent (Table 12.3). Although China does appear to take a bigger share of FDI at the expense of its neighboring countries, FDI promotion could come from the internal economic policy of each country, such as a lower level of corporate tax and higher degree of openness in international trade. The influence of openness on FDI is at least twice as large as that of the China effect in specifications (12.1), (12.2) and (12.4). Similarly, the influence of corporate taxes on FDI can be more than three times as large as that of the China effect.

Corporate tax rates as well as level of corruption are also generally significant and have large effects. These variables tend to have larger coefficients than the China effect proxy.

4.3. Regressions Using Individual Countries' Shares in the World FDI Inflows of Individual Countries' Share in FDI to Asia

In this last empirical exercise, our dependent variable is individual countries' share in FDI to the world. Although the eight East Asian countries account for a bulk of FDI that goes to Asia, together their share in the world FDI inflows are only marginal. Therefore, we expect that the presence of China will not affect the Asian individual country's share in the world FDI to a great extent. In fact, our results show that none of the *CLNFDI* coefficients is significant (Table 12.4).

Now that *CLNFDI* has lost its influential momentum on shares in the world FDI inflows, many variables gained their significance. Corruption has become much more significant in all specifications; magnitudes of the coefficient have become higher. A 10 percent improvement in the level of corruption increases the East Asian country's share in the world FDI inflows somewhere from 6.2 to 10 percent.[10] Other factors that remain significant are openness, corporate income tax rates and income. Corporate tax rates exert a consistently large and negative influence on FDI. Market size variable, as measured by *AINCOME*, is significant in column (5).

5. CONCLUSION

China's development strategy to attract foreign firms has been a huge success. But is China's FDI policy detrimental or complementary to its neighbors' attempts to attract more foreign investment? In other words, is China diverting FDI away from other Asian economies? This is a paramount question on the minds of many academic researchers as well as Asian policymakers.

Table 12.4:   *Panel Regression with Individual Countries' Shares in the World FDI*

Independent Variables	(1)	(2)	(3)	(4)	(5)
CHINA_FDI	−0.0052	−0.0166	0.0288	−0.0084	−0.0019
	(0.078)	(0.246)	(0.416)	(0.131)	(0.029)
AGROWTH	0.5220	0.5743	0.4225	0.4853	0.3557
	(0.661)	(0.736)	(0.521)	(0.621)	(0.451)
ACORRUPT	0.7288	0.8331	1.0057	0.6203	0.7639
	(3.072)***	(3.440)***	(4.094)***	(2.593)**	(3.314)***
ADUTY	0.0013	0.0192	−0.3006	0.0650	−0.0700
	(0.006)	(0.094)	(1.604)	(0.305)	(0.343)
AGOV	0.0451	0.1012	0.0300	0.0099	0.0102
	(0.270)	(0.584)	(0.167)	(0.059)	(0.060)
AWAGE	−0.0513	–	–	–	–
	(0.441)	–	–	–	–
AOPEN	0.5164	0.6354	–	0.3556	–
	(2.951)***	(3.257)***	–	(1.939)*	–
AILLIT	0.4283	0.3428	0.5898	0.5845	0.6985
	(2.428)**	(1.938)*	(3.537)***	(3.445)***	(4.358)***
ACPTAX	−1.1093	−1.2686	−0.6879	−0.9633	−0.6657
	(2.937)***	(3.241)***	(1.898)*	(2.535)**	(1.893)*
ATEL	–	−0.1251	0.0683	–	–
	–	(1.327)	(0.896)	–	–
AINCOME	–	–	–	0.1361	0.2624
	–	–	–	(1.164)	(2.677)***
Constant	−1.0717	−0.8328	−1.3903	−2.3720	−3.0613
	(0.662)	(0.558)	(0.901)	(1.391)	(1.819)*
R-square	0.4999	0.5107	0.4665	0.5087	0.4935
F-test: p-value	0.0000	0.0000	0.0000	0.0000	0.0000
Observations	130	131	131	131	131

Notes: Absolute value of t statistics in parentheses, * significant at 10%; ** significant at 5%; *** significant at 1%.

Theoretically, the emergence of China can have both an investment-creating effect as well as an investment-diverting effect. In this chapter, we examine this issue empirically. We use data for eight Asian economies (Hong Kong, Taiwan, Republic of Korea, Singapore, Malaysia, Philippines, Indonesia and Thailand) and estimate the impacts of FDI determinants in these economies. The standard determinants we consider include GDP growth rates, degree of openness, corporate tax rates, level of corruption, degree of government stability, illiteracy rates, per capita GDP, tariff rates, wage rates, proxies of infrastructure and the global supply of FDI. To estimate the China effect, we utilize the level of China's inward FDI. As China's FDI should also be dependent on FDI in other Asian economies and other similar policies and institutional factors, we use simultaneous equations to estimate the coefficients.

The main results of our chapter are as follows. First, in terms of levels of FDI, the China effect is positive, i.e. FDI to the Asian economies are positively related to China's FDI. Second, in terms of the shares of FDI, the China effect is negative. Thus while both the level of China's FDI and levels of FDI to the Asian economies are increasing together, an increase in China's FDI is associated with a decline in the shares in FDI that each of the Asian economies receives. Third, the China effect is not the most important determinant of FDI inflows in these Asian economies. Specifically, policy variables such as lower corporate taxes, lower degree of corruption and higher degrees of openness play a larger role in attracting investment.

From a development policy perspective, it seems that if Asian governments care more about the absolute levels of FDI they can obtain, they should focus on reforming their internal institutional and policy factors. In terms of relative importance of FDI destination with respect to China, our empirical evidence suggests that China is rising while the others are falling behind.

APPENDIX A: DEFINITION AND SOURCE OF VARIABLES

AFDI and *CHINA_FDI*: Data on aggregate FDI inflows of each country, aggregate FDI inflows to Asia, and aggregate FDI to the world are from UNCTAD.

ACORRUPT and *CCORRUPT*: An index of corruption from the International Country Risk Guide (ICRG) by the PRS Group. It ranges from 0 to 6. A higher number means a lower level of corruption.

AGOV and *CGOV*: An index of government stability from the International Country Risk Guide (ICRG) by the PRS Group. The range is from 0 to 12. A higher score means higher stability of a government.

ADUTY and *CDUTY*: Import duties are from the IMF's *Government Finance Statistics Yearbook*.

AWAGE and *CWAGE*: Average wages in manufacturing; from UN Common Database, LABORSTA, and countries' official websites.

AOPEN and *COPEN*: Openness = (export + import)/GDP. Export and import data are from IMF's *Direction of Trade Statistics*.

AILLIT: The illiteracy rate is the percentage of people aged 15 years and above who cannot, with understanding, read and write a short, simple statement on their everyday life. Data are from World Bank, World Development Indicators.

ACPTAX: Corporate income tax rate, measured in percentage points, from Price Waterhouse' s Worldwide summary book.

ATEL: Telephone mainlines per 1000 people. Data are from World Bank, World Development Indicators.

AINCOME and *CINCOME*: Per capita GDP (GDP/population). GDP data are from EconStats. Population data are from World Bank, World Development Indicators (various years).

AGROWTH and *CGROWTH*: GDP growth, measured in percentage point. Data are from EconStats.

OUTFLOW: Total supply of FDI, from UNCTAD.

APPENDIX B: LIST OF COUNTRIES IN ASIA

Israel, Japan, Bahrain, Cyprus, Iran (Islamic Rep. of), Iraq, Jordan, Kuwait, Lebanon, Oman, Palestinian territory, Qatar, Saudi Arabia, Syrian Arab Republic, Turkey, United Arab Emirates, Yemen, Armenia, Azerbaijan, Georgia, Kazakhstan, Kyrgyzstan, Tajikistan, Turkmenistan, Uzbekistan, Bangladesh, Bhutan, Brunei Darussalam, Cambodia, China, China Hong Kong SAR, China Macao SAR, China (Taiwan Province of), India, Indonesia, Korea (Dem. People's Rep. of), Korea (Republic of), Lao People's Dem. Rep., Malaysia, Maldives, Mongolia, Myanmar, Nepal, Pakistan, Philippines, Singapore, Sri Lanka, Thailand, Vietnam.

Definition of Asia is from UNCTAD.

NOTES

1. ChinaOnline, 14 November 2002.
2. Sung-jin, Kim (2002).
3. *New Straits Times–Management Times,* 9 March 2002.
4. Taiwanese Central News Agency, 21 November 2002.
5. Other related literature includes Zhang and Song (2001), Bao et al. (2002), Fung et al. (2003).
6. In future studies, we intend to include other Asian economies such as India and Pakistan.
7. $AFDI_{i,t}$ = the level of inward FDI in the i Asian economy in year t; $CLNFD_{lt}$ = inward FDI into China in year t; $AGROWTH_{i,t}$ = growth rate of GDP of country i at time t; $CGROWTH_t$ = growth rate of GDP of China at time t; $ACORRUPT_{i,t}$ = index of corruption of county i at time t; $CCORRUPT_t$ = index of corruption of China at time t; $ADUTY_{i,t}$ = import duty of country i at time t; $CDUTY_t$ = import duty of China at time t; $AWAGE_{i,t}$ = average wage in manufacturing of country i at time t; $CWAGE_t$ = average wage in manufacturing of China at time t; $AOPEN_{i,t}$ = share of exports and imports in GDP of country i at time t; $COPEN_t$ = share of exports and imports in GDP of China at time t; $AILLIT_{i,t}$ = percentage of people who are illiterate in country i at time t; $ATAX_{i,t}$ = corporate tax rate of country i at time t; $AGOV_{i,t}$ = index of government stability of country i at time t; $CGOV_t$ = index of government stability of China at time t; $ATEL_{i,t}$ = number of telephone mainlines per 1000 people of country i at time t; $AINCOME_{i,t}$ = per capita GDP of country i at time t; $CINCOME_t$ = per capita GDP of China at time t; $OUTFLOW_t$ = total world FDI outflows at time t.
8. Another possible determinant of FDI is the level of exchange rates. However, as highlighted by Russ (2004), there are many conflicting empirical studies concerning the significance and even the sign of the exchange rate variable.
9. As a robustness check, we experimented with running the regressions without Hong Kong. The results remain very similar to those with Hong Kong in the sample.
10. That is 10 percent less corruption.

REFERENCES

Bao, Shuming, Gene Hsing Chang, Jeffrey D. Sachs and Wing Thye Woo (2002), 'Geographic factors and China's regional development under market reforms, 1978–98', *China Economic Review,* **13** (1), 89–111.

Brainard, Lael S. (1997), 'An empirical assessment of the proximity-concentration trade-off between multinational sales and trade', *American Economic Review*, **87** (4), 520–44.

Carr, David L., James R. Markusen and Keith E. Maskus (2001), 'Estimating the knowledge-capital model of the multinational enterprise', *American Economic Review*, **91** (3), 693–708.

China's Custom Statistics Monthly (2004), General Administration of Customs, Economic Information and Agency, Hong Kong.

ChinaOnline (2002), 'China's rise is the most dramatic change in Asia', 14 November.

EconStats, http://www.econstats.com.

Fung, K.C., Hitomi Iizaka and Alan Siu (2003), 'Japanese direct investment in China', *China Economic Review*, **14**, 304–15.

Gastanaga, Victor M., Jeffrey B. Nugent and Bistra Pashamova (1998), 'Host country reforms and FDI inflows: How much difference do they make?', *World Development*, **26** (7), 1299–314.

Hines, James R. Jr. (1995), 'Forbidden payment: Foreign bribery and American business after 1977', NBER Working Paper: No. 5266.

Horst, Thomas (1971), 'The theory of the multinational firm: Optimal behavior under different tariff and tax rates', *Journal of Political Economy*, 79(5), 1959–72.

Hsiao, Cheng (2001), 'Efficient estimation of dynamic panel data models – with an application to the analysis of foreign direct investment to developing countries', Paper prepared for the 2001 Econometric Society Far Eastern Meeting in Kobe, Japan.

International Labor Organization Bureau of Statistics, LABORSTA: an International Labour Office database, http://laborsta.ilo.org/.

International Monetary Fund, *Direction of Trade Statistics* (CD-ROM), Washington, DC: International Monetary Fund.

International Monetary Fund (various years), *Government Finance Statistics Yearbook*, Washington, DC: International Monetary Fund.

New Straits Times–Management Times (2002), 'Future flows of FDI into Asian economies to depend on China', 9 March.

Price Waterhouse (various years), *Corporate Taxes, a Worldwide Summary*, New York, NY: Price Waterhouse Center for Transnational Taxation.

Price Waterhouse (various years), *Individual Taxes, a Worldwide Summary*, New York, NY: Price Waterhouse Center for Transnational Taxation.

PricewaterhouseCoopers (various years), *Individual Taxes: Worldwide Summaries*, Hoboken, NJ: John Wiley & Sons.

PRS Group, International Country Risk Guide (ICRG) database, Table 3B.

Russ, Kathryn (2004), 'The endogeneity of the exchange rate as a determinant of FDI: A model of money, entry and multinational firms', mimeo, UC, Davis.

Taiwanese Central News Agency (2002), 'Taiwan to improve competitiveness', 21 November.

Sung-jin, Kim (2002), 'Foreign investment likely to fall', *The Korea Times*, 26 August.

United Nations Conference on Trade and Development (UNCTAD), UNCTAD Database On-line.

UNCTAD (2004), *World Investment Report*, Geneva: Switzerland.

United Nations Statistic Division, UN Common Database (UNCDB).

Wei, Shang-Jin (1997), 'Why is corruption so much more taxing than tax? Arbitrariness kills', NBER Working Paper: No. 6255.

World Bank (2002), *Global Development Finance 2002*, **41**, Washington, DC.

Zhang, Kevin Honglin and Shunfeng Song (2001), 'Promoting exports: The role of inward FDI in China', *China Economic Review*, **12**(1), 385–96.

Index